HOSEA

BHB
Baylor Handbook
on the Hebrew Bible

General Editor

W. Dennis Tucker Jr.

HOSEA
A Handbook on the Hebrew Text

Eric J. Tully

BAYLOR UNIVERSITY PRESS

© 2018 by Baylor University Press
Waco, Texas 76798

All Rights Reserved. No part of this publication may be reproduced, stored in a retrieval system, or transmitted, in any form or by any means, electronic, mechanical, photocopying, recording, or otherwise, without the prior permission in writing of Baylor University Press.

Cover Design by Pamela Poll

Cover photograph by Bruce and Kenneth Zuckerman, West Semitic Research, in collaboration with the Ancient Biblical Manuscript Center. Courtesy Russian National Library (Saltykov-Shchedrin).

This book has been cataloged by the Library of Congress with ISBN 978-1-4813-0282-1.

Printed in the United States of America on acid-free paper with a minimum of 30 percent recycled content.

For Traci, Lauren, and Kate
God's greatest gifts to me

TABLE OF CONTENTS

Acknowledgments	ix
Abbreviations	xi
Introduction	1
1:1 Superscription	17
1:2–2:3 Gomer and Israel Are Two Adulterous Wives, But There Is Hope	19
2:4-10 She Goes to Adulterous Lovers for Gifts	35
2:11-15 He Will Take Away Her Gifts and Leave Her Desolate	46
2:16-25 He Will Put Away Her Lovers and Establish a New Relationship	55
3:1-5 Gomer and Israel Are Two Wives, Awaiting Full Restoration	68
4:1-3 Introduction to YHWH's Case	77
4:4-19 The Wicked Priest and the Illegitimate Cult	81
5:1-15 Israel Does Not Truly Seek YHWH	110
6:1-3 Call to Return to YHWH (Rejected)	135
6:4–7:2 Israel and Judah Are Entrenched in Covenant Violations	140
7:3-10 Israel Is Like an Oven and a Cake	156
7:11-16 Israel Is Like a Dove and a Bow	168
8:1-3 Israel Has Rejected the Good	179
8:4-14 Summation: Idols, Political Schemes, and Manipulative Worship	184

9:1-9 YHWH Will Destroy Their Hope: No Food	205
9:10-17 YHWH Will Destroy Their Hope: No Children	220
10:1-8 YHWH Will Destroy Their Cult Sites	235
10:9-15 YHWH Will Destroy the Nation Itself	250
11:1-11 YHWH's Resolve and Israel's Repentance Will Lead to Relationship	265
12:1-15 Accusation: Israel Is Not Like Their Father Jacob	286
13:1-14:1 YHWH Has Become Israel's Enemy	311
14:2-9 Relationship Will Be Restored through Repentance	337
14:10 Epilogue	352
Works Cited	355
Index of Linguistic Issues	363

ACKNOWLEDGMENTS

I am grateful to a number of people who have assisted me in various, crucial ways throughout the process of researching and writing this volume. My work on the Hebrew text of Hosea began as a component of my dissertation at the University of Wisconsin-Madison under the direction of Michael V. Fox, who modeled careful and insightful exegesis and high expectations, which he applied to himself first. During my time at UW, I was also significantly formed by Cynthia Miller-Naude. She taught me to love linguistics and played a key role in shaping my academic interests and methodology.

In the spring semester of 2014, I taught "Advanced Hebrew Exegesis: Hosea" at Trinity Evangelical Divinity School. As we worked through the entire book of Hosea in Hebrew, the students made excellent observations and raised numerous helpful questions. I appreciate the good work of Ken Clewett, Kirk Miller, Samuel "Cooper" Smith, Kevin Sprague, Stacey Swanson, Chew Suan Tan, and Seiichi Yaginuma.

I am grateful to the faculty and administration of TEDS for granting me a sabbatical in the fall of 2015, during which I was able to research and write the bulk of this book.

My T.A., Jeremiah Zuo, has helped in invaluable ways, from researching particular problems to careful editing and assistance with bibliography. John Cook, Dennis Magary, and K. Lawson Younger generously provided guidance on specific questions.

I offer my sincere thanks to Carey Newman at Baylor University Press for the opportunity to participate in this excellent series. Dennis Tucker, the series editor, and Diane Smith were extremely helpful in guiding the process, offering suggestions, and catching errors. The volume is better because of their good work.

The book of Hosea is complex and sophisticated, but ultimately everything revolves around gifts. God gives generous gifts to Israel because they are his special, covenant people. Israel takes those gifts and uses them to foster new relationships with other gods. Israel also mistakenly assumes that those other gods are the source of the gifts in the first place. God will not share Israel's loyalty, so he takes away his gifts. But the prophet promises that when Israel turns back to God he will restore his gifts and show his generosity once more.

As I worked through the text of Hosea and then wrote this book, I came to a new understanding of God as a giver, and I reflected on his great and undeserved generosity toward me. I have been given many things, but the most precious blessings are my wife, Traci, and my two daughters, Lauren and Kate. They fill my life with joy and are constant reminders of God's goodness. It is to them that I lovingly dedicate this book.

ABBREVIATIONS

abl	ablative
abs	absolute
AF	Francis I. Anderson, and David Noel Freedman. 1980. *Hosea*. New York: Doubleday.
acc	accusative
BDB	Francis Brown, S. R. Driver, and Briggs Charles. 2000. *The Brown-Driver-Briggs Hebrew and English Lexicon*. Peabody, Mass.: Hendrickson.
BH	Biblical Hebrew
BHQ	Anthony Gelston. 2010. *Biblia Hebraica Quinta*. Stuttgart: Deutsche Bibelgesellschaft.
BHS	Karl Elliger, and Wilhelm Rudolph. 1997. *Biblia Hebraica Stuttgartensia*. Stuttgart: Deutsche Bibelstiftung.
c	common
compl	complement
constr	construct
f	feminine
G	Greek Septuagint
GKC	Emil Kautzsch, ed. 1910. *Gesenius' Hebrew Grammar*. Translated and revised by A. E. Cowley. 2nd Engl. ed. Oxford: Clarendon.
HALOT	Ludwig Koehler and Walter Baumgartner. 2001. *The Hebrew and Aramaic Lexicon of the Old Testament*. Boston: Brill.
Hiph	Hiphil
Hith	Hithpael
Hoph	Hophal

impv	imperative
inf	infinitive
interr	interrogative
JM	Paul Joüon. 1993. *A Grammar of Biblical Hebrew*. Translated and revised by T. Muraoka. 2 vols. Subsidia Biblica 14. Rome: Pontifical Biblical Institute.
juss	jussive
m	masculine
MNK	Christo H. J. van der Merwe, Jackie A. Naudé, and Jan H. Kroeze. 1999. *A Biblical Hebrew Reference Grammar*. Biblical Languages: Hebrew 3. Sheffield: Sheffield Academic.
Mp	Masorah parva
MT	Masoretic Text
NIDOTTE	Willem VanGemeren. 1997. *New International Dictionary of Old Testament Theology & Exegesis*. 5 vols. Grand Rapids: Zondervan.
Niph	Niphal
OT	Old Testament/Hebrew Bible
p	plural
pass	passive
poss	possessive
PN	proper noun
PP	prepositional phrase
prep	preposition
ptc	participle
R	root letter
s	singular
S	Syriac Peshitta
SV	subject verb
T	Aramaic Targum
V	Latin Vulgate
VS	verb subject
WHS	Ronald J. Williams. 2007. *Williams' Hebrew Syntax*. Revised and Expanded by John C. Beckman. Toronto: University of Toronto.
WO	Bruce K. Waltke and Michael O'Connor. 1990. *An Introduction to Biblical Hebrew Syntax*. Winona Lake, Ind.: Eisenbrauns.

INTRODUCTION

The book of Hosea is known for its difficult language, uncertain historical references, and frequently obscure oracles. Yet, the captivating picture it presents of God's radical love for his people makes it one of the most beloved of the prophetic books in the Old Testament/Hebrew Bible.

The superscription (Hos 1:1) dates Hosea's ministry to the reigns of "Uzziah, Jotham, Ahaz, and Hezekiah, kings of Judah" and to "Jeroboam the son of Joash, king of Israel." This would put the date of his ministry, and the oracles contained in the book, to a period between 755 and 725 BC. Most scholars assume a terminus ad quem of about 725 BC since Hosea does not mention the destruction of Samaria and the effective end of the northern kingdom in 722 BC. At the beginning of Hosea's ministry, eighth-century Israel was characterized by wealth and prosperity, but also great spiritual darkness. Separated from Judah, the temple, and sanctioned worship of YHWH, the nation was trapped in systemic syncretism and heterodoxy. By the end of Hosea's ministry, life in Israel was marked by political and military instability. The nation's mounting problem led to various kinds of attempts at religious and political solutions.

We are told no biographical details about the prophet except for his father's name (בְּאֵרִי) and the story of his wife and children that emerges in the book. He is the only writing prophet who was a native of the northern kingdom. His ministry was primarily directed at its people and centers of power at Samaria and Bethel, but it also concerned the kingdom of Judah and makes reference to it.

Chapters 1–3 are among the most well-known portions of the Latter Prophets. Hosea's marriage to Gomer, her incorrigible infidelity, and his amazing faithfulness is an intense and personal picture of God's mercy and his refusal to abandon his people in spite of their rebellion. These chapters capture our imagination and give us a concrete way to grapple with God's grace.

By comparison, chapters 4–14 are often neglected, especially in the church. But it is here that the detail and substance of YHWH's redemptive program is set forth by Hosea. YHWH brings a case against Israel for her unfaithfulness. She has abandoned the exclusive worship of YHWH for syncretistic religion and the worship of Canaanite fertility deities. Furthermore, she insists on solving national problems without YHWH's covenant protection and blessing. Refusing to trust him, she turns to alliances with foreign nations, another form of idolatry. Hosea announces imminent destruction and death as a consequence of this defiance. However, because of YHWH's love for Israel, he will not allow judgment to be the last word. He is determined to redeem his people and restore the relationship permanently. The book concludes with a presentation of Israel's redemption as an accomplished fact. This is what G. Campbell Morgan called *The Heart and Holiness of God* (n.d.). It is the passionate love of a God who glories in his holiness and yet woos his beloved until she realizes her need and turns back to him.

The book is structured as follows:

Superscription (1:1)

PART 1: Hosea's Sign-Act and Its Application to Israel (1:2–3:5)
- 1:2–2:3 Gomer and Israel Are Two Adulterous Wives, But There Is Hope
- 2:4-10 She Goes to Adulterous Lovers for Gifts
- 2:11-15 He Will Take Away Her Gifts and Leave Her Desolate
- 2:16-25 He Will Put Away Her Lovers and Establish a New Relationship
- 3:1-5 Gomer and Israel Are Two Wives, Awaiting Full Restoration

PART 2: YHWH's First Case Against Israel (4:1–11:11)
4:1–8:14 Accusation (ריב): Idols, Political Schemes, and Manipulative Worship
  Introduction to YHWH's Case (4:1-3)
  The Wicked Priest and the Illegitimate Cult (4:4-19)
  Israel Does Not Truly Seek YHWH (5:1-15)
  Call to Return to YHWH (Rejected) (6:1-3)
  Israel and Judah Are Entrenched in Covenant Violations (6:4–7:2)
  Israel Is Like an Oven and a Cake (7:3-10)

    Israel Is Like a Dove and a Bow (7:11-16)
    Israel Has Rejected the Good (8:1-3)
    Summation: Idols, Political Schemes, and Manipulative Worship (8:4-14)
  9:1–10:15 YHWH Will Destroy Israel's Food, Cult Sites, and the Nation Itself
    YHWH Will Destroy Their Hope: No Food (9:1-9)
    YHWH Will Destroy Their Hope: No Children (9:10-17)
    YHWH Will Destroy Their Cult Sites (10:1-8)
    YHWH Will Destroy the Nation Itself (10:9-15)
  11:1–11 YHWH's Resolve and Israel's Repentance Will Lead to Relationship
PART 3: YHWH's Second Case Against Israel (12:1–14:9)
  12:1-15 Accusation (ריב): Israel Is Not Like Their Father Jacob
  13:1–14:1 YHWH Has Become Israel's Enemy
  14:2-9 Relationship Will Be Restored through Repentance

Epilogue (14:10)

The pre-exilic prophets typically speak on behalf of YHWH in reference to five time periods: past accusation, (near) future judgment, (near) future restoration, eschatological judgment, and eschatological restoration. Hosea's oracles are organized according to the first, second, and fifth of these periods or phases. The first three chapters are a microcosm of the book, introducing the pain and consequences of unfaithfulness as well as a husband's resolve to love his wife and bring her back under his care. The sign-act in 1:2–2:3 and 3:1-5 forms an inclusio around the introduction, inviting the reader to consider God's relationship with Israel in light of Hosea's relationship to his family. In 2:4-25 the prophet applies the sign-act to Israel in three phases: Accusation, Temporary Judgment, and Ultimate Reconciliation. Having established the structural pattern, the prophet repeats this cycle twice more in the oracles found in 4:1–14:9. The correspondences between the structural panels are identified by topic as well as lexical patterns. The table on the next page summarizes the correspondences within the book.

The primary focus of this commentary is the Hebrew text of Hosea including translation, linguistic analysis, and issues in the text that are particularly significant for interpretation. Discussions of social and historical context and theology are secondary and are addressed only in reference to understanding the Hebrew text.

	1:1—Superscription	
Sign-act:	Gomer and Israel are Two Adulterous Wives, but There is Hope (1:2-2:3)	
Accusation	She Goes to Adulterous Lovers for Gifts (כי) (2:4-10)	Accusation (כי): Idols, Political Schemes and Manipulative Worship (4:1-8:14)	Accusation (כי): Israel is Not Like Their Father Jacob (12:1-15)
Temporary Judgment	He will Take Away Her Gifts and Leave her Desolate (2:11-15)	YHWH will Destroy Israel's Food, Children, Cult Sites, and the Nation Itself (9:1-10:15)	YHWH has Become Israel's Enemy
Ultimate Reconciliation	He will Put Away Her Lovers and Establish a New Relationship (2:16-25)	YHWH's Resolve and Israel's Repentance will Lead to Relationship (11:1-11)	Relationship will be Restored Through Repentance (14:2-9)
Sign-act:	Gomer and Israel are Two Wives, Awaiting Full Reconciliation (3:1-5)		
	Application of the Sign-Act to Israel		14:10 [14:9]—Epilogue

Linguistic Background

In the following four subsections, I will briefly describe the linguistic approach with which I analyze the text of Hosea and the accompanying terminology that I use in the handbook.

Syntactic Roles

In my description of various constituents in Hebrew phrases and clauses, I follow Holmstedt in his commentaries on Ruth (2010) and Esther (Screnock and Holmstedt 2015) in the present series as well as his other studies. A "head" is the constituent in a phrase that is being modified. There are three basic types of modifiers: complements, adjuncts, and specifiers (Holmstedt 2009:113).

First, a complement is a constituent that is required by the semantics of the head (Screnock and Holmstedt 2015:3). Complements are "licensed or limited by the verb"; that is, they fulfill a limited number of roles for the verb and are sometimes required for grammaticality (Cook 2017). For example, verbs take different numbers and types of complements depending upon their valency, or what is required to make them semantically complete. A stative verb does not take a complement at all since it is semantically complete on its own. Likewise, an intransitive (or *monovalent*) verb expresses an action that does not act upon anything else, so it does not take a complement. However, transitive (or *bivalent*) verbs require at least one complement such as a noun phrase, prepositional phrase, infinitive, or direct speech. The verb in example (1) has one complement: the noun phrase גֹּמֶר ("Gomer").

(1) A Qal bivalent verb
וַיִּקַּח אֶת־גֹּמֶר
"he took Gomer" (Hos 1:3)

Certain verbs take oblique complements which are marked with prepositions.

(2) The verb √נגע
וְדָמִים בְּדָמִים נָגָעוּ
"and bloodshed touches bloodshed" (Hos 4:2)

In example (2), the first דָמִים is the plural subject of the verb נָגָעוּ. The verb √נגע requires a complement marked with a בְּ preposition, found here as the second occurrence of דָמִים.

In example (3) below, the verb √פקד, used in a particular idiom, is *trivalent*, meaning that it takes two complements: an accusative (here marked with אֶת), which specifies the reason for punishment, and a PP (introduced with עַל), which specifies the recipient of the punishment.

(3) The verb √פקד in the sense of "punish"
וּפָקַדְתִּי אֶת־דְּמֵי יִזְרְעֶאל עַל־בֵּית יֵהוּא
"I will visit the bloodshed of Jezreel (*compl 1*) upon the house of Jehu (*compl 2*)" (Hos 1:4)

In contrast to complements, adjuncts are modifiers which have roles that are not dictated by the verb. Therefore, they can be added (theoretically) without limit (Cook 2017). Adjuncts include adjectives, adverbs, or prepositional phrases (Holmstedt 2005:139). An adjunct provides additional information about the head but is not limited by the verb. In example (4), the prepositional phrase אֵלַי identifies the addressee of YHWH's speech:

(4) Adjunct PP
וַיֹּאמֶר יְהוָה אֵלַי
"and YHWH said to me" (Hos 3:1)

The third type of modifier is a specifier, which includes explicit verbal subjects, articles, demonstratives, and possessive pronouns (Holmstedt 2005:139). In Hebrew, verbs are marked for person, number, and gender and do not require an explicit subject. When a subject is included in the clause, it specifies information salient for the author's purpose. Other specifiers are used for similar reasons.

Word Order

Presently, the majority view among Hebrew grammarians is that the basic word order of BH is verb–subject (VS) (see GKC §142a; Brockelmann 1956:§48; JM §155k; WO §8.3). GKC states, "the natural order of words within the verbal sentence is Verb–Subject, or Verb–Subject–Object. But as in the noun-clause so also in the verbal-clause, a variation of the usual order of words frequently occurs when any member of the sentence is to be specially emphasized by priority of position" (§142f). In other words, though the default word order is VS, that order can be manipulated by an author for pragmatic reasons, and thus there are sentences that exhibit word order in which the subject precedes the verb. VS word order is statistically dominant in BH. For example, in Genesis the verb precedes the subject in 84 percent of verbal clauses (Moshavi 2010:11–12).

An alternate view, followed in the present commentary, is grounded in a generative approach to syntax. This view holds that the basic word order of the clause in BH is subject—verb (SV) (see Holmstedt 2005, 2009, 2011, 2016). Accordingly, the basic (or "deep structure") order is SV, which is then realized as SV or VS depending upon various syntactic rules. These different realizations are explained by constituent movement in the sentence. For example, English demonstrates this kind of constituent movement in certain interrogative clauses that contain so-called "Wh" words.

(5a) Declarative: "Traci purchased a car"
(subj) (verb) (infl) (compl)
(5b) Interrogative: "What did Traci purchase?"
(compl) (infl) (subj) (verb)

In example (5a), the declarative sentence has an expected SV word order for English. But the presence of the interrogative "What" has triggered constituent movement in example (5b). The complement and the inflection (past tense) have both been raised to a higher position, preceding the verb.

In BH, clauses with VS word order have undergone constituent movement; that is, the constituents in the clause have been "triggered" from SV to VS word order for one of several reasons. First, syntactic features trigger VS word order, such as subordinating particles (e.g., כִּי), relative words (e.g., אֲשֶׁר), interrogatives (e.g., לָמָּה or מָה), and *wayyiqtol* verbs. *Wayyiqtols* have an obligatory VS word order, probably accounted for by the geminated prefix. Holmstedt (2009:125) argues that the gemination apparently preserves a particle or other function word that triggers word order inversion.

Second, there are semantic triggers that result in VS word order such as negation (e.g., לֹא) or irrealis mood (*weqatal* or jussive verbs; see the discussion below). These syntactic and semantic triggers are extremely common in BH, especially in narrative, and account for the statistical predominance of VS word order, even though SV is basic in BH.

Verbal Semantics

My approach to the BH verbal system follows Cook (2006, 2008, 2012, 2013). For a full discussion of the semantics of the BH verb, see especially Cook 2012. According to Cook (2012:263–64), Hebrew verbs primarily express aspect. However, the *wayyiqtol* is an older form which is tensed and mostly restricted to narrative. Three elements work together in the verbal system to indicate the type and temporal nature of the verbal system: tense (temporal location), aspect (temporal structure), and modality (temporal existence)—or TAM.

Aspect refers to several different and distinct phenomena. "Situation" aspect refers to the differences in the temporal structure of events such as a state, activity, accomplishment, or achievement (Cook 2012:22). "Phasal" aspect refers to the development through which a situation progresses. For example, a verb may focus on the initial phase of the action ("began writing") or the middle phase ("continued writing") (2012:25).

"Viewpoint" aspect refers to the "different ways of viewing the internal temporal constituency of a situation" (Comrie 1976:3). A common analogy for viewpoint aspect is that of varying focal lengths of camera lenses. Imperfective viewpoint aspect is like a telephoto lens. It considers the action in close-up with a focus on details but without an overall view of the situation. If an action is viewed as a linear progression, imperfective aspect presents the progress of a situation but the beginning and end of the situation are not in view. Therefore, it is "unbounded" (Cook 2012:27).

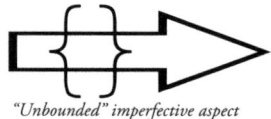

"Unbounded" imperfective aspect

By contrast, perfective situation aspect is analogous to a wide-angle camera lens. It presents the endpoints of the situation, but not the details of the situation. Thus, it is "bounded" (Cook 2012:27).

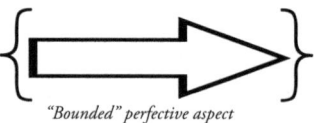

"Bounded" perfective aspect

The third element of TAM is modality. Cook defines modality as "the conceptual or semantic domain consisting of the theoretically limitless ways in which speakers might choose to relate an event or proposition to alternative situations" (2012:234). Modal verbs refer to multiple possible states of affairs or other possible worlds; that is, "alternative situations or situations that are not necessarily real" (2012:45). Modal, or irrealis, verbs refer to non-indicative situations such as obligation, volition, contingency, or habitual actions.

Cook (2012:270) argues that there are therefore three primary oppositions in the BH verbal system. The first opposition involves stative vs. dynamic verbs (situation aspect). The second opposition is *qatal* (perfective) vs. *yiqtol* (imperfective) verbs (viewpoint aspect). The third opposition is real (indicative) vs. irreal (modal). These oppositions, combined with the above discussion of word order, explain the semantics of the verb in BH.

The *qatal* (perfective) verb is used to present both indicative and irrealis situations. In the indicative, the *qatal* verb has SV word order. Its bounded viewpoint aspect (i.e., it presents situations as a completed whole) means that it frequently describes situations in the past. However, *qatal* verbs can present perfective actions in the future as well, depending upon the context. In example (6) the context, as well as the *yiqtol* verbs (יָגוּרוּ and יָגִילוּ), suggest that the prophet is referring to a situation in the future. Thus, the two *qatal* verbs (אָבַל and גָּלָה) are translated as completed acts in the future.

(6) *Qatal* verb expressing completed action in the future
לְעֶגְלוֹת֙ בֵּ֣ית אָ֔וֶן יָג֖וּרוּ שְׁכַ֣ן שֹׁמְר֑וֹן כִּי־אָבַ֤ל עָלָיו֙
עַמּ֔וֹ וּכְמָרָיו֙ עָלָ֣יו יָגִ֔ילוּ עַל־כְּבוֹד֖וֹ כִּי־גָלָ֥ה מִמֶּֽנּוּ׃
"For the calves of Beth Aven, the inhabitants of Samaria will be afraid. It's people will mourn over it and its idolatrous priests over it—who rejoice over its glory—for it will have gone into exile from them." (Hos 10:5)

In the irrealis mood, the *qatal* verb triggers word order inversion and has VS word order. If there is no explicit subject, the verb will be clause-initial and will be preceded by a וְ conjunction (*weqatal*). Irrealis *qatal* verbs are frequently used in Hosea for prophetic predictions, such as the verb וְשָׁבַרְתִּי in example (7).

(7) Irrealis *qatal* in predictive discourse
וְהָיָה֙ בַּיּ֣וֹם הַה֔וּא וְשָׁבַרְתִּי֙ אֶת־קֶ֣שֶׁת יִשְׂרָאֵ֔ל
"And on that day I will break the bow of Israel." (Hos 1:5)

Irrealis *qatal* verbs are also used to express other irreal situations such as contingent modality, habitual modality, and volition.

The *yitqol* (imperfective) verb is similar to the *qatal* in that it is used indicatively (with SV word order) or to express irreal situations (with VS word order). In the indicative its unbounded aspect means that it frequently refers to nonpast situations (present or future). However, depending upon the context, it can be used for frequentative or habitual actions in the past, such as the verb יְזַבֵּחוּ in example (8).

(8) Frequentative *yiqtol* in the past
לַבְּעָלִים יְזַבֵּחוּ וְלַפְּסִלִים יְקַטֵּרוּן
"They kept sacrificing to the Ba'als, and to the idols they were burning incense." (Hos 11:2)

Unlike other verbs in BH that primarily denote aspect, the *wayyiqtol* is a carry-over from an earlier period in the development of BH. It denotes tense; Cook (2012:256) states that over 90 percent of more than 15,000 occurrences appear in prose narrative and are used for past temporality. As noted above, the indicative *wayyiqtol* always occurs in VS word order.

The following chart presents a simplified overview of the BH verbal system:

Form	Modality	Aspect	Tense
Qatal (קָטַל) "Perfect"	Indicative	Perfective (bounded)	Depends upon context (typically past)
	Irreal (VS word order)		
Yiqtol (יִקְטֹל) "Imperfect"	Indicative	Imperfective (unbounded)	Depends upon context (typically nonpast)
	Irreal (VS word order)		
Juss/Impv (יִקְטֹל)/(קְטֹל)	Irreal		
Wayyiqtol (וַיִּקְטֹל) "Past Narrative"	Indicative		Past (tensed)
Participle	Verbal adjective	Progressive	Depends upon context

Pragmatics

As noted above, basic BH word order is SV. The word order inverts to VS for either syntactic (e.g., subordination) or semantic (e.g., irrealis mood) reasons. Additionally, authors adjust the word order for pragmatic reasons. That is, they front, or move words forward, in order to highlight them for topic or focus. While constituents marked for topic or focus can exhibit the default or expected word order, it is much more common for authors to "front" the constituent (i.e., to move it to the front of the clause) (Screnock and Holmstedt 2015:9).

Words fronted for *topic* highlight thematic information. The theme is information in the discourse that is already known; it is the anchor to which new information can be added. Authors front words for topic in order to isolate one theme and indicate that that information is salient. In other words, fronting for topicalization signals a shift in what the discourse is about (Holmstedt 2009:126–28). In example (9) below, the independent pronoun היא is not obligatory and indicates the topic in the discourse. In the preceding context, the reader is made aware of Israel (personified as a woman), her adulterous "lovers," and her first husband (YHWH). Now, in v. 10 the author uses and fronts the 3fs pronoun to signal that it is "*she*" that is of primary concern.

(9) Personal pronoun used for topicalization
וְהִיא לֹא יָדְעָה
"But she does not know ... ." (Hos 2:10a)

Constituents fronted for *focus* signal information that contrasts with possible alternatives either in the discourse or in the knowledge shared between the author and reader (Screnock and Holmstedt 2015:9). Consider the next clause in Hos 2:10:

(10) Personal pronoun fronted for focus
כִּי אָנֹכִי נָתַתִּי לָהּ הַדָּגָן
"... that I have given her the grain." (Hos 2:10b)

In example (10) we would expect the clause to exhibit VS word order because it is preceded by כִּי. However, the pronoun אָנֹכִי is fronted in the clause for focus. The author is contrasting the behavior of YHWH ("I") with that of Israel ("she") in the previous line. Fronting for topic or focus occurs after syntactic or semantic triggering that produces VS word order. Therefore, in a VS clause without a syntactic trigger, such as כִּי or אֲשֶׁר, the verb may be fronted and marked for pragmatic reasons.

Or, a clause with SV order that contains an irrealis verb (in which we would expect triggered VS order) has the subject fronted for topic or focus (Holmstedt 2009:138).

In this commentary, I do not explain the word order in every clause but attempt to draw attention to those examples of pragmatic marking which may be significant for exegesis. For more discussion on these matters, see Holmstedt 2009 and 2011 and Screnock and Holmstedt 2015.

Poetry

Like many of the prophets in the OT, most of the book of Hosea consists of poetry. It is not always easy to distinguish between Hebrew prose and poetry, and yet the identification of a text as one or the other, and analysis on that basis, can have significant exegetical ramifications.

Watson (1986:46–47) lists features of Hebrew poetry including established line forms, ellipsis (esp. of the verb), unusual vocabulary or word order, conciseness, and regularity and symmetry. In addition, structural features such as parallelism, word pairs, chiasm, and sound patterns indicate poetry. Finally, Watson looks for the absence or rarity of elements normally associated with prose.

In this commentary, I analyze and present the text of Hosea according to the existence of poetic lines, parallelism, and features such as ellipsis. Hosea 1:1-6, 8-9, and 3:1-5 are presented in paragraph format and analyzed clause by clause. The rest of the book is presented and analyzed as poetry, line by line. I label each line with successive letters for reference and cross-reference.

A word about terminology. I follow Berlin 2008, Watson 1986, and Dobbs-Allsopp 2015 in calling a "line" what others call a half-verse, verset, stich, or colon (e.g., Fokkelman 2001; Alter 2011). Dobbs-Alsopp states, "the only term in English with currency both in common usage and in the vernacular of literary critical discourse is *line*" (2015:27). Therefore, the levels in a poem are the stanza (the largest division), the strophe, the verse (i.e., a verse of poetry such as a bicolon, not necessarily a biblical verse), the line, and the word.

I acknowledge that the primary challenge to using "line" in this way is that the normal convention in BHS is for one verse of poetry to be written as one line of text on the page. However, the Masoretes did recognize the individual segments (or lines) of poetry and indicated them by means of disjunctive accents. Lines conclude with *Rᵉbîaʿ*, *Zaqep parvum*, *'Atnaḥ*, and *Silluq*. The stronger accents such as *'Atnaḥ*, and *Silluq* frequently divide between poetic verses. In this commentary I do not regard the MT accents as inviolable in determining how lines break. They indicate the interpretation of the Masoretes (which should, of course, be taken seriously), but there are times when I go against these accents for various reasons.

Poetic verses are found with varying numbers of lines. A monocolon is a single, independent line of poetry. This is not common and usually introduces or concludes a section or poem. The bicolon—two lines usually exhibiting some form of parallelism—is the most common verse and the standard in BH poetry. Three lines make a tricolon. Due to the odd number, it is typical for two of the lines to be parallel while the first or third (whichever is left out) stands apart as an introduction or conclusion. A tetracolon or quatrain is four lines. Tricola and quatrains are not nearly as common as bicola and frequently signal a transition in the poem or some other structural feature.

According to Berlin, "Parallelism promotes the perception of a relationship ... and this relationship is one of correspondence. The nature of the correspondence varies, but in general it involves repetition or the substitution of things which are equivalent on one or more linguistic levels" (2008:2). Berlin speaks of several aspects of parallelism. There can be grammatical parallelism, in which lines correspond through morphological (e.g., noun//pronoun; Qal//Niph) or syntactic (nominal//verbal; positive//negative; subject//compl) contrasts. For instance, in example (11) the same root (שכח√) occurs in two different conjugations (*wayyiqtol* and *yiqtol*), thus binding the lines together.

(11) Grammatical parallelism: conjugation
וַתִּשְׁכַּח תּוֹרַת אֱלֹהֶיךָ
אֶשְׁכַּח בָּנֶיךָ גַּם־אָנִי
You *forgot* the law of your God;
I also will *forget* your children. (Hos 4:6)

Berlin (2008:65–80) also refers to the lexical aspect of parallelism, in which naturally occurring word pairs create a correspondence between lines (see also Watson 1986:128–43). In example (12), the lines in Hos 13:14 contain two word pairs (מָוֶת//שְׁאוֹל and גאל√//פדה√) as well as repetition of the preposition מִן and the 3mp acc suffix.

(12) Lexical parallelism
מִיַּד שְׁאוֹל אֶפְדֵּם
מִמָּוֶת אֶגְאָלֵם
Will I ransom them from the power of Sheol?
Will I redeem them from death? (Hos 13:14)

Ellipsis is another technique that is common in poetry, used to connect two parallel lines. Miller states, "ellipsis involves constructions in which a grammatically required element is omitted by the speaker, thus creating a structural hole or gap" (2003:252). The earlier view of grammarians was that a word or words in the first line stand in for—or do "double duty" for—words in a subsequent line. Alternatively, we can say that the word or words in the second line are gapped or elided since that sentence is not grammatical without the word that is found in the previous line (2003:260). Ellipsis can involve multiple words, but it frequently involves only the verb of a clause, as in example (13).

(13) Ellipsis
אִמְרוּ לַאֲחֵיכֶם עַמִּי
וְלַאֲחוֹתֵיכֶם רֻחָמָה׃
Say to your brothers, "My people"
and to your sisters, "Pitied" (Hos 2:3)

In this example the imperative אִמְרוּ is not written or phonologically present in the second line, but it is in reality just as present as the אִמְרוּ in the first line. The identity of the gapped verb in the second line is obvious and completes the sentence. In this commentary I indent the Hebrew text in order to show which elements in a line are gapped. For more on ellipsis, see Miller (2005).

Perhaps the most significant characteristic of parallelism for exegesis is the semantic correspondence between lines. This relationship between items in parallel lines is not static. Kugel (1981:12–15) uses the expression "A, what's more, B" to describe the ways that the second line goes beyond the meaning of the first line in any number of ways. Alter (2011) prefers the word "intensification" to describe the dynamic movement from one line to the next. He states that "the characteristic movement of meaning is one of heightening or intensification ... of focusing, specification, concretization, even what could be called dramatization" (2011:20). For example, if the first line contains a spatial or geographical entity, the second line may contain a smaller entity contained within the first. Or, a literal statement in the first line is echoed with a metaphorical statement in the second (2011:21). Fokkelman prefers the term "amplification" which includes the idea of "intensification" as well as other relationships. He states that competent readers must determine the exact relationship between lines in each case. The second line can do all sorts of things with the first, including "expand it, intensify it, underline it, embellish it. These are all variations within a process of amplification" (2001:75).

The semantic relationship or development between one line and a subsequent parallel line is a poetic strategy that allows for a concept to be presented with additional depth and sophistication. The meaning intended by the poetic is not limited to the combination of the sense in the two lines but rather exists in the interplay between corresponding terms.

(14) Semantic development in parallel lines
עַל־כֵּן תִּזְנֶינָה בְּנוֹתֵיכֶם
וְכַלּוֹתֵיכֶם תְּנָאַפְנָה
Therefore, your daughters fornicate,
and your daughters-in-law commit adultery (Hos 4:13)

In example (14), the sin (and victimization) of the women of Israel is heightened in the parallelism. "Daughters" in the first line becomes "daughters-in-law" in the second: the scope of transgression is comprehensive. Also, "fornicate" becomes "commit adultery" which is a sexual sin with more serious social consequences.

Text

Hosea is one of the most difficult books in the OT, with a high number of syntactic difficulties and *hapax legomena*. While some scholars suppose that these difficulties reflect the prophet's distinctive Hebrew dialect and the book's northern provenance (e.g., Stuart 1987:13; Garrett 1997:26; Macintosh 2014:liii), this is ultimately speculation without substantive support. No solid evidence is given. Furthermore, difficulty and dialect are not the same thing. Inscriptions such as the Samaria ostraca have a northern provenance but they do not prove to be unduly difficult, nor are inscriptions in other Canaanite dialects such as Phoenician and Moabite. Difficulties in Hosea are not limited to specific morphological isoglosses or uncertain words here or there. Rather, entire verses defy a straightforward reading.

It seems more likely that the difficulties in the book represent textual corruption (see AF 66–67; Dearman 2010:9). However, many of the same apparent problems are also found in the major textual witnesses such as the Greek Septuagint and the Syriac Peshitta as well. At times the translators were wrestling with the same textual challenges that we do. This would suggest that corruptions must be quite early.

In my analysis of the text, I maintain an open stance toward solving difficulties either as unusual Hebrew constructions (perhaps even idiosyncrasies of the author?) or as textual corruptions. I resolve each problem on a case-by-case basis, sometimes making the best sense possible from the Hebrew text as it stands, and at other times looking at possible textual variants as providing superior readings that solve the problem.

The Qumran texts of Hosea are very limited and only fragmentary. For a good reader-friendly edition of the texts, see Ulrich 2013. For the critical edition of the Septuagint (G), see Ziegler 1984. Glenny 2013 provides a commentary on Hosea in Codex Vaticanus. For the critical edition of the Syriac Peshitta (S), see Gelston 1980 and the comprehensive study of the Peshitta of Hosea in Tully 2015. For the critical edition of Targum Jonathan (T), see Sperber 2004 and the translation notes concerning Hosea in Cathcart and Gordon 1989. For the Vulgate (V), see Weber 2007. On my approach to adjudicating between possible variants and possible interference from the translators of versions, see Brotzman and Tully 2016:90–96.

Due to the focus of the commentary on the Hebrew text of Hosea, I do not attempt to discuss versional evidence of variants except as they may solve particular textual problems in the Hebrew. The primary focus is on the MT, and specifically the text of BHS. The apparatus of BHS is notoriously problematic and unhelpful. Many of the notes are literary judgments of the editors and those notes which relate to textual evidence are uneven and inconsistent. They draw attention to insignificant matters and fail to note significant readings. However, because BHS is still the most often used critical text, in the commentary I do refer to notes in the BHS apparatus. In addition, I sometimes comment on key issues in the Masorah parva as well as other masoretic marks and symbols presented in BHS.

A HANDBOOK ON THE HEBREW TEXT OF HOSEA

Superscription (1:1)

The opening verse of Hosea is a superscription which functions as a title, identifies the prophet, and locates the oracles in their particular historical context. This title makes the theological claim that the entire book is the "word" of YHWH, including both the prophetic sign-act of Hosea's family (chs. 1–3) and the oracles which further expound on YHWH's present and future relationship with Israel (chs. 4–14).

¹*The word of YHWH which came to Hosea, the son of Be'eri in the days of Uzziah, Jotham, Ahaz [and] Hezekiah, kings of Judah, and in the days of Jeroboam the son of Joash, king of Israel.*

1:1 דְּבַר־יְהוָה ׀ אֲשֶׁר הָיָה אֶל־הוֹשֵׁעַ בֶּן־בְּאֵרִי בִּימֵי עֻזִּיָּה יוֹתָם אָחָז יְחִזְקִיָּה מַלְכֵי יְהוּדָה וּבִימֵי יָרָבְעָם בֶּן־יוֹאָשׁ מֶלֶךְ יִשְׂרָאֵל׃

סְא. In the margin, to the right of the first line of text, a ס with a subscript א marks the beginning of a *seder*. In Palestinian manuscripts the Torah was divided into *sedarim* (sections) so that it could be read in the synagogue in the course of a year. The significance of the division in the Prophets and Writings is uncertain (Yeivin 1980:40; Kelley et al. 1998:155). See 6:2; 10:12; 14:6.

דְּבַר־יְהוָה ׀ אֲשֶׁר הָיָה אֶל־הוֹשֵׁעַ בֶּן־בְּאֵרִי. This prose superscription is a sentence fragment with no predicate. It consists of a construct phrase (דְּבַר־יְהוָה) which is the head of an embedded relative clause. As such, the verb הָיָה and the PP אֶל־הוֹשֵׁעַ (within the relative clause) merely describe the "Word of YHWH." These first six words in Hosea are identical to the openings of Joel (1:1), Micah (1:1), and Zephaniah (1:1). By contrast, the opening words of Jeremiah (1:2), Ezekiel (1:3), Haggai (1:1) and Zechariah (1:1) have דְּבַר־יְהוָה as the subject of the verb הָיָה either within a relative clause (Jer 1:2) or without a relative clause at all. The difference is that the latter books focus on the revelation as an event, whereas the former books are more interested in its identity.

אֲשֶׁר הָיָה אֶל־הוֹשֵׁעַ בֶּן־בְּאֵרִי. Relative clause headed by דְּבַר־יְהוָה. The verb הָיָה is a Qal *qatal* 3ms √היה. אֶל־הוֹשֵׁעַ is a PP. The prep אֶל indicates direction: in this case the receiver of the "word." The name הוֹשֵׁעַ comes from √ישע ("to deliver, save") and represents either a Hiph *qatal* 3ms ("he has delivered") or a Hiph inf abs, possibly to be translated as an imperative ("Deliver!"). It is closely related to the name יְהוֹשׁוּעַ ("Joshua") which has the same meaning. Joshua, the son of Nun, is even called הוֹשֵׁעַ several times in the Pentateuch (Num 13:8, 16; Deut 32:44). The construct phrase בֶּן־בְּאֵרִי is in apposition to הוֹשֵׁעַ and identifies the father of the prophet. The name בְּאֵרִי means "my well" and might refer to a location or to the joy of the parents as they welcome new life into the family (Macintosh 2014:5).

בִּימֵי עֻזִּיָּה יוֹתָם אָחָז יְחִזְקִיָּה מַלְכֵי יְהוּדָה. PP with בְּ attached to the mp construct form of יוֹם. The construct governs all four names of the kings, which are coordinated without a conjunction (WO §9.3b). One usually finds a וְ conjunction on each item in a series and sometimes only on the last item. It is very rare to omit the conjunction entirely, as is the case here (WO §39.2.1b). The construct phrase מַלְכֵי יְהוּדָה with a plural construct noun (or, *nomen regens*) is in apposition to the proper nouns which precede it.

וּבִימֵי יָרָבְעָם בֶּן־יוֹאָשׁ מֶלֶךְ יִשְׂרָאֵל. This PP is parallel to the preceding one and is constructed in the same way. The mp construct form of יוֹם governs the PN יָרָבְעָם. Two construct phrases in apposition to יָרָבְעָם follow: בֶּן־יוֹאָשׁ provides the name of Jeroboam's father and מֶלֶךְ יִשְׂרָאֵל describes the location of his rule.

Part 1: Hosea's Sign-Act and Its Application to Israel (1:2–3:5)

The book of Hosea begins in 1:2-9 with a prophetic sign-act illustrating the broken relationship between YHWH and his people. The sign-act has two parts: Hosea's marriage to Gomer and the names of his three children, "Jezreel," "Not Pitied," and "Not My People." Each name is a message to Israel of sin, rejection, and forthcoming consequences.

However, in the next short section (2:1-3), Hosea announces that in the future the names will be reversed. After judgment, hope lies beyond. This alternation of judgment and hope is a pattern that will continue throughout the book.

In 2:4-25 the associations and emotional undertones of the sign-act continue while the prophet applies it to Israel. A marriage relationship entails both a commitment to fidelity as well as social and financial benefits. In the same way, Israel was to be committed to the exclusive worship of YHWH. In turn, he would bless her with agricultural wealth and protection from her enemies. However, Israel has broken faith with her "husband" and credited her lovers for her prosperity (2:4-10). Therefore, he will remove those benefits and leave her desolate (2:11-15). But this is not the final word (2:16-25). Like a husband in a broken marriage who makes a fresh start, YHWH will take Israel back to the wilderness. This will be like returning to the place of the honeymoon in order to signal a new beginning. He will put away her lovers and establish a new relationship. At that time, in the eschatological future, YHWH will restart the agricultural processes which he had stopped up in judgment. The land will once again provide Israel with its gifts of grain, wine, and oil.

In 3:1-5 Hosea returns once again to the sign-act. He finds Gomer and brings her back into his house, but refrains from sexual activity until there is full reconciliation in the future. Likewise, Israel will live estranged from YHWH for a time, but in the last days they will again seek him and know his goodness.

1:2–2:3: Gomer and Israel Are Two Adulterous Wives, But There Is Hope

The sign-act begins when YHWH commands the prophet to marry a woman characterized by illicit sexual behavior. The union produces three children (although the text is not explicit that the second and third were actually from Hosea). The focus of this unit is on the meaning of the names of the three children, which are symbolic and point to Hosea's prophetic message. Beyond this, there are scant biographical details and it is impossible to reconstruct the specifics of Hosea's life and family. In 2:1-3 the negative symbolism of the names is reversed as the prophet announces future hope. The scattered Israelites will once again be the unified people of God (vv. 1-2) and will experience forgiveness and relationship with him once more (v. 3). This juxtaposition of judgment (1:2-9) and hope (2:1-3) is continued in the rest of the book. The prophet frequently switches between judgment and salvation oracles without an explicit transition.

> ²*The beginning of that which YHWH spoke with Hosea. YHWH said to Hosea, "Go, take for yourself a wife of fornication and children of fornication, for the land surely fornicates away from YHWH." ³And he went and married Gomer, the daughter of Diblaim, and she conceived and bore him a son. ⁴And YHWH said to him, "Call his name 'Jezreel' for in a little while I will visit the bloodshed of Jezreel upon the house of Jehu and I will bring to an end the rule of the house of Israel. ⁵And on that day I will break the bow of Israel in the Valley of Jezreel." ⁶And she conceived again and bore a daughter and he said to him, "Call her name 'Not Pitied' for I will no longer pity the house of Israel, but I will annihilate them.*
>
> ⁷*But the house of Judah I will pity*
> *and I will save them by YHWH their God,*
> > *but I will not save them by bow or by sword or by war, by horses or by horsemen."*
>
> ⁸*And she weaned "Not Pitied" and she conceived and bore a son. ⁹And he said, "Call his name 'Not My People' for you are 'Not My People' and I am 'Not I Am' to you."*
>
> ²:¹*And the number of the Israelites will be like the sand of the sea*
> *which is not measured and is not counted.*
> *And it will be: in the place where it was said to them, "You are not my people,"*
> *it will be said to them, "Sons of the living God."*
> ²*And the Judahites and the Israelites will gather together,*
> *and they will establish one head for themselves,*
> *and they will go up from the land.*
> *Great is the day of Jezreel!*
> ³*Say to your brothers, "My people"*
> *and to your sisters, "Pitied."*

1:2 תְּחִלַּ֥ת דִּבֶּר־יְהוָ֖ה בְּהוֹשֵׁ֑עַ פ וַיֹּ֨אמֶר יְהוָ֜ה אֶל־הוֹשֵׁ֗עַ לֵ֣ךְ קַח־לְךָ֞ אֵ֤שֶׁת זְנוּנִים֙ וְיַלְדֵ֣י זְנוּנִ֔ים כִּי־זָנֹ֤ה תִזְנֶה֙ הָאָ֔רֶץ מֵאַחֲרֵ֖י יְהוָֽה׃

תְּחִלַּת דִּבֶּר־יְהוָה בְּהוֹשֵׁעַ. Title and introduction to the prophetic sign-act in chapters 1–3. The title in 1:1 introduces the book of Hosea as a whole, whereas this title introduces the beginning of Hosea's prophecy proper.

תְּחִלַּת. While it is usual for time determinations to be in the construct state (GKC §130d), here the *nomen rectum* is an unmarked relative clause: דִּבֶּר־יְהוָה בְּהוֹשֵׁעַ (see Holmstedt 2016:112, n. 9; 213, n. 12).

דִּבֶּר־יְהוָה. Piel *qatal* 3ms √דבר. Its subject is יְהוָה.

בְּהוֹשֵׁעַ. PP with בְּ. Normally one would expect the prep אֶל or לְ with the verb דִּבֶּר (cf. Ezek 1:3; Joel 1:1; Jon 1:1). The use of בְּ might indicate that YHWH spoke "through" Hosea and that he is not the primary audience (Stuart 1987:26). Alternatively, because this constitutes the instructions for Hosea's family to serve as a sign-act, it might indicate that it is a conversation "with" Hosea rather than delivery of an oracle to him.

וַיֹּאמֶר יְהוָה אֶל־הוֹשֵׁעַ. Independent clause, main narrative line.

וַיֹּאמֶר. Qal *wayyiqtol* 3ms of √אמר. Following the two titles to the book, this verb signals the beginning of the sequential narrative.

יְהוָה. Subject of the verb וַיֹּאמֶר.

אֶל־הוֹשֵׁעַ. PP with אֶל. PPs introduced by אֶל and לְ commonly indicate the addressee of verbs of speaking (e.g., √דבר, √אמר).

לֵךְ קַח־לְךָ אֵשֶׁת זְנוּנִים וְיַלְדֵי זְנוּנִים. Independent clause, direct speech. Two verbs are included in this clause because לְךָ functions as an auxiliary verb to modify קַח.

לֵךְ. Qal impv ms √הלך (the ה is lost in the imperative due to aphaeresis, analogous with I-ו/י verbs). The use of √הלך does not suggest a journey, it initiates and intensifies the command of the following imperative.

קַח־לְךָ. Qal impv ms √לקח (the ל is lost in the imperative due to aphaeresis, analogous to I-נ verbs). This is the usual verb for taking a wife in marriage (cf. Gen 4:19; 11:29; 21:21). The PP לְךָ is an adjunct indicating the person for whom the action is directed (dative of advantage).

אֵשֶׁת זְנוּנִים. אֵשֶׁת is an acc complement of the impv קַח. The genitive זְנוּנִים is adjectival (WO §9.5.3a), indicating that אִשָּׁה is characterized by זְנוּנִים. McComiskey (2009:13) argues that characteristic genitives always describe the present state of the *nomen regens*. This would indicate that she was promiscuous before she was married. It does not mean adultery nor does it mean a professional prostitute (זוֹנָה); it is a general term of fornication and illegitimate sexual activity. For a helpful list of interpretive options on this phrase, see Garrett 1997:44–46. GKC [§124f] supposes that זְנוּנִים is an abstract plural because it describes several parts of an action.

וְיַלְדֵי זְנוּנִים. Constr phrase coordinated with אֵשֶׁת זְנוּנִים and serving as a second acc compl of the verb קַח. If we understand this phrase in the same way as the previous one, in what way are the children characterized by זְנוּנִים? It cannot mean that they were a result of fornication, because 1:3 indicates that the first child (at least) was Hosea's. It is most likely that the character of the mother and children are linked because they both serve as a sign-act for the corrupt northern kingdom (AF 168). It is precarious to press the first three chapters for biographical details of Hosea's family since he does not carefully keep the signs and the referents distinct.

כִּי־זָנֹה תִזְנֶה הָאָרֶץ מֵאַחֲרֵי יְהוָה. Subordinate causal clause giving the reason that Hosea should marry an אֵשֶׁת זְנוּנִים.

זָנֹה. Qal inf abs √זנה used to intensify the cognate finite verb which follows as an absolute complement (WO §35.3.1).

תִזְנֶה. Qal *yiqtol* 3fs √זנה. There are a total of four occurrences of the root √זנה in this verse, emphasizing the surprising and emotionally painful nature of the sign-act.

הָאָרֶץ. Feminine subject of תִזְנֶה.

מֵאַחֲרֵי יְהוָה. PP with compound prep מִן and אַחַר (אַחֲרֵי) is an alternate form, apparently plural, WO §11.2.1a). The compound preposition occurs sixty-two times in the MT and it is usually used of someone following someone else. The image is a combination of a metonymy ("land" represents the people who live on the land) and the common biblical metaphor: life is a path. The land is pictured as leaving her position as a follower of YHWH and deviating from the path in disloyalty and spiritual fornication.

1:3 וַיֵּלֶךְ וַיִּקַּח אֶת־גֹּמֶר בַּת־דִּבְלָיִם וַתַּהַר וַתֵּלֶד־לוֹ בֵּן׃

וַיֵּלֶךְ. Independent clause, main narrative line. The verb is a Qal *wayyiqtol* 3ms √הלך. This verb picks up the narrative again after YHWH's dialogue in 1:2.

וַיִּקַּח אֶת־גֹּמֶר בַּת־דִּבְלָיִם. Independent clause, main narrative line.

וַיִּקַּח. Qal *wayyiqtol* 3ms √לקח (the ל-I assimilates to the ק, analogous to I-נ verbs). YHWH's command in 1:2 had been לֵךְ קַח. Now the narrator repeats those verbs in sequence (וַיֵּלֶךְ וַיִּקַּח) in order to indicate Hosea's full compliance.

אֶת־גֹּמֶר. Acc compl of וַיִּקַּח. This is the only time that Hosea's wife is named in the book. Elsewhere גֹּמֶר is the name of one of Japheth's sons (Gen 10:2-3; 1 Chr 1:5-6) and one of Gog's allies in the book of Ezekiel (38:6). The name has a segolate noun pattern based on the root √גמר which means "to come to an end" or "complete" (BDB 170). There is no further wordplay on the name in Hosea and thus there does not seem to be any implied symbolic meaning (AF 171).

בַּת־דִּבְלָיִם. Constr phrase in apposition to גֹּמֶר, which tells us the name of her father. דִּבְלָיִם has a dual ending.

וַתַּהַר. Independent clause, main narrative line. The verb is a Qal *wayyiqtol* 3fs √הרה. This verb is commonly preceded in narratives by a report of sexual intercourse with √בוא or √ידע (e.g., Gen 4:1, 17; 16:4; 1 Sam 1:19-20). That neither verb appears here might suggest that even in bearing Hosea's three children, Gomer was living up to her reputation as a sexually promiscuous woman, and it was not Hosea who caused her to conceive. However, the following clause states that "she bore a son *to him*," suggesting that the child was Hosea's.

וַתֵּלֶד־לוֹ בֵּן. Independent clause, main narrative line.

וַתֵּלֶד־לוֹ. Qal *wayyiqtol* 3fs √ילד. The I-י is actually a I-ו (cf. Hiph יוֹלִיד), which contracts with the vowel under the preformative ת and becomes a *tsere*. The adjunct PP לוֹ specifies the person to whom a son was born (a dative of advantage).

בֵּן. Acc compl of וַתֵּלֶד.

וַיֹּאמֶר יְהוָה אֵלָיו קְרָא שְׁמוֹ יִזְרְעֶאל כִּי־עוֹד מְעַט 1:4
וּפָקַדְתִּי אֶת־דְּמֵי יִזְרְעֶאל עַל־בֵּית יֵהוּא וְהִשְׁבַּתִּי
מַמְלְכוּת בֵּית יִשְׂרָאֵל:

וַיֹּאמֶר יְהוָה אֵלָיו. Independent clause, main narrative line.

וַיֹּאמֶר. Qal *wayyiqtol* 3ms √אמר.

יְהוָה. Subject of וַיֹּאמֶר.

אֵלָיו. PP with אֶל indicating the addressee of וַיֹּאמֶר.

קְרָא שְׁמוֹ יִזְרְעֶאל. Independent clause, direct speech.

קְרָא. Qal impv ms √קרא.

שְׁמוֹ. Acc compl of קְרָא. The complement of an imperative is often not marked with אֶת, even in prose.

יִזְרְעֶאל. The name "Jezreel" consists of a *yiqtol* or juss of √זרע and the theophoric element אל meaning, "God sows/will sow" or "may God sow." The prophet will play with this meaning later in 2:23. יִזְרְעֶאל is also the name of a valley in the northern kingdom (cf. Josh 17:16) and a royal city in the northern kingdom. It was this city where Jehu, after he was anointed, slaughtered the family of Ahab and famously had Jezebel thrown down so that she was trampled by horses (2 Kgs 9–10). These actions are sanctioned by Elisha the prophet (2 Kgs 9:7) and YHWH (2 Kgs 10:30).

כִּי־עוֹד מְעַט וּפָקַדְתִּי אֶת־דְּמֵי יִזְרְעֶאל עַל־בֵּית יֵהוּא. Subordinate causal clause giving the reason that Hosea should name his son "Jezreel." עוֹד ("yet") is a temporal adverb and מְעַט ("little") is an adjective; together they modify the time of the following three clauses (to the end of v. 5).

וּפָקַדְתִּי. Qal *qatal* (irrealis) 1cs √פקד. The combination of the verb √פקד and the prep עַל can mean "to commission, instruct" (e.g., Num 4:27), "to accuse" (e.g., 2 Sam 3:8) or "to bring punishment upon" (e.g., Exod 32:34). The verb √פקד in the idiom here (cf. 2:15), takes two complements: an accusative (here marked with אֵת), which specifies the reason for the punishment or the form that punishment will take, and a PP (introduced by עַל), which specifies the recipient of the punishment. McComiskey (1993:93–101) has argued that in this context, the collocation does not have an inherent sense of reciprocal punitive action. Jehu is not being punished for the bloodshed he committed at Jezreel, an act he was instructed to do by Elisha (2 Kgs 9:7). Rather, just as he inflicted bloodshed on evil king Ahab in Jezreel, he will be visited with similar bloodshed because he is now an evil king as well.

אֶת־דְּמֵי יִזְרְעֶאל. The construct form דְּמֵי is the acc compl of וּפָקַדְתִּי. Whereas the singular דָּם refers more generally to blood, the plural refers to blood that has been shed or to blood-guilt. Knowledge of the historical reference would indicate that יִזְרְעֶאל is an objective genitive. It is not bloodshed *by* Jezreel but bloodshed *against* Jezreel.

עַל־בֵּית יֵהוּא. This PP with עַל is a complement of √פקד specifying the recipient.

וְהִשְׁבַּתִּי מַמְלְכוּת בֵּית יִשְׂרָאֵל. Independent clause, direct speech.

וְהִשְׁבַּתִּי. Hiph *qatal* (irrealis) 1cs √שבת. The final ת of the root has geminated with the ת of the 1cs suffix.

מַמְלְכוּת בֵּית יִשְׂרָאֵל. Constr chain. מַמְלְכוּת is the acc compl of וְהִשְׁבַּתִּי. It means "rule" or "dominion" and the whole construct chain refers to the broader institution and power of the northern kingdom. This clause is parallel to the previous one and represents an expansion in scope. Not only will YHWH visit bloodshed back on the dynasty of Jehu, he will bring to an end the entire monarchy.

1:5 וְהָיָה בַּיּוֹם הַהוּא וְשָׁבַרְתִּי אֶת־קֶשֶׁת יִשְׂרָאֵל בְּעֵמֶק יִזְרְעֶאל׃

וְהָיָה בַּיּוֹם הַהוּא. Independent clause, direct speech.

וְהָיָה. Qal *qatal* (irrealis) 3ms √היה. This verb frequently used in scene-setting clauses (see Holmstedt 2010:52–53, 160). In this use it does not have an explicit subject and instead provides the temporal setting for the next main clause. The irrealis *qatal* indicates that this clause is contingent upon the preceding event (YHWH's ending of the monarchy of the northern kingdom) (see Holmstedt 2010:168).

בַּיּוֹם הַהוּא. PP with בְּ indicating the temporal setting for the following clause. הַהוּא is an attributive (hence the article) and functions here as a far demonstrative (JM §143j; WO §17.3a). When spoken by a prophet (even outside the Latter Prophets), the phrase בַּיּוֹם הַהוּא refers to an event in the indeterminate future. While the phrase here appears to refer to an event within the prophet's lifetime (the Assyrian conquest), the other three occurrences in the book (2:18, 20, 23) refer to an eschatological event—when YHWH's relationship with Israel is fully restored.

וְשָׁבַרְתִּי אֶת־קֶשֶׁת יִשְׂרָאֵל בְּעֵמֶק יִזְרְעֶאל. Independent clause, direct speech.

וְשָׁבַרְתִּי. Qal *qatal* (irrealis) 1cs √שבר. The irrealis *qatal* indicates a prophetic prediction.

אֶת־קֶשֶׁת יִשְׂרָאֵל. Constr noun קֶשֶׁת is the acc compl of וְשָׁבַרְתִּי. The קֶשֶׁת ("bow") is a weapon often used as a metaphor for military strength (see 1 Sam 2:4; Ezek 39:3).

בְּעֵמֶק יִזְרְעֶאל. PP with בְּ indicating the location of the verbal action. Whereas the previous reference was to the city of Jezreel (1:4), this verse locates YHWH's action in the "Valley of Jezreel." This valley is frequently mentioned in the Bible as the location of significant battles including Deborah and Barak's defeat of the Canaanites by the river Kishon (Judg 4:13), Gideon's defeat of the Midianites (Judg 6:33), and the death of Josiah in the battle against Egypt at Megiddo (2 Kgs 23:29). In 733 BCE the armies of Tiglath-Pileser captured the valley in their conquest of the northern kingdom, leaving only Samaria and Ephraim under Israelite control. Thus, the Valley of Jezreel was the location of the defeat of the northern kingdom.

1:6 וַתַּהַר עוֹד וַתֵּלֶד בַּת וַיֹּאמֶר לוֹ קְרָא שְׁמָהּ לֹא רֻחָמָה כִּי לֹא אוֹסִיף עוֹד אֲרַחֵם אֶת־בֵּית יִשְׂרָאֵל כִּי־נָשֹׂא אֶשָּׂא לָהֶם׃

וַתַּהַר עוֹד. Independent clause, main narrative line. The verb is Qal *wayyiqtol* 3fs √הרה. עוֹד is a constituent adverb modifying the predicate וַתַּהַר (WO §39.3.1d).

וַתֵּלֶד בַּת. Independent clause, main narrative line. The verb is Qal *wayyiqtol* 3fs √ילד. Unlike 1:3 above, the narrator does not say that she bore the child לוֹ ("to him"). However, the adverb עוֹד in the previous clause links this pregnancy to that of יִזְרְעֶאל and suggests similarity (AF 187).

וַיֹּאמֶר לוֹ. Independent clause, main narrative line. The verb is a Qal *wayyiqtol* 3ms √אמר. לוֹ is a PP with לְ indicating the addressee of וַיֹּאמֶר. In 1:2 and 1:4 above, YHWH speaks אֶל־ Hosea, but there is no discernible difference between the two prepositions when used with verbs of speaking.

קְרָא שְׁמָהּ לֹא רֻחָמָה. Independent clause, direct speech.

קְרָא. Qal impv ms √קרא.

שְׁמָהּ. Acc compl of קְרָא.

לֹא רֻחָמָה. The name of Hosea's daughter consists of לֹא (an adverb, which is the negative particle) and רֻחָמָה, a Pual *qatal* 3fs √רחם. The two words form a compound which means "Not Pitied" (see GKC §152a, n. 1). Showing "pity" (√רחם) is one of YHWH's essential attributes in other parts of the OT (cf. Exod 34:6; Neh 9:17; Pss 86:15; 103:8; 145:8;

Joel 2:13; Jonah 4:2). The connection between the verb רחם√ and the noun רֶחֶם ("womb") is found throughout Semitic cognate languages and probably arises from the emotional, tender care associated with childbirth and an infant (cf. 1 Kgs 3:26). The verb is usually used of God having (or not having) compassion on his people or of the behavior of conquerors toward those whom they have subjugated (cf. Jer 42:12). Thus, the verb denotes mercy toward someone who is in a vulnerable position.

כִּי לֹא אוֹסִיף עוֹד אֲרַחֵם אֶת־בֵּית יִשְׂרָאֵל. Subordinate causal clause indicating the reason that Hosea should name his daughter, "Not Pitied." Waltke and O'Connor (§39.3.1d) understand the כִּי instead as a clausal adverb of emphasis. This is also known as an "asseverative" כִּי (cf. JM §164b).

לֹא אוֹסִיף. Hiph *yiqtol* 1cs יסף√. This verb is negated by the adverb לֹא. It is often used as an auxiliary, meaning "to do again" with an infinitival complement (JM §177b).

עוֹד. Constituent adverb qualifying the time extent of the predicate, "again" (WO 39.3.1d). Because the action of אֲרַחֵם is already qualified by אוֹסִיף, the use of this word signals additional emphasis. We could translate, "I will not show mercy again … ever."

אֲרַחֵם. Piel *yiqtol* 1cs רחם√. Although the complement of the auxiliary יסף√ is usually an infinitive in this construction, here it is a *yiqtol* without the copula. GKC states that this is "more vigorous and bold and belongs to poetic or elevated style" (§120h).

אֶת־בֵּית יִשְׂרָאֵל. Constr noun בֵּית serves as the acc compl of אֲרַחֵם.

כִּי־נָשֹׂא אֶשָּׂא לָהֶם. Subordinate adversative clause in direct speech.

נָשֹׂא. Qal inf abs of נשׂא√ intensifying אֶשָּׂא as an abs compl (WO §35.3.1).

אֶשָּׂא. Qal *yiqtol* 1cs נשׂא√.

לָהֶם. Oblique compl of אֶשָּׂא (cf. WO §11.2.10g).

This difficult clause elicits contradictory translations from commentators. Garrett (1997:60–62) translates, "but I shall completely forgive them," understanding the כִּי as adversative ("but") and translating נשׂא√ as "forgive" because its complement is marked with a לְ prep. He acknowledges that this is a surprising statement in the context of judgment on Israel. AF (143, 189) also translate נשׂא√ as "forgive" though, in light of the context of judgment, they understand the negative opening words

לֹא אוֹסִיף עוֹד to be governing every clause in vv. 6-7 so that the clause means, "or forgive them at all." Others, such as Wolff 1974 and Macintosh 2014 understand √נשׂא negatively. Wolff (1974:8) understands √נשׂא as "to carry off, take away" (cf. 5:14; Jer 49:29; Mic 2:2). Against AF, Macintosh argues that there is "considerable difficulty" in supposing that the negative לֹא can carry over the intervening כִּי. He translates √נשׂא as "annihilate" with support from Job 32:22, a view first proposed by Ibn Ezra and similar to the understanding of Kimchi (2014:21–22). The similar views of Wolff 1974 and Macintosh 2014 are attractive because they assume consistency in the negative context (which is accentuated by the contrasting mercy for Judah in 1:7a below) while still understanding √נשׂא in a way that occurs elsewhere.

1:7 a וְאֶת־בֵּית יְהוּדָה אֲרַחֵם
b וְהוֹשַׁעְתִּים בַּיהוָה אֱלֹהֵיהֶם
c וְלֹא אוֹשִׁיעֵם בְּקֶשֶׁת וּבְחֶרֶב וּבְמִלְחָמָה בְּסוּסִים וּבְפָרָשִׁים׃

וְאֶת־בֵּית יְהוּדָה אֲרַחֵם. *Line a.* Independent clause, direct speech. Although the first chapter of Hosea is essentially written in prose, this verse is a tricolon; the three lines are coordinated with ו and are marked by *Zaqep parvum*, *'Atnaḥ*, and *Silluq* disjunctive accents.

וְאֶת־בֵּית יְהוּדָה. Constr noun בֵּית is the acc compl of אֲרַחֵם. It is fronted in the word order for focus, to emphasize the contrast with the preceding clause. YHWH says, "I will no longer pity the house of Israel ..." (1:6b), but "I will pity *the house of Judah*."

אֲרַחֵם. Piel *yiqtol* 1cs √רחם. This verb continues the wordplay on the name לֹא רֻחָמָה.

וְהוֹשַׁעְתִּים בַּיהוָה אֱלֹהֵיהֶם. *Line b.* Independent clause, direct speech.

וְהוֹשַׁעְתִּים. Hiph *qatal* (irrealis) 1cs √ישע with 3mp acc suffix. The irrealis *qatal* indicates intent and volition. The verb √ישע occurs only in the Niphal (pass) and the Hiphil (active, transitive). It is used of helping or saving someone who is in danger. Both people (e.g., Deut 22:27) and YHWH (e.g., Exod 14:30) serve as subjects of this verb.

בַּיהוָה אֱלֹהֵיהֶם. PP with בְּ used instrumentally to indicate the means by which YHWH, the speaker of the 1cs verb וְהוֹשַׁעְתִּים, will save. The awkwardness of the speaker referring to himself in the third person motivates AF (194–95) to understand the preposition as a *beth essentiae*, marking the subject of the verb in apposition (cf. GKC §119i). However, line b is formally parallel to line c, where the prep בְּ is best understood as instrumental. Each of the lines has the verb ישׁע√, a 3mp acc suffix, a prep בְּ, and complement(s) of that preposition. This similarity suggests that they should be understood in the same way. Therefore, line b is intentionally unusual and highlights the first of two competing options. YHWH is presenting himself as a *means* of salvation in contrast to basic weapons of war (line c) which fail those who wield them and cannot ultimately save.

וְלֹא אוֹשִׁיעֵם בְּקֶשֶׁת וּבְחֶרֶב וּבְמִלְחָמָה בְּסוּסִים וּבְפָרָשִׁים. *Line c.* Independent clause, direct speech.

וְלֹא אוֹשִׁיעֵם. Following the negative particle, the verb is a Hiph *yiqtol* 1cs ישׁע√ with a 3mp acc suffix.

בְּקֶשֶׁת וּבְחֶרֶב וּבְמִלְחָמָה בְּסוּסִים וּבְפָרָשִׁים. PP with בְּ used instrumentally to indicate potential means of deliverance (GKC §119o). The preposition is commonly repeated on each item in a list (JM §132g). Additionally, the וְ conjunction is usually repeated on each item in the list (WO §39.2.1b). This is the case here, except with בְּסוּסִים following the disjunctive *Zaqep parvum* accent; the omission is probably for stylistic purposes. After a clausal negative, this use of וְ has an "alternative force" (WO §39.2b), meaning "or."

1:8 וַתִּגְמֹל אֶת־לֹא רֻחָמָה וַתַּהַר וַתֵּלֶד בֵּן׃

וַתִּגְמֹל אֶת־לֹא רֻחָמָה. Independent clause, main narrative line.

וַתִּגְמֹל. Qal *wayyiqtol* 3fs גמל√. Because children nursed longer in the ancient world, the statement that Gomer weaned לֹא רֻחָמָה and then conceived again may indicate that three years have passed in the span of this verse (cf. Garrett 1997:69).

אֶת־לֹא רֻחָמָה. Name of Hosea's daughter (see 1:6) and acc compl of וַתִּגְמֹל.

וַתַּהַר. Independent clause, main narrative line with a Qal *wayyiqtol* 3fs הרה√.

וַתֵּלֶד בֵּן. Independent clause, main narrative line with a Qal *wayyiqtol* 3fs ילד√.

בֵּן. Acc compl of וַתֵּלֶד. This is the third and final occurrence of this construction in Hosea, and each is somewhat different (see 1:3, 6). In 1:3 the narrator states that Gomer bore a son לוֹ (i.e., to Hosea). In 1:6 the second report of conception and birth, the narrator says that Gomer conceived עוֹד ("again"). This third report is the most simple, containing only three words. The lack of interest in consistency or providing specific biographical details only reinforces that it is the *names* of the children that are significant in the prophetic sign-act.

1:9 וַיֹּאמֶר קְרָא שְׁמוֹ לֹא עַמִּי כִּי אַתֶּם לֹא עַמִּי וְאָנֹכִי לֹא־אֶהְיֶה לָכֶם: ס

וַיֹּאמֶר. Independent clause, main narrative line. This short clause introduces the direct speech which follows. The verb is a Qal *wayyiqtol* 3ms √אמר.

קְרָא שְׁמוֹ לֹא עַמִּי. Independent clause, direct speech.

קְרָא. Qal impv ms √קרא.

שְׁמוֹ. Acc compl of קְרָא.

לֹא עַמִּי. The name of Hosea's third child consists of the negative particle לֹא and the noun עַם with a 1cs pronominal suffix. לֹא usually negates verbal clauses except in the case of single words or compounds (GKC §152a, n. 1). The name means "Not My People."

כִּי אַתֶּם לֹא עַמִּי. Subordinate causal clause which indicates the reason for the instruction in the main clause. This is a verbless clause in which the subject is the pronoun אַתֶּם and the predicate is the noun phrase לֹא עַמִּי. The word לֹא is not negating the predicate (i.e., "you *are not* 'my people'"). Rather, the negative particle stands within the predicate, negating the noun עַם and pronominal suffix (i.e., you *are* "Not My People"). The designation עַמִּי ("my people") was incredibly significant in Israelite experience and theology. YHWH uses the expression in Exod 3:7 when he initiates their exodus from Egypt. Perhaps the clearest statement of the relationship, borne out of covenant and now undone in Hosea, is found in Lev 26:12, וְהָיִיתִי לָכֶם לֵאלֹהִים וְאַתֶּם תִּהְיוּ־לִי לְעָם ("and I will be God to you, and you will be a people to me").

וְאָנֹכִי לֹא־אֶהְיֶה לָכֶם. Verbless clause in which the subject is the pronoun אָנֹכִי and the predicate is the noun phrase לֹא־אֶהְיֶה.

לֹא־אֶהְיֶה. The word אֶהְיֶה is a Qal *yiqtol* 1cs √היה meaning "I am." It is used here as a divine name for YHWH (perhaps an alternate form of the tetragrammaton) but negated because of the broken relationship between YHWH and his people. This verb also appears as a divine name in Exod 3:14: וַיֹּאמֶר אֱלֹהִים אֶל־מֹשֶׁה אֶהְיֶה אֲשֶׁר אֶהְיֶה וַיֹּאמֶר כֹּה תֹאמַר לִבְנֵי יִשְׂרָאֵל אֶהְיֶה שְׁלָחַנִי אֲלֵיכֶם ("And God said to Moses, 'I am who I am.' And he said, 'Thus you will say to the Israelites, "I am has sent me to you."'") This verbless clause, like the previous one, indicates identification. In the same way that the people are now "Not My People," YHWH is now "Not I Am" to them.

לָכֶם. A PP with ל functioning as a *lamed* of interest (*dativus commodi*) which marks the person for whom the verbless clause is directed (WO §11.2.10d).

2:1 a וְהָיָה מִסְפַּר בְּנֵי־יִשְׂרָאֵל כְּחוֹל הַיָּם
b אֲשֶׁר לֹא־יִמַּד וְלֹא יִסָּפֵר
c וְהָיָה בִּמְקוֹם אֲשֶׁר־יֵאָמֵר לָהֶם לֹא־עַמִּי אַתֶּם
d יֵאָמֵר לָהֶם בְּנֵי אֵל־חָי׃

Lines a-b and c-d are bicola. Each bicolon is one sentence in which the second line completes the first. In the first bicolon, line b contains two relative clauses which are headed by מִסְפַּר in line a. The lines are marked by *Zaqep parvum* and *'Atnaḥ*. In the second bicolon, line d presents a contrast of line c. The lines are marked by *Zaqep parvum* and *Silluq*.

וְהָיָה מִסְפַּר בְּנֵי־יִשְׂרָאֵל כְּחוֹל הַיָּם. *Line a.* Independent clause. Whereas 1:2-9 consisted of narrative and reported speech from YHWH, this verse begins oracular material. Therefore, the main line of the discourse is indicated with irrealis *qatal* verbs rather than *wayyiqtol* verbs.

וְהָיָה. Qal *qatal* (irrealis) 3ms √היה.

מִסְפַּר בְּנֵי־יִשְׂרָאֵל. The ms constr noun מִסְפַּר is the subject of the verb וְהָיָה. The rest of the construct chain (בְּנֵי־יִשְׂרָאֵל) is a genitive of measure (cf. WO §9.5.3f). Hosea used בֵּית יִשְׂרָאֵל to refer to the northern kingdom in 1:4, 6 in contrast to בֵּית יְהוּדָה (Judah) in 1:7. Here the combination of מִסְפַּר ("number") and the gentilic בְּנֵי־יִשְׂרָאֵל indicates that he has in mind the entire nation, north and south.

כְּחוֹל הַיָּם. PP consisting of כְּ used to indicate agreement in kind (WO §11.2.9) and construct phrase expressing an adjectival genitive.

אֲשֶׁר לֹא־יִמַּד. *Line b.* Relative clause headed by חוֹל. The verb is Niph *yiqtol* 3ms √מדד.

וְלֹא יִסָּפֵר. *Line b.* Relative clause headed by חוֹל. This clause is coordinated with the previous one and both are embedded in the main clause together and marked by the אֲשֶׁר. Unlike English, Hebrew allows the stacking of multiple relative clauses on the same head (Holmstedt 2016:211). It is the sand (חוֹל) of the sea which cannot be measured or counted, and the number of the Israelites is like that sand. The verb is Niph *yiqtol* 3ms √ספר. The two Niphal verbs in these clause are *Niphal tolerativum* that "express actions which the subject allows to happen to himself" (GKC §51c). The sand does not allow itself to be measured or counted.

וְהָיָה בִּמְקוֹם. *Line c.* Independent clause. The verb is Qal *qatal* (irrealis) 3ms √היה. It does not have an explicit subject and, with the PP בִּמְקוֹם, indicates the temporal and spatial setting of the next main clause (the second occurrence of יֵאָמֵר).

אֲשֶׁר־יֵאָמֵר לָהֶם. *Line c.* Relative clause headed by מְקוֹם, which is in the bound or construct form. This is common in BH and indicates that the relative clause has a restrictive sense, meaning that the relative clause is supplying crucial information for distinguishing between this מָקוֹם and another one (see Holmstedt 2016:205, 211).

יֵאָמֵר. Niph *yiqtol* 3ms √אמר. The *yiqtol* conjugation indicates the imperfective aspect. It typically refers to an action that is temporally non-past, but here it apparently refers to iterative action in the past (cf. Cook 2012:218, n. 51). If the prophet had used the *qatal* conjugation, he might have meant that "you are not my people" was said once and no longer applies. Instead, his use of the *yiqtol* gives the saying an immediacy and suggests that it is still current and applicable.

לָהֶם. PP indicating the addressee of the speech verb.

לֹא־עַמִּי אַתֶּם. *Line c.* Independent clause, direct speech. This is a verbless clause in which the subject is the pronoun אַתֶּם and the predicate is the noun phrase לֹא עַמִּי (see 1:9).

יֵאָמֵר לָהֶם בְּנֵי אֵל־חָי. *Line d.* Independent clause.

יֵאָמֵר. Niph *yiqtol* 3ms √אמר. This central clause in the verse corresponds to the previous relative clause in root (אמר) and conjugation (*yiqtol*), the PP לָהֶם, and the action occurs at the same location (מָקוֹם). This link conveys a transformation from what *is* (they are not YHWH's people) to what *will be* (children of the living God).

2:2 a וְנִקְבְּצוּ בְּנֵי־יְהוּדָה וּבְנֵי־יִשְׂרָאֵל יַחְדָּו
b וְשָׂמוּ לָהֶם רֹאשׁ אֶחָד
c וְעָלוּ מִן־הָאָרֶץ
d כִּי גָדוֹל יוֹם יִזְרְעֶאל׃

Lines a-d are a quatrain. Line d provides the summary and conclusion to the first three lines which resent three successive actions. Each of the first three lines begins with a 3cp irrealis *qatal*; בְּנֵי־יְהוּדָה in line a is the subject of all three verbs. The lines are marked by *Zaqep parvum*, *Ṭipḥa*, *'Atnaḥ*, and *Silluq*.

וְנִקְבְּצוּ בְּנֵי־יְהוּדָה וּבְנֵי־יִשְׂרָאֵל יַחְדָּו. *Line a*. Independent clause.

וְנִקְבְּצוּ. Niph *qatal* (irrealis) 3cp √קבץ. The Niphal must have a reflexive sense here ("they will gather themselves together"); if it were passive there would be no agent (AF 143). The irrealis use of *qatal* (along with the following two verbs) is used for predictive prophecy.

בְּנֵי־יְהוּדָה וּבְנֵי־יִשְׂרָאֵל. These two construct phrases are gentilics referring to the "Judahites" and the "Israelites" respectively. The latter must refer to the people of the northern kingdom in contrast to Judah in the south. Together they constitute all Israel referred to in 2:1.

יַחְדָּו. Adverb modifying וְנִקְבְּצוּ.

וְשָׂמוּ לָהֶם רֹאשׁ אֶחָד. *Line b*. Independent clause.

וְשָׂמוּ. Qal *qatal* (irrealis) 3cp √שׂים.

לָהֶם. Adjunct PP specifying the recipient of the action (dative of advantage).

רֹאשׁ אֶחָד. Acc compl of וְשָׂמוּ. אֶחָד is an attributive adjective modifying רֹאשׁ. The idiom שִׂים ... רֹאשׁ means either to appoint leadership (Deut 1:13; Judg 11:11; 1 Chr 26:10; Ps 18:44) or, by extension, to divide into several battle groups (1 Sam 11:11; Job 1:17). The former must be intended in this context.

וְעָלוּ מִן־הָאָרֶץ. *Line c.* Independent clause.

וְעָלוּ. Qal *qatal* (irrealis) 3cp √עלה.

מִן־הָאָרֶץ. PP. The מִן prep has an ablative sense, designating movement away from הָאָרֶץ (WO §11.2.11b). The basic linguistic meaning of this clause is straightforward, but it is difficult to interpret. S, T, and some medieval Jewish exegetes understood it as a return from exile. This is supported by Stuart (1987:36). AF (208–9) interprets it as release from captivity, but in the historical Exodus. However, "the land" (הָאָרֶץ) is not used in the Hebrew Bible to refer to foreign nations. Therefore, Macintosh (2014:33) and Garrett (1997:73) understand the clause to mean that Israel will grow and flourish like a metaphorical plant, sprouting from the land (cf. "sowing" in Hos 2:25). The restoration therefore would involve repopulation. If so, the metaphor would relate to the name "Jezreel" at the end of the verse which means "God sows" (Garrett 1997:73).

כִּי גָדוֹל יוֹם יִזְרְעֶאל. *Line d.* Independent, verbless clause with asseverative כִּי. Translators commonly interpret this כִּי as marking a causal clause, "for great is the day of Jezreel" on analogy with the explanation of the names in 1:2, 4, 6, and 9. However, there is not really a causal logic in the verse; it makes more sense to understand the כִּי as asseverative (AF 209). On the asseverative use of כִּי, see JM §164b and Kugel 1980.

גָדוֹל. Adjective modifying יוֹם and the predicate of the verbless clause.

יוֹם יִזְרְעֶאל. This is probably a construct phrase, but the name יִזְרְעֶאל could be understood as a vocative ("Great is the day, O Jezreel"). Jezreel was a place of bloodshed and death (cf. 1:5), but now it will once again refer to populating and flourishing as originally intended.

2:3 a אִמְרוּ לַאֲחֵיכֶם עַמִּי
     b וְלַאֲחוֹתֵיכֶם רֻחָמָה:

Lines a-b are a bicolon identified by ellipsis of the imperative אִמְרוּ which is elided in line b. The lines are marked by *'Atnaḥ* and *Silluq*.

אִמְרוּ לַאֲחֵיכֶם עַמִּי. *Line a.* Independent clause.

אִמְרוּ. Qal impv mp √אמר. The addressee of this plural imperative is unspecified. AF (211) argue that the prophet is continuing the description of his own family and is here speaking to his three children.

However, the prophet's focus is now on the nation of Israel, which Hosea's family represents. It is more likely that he is speaking rhetorically to the restored people of God and inviting them to acknowledge their renewed status.

לַאֲחֵיכֶם. PP with לְ indicating the addressee of the verb אִמְרוּ.

עַמִּי. Vocative and the direct speech commanded by the verb אִמְרוּ.

וְלַאֲחוֹתֵיכֶם רֻחָמָה. *Line b.* Independent clause. The verb אִמְרוּ is elided. The lines are very terse and focus on the reversal of the names in chapter 1. The order of the lines in this verse represent a reversal of 1:6-9. Line a ("my people") corresponds to 1:8-9 ("not my people") and line b ("mercy") corresponds to 1:6-7 ("no mercy").

וְלַאֲחוֹתֵיכֶם. PP indicating the addressee of the verb אִמְרוּ in line a.

רֻחָמָה. Pual *qatal* 3fs √רחם. Direct speech commanded by אִמְרוּ in line a. On this name, see the discussion on 1:6.

2:4-10: She Goes to Adulterous Lovers for Gifts

The prophet continues to use the familial language of wife, mother, husband, children, and adulterous lovers in continuity with his sign-act in chapter 1. Like a visual dissolve in a film, in which two images are temporarily overlaid and interpreted in light of each other, Hosea speaks to the nation of Israel even as he maintains the image of his wife and three children in the background. He increasingly uses in reference to the nation plural forms and images which are not really relevant to his family. Nevertheless, we are still meant to draw upon the social, moral, and emotional associations of family as we consider Israel's actions. My use of "she" and "he" in this and following unit titles is meant to reflect this intentional blurring of the sign-act and referent. In 2:4-10 Hosea describes a woman (Israel) who goes to lovers for gifts not realizing that they have really come from her husband (YHWH). In the next part, 2:11-15, the husband (YHWH) will take away those gifts as punishment.

[4]Contend against your mother, contend:
that she is not my wife,
and I am not her husband.

And let her put away her fornication from her face,
and her adulteries from between her breasts.

⁵*lest I strip her naked,*
and make her like the day she was born,

I will make her like a wilderness,
and render her like a parched land,
and kill her with thirst.

⁶*And her children I will not pity,*
for they are children of fornication.

⁷*Indeed their mother has fornicated,*
the one who conceived them has acted shamefully,

for she said, "I will go after my lovers
who give my bread, my water, my wool and my flax, my oil and my drink."

⁸*Therefore, behold, I will hedge in your way with thorns,*
and I will build up her wall,
so that she will not find her paths.

⁹*And she will pursue her lovers but will not overtake them,*
and she will seek them, but she will not find them.
And she will say, "I will go and return to my first man,
for it was better for me then than now."

¹⁰*But she does not know*
that I have given her the grain and the new wine and the oil,

and I multiplied silver for her
and gold which they made into the Ba'al.

2:4 a רִיבוּ בְאִמְּכֶם רִיבוּ
b כִּי־הִיא לֹא אִשְׁתִּי
c וְאָנֹכִי לֹא אִישָׁהּ
d וְתָסֵר זְנוּנֶיהָ מִפָּנֶיהָ
e וְנַאֲפוּפֶיהָ מִבֵּין שָׁדֶיהָ:

Lines a-c are a tricolon. The lines are linked via grammatical parallelism in which the noun אֵם in line a is the antecedent of the 3fs pronouns in lines b and c. The lines are marked by *Zaqep parvum, Zaqep parvum,* and *'Atnaḥ*. Lines d-e are a bicolon identified by ellipsis of the verb וְתָסֵר in line d. The lines are marked by *Zaqep parvum* and *Silluq*.

רִיבוּ בְאִמְּכֶם. *Line a*. Independent clause.

רִיבוּ. Qal impv mp √ריב. The noun and verb forms of the root √ריב refer to a quarrel or informal dispute (e.g., Gen 26:20) or an official case before authorities (e.g., Deut 19:17). In the prophets the word is often used to express YHWH's formal complaint against his people (Jer 2:5-9; Hos 4:1-3; Mic 6:1-8) (see NIDOTTE 3:1105–6). The addressee of this plural imperative is the people of the northern kingdom. Whereas in 2:3 Hosea urges the future people of God to proclaim their restored status, here he returns to the present time and urges the people to contend with their "mother." The prophet frequently alternates between present and future, judgment and hope, without an explicit transition.

בְאִמְּכֶם. PP which states the addressee of the רִיב. The verb √ריב is frequently followed by the prep עִם ("contend *with*"), suggesting a dispute in which both parties are participants and quarrel with each other (e.g., Gen 26:20; Exod 17:2). The use of the prep בְּ here indicates that the dispute is unidirectional: one party is angry at the other ("contend *against*") (e.g., Gen 31:36; Judg 6:32). Garrett (1997:39) makes a compelling argument that the "mother" here is the leadership, institutions, and culture of the nation. Hosea tells the people to contend against her because she has exploited them and taught them to be unfaithful.

רִיבוּ. *Line a*. Independent clause. The verb is a Qal impv mp √ריב.

כִּי־הִיא לֹא אִשְׁתִּי. *Line b*. Complement clause stating the content of רִיבוּ at the end of the previous line.

וְאָנֹכִי לֹא אִישָׁהּ. *Line c*. Verbless clause. Because it is coordinated with the previous clause, it also a complement clause marked by the כִּי. YHWH is stating that the covenant relationship between himself and Israel is broken.

וְתָסֵר זְנוּנֶיהָ מִפָּנֶיהָ. *Line d*. Independent clause.

וְתָסֵר. Hiph juss 3fs √סור. The *yiqtol* and jussive are indistinguishable in most *binyanim*. In the Hiphil, however, the *yiqtol* has a ִי (*hireq yod*) theme vowel, whereas the jussive has a ֵ (*tsere*).

זְנוּנֶיהָ. This noun meaning "fornication" is an abstract plural. See the discussion at 1:2.

מִפָּנֶיהָ. PP with מִן having an ablative sense. The noun פָּנֶה ("face") is singular and has a 3fs pronominal suffix. This noun takes the plural forms of pronominal suffixes. The form in the Leningrad Codex (and thus, BHS) is a spelling error. Note [b] in the apparatus gives the correct spelling according to multiple medieval Hebrew manuscripts.

וְנַאֲפוּפֶיהָ מִבֵּין שָׁדֶיהָ. *Line e.* Independent clause. The verb תָּסַר (line d) is elided here. The noun נַאֲפוּף (with two פs) is a *hapax* derived from √נאף ("to commit adultery").

מִבֵּין שָׁדֶיהָ. PP paralleling מִפָּנֶיהָ in line d.

2:5 a פֶּן־אַפְשִׁיטֶנָּה עֲרֻמָּה
b וְהִצַּגְתִּיהָ כְּיוֹם הִוָּלְדָהּ
c וְשַׂמְתִּיהָ כַמִּדְבָּר
d וְשַׁתִּהָ כְּאֶרֶץ צִיָּה
e וַהֲמִתִּיהָ בַּצָּמָא:

Lines a-b are a bicolon identified by word pairs (הִצַּגְתִּיהָ//אַפְשִׁיטֶנָּה and יוֹם הִוָּלְדָהּ//עֲרֻמָּה). The lines are marked by *Zaqep parvum* and *'Atnaḥ*. Lines c-e are a tricolon. Lines c-d are more formally parallel with desert imagery while line e is an intensified conclusion. The lines are marked by *R^ebi^aʿ*, *Zaqep parvum*, and *Silluq*.

פֶּן־אַפְשִׁיטֶנָּה עֲרֻמָּה. *Line a.* A negative final clause introduced by the conjunction פֶּן (WO §38.3c). This clause is subordinate to the main clauses in 2:4, lines d and e, "And let her put away her fornication… ." A final clause describes the result of the main clause; this negated final clause describes what will *not* happen if the main clause comes to pass.

אַפְשִׁיטֶנָּה. Hiph *yiqtol* 1cs √פשט with a 3fs (energic) acc suffix. The Qal often refers to the removal of one's own clothing (Lev 16:23; 1 Sam 18:4). In the Hiphil, when used of removing the clothing of someone else, it is generally in contexts of theft (Gen 37:23; 1 Sam 31:9; Job 22:6) or taking another's clothes in judgment (Num 20:26). Even in the judgment passage in Ezek 23:26, the word is used in parallel with taking beautiful jewels. It seems likely that here in Hosea, the emphasis is on taking away her clothes (which are beautiful and valuable) as opposed to displaying her nakedness. The point is that he is impoverishing her, not that he is exhibiting her.

עֲרֻמָּה. This predicate adjective (fs) refers to the suffix of אַפְשִׁיטֶנָּה and thus functions as an adverbial accusative (see JM §126).

וְהִצַּגְתִּיהָ כְּיוֹם הִוָּלְדָהּ. *Line b.* Negative final clause. This clause and the following clauses in lines c, d, and e are all subordinate to the main clauses in 2:4, lines d and e. Although the conjunction פֶּן occurs only at the beginning of this verse, the clauses are all coordinated on the same syntactic level. The clauses are in two separate cola, but they comprise one long sentence with 2:4.

וְהִצַּגְתִּיהָ. Hiph *qatal* (irrealis) 1cs √יצג with a 3fs acc suffix. The irrealis *qatal* expresses contingent modality in the final clause (see line a). This is one of six י׳ verbs in which the י assimilates to the second radical like I-נ verbs (JM §77). The verb occurs only in the Hiphil and its meaning is similar to √שׂים or √שׁית ("to set, place").

כְּיוֹם הִוָּלְדָהּ. PP indicating agreement in kind. הִוָּלְדָהּ is a Niph inf constr with a 3fs suffix. It is the genitive of the construct phrase: "like the day when she was born."

וְשַׂמְתִּיהָ כַמִּדְבָּר. *Line c.* Negative final clause. The verb is a Qal *qatal* (irrealis) 1cs √שׂים with a 3fs acc suffix. כַמִּדְבָּר is a PP with כְּ indicating agreement in kind.

וְשַׁתִּהָ כְּאֶרֶץ צִיָּה. *Line d.* Negative final clause. The verb is a Qal *qatal* (irrealis) 1cs √שׁית with a 3fs acc suffix. It is spelled defectively, without the י *mater* of the 1cs inflectional suffix. כְּאֶרֶץ צִיָּה is a PP consisting of כְּ indicating agreement in kind and a construct phrase.

וַהֲמִתִּיהָ בַּצָּמָא. *Line e.* Negative final clause. The verb is a Hiph *qatal* (irrealis) 1cs √מות with a 3fs acc suffix. It is spelled defectively, without the י *mater*. בַּצָּמָא is a PP with instrumental בְּ (WO §11.2.5d). This is how YHWH will kill her. Ironically, she went after other lovers to gain blessing and fertility, but she will die because basic needs will be removed.

2:6 a וְאֶת־בָּנֶיהָ לֹא אֲרַחֵם
b כִּי־בְנֵי זְנוּנִים הֵמָּה

Lines a–b are a bicolon indicated by noun//pronoun grammatical parallelism (הֵמָּה//בָּנֶיהָ). In addition, line b is syntactically subordinate to the clause in line a. The lines are marked by *'Atnaḥ* and *Silluq*.

וְאֶת־בָּנֶיהָ לֹא אֲרַחֵם. *Line a.* Independent clause.

וְאֶת־בָּנֶיהָ. Acc compl of אֲרַחֵם. בָּנֶיהָ is a mp noun with a 3fs poss suffix.

אֲרַחֵם. Piel *yiqtol* 1cs √רחם. This echoes 1:6 and 7.

כִּי־בְנֵי זְנוּנִים הֵמָּה. *Line b.* Causal clause subordinate to the clause in line a and indicating the reason that YHWH will not pity. This is a verbless clause. The predicate is the construct phrase בְנֵי זְנוּנִים, and the subject is the independent personal pronoun הֵמָּה. The accusation "they are children of fornication" seems overly harsh at first glance. However, the point is likely that they have inherited a proclivity to waywardness from their mother and will therefore share the same punishment (Macintosh 2014:46). As mentioned above, the children are the people of Israel, and the mother represents the political and religious institutions and culture of the nation.

2:7 a כִּי זָנְתָה אִמָּם
b הֹבִישָׁה הוֹרָתָם
c כִּי אָמְרָה אֵלְכָה אַחֲרֵי מְאַהֲבַי
d נֹתְנֵי לַחְמִי וּמֵימַי צַמְרִי וּפִשְׁתִּי שַׁמְנִי וְשִׁקּוּיָי:

Lines a-b is a bicolon, identified by word pairs (הֹבִישָׁה//זָנְתָה and הוֹרָתָם//אִמָּם) as well as the correspondence of 3fs *qatal* verbs and 3mp poss suffixes. The lines are marked by *Zaqep parvum* and *'Atnaḥ*. Lines c-d are a second bicolon consisting of one sentence; the second line is in apposition to the first. The lines are marked by *Pašṭa* and *Silluq*.

כִּי זָנְתָה אִמָּם. *Line a.* Independent, asseverative clause with כִּי. It is possible to analyze this as a causal clause in apposition to the causal clause in line b of 2:6. In that analysis, 2:6b and 2:7a are *both* reasons that YHWH will not pity (2:6a). However, we must also deal with another כִּי clause in line c of this verse. It seems unlikely that this would be a second clause in apposition. Rather, the present clause is asseverative or intensifying as the prophet shifts attention back to the mother (see JM §164b; Kugel 1980).

זָנְתָה. Qal *qatal* 3fs √זנה. In III-ה verbs, the feminine is formed directly on the masculine with a ת feminine morpheme and usually an additional ה feminine ending, as here (see JM §79d). This is the second use of this verb in the book. In 1:2 Hosea is told to marry a woman of fornication because the land has fornicated (זָנֹה תִזְנֶה הָאָרֶץ) away from YHWH.

אִמָּם. אֵם with a 3mp poss suffix; subject of זָנְתָה. The antecedent of the suffix is the children in 2:6b.

הֹבִישָׁה הוֹרָתָם. *Line b.* Independent clause.

הֹבִישָׁה. Hiph *qatal* 3fs √בושׁ. This is a so-called "B form" of this verb, probably formed on the basis of confusion with √יבשׁ (HALOT 117). This root is intransitive in the Qal ("be ashamed"), and it can be transitive ("put to shame") or intransitive ("act shamefully") in the Hiphil.

הוֹרָתָם. Qal ptc fs √הרה with a 3mp acc suffix (see JM §66). This is the subject of הֹבִישָׁה.

כִּי אָמְרָה. *Line c.* Causal clause explaining the reason that the mother has fornicated and acted shamefully: she has decided that other lovers are responsible for the gifts that she enjoys. The verb is a Qal *qatal* 3fs √אמר.

אֵלְכָה אַחֲרֵי מְאַהֲבַי. *Line c.* Independent clause; direct speech. This is one clause divided into two poetic lines (c and d).

אֵלְכָה. Qal juss (cohortative) 1cs √הלך. The cohortative is a long form of the jussive, with a paragogic ה, and indicates a first-person volative. Here, the mother is not predicting that she will go after other lovers, she is declaring her intention to do so.

אַחֲרֵי מְאַהֲבַי. PP with אַחֲרֵי, which has a metaphorical locational sense: to walk after is to behave like (WO §11.2.1a).

מְאַהֲבַי. Piel ptc mp √אהב with a 1cs poss suffix. This is a substantival participle in the construct state governing a complement in the genitive case, here a suffix (WO §37.3c). This word always occurs in the plural in Hosea (cf. 2:9, 12, 14, 15), suggesting a multiplicity of lovers (AF 230). The Piel participle is exclusively used in the OT of illegitimate lovers (cf. Jer 30:14; Ezek 16:33-37; 23:5, 9, 22).

נֹתְנֵי לַחְמִי וּמֵימַי צַמְרִי וּפִשְׁתִּי שַׁמְנִי וְשִׁקּוּיָי. *Line d.* A continuation of the clause begun in line c.

נֹתְנֵי. Qal ptc mp √נתן. This is a substantival participle, in the construct state, governing the complements which follow. It is in apposition to the previous substantival participle: מְאַהֲבַי. Two nominals in apposition are juxtaposed and agree in definiteness and reference. Here the appositive "givers of" provides further information about the leadword "lovers of" (see WO §12.3b).

לַחְמִי וּמֵימַי צַמְרִי וּפִשְׁתִּי שַׁמְנִי וְשִׁקּוּיָי. These nouns constitute a coordinated noun phrase which is governed by the construct נֹתְנֵי.

Typically, the construct is repeated with each genitive noun, but here they are all joined, probably because of the close semantic relationship among them (WO §9.3b). We also expect a וְ on each item in the list; it is rare that the וְ is irregularly distributed (WO §39.2.1b). The word וְשִׁקּוּי means "drink," and is related to the verbal root שׁקה√ ("to provide drink for"). It occurs only three times in the Hebrew Bible (Ps 102:10; Prov 3:8).

2:8 a לָכֵן הִנְנִי־שָׂךְ אֶת־דַּרְכֵּךְ בַּסִּירִים
b וְגָדַרְתִּי אֶת־גְּדֵרָהּ
c וּנְתִיבוֹתֶיהָ לֹא תִמְצָא׃

Lines a-c are a tricolon. The first two lines are parallel with semantic correspondence of the verbs גדר√//שׂוך√ and the imagery of obstruction. Each verb in lines a-b has a 1cs subject, while the third line shifts to a 3fs verb in order to describe the result. The lines are marked by 'Atnaḥ, Zaqep parvum, and Silluq.

לָכֵן הִנְנִי־שָׂךְ אֶת־דַּרְכֵּךְ בַּסִּירִים. *Line a.* Independent clause. The prophet, speaking for YHWH, responds to the mother's decision in 2:7.

לָכֵן. Adverb introducing the logical consequence of the preceding clause.

הִנְנִי־שָׂךְ. הִנֵּה is an interjection with a 1cs suffix. It is used to redirect or focus the attention of the addressee to something that is new or surprising (Berlin 1994:91–92). The 1cs suffix is the subject of the following participle. שָׂךְ is a Qal ptc ms שׂוך√/סוך√. Participles have a durative aspect but can refer to situations in the future, often with a sense of immediacy. Here, the participle means something like "I am going to." The roots שׂוך√ or סוך√ (II) occur elsewhere only in Job in reference to creating a protective barrier or trapping something within limits. The related noun שׂוֹךְ ("branches, twigs") is a *hapax*.

אֶת־דַּרְכֵּךְ. Acc compl of שָׂךְ. The noun דֶּרֶךְ is a key metaphor in wisdom literature for the character and culmination one's life choices. Hosea uses the word frequently (cf. 4:9; 6:9; 9:8; 10:13; 12:3; 13:7; 14:10).

בַּסִּירִים. PP with בְּ indicating the instrument (material) of the verbal action.

וְגָדַרְתִּי אֶת־גְּדֵרָהּ. *Line b.* Independent clause.

וְגָדַרְתִּי. Qal *qatal* (irrealis) 1cs √גדר. The verb simply means to build a wall, and it frequently takes a cognate accusative. It is used of keeping someone in (Job 19:8; Lam 3:7, 9) or keeping the enemy out (Ezek 13:5; Amos 9:11).

אֶת־גְּדֵרָהּ. Acc compl of וְגָדַרְתִּי. The antecedent of the 3fs poss suffix on גְּדֵר might be the דֶּרֶךְ in the previous clause (it can be feminine) referring to the sides of the path. It more likely refers to the mother: it is "her" wall because it is barring her from leaving. This would correspond to the 3fs suffix on a plural noun in the next clause.

וּנְתִיבוֹתֶיהָ לֹא תִמְצָא. *Line c.* Subordinate purpose clause.

וּנְתִיבוֹתֶיהָ. Acc compl with a 3fs poss suffix referring to the mother (see line b). Although this clause is syntactically coordinate to the previous clause (with וּ), semantically it is subordinate and has the sense of a purpose clause, "*so that* she cannot find her paths."

תִמְצָא. Qal *yiqtol* 3fs √מצא.

2:9 a וְרִדְּפָה אֶת־מְאַהֲבֶיהָ וְלֹא־תַשִּׂיג אֹתָם
b וּבִקְשָׁתַם וְלֹא תִמְצָא
c וְאָמְרָה אֵלְכָה וְאָשׁוּבָה אֶל־אִישִׁי הָרִאשׁוֹן
d כִּי טוֹב לִי אָז מֵעָתָּה:

Lines a-b are a bicolon. Each line has two clauses: one of an attempted action, and one describing its failure. The lines are marked by *Zaqep parvum* and *'Atnaḥ*. The second bicolon (lines c-d) consists of direct speech including a main clause (line c) and a subordinate clause (line d). The lines are marked by *Zaqep parvum* and *Silluq*.

וְרִדְּפָה אֶת־מְאַהֲבֶיהָ. *Line a.* Independent clause.

וְרִדְּפָה. Piel *qatal* (irrealis) 3fs √רדף. BDB suggests that the relatively rare Piel is intensive and means "to pursue ardently" (922). With the irrealis *qatal*, the prophet is describing a situation hypothetically; all of these statements are contingent upon the conditions in 2:4-5.

אֶת־מְאַהֲבֶיהָ. Acc compl of וְרִדְּפָה. This is a Piel ptc mp √אהב with a 3fs poss suffix. See the comment in 2:7.

וְלֹא־תַשִּׂיג אֹתָם. *Line a.* Independent clause.

תַשִּׂיג. Hiph *yiqtol* 3fs √נשׂג. This verb is common and refers to following someone and catching up.

אֹתָם. Acc compl of תַּשִּׂיג. The antecedent of the 3mp suffix is the lovers in the previous clause.

וּבִקְשָׁתַם. Line b. Independent clause. The verb is a Piel *qatal* (irrealis) 3fs √בקשׁ with a 3mp acc suffix. The *dagesh,* characteristic of the Piel, has dropped out of the ק because it is followed by a vocal *shewa* (JM §20m).

וְלֹא תִמְצָא. Line b. Independent clause. The verb is a Qal *yiqtol* 3fs √מצא. This verb requires an accusative complement, which is assumed here ("them").

וְאָמְרָה. Line c. Independent clause. The verb is a Qal *qatal* (irrealis) 3fs √אמר.

אֵלְכָה. Line c. Independent clause, direct speech. The verb is a Qal juss (cohortative) 1cs √הלך. With this volative verb, the speaker declares her intention to return to her legitimate husband.

וְאָשׁוּבָה אֶל־אִישִׁי הָרִאשׁוֹן. Line c. Independent clause.

וְאָשׁוּבָה. Qal juss (cohortative) 1cs √שׁוב. If the verb √שׁוב *precedes* another verb, it frequently functions as an auxiliary meaning "to do again" (HALOT 1430; JM §177b). However, the present verb is coordinated with the preceding אֵלְכָה so it should be translated as an independent clause. Hosea frequently uses the verb √שׁוב with the meaning of "repent" (cf. 2:11; 3:5; 4:9; 5:4; 6:1; 7:10; 14:2, 3, 5, 8).

אֶל־אִישִׁי הָרִאשׁוֹן. This PP is the complement of וְאָשׁוּבָה. הָרִאשׁוֹן is an attributive adjective modifying אִישׁ. The noun אִישׁ can mean "man" or "husband" (analogous to אִשָּׁה). In Deut 24:4 "first husband" is בַּעְלָהּ הָרִאשׁוֹן with the word בַּעַל. However, the lovers in the present passage are not husbands and nothing in the metaphor suggests a divorce or other marriages. They are "pseudo-husbands"—illegitimate substitutes. The use of אִישׁ to denote a husband here anticipates the change in terminology in 2:18-19 below (AF 239).

כִּי טוֹב לִי אָז מֵעָתָּה. Line d. Causal clause indicating the reason that the mother has decided to return to her legitimate husband. This is a verbless clause with only the adjectival predicate טוֹב and an implied subject ("it is"). Hebrew has no inflectional scheme for distinguishing among absolute, comparative, and superlative adjectives (WO §14.4a). The comparative מִן prep on מֵעָתָּה suggests that we should understand טוֹב as comparative: "[it was] better for me then than now." She now recognizes that although she has given the credit for her material wealth to her lovers *now*, she was better off with her first husband *then*.

2:10 a וְהִיא֙ לֹ֣א יָֽדְעָ֔ה
b כִּ֤י אָֽנֹכִי֙ נָתַ֣תִּי לָ֔הּ הַדָּגָ֖ן וְהַתִּיר֣וֹשׁ וְהַיִּצְהָ֑ר
c וְכֶ֨סֶף הִרְבֵּ֤יתִי לָ֔הּ
d וְזָהָ֖ב עָשׂ֥וּ לַבָּֽעַל׃

Lines a-b are a bicolon; line b is a complement clause embedded in the clause in line a. The lines are marked by *Zaqep parvum* and *'Atnaḥ*. The second bicolon is identified by the word pairs זָהָב//כֶּסֶף as well as first-person//third-person contrast of the verbs. In addition, the verb הִרְבֵּיתִי is elided in line d. The lines are marked by *Tebir* and *Silluq*.

וְהִיא לֹא יָדְעָה. **Line a.** Independent clause.

הִיא. Independent personal pronoun and subject of the clause. This pronoun is not obligatory in the syntax because the finite verb יָדְעָה is intrinsically marked for person, gender, and number. It marks the topic within the discourse and, with the pleonastic pronoun אָנֹכִי in the next clause (line b), contrasts what the mother knew with what YHWH had done.

יָדְעָה. Qal *qatal* 3fs √ידע. The verb should be translated in the present tense. All of the mother's actions are a result of what she does not know: that the credit for the things that she enjoys should be given to her husband (YHWH). Therefore, this verse supplies a summary of this subsection (2:4-10).

כִּי אָנֹכִי נָתַתִּי לָהּ הַדָּגָן וְהַתִּירוֹשׁ וְהַיִּצְהָר. **Line b.** Complement clause serving as the complement of יָדְעָה.

אָנֹכִי. Pleonastic independent personal pronoun and subject of the clause. We would expect VS word order following the כִּי. Therefore, in the SV word order the pronoun is pragmatically marked for focus, contrasting with הִיא in the previous line (see line a). It was YHWH, not the lovers, who gave her the gifts.

נָתַתִּי. Qal *qatal* 1cs √נתן. The III-נ has assimilated to the ת in the inflectional suffix.

לָהּ. The verb √נתן typically takes two complements. This first complement is a PP with לְ which specifies the recipient; the second, accusative complements, follow. The antecedent of the 3fs suffix is the mother (2:7).

הַדָּגָן וְהַתִּירוֹשׁ וְהַיִּצְהָר. These three coordinated nouns are the accusative complements of נָתַתִּי. They occur in this same order sixteen times in the Hebrew Bible with an especially prominent cluster in Deuteronomy (6×). The grain, new wine, and oil are gifts from God based on their adherence to covenant faithfulness (Deut 7:13; 11:14) and will be taken away if that covenant is broken (Deut 28:51).

וְכֶסֶף הִרְבֵּיתִי לָהּ. *Line c.* Independent clause.

וְכֶסֶף. Acc compl of הִרְבֵּיתִי.

הִרְבֵּיתִי. Hiph *qatal* 1cs √רבה. In another possible allusion, Deut 8:13 speaks of forgetting YHWH once כֶּסֶף and זָהָב are multiplied (√רבה).

לָהּ. Adjunct PP specifying the person to whom the action is directed. The 3fs suffix refers to the mother (see 2:7).

וְזָהָב. *Line d.* Acc compl of the verb הִרְבֵּיתִי, which is elided. This enables parallelism in the bicolon based on a well-known word pair (זָהָב//כֶּסֶף).

עָשׂוּ לַבַּעַל. *Line d.* Unmarked relative clause headed by כֶּסֶף and זָהָב in the main clause.

עָשׂוּ. Qal *qatal* 3cp √עשה. This verb has an unidentified, impersonal subject (JM §155b). Perhaps this is an instance when the referent of the metaphor emerges and Hosea refers directly to the people represented by the "mother."

לַבַּעַל. Adjunct PP with לְ specifying the person for whom the action is directed. Similar language in Hos 8:4-6 encourages us to interpret this as making the silver and gold (the word pair is used there) *into* an idol rather than serving as offerings *to* it. The irony is thick: "deluded into thinking that Baal is generous, his worshipers have to supply the metals to make him" (AF 243).

2:11-15: He Will Take Away Her Gifts and Leave Her Desolate

As noted in the introduction, the book is organized by the repeating pattern of three phases: Accusation, Temporary Judgment, and Ultimate Reconciliation. Hosea 2:4-25 is the first occurrence of this pattern. In its present position, the passage forecasts the structure of the oracles in chapters 4–14. The accusation came in 2:4-10 above. Israel, bound to YHWH in covenant, was supposed to look to him for security and flourishing but instead she looked elsewhere, to foreign gods and foreign nations. In the present unit, 2:11-15, YHWH announces judgment: he will take away those gifts—which have actually come from him—and leave her without the things that motivated her infidelity.

11 Therefore, I will return
and take my grain in its time
and my new wine in its season,

and I will take my wool and my flax
which were intended to cover her nakedness.

12 And now I will reveal her folly to the eyes of her lovers,
and no one will take her from my hands.

13 And I will put an end to all of her rejoicing:
her feasts, new moons, and her Sabbaths,
and all of her appointed times.

14 And I will devastate her vines and her fig trees,
of which she said, "They are my pay
which my lovers have given to me."

And I will make them into a forest,
and the wild animals of the field will devour them.

15 And I will visit upon her the days of the Ba'als
to whom she offered sacrifices.

She wore her rings and her jewelry,
and she went after her lovers,
but she forgot me.
A declaration of YHWH.

2:11 a לָכֵן אָשׁוּב
b וְלָקַחְתִּי דְגָנִי בְּעִתּוֹ
c וְתִירוֹשִׁי בְּמוֹעֲדוֹ
d וְהִצַּלְתִּי צַמְרִי וּפִשְׁתִּי
e לְכַסּוֹת אֶת־עֶרְוָתָהּ׃

Verses 11-15 are a new subsection. YHWH will take away his gifts since the mother (Israel) does not acknowledge him.

Lines a-c are a tricolon. A tricolon usually has two lines which are more formally parallel while the first or third line is more loosely related. Here lines b and c are parallel. They contain word pairs (תִּירוֹשׁ//דָּגָן and מוֹעֵד//עֵת) and the verb וְלָקַחְתִּי is elided in line c. Tricola often signal a contrast or shift in topic in a poem, as here. The lines are marked with *Zaqep parvum, Zaqep parvum,* and *'Atnaḥ*. Lines d-e are a bicolon consisting of one sentence; line e is a final clause completing the sentence. The lines are marked by *Zaqep parvum* and *Silluq*.

לָכֵן אָשׁוּב. *Line a.* Independent clause. לָכֵן is an adverb which introduces the consequence of the mother's actions and ignorance in the preceding lines.

אָשׁוּב. Qal *yiqtol* 1cs √שוב. This is usually understood as an auxiliary modifying the following verb לָקַחְתִּי ("I will take back") (JM §177b). However, the disjunctive accent (*Zaqep parvum*) indicates a break here, and the ו on the following verb may indicate a new clause. In addition, poetic analysis urges us to see this as a tricolon rather than as a bicolon with an overloaded first line. AF (244–45) argue that YHWH is not taking back anything from Ba'al. Rather, this is a play on words with וְאָשׁוּבָה in 2:9. The "mother" is changing her mind about her lovers and returning to her husband. However, it is too late and the husband (YHWH) is changing his mind as well. He will no longer give her the fertile produce to which she is accustomed.

וְלָקַחְתִּי דְגָנִי בְּעִתּוֹ. *Line b.* Independent clause.

וְלָקַחְתִּי. Qal *qatal* (irrealis) 1cs √לקח.

דְגָנִי. Acc compl of וְלָקַחְתִּי. This is a reversal of 2:10.

בְּעִתּוֹ. PP with בְּ used temporally. The antecedent of the 3ms poss suffix is דָּגָן. At the time that the דָּגָן is mature and ready for use, it will be taken before she can enjoy it.

וְתִירוֹשִׁי בְּמוֹעֲדוֹ. *Line c.* Independent clause in which the verb וְלָקַחְתִּי is elided.

וְתִירוֹשִׁי. Acc compl of the elided verb with a 1cs poss suffix.

בְּמוֹעֲדוֹ. PP with בְּ used temporally. The antecedent of the 3ms poss suffix is תִּירוֹשׁ. The noun מוֹעֵד is usually associated with cultic contexts for the tent of meeting (אֹהֶל מוֹעֵד) or religious festivals. However, a few occurrences have a noncultic use refering to a time appointed in the future, such as the birth of a child (Gen 17:21) or the time that a bird migrates (Jer 8:7). Here, in Hos 2:11 it refers to the anticipation of new wine, which will be taken away just as it is ready to be enjoyed.

וְהִצַּלְתִּי צַמְרִי וּפִשְׁתִּי. *Line d.* Independent clause.

וְהִצַּלְתִּי. Hiph *qatal* (irrealis) 1cs √נצל. The I-נ has assimilated to the צ. The verb √נצל means to "take away" in two senses. First, it can mean "to take away" from danger or to save from harm. Or, it can mean "to take away" without the permission of the owner (see Gen 31:9; 1 Sam 17:35; Amos 3:12). The semantic nuance here suggests that YHWH is taking back his wool and flax without her consent. It is not theft (it is his property); but it is against her will.

צַמְרִי וּפִשְׁתִּי. Acc compls of וְהִצַּלְתִּי with 1cs poss suffixes.

לְכַסּוֹת אֶת־עֶרְוָתָהּ. *Line e.* The syntax seems truncated here. The infinitive cannot introduce a purpose clause, because the verb √נצל would expect a negative sense ("so that she *cannot* cover her nakedness"), but there is no מִן or לְבִלְתִּי or other negating particle. JM (§124d) understands the infinitive as a genitive, "flax of covering." The best approach is to analyze it as an elliptical relative clause, "*which were intended* to cover. ..." The clause is not subordinate to the verb, rather it modifies the wool and flax.

לְכַסּוֹת. Piel inf constr √כסה.

עֶרְוָתָהּ. Acc compl of לְכַסּוֹת. The antecedent of the 3fs poss suffix is the mother in 2:7. The noun עֶרְוָה refers to genitals or sexual relations (cf. Lev 20:17-18).

2:12

a וְעַתָּה אֲגַלֶּה אֶת־נַבְלֻתָהּ לְעֵינֵי מְאַהֲבֶיהָ
b וְאִישׁ לֹא־יַצִּילֶנָּה מִיָּדִי׃

Lines a-b are a bicolon. It is one sentence with two coordinated clauses. The lines are marked with *'Atnaḥ* and *Silluq*.

וְעַתָּה אֲגַלֶּה אֶת־נַבְלֻתָהּ לְעֵינֵי מְאַהֲבֶיהָ. *Line a.* Independent clause.

וְעַתָּה. Temporal adverb that introduces "a shift in argumentative tack with a continuity in subject and reference" (WO §39.3.4f). It frequently divides an argument into segments. He has said that he will "strip" the land (2:11); now he will go further and strip her.

אֲגַלֶּה. Piel *yiqtol* 1cs √גלה. This verb means "to expose" or "to uncover" what was hidden.

אֶת־נַבְלֻתָהּ. Acc compl with a 3fs suffix still referring to the "mother" from 2:7. נַבְלוּת is a *hapax*. The verb √גלה commonly has nakedness (עֶרְוָה) as its complement (cf. Lev 18; Ezek 16:36-37; 23:10, 29), thus some commentators see this as the exposing of the mother's genitals (cf. Wolff 1974:37–38). While עֶרְוָה occurs at the end of the previous verse, נַבְלוּת is probably related to √נבל ("to be futile, foolish") (HALOT 664). Therefore, while the image may be that of exposing nakedness, the clause here primarily refers to exposing *actions* which are foolish and shameful (cf. Macintosh 2014:59–60; AF 248–49). The question since 2:4 has been which of her "men" is best suited to give her what she wants.

לְעֵינֵי מְאַהֲבֶיהָ. PP with לְ indicating to whom she will be exposed. עֵינֵי is a construct form. מְאַהֲבֶיהָ is a Piel ptc mp √אהב with a 3fs suffix.

וְאִישׁ לֹא־יַצִּילֶנָּה מִיָּדִי. *Line b*. Independent clause.

וְאִישׁ. This impersonal use of אִישׁ ("anyone," "someone") is the subject of יַצִּילֶנָּה. Because the following verb is negated, we should translate "no one."

לֹא־יַצִּילֶנָּה. Hiph *yiqtol* 3ms √נצל with a 3fs acc suffix. There is wordplay with the previous verse (2:11). There, YHWH will take (√נצל—without her consent) all his gifts from her. In this verse, no one will take her from his hand. The stakes have been raised and the judgment is certain.

מִיָּדִי. PP with abl מִן. The noun has a collective sense; it always occurs in the singular with a pronominal suffix except for eight technical uses in Exodus and 1 Kings referring to tabernacle or temple furnishings. The antecedent of the 1cs poss suffix is the speaker YHWH (via the prophet).

2:13 a וְהִשְׁבַּתִּי כָּל־מְשׂוֹשָׂהּ
b חַגָּהּ חָדְשָׁהּ וְשַׁבַּתָּהּ
c וְכֹל מוֹעֲדָהּ׃

Lines a-c are a tricolon comprising one independent clause. The poetic division is based on the masoretic accents (*Zaqep parvum* and *'Atnaḥ*) and the grouping of the terms according to content (see below).

וְהִשְׁבַּתִּי. Hiph *qatal* (irrealis) 1cs √שבת. He has stripped the land of her gifts (2:11), and stripped her (2:12). Now he is putting an end to her religious festivals. This is another way of taking back what she had wrongly attributed to competing "lovers."

כָּל־מְשׂוֹשָׂהּ חַגָּהּ חָדְשָׁהּ וְשַׁבַּתָּהּ וְכֹל מוֹעֲדָהּ. These six nouns, each with a 3fs poss suffix referring to the "mother" (cf. 2:7), are accusative complements of וְהִשְׁבַּתִּי. Each noun is singular but should be understood as collective. The poetic lines in the tricolon organize the nouns in three groups. The first term מָשׂוֹשׂ (line a) is used generally for rejoicing in contrast to gloom. It introduces the tone and the value of what is being taken away. The three center terms (line b) refer to cultic festivals or days. These are actually what is coming to an end. The last term מוֹעֵד (line c) is used for established times (cf. 2:11). It includes the preceding holy days as well as others.

2:14 a וַהֲשִׁמֹּתִי גַּפְנָהּ וּתְאֵנָתָהּ
b אֲשֶׁר אָמְרָה אֶתְנָה הֵמָּה לִי
c אֲשֶׁר נָתְנוּ־לִי מְאַהֲבָי
d וְשַׂמְתִּים לְיָעַר
e וַאֲכָלָתַם חַיַּת הַשָּׂדֶה:

Lines a-c are a tricolon consisting of a main clause and two embedded relative clauses, which use the imagery of gifts and wages. The lines are marked by *Zaqep parvum*, *Zaqep parvum*, and *'Atnaḥ*. Lines d-e are a bicolon that changes the imagery to that of wild animals in an uncultivated land. The lines are marked by *Zaqep parvum* and *Silluq*.

וַהֲשִׁמֹּתִי גַּפְנָהּ וּתְאֵנָתָהּ. *Line a*. Independent clause.

וַהֲשִׁמֹּתִי. Hiph *qatal* (irrealis) 1cs √שמם. The irrealis *qatal* expresses volition and intention. The Qal of √שמם means "to be uninhabited" and the Hiphil means "to cause to be deserted" (HALOT 1565). He will decimate her agriculture so that it is untended and unproductive. This anticipates his changing the vines and fig trees into a wild forest at the end of the verse.

גַּפְנָהּ וּתְאֵנָתָהּ. Acc compls of וַהֲשִׁמֹּתִי with 3fs poss suffixes referring to the mother (2:7). They should be translated as collectives.

אֲשֶׁר אָמְרָה. *Line b*. Embedded relative clause headed by גַּפְנָהּ and וּתְאֵנָתָהּ in the main clause. The relative clause occupies the function of a PP ("... vines and fig trees, *concerning* which she said ...") but the preposition is frequently omitted with verbs of saying (JM §158i). The verb is a Qal *qatal* 3fs √אמר.

אֶתְנָה הֵמָּה לִי. *Line b.* Independent, verbless clause. This is direct speech introduced by the verb in the relative clause. The word order of this verbless clause is predicate-subject-PP. The author could have used a possessive suffix with a subject-predicate word order: הֵמָּה אֶתְנָתִי ("they are my pay"). In the present order, the predicate אֶתְנָה is in a fronted position for focus (JM §154fa). YHWH will devastate her vines and fig trees because she identifies them as *payment* from lovers.

אֶתְנָה. Predicate of the verbless clause. This is also the head of the following relative clause, and thus the accusative complement of the following verb נָתְנוּ in line c. This noun is a *hapax*. The similar noun אֶתְנַן occurs twelve times in the Hebrew Bible, including Hos 9:1 and means, "the fee of a prostitute" (HALOT 103). Hosea may be avoiding this usual term here because the imagery is not one of technical prostitution. Rather, her relationships with lovers result in gifts (AF 254). Wolff (1974:38) suggests that אֶתְנָה is a coined term, perhaps for wordplay with תְּאֵנָה ("fig tree") and נָתְנוּ ("they have given me") elsewhere in the verse.

הֵמָּה. Subject of the verbless clause. The antecedent of this pronoun is the גֶּפֶן and תְּאֵנָה in line a. This presents us with an apparent problem since the pronoun is masculine but תְּאֵנָה is feminine and גֶּפֶן is usually feminine. However, גֶּפֶן sometimes concords with masculine participles (Hos 10:1) or suffixes (2 Kgs 4:39). This is likely an example of preference for mp forms (cf. GKC §135o; JM §149). In addition, this clause is introduced by the relative clause which is headed by גֶּפֶן and תְּאֵנָה, reinforcing the analysis that those nouns are the antecedents of the pronoun.

לִי. PP with לְ and a 1cs suffix indicating possession.

אֲשֶׁר נָתְנוּ־לִי מְאַהֲבָי. *Line c.* Embedded relative clause headed by אֶתְנָה ("pay") in line b. Thus, the relative clause in line b is embedded within the main clause in line a, and the relative clause in line c is embedded within the direct speech in line b.

נָתְנוּ־לִי. Qal *qatal* 3cp √נתן with a PP לִי indicating the recipient. The verb √נתן is a trivalent verb taking two complements. The accusative complement is אֶתְנָה (see above). The second complement, indicating the recipient of the action, is the PP with לְ and a 1cs suffix referring to the mother.

מְאַהֲבַי. Piel ptc mp √אהב with a 1cs pronominal suffix. This is the subject of נָתְנוּ.

וְשַׂמְתִּים לְיַעַר. *Line d*. Independent clause.

וְשַׂמְתִּים. Qal *qatal* (irrealis) 1cs √שׂים with a 3mp acc suffix. The verb √שׂים requires two complements: an accusative as well as a PP specifying location or the thing produced.

לְיַעַר. PP with לְ indicating the goal of the verb (cf. WO §11.2.10d). יַעַר here refers to a place which was once cultivated and now is deserted and wild (cf. Isa 32:15; Mic 3:12).

וַאֲכָלָתַם חַיַּת הַשָּׂדֶה. *Line e*. Independent clause.

וַאֲכָלָתַם. Qal *qatal* (irrealis) 3fs √אכל with a 3mp acc suffix. This verb continues the sequence of irrealis *qatal* verbs which express YHWH's intention to punish her in the future.

חַיַּת הַשָּׂדֶה. Subject of וַאֲכָלָתַם. The construct noun חַיָּה is morphologically and syntactically singular, but should be translated as a collective plural.

2:15 a וּפָקַדְתִּי עָלֶיהָ אֶת־יְמֵי הַבְּעָלִים
b אֲשֶׁר תַּקְטִיר לָהֶם
c וַתַּעַד נִזְמָהּ וְחֶלְיָתָהּ
d וַתֵּלֶךְ אַחֲרֵי מְאַהֲבֶיהָ
e וְאֹתִי שָׁכְחָה
f נְאֻם־יְהוָה: פ

Lines a-b are a bicolon comprising a main clause and an embedded relative clause. The lines are marked with *Pašṭa* and *Zaqep parvum*. Lines c-e are a tricolon, with parallelism of past narrative verbs and 3fs suffixes in lines c and d. Line e concludes the tricolon and is less formally parallel to the first two lines. The lines are marked by *Zaqep parvum*, *ʾAtnaḥ*, and *Ṭipḥa*. Line f is an editorial comment that stands outside the poetic structure.

וּפָקַדְתִּי עָלֶיהָ אֶת־יְמֵי הַבְּעָלִים. *Line a*. Independent clause.

וּפָקַדְתִּי. Qal *qatal* (irrealis) 1cs √פקד. The irrealis *qatal* is predictive.

עָלֶיהָ. This PP indicating the recipient of the punishment is the first of two complements of וּפָקַדְתִּי (see discussion in 1:4). The antecedent of the 3fs suffix is once again the mother (2:7).

אֶת־יְמֵי הַבְּעָלִים. The collocation of the verb √פקד with the prep עַל has the sense "to bring punishment for X upon Y." The second complement (here marked with אֶת) indicates the reason for the punishment. The plural הַבְּעָלִים likely refers to local deities or multiple cult sites, due to the resumptive 3mp suffix at the end of the following relative clause.

אֲשֶׁר תַּקְטִיר לָהֶם. *Line b.* Embedded relative clause. Many translators understand the head of the relative to be יְמֵי ("days of") and translate, "... the days of the Ba'als *when* she offered sacrifices to them" (e.g., Macintosh 2014:65). This would mean that the head of אֲשֶׁר and the suffix on לָהֶם would have different referents. However, it is more convincing to analyze לָהֶם as a resumptive element within the relative clause, which is headed by הַבְּעָלִים ("the Ba'als"). Hebrew relative clauses frequently contain a resumptive element that refers back to the head of the clause and specifies the role of the relative pronoun (WO §19.3a). In this case, the resumptive element לָהֶם is necessary because it serves as the complement of the verb תַּקְטִיר within the clause, indicating *to whom* sacrifice is made (i.e., "the Ba'als"). Relative clauses headed by nouns pertaining to time (i.e., if the head were יְמֵי) do not use resumptive elements (JM §158k).

תַּקְטִיר. Hiph *yiqtol* 3fs √קטר. This verb can refer to burning incense (קְטֹרֶת) in a priestly context (Exod 30:7). In other contexts it is frequently used in parallel with the verb √זבח ("to slaughter" or "make sacrifice") (cf. Hos 4:13; 11:2), and as a general term for sacrifice (HALOT 1095).

וַתַּעַד נִזְמָהּ וְחֶלְיָתָהּ. *Line c.* Independent clause.

וַתַּעַד. Qal *wayyiqtol* 3fs √עדה. This and the following וַתֵּלֶךְ are the first *wayyiqtol* verbs since chapter 1. In this last colon of the subsection, the prophet breaks from his prophetic discourse and uses *wayyiqtol* past narrative verbs to introduce a very short narrative summary. In the past Israel purposefully went after competing gods and forgot YHWH. That is why she is destined for judgment now. The verb וַתַּעַד is differentiated from √לבש in that it usually refers to adorning oneself with ornaments or jewelry rather than clothing.

נִזְמָהּ וְחֶלְיָתָהּ. Acc compls of וַתַּעַד with 3fs poss suffixes.

וַתֵּלֶךְ אַחֲרֵי מְאַהֲבֶיהָ. *Line d.* Independent clause.

וַתֵּלֶךְ. Qal *wayyiqtol* 3fs √הלך.

אַחֲרֵי מְאַהֲבֶיהָ. Adjunct PP with אַחֲרֵי indicating metaphorical locational sense (cf. 2:7). מְאַהֲבֶיהָ is a Piel ptc mp √אהב with a 3fs poss suffix.

וְאֹתִי שָׁכְחָה. *Line e.* Independent clause. The accusative אֹתִי is fronted in the clause for focus to contrast with the preceding מְאַהֲבֶיהָ. "She went after lovers, but *me* she forgot."

שָׁכְחָה. Qal *qatal* 3fs √שכח. In contrast to the preceding *wayyiqtol* verbs which refer to a narrative past tense, this *qatal* has a perfective aspect and is summative in nature.

נְאֻם־יְהוָה. *Line f.* This construct phrase is a typical editorial formula in the prophetic books that identifies YHWH as the speaker of the preceding passage. In Hosea it occurs only four times: in a cluster in 2:15, 18, and 23 and one more time at the end of chapter 11 (v. 11). (On this phrase, see Baumgärtel 1961.)

2:16-25: A New Relationship and a New Covenant

Hosea continues to use the image of his own unfaithful wife and broken marriage to describe Israel, but now he turns to third phase of the structural pattern: Ultimate reconciliation. These verses reverse specific language from chapter 1. YHWH will make a fresh start, like when he brought her out of Egypt (vv. 16-17). He will put away competing "lovers" (vv. 18-19), give her security (v. 20), and betroth her again (vv. 21-22). This restored relationship will result in new fertility and blessing, the very things that she had wanted so desperately and which had motivated her unfaithfulness. YHWH will reactivate her agriculture which he had previously stopped in judgment (vv. 23-24a). Finally, he reverses the names of Hosea's children as they apply to Israel (vv. 24b-25).

16 Therefore, behold, I will entice her,
and I will take her to the desert,
and I will coax her.

17 And I will give to her there her vineyards,
and [make] the Valley of Achor a door of hope.
And she will answer there as in the days of her youth,
and like the day when she came up from the land of Egypt.

¹⁸And it will be on that day (A declaration of YHWH),
you will call me "My husband,"
and you will no longer call me, "My Ba'al."

¹⁹And I will put away the names of the Ba'als from her mouth,
and they will no longer be remembered by their names.

²⁰And I will make for them a covenant on that day,
with the animals of the field and with the birds of the sky and the creeping things of the ground.

And bow and sword and war I will abolish from the land,
and I will make them lie down in safety.

²¹And I will betroth you to myself forever,
and I will betroth you to myself in righteousness, and in justice
and in covenant love and in compassion.
²²And I will betroth you to myself in faithfulness,
and you will know YHWH.

²³And it will be on that day,
I will answer (A declaration of YHWH)

I will answer the heavens,
and they will answer the land.

²⁴And the land will answer the grain and the new wine and the oil,
and they will answer Jezreel.

²⁵And I will sow her for myself in the land,
and I will have pity on "Not Pitied"
and I will say to "Not My People" you are my people,
and he will say, "My God!"

2:16 a לָכֵ֗ן הִנֵּ֤ה אָֽנֹכִי֙ מְפַתֶּ֔יהָ
b וְהֹֽלַכְתִּ֖יהָ הַמִּדְבָּ֑ר
c וְדִבַּרְתִּ֖י עַל־לִבָּֽהּ׃

Lines a-c are a tricolon. The lines are marked with disjunctive accents (*Zaqep parvum* and *'Atnaḥ*).

Hosea 2:16

לָכֵן הִנֵּה אָנֹכִי מְפַתֶּיהָ. *Line a*. Independent clause.

לָכֵן. Adverb indicating the logical consequences of the previous clause. This move is surprising: the consequence of her forgetting him (2:15) is that now he will woo her back and restore her.

הִנֵּה. Interjection used to redirect the attention of the addressee to something that is new or surprising. The addressee is the audience of the prophet and now the reader of the book.

אָנֹכִי. 1cs independent personal pronoun providing the subject of the participle מְפַתֶּיהָ. The use of the independent pronoun as subject rather than הִנֵּה + 1cs suffix (see the very similar construction in 2:8) brings additional contrastive focus to the subject. She has forgotten (2:15), but *he* is going to entice her once again.

מְפַתֶּיהָ. Piel ptc ms √פתה with a 3fs acc suffix. The participle, used predicatively, refers to a situation in the future, meaning something like "I am going to" (WO §37.6f; cf. 2:8). The root √פתה often has the sense of "lure" or "deceive." It is remarkable that the prophet uses it in this context. Perhaps he is acknowledging that Israel will not want to return, but YHWH intends to pursue her anyway.

וְהֹלַכְתִּיהָ הַמִּדְבָּר. *Line b*. Independent clause.

וְהֹלַכְתִּיהָ. Hiph *qatal* (irrealis) 1cs √הלך with a 3fs acc suffix.

הַמִּדְבָּר. PP indicating the location of the action of וְהֹלַכְתִּיהָ. Based on other uses of √הלך in the Hiphil, we expect the prep אֶל or בְּ or a locative ה on the noun. However, here the preposition is omitted. (cf. JM §133i). The verb √הלך occurs forty-five times in the Hiphil and the preposition is omitted in four instances where it is expected (2 Chr 35:24; Jer 32:5; Ezek 40:24; 47:6).

וְדִבַּרְתִּי עַל־לִבָּהּ. *Line c*. Independent clause.

וְדִבַּרְתִּי. Piel *qatal* (irrealis) 1cs √דבר.

עַל־לִבָּהּ. PP with עַל indicating the object of interest. The idiom דִּבֶּר עַל לֵב occurs a total of eight times in the Hebrew Bible. It is used when someone in a position of power is coaxing or attempting to gain the trust of someone who is very vulnerable, either because they have suffered (e.g., Gen 34:3; Isa 40:2) or because their situation is perilous (e.g., Gen 50:21; Ruth 2:13).

Hosea 2:17

וְנָתַתִּי לָהּ אֶת־כְּרָמֶיהָ מִשָּׁם a 2:17
וְאֶת־עֵמֶק עָכוֹר לְפֶתַח תִּקְוָה b
וְעָנְתָה שָּׁמָּה כִּימֵי נְעוּרֶיהָ c
וּכְיוֹם עֲלֹתָהּ מֵאֶרֶץ־מִצְרָיִם: ס d

Lines a-b and c-d are bicola, indicated by the elided verbs in each respective second line. The first bicolon is marked with *Zaqep parvum* and *'Atnaḥ*. The second is marked with *Zaqep parvum* and *Silluq*.

וְנָתַתִּי לָהּ אֶת־כְּרָמֶיהָ מִשָּׁם. *Line a*. Independent clause.

וְנָתַתִּי. Qal *qatal* (irrealis) 1cs √נתן.

לָהּ. This PP with לְ is the first complement of √נתן which specifies to whom her vineyards are given (see 2:10b).

אֶת־כְּרָמֶיהָ. Acc compl of √נתן specifying what is given. The antecedent of both 3fs suffixes in this clause is the "mother" (representing Israel), who has been in view all along.

מִשָּׁם. PP with מִן indicating the location of the vineyards. The antecedent of the locative adverb שָׁם must be הַמִּדְבָּר ("the desert") in the previous verse (2:16). She has desired agricultural fertility, but she went to competing lovers for it. Therefore, YHWH will make her vines and fig trees a wasteland (2:14). Now, YHWH will give *her* vineyards (i.e., the ones that she longs for) to her out of the desert.

וְאֶת־עֵמֶק עָכוֹר לְפֶתַח תִּקְוָה. *Line b*. Independent clause. The verb וְנָתַתִּי in line a is elided in this line but with a slightly different sense. In this line the assumed verb √נתן again takes two complements, but it means "to turn something into something else."

וְאֶת־עֵמֶק עָכוֹר. This first complement of the elided √נתן indicates what will be converted. The "Valley of Achor" is only found five times in the Hebrew Bible. In Joshua (7:24, 26; 15:7) it is the location where Achan was stoned for violating the חֵרֶם ("ban"). Thus, it is a prototypical place of rebellion and then judgment. In Isa 65:10 it is reversed into a place of restoration, as here.

לְפֶתַח תִּקְוָה. This second complement of √נתן specifies what the Valley of Achor will become. The פֶּתַח ("door") may be a reversal of 2:8 when she is hedged in and cannot find her paths, or it may refer to the transition from judgment to hope.

וְעָ֤נְתָה שָׁ֙מָּה֙ כִּימֵ֣י נְעוּרֶ֔יהָ. *Line c*. Independent clause.

וְעָ֤נְתָה. Qal *qatal* (irrealis) 3fs √ענה. "She will answer" refers to her responding to YHWH's previous coaxing (cf. 2:16). In the wilderness she responded to YHWH's protection and provision with fidelity, now she will do so again. This renewed relationship is further described in vv. 18 and following. This nuance of √ענה, "to answer," works well in the occurrences in 2:23-24 below, which is connected to this verse via wordplay.

שָׁ֙מָּה֙. Adverb with a locative ה indicating the location of her response. The referent of this adverb is once again הַמִּדְבָּר ("the desert") in 2:16. He will take her back to the desert and give her what she wanted all along, and she will respond favorably. The *dagesh* in the שׁ is a "conjunctive" *dagesh* (MNK 39–40).

כִּימֵ֣י נְעוּרֶ֔יהָ. PP with כְּ indicating correspondence between her response now and her initial response.

וּכְי֖וֹם עֲלֹתָ֥הּ מֵאֶֽרֶץ־מִצְרָֽיִם. *Line d*. Independent clause. The verb and adverb are elided (from line c).

וּכְי֖וֹם עֲלֹתָ֥הּ. This PP with כְּ indicates the same correspondence as the previous line. The genitive of the construct phrase is a substantival Qal inf constr √עלה with a 3fs pronominal suffix functioning as the subject. It should be translated temporally, "when she went up."

מֵאֶֽרֶץ־מִצְרָֽיִם. PP with מִן indicating a locative, ablative sense. We now learn the location of the desert mentioned in 2:16 and referred to twice with שָׁם in this verse. He is taking her back to the beginning of their relationship, to the wilderness when he brought her out of Egypt. Although that was a time of grumbling and complaining, the prophet must have in mind YHWH's tender care and Israel's response of dependence and trust.

2:18 a וְהָיָ֤ה בַיּוֹם־הַהוּא֙ נְאֻם־יְהוָ֔ה
b תִּקְרְאִ֖י אִישִׁ֑י
c וְלֹֽא־תִקְרְאִי־לִ֥י ע֖וֹד בַּעְלִֽי׃

Lines a-c are a tricolon. Line a introduces the verse, setting the scene and providing the temporal reference. Lines b-c are parallel with positive and negative commands using the same verb (√קרא) as well as a contrast between synonyms (אִישׁ//בַּעַל). The lines are marked by *Zaqep parvum*, *'Atnaḥ*, and *Silluq*.

וְהָיָה בַיּוֹם־הַהוּא. *Line a*. Independent, scene-setting clause (see 1:5).

וְהָיָה. Qal *qatal* (irrealis) 3ms √היה. This verb does not have an explicit subject; it provides the temporal setting for the next main clause (line b).

בַיּוֹם־הַהוּא. PP with בְּ indicating the temporal setting for the following clause (see 1:5). In 1:5 the prophet spoke of a day of judgment in the indeterminate future, here he speaks of an eschatological day of promise and renewal (cf. 2:20, 23).

נְאֻם־יְהוָה. *Line a*. Editorial formula (see 2:15).

תִּקְרְאִי אִישִׁי. *Line b*. Independent clause.

תִּקְרְאִי. Qal *yiqtol* 2fs √קרא. With this indicative verb, YHWH is not commanding her to call him "my husband" but *predicting* it. The context (vv. 16-25) is one of a new status and relationship and this includes a change in her perspective. When it has the sense indicated by the context, "to name someone," the verb √קרא takes two complements: the first marked by לְ is the person named, and the second is the name given (cf. Gen 1:5; 2:19; HALOT 1129). In this clause the first accusative is omitted.

אִישִׁי. Second compl of תִּקְרְאִי, specifying the name given, with a 1cs poss suffix. With a possessive suffix, the noun אִישׁ generally means "husband" (cf. Gen 3:6; 29:32; Ruth 1:3; Hos 2:4, 9).

וְלֹא־תִקְרְאִי־לִי עוֹד בַּעְלִי. *Line c*. Independent clause.

תִקְרְאִי־לִי. Qal *yiqtol* 2fs √קרא. לִי indicates the first complement of קרא, which is the person named. The imperfective verb has a habitual sense, restricted by the temporal adverb עוֹד because it is negated.

בַּעְלִי. Second compl of תִּקְרְאִי, specifying the name given. The noun בַּעַל frequently refers to an "owner" (Exod 21:28, 34; Eccl 5:12) or "husband" (see Gen 20:3). In 2 Sam 11:26 אִישׁ and בַּעַל are used in parallel, "When the wife of Uriah her husband (אִישָׁהּ) was dead, she mourned over her husband (בַּעְלָהּ)." בַּעַל is also the name of the Canaanite fertility deity. Thus, there is a play on words here. Under other circumstances it would have been linguistically appropriate to call him בַּעְלִי ("my husband"). But in her syncretistic worship she used the name "Ba'al" in spiritual adultery. In the eschatological restoration, she will be faithful to YHWH and will cease to use the word "Ba'al" at all.

2:19

a וַהֲסִרֹתִ֛י אֶת־שְׁמ֥וֹת הַבְּעָלִ֖ים מִפִּ֑יהָ
b וְלֹֽא־יִזָּכְר֥וּ ע֖וֹד בִּשְׁמָֽם׃

Lines a-b are a bicolon. The lines demonstrate several aspects of parallelism: positive//negative, active//passive, syntactic role of the noun שְׁמוֹת, and noun (הַבְּעָלִים)//pronoun (ם). The lines are marked by *'Atnaḥ* and *Silluq*.

וַהֲסִרֹתִי אֶת־שְׁמוֹת הַבְּעָלִים מִפִּיהָ. *Line a*. Independent clause.

וַהֲסִרֹתִי. Hiph *qatal* (irrealis) 1cs √סור.

אֶת־שְׁמוֹת הַבְּעָלִים. This acc compl of וַהֲסִרֹתִי is a construct phrase with two plural nouns. The plural, like 2:15, refers to multiple deities or local manifestations of Ba'al at multiple religious sites.

מִפִּיהָ. This PP is an adjunct of וַהֲסִרֹתִי; מִן has an ablative sense.

וְלֹא־יִזָּכְרוּ עוֹד בִּשְׁמָם. *Line b*. Independent clause.

יִזָּכְרוּ. Niph *yiqtol* 3mp √זכר. It is syntactically possible for the subject of this verb to be either שְׁמוֹת (mp) or הַבְּעָלִים in the preceding construct phrase. However, because שֵׁם occurs again in an adjunct PP in this second clause and both occurrences have the same referent, the subject of the verb must be הַבְּעָלִים. It would not make sense to say, "their names will not be remembered by their name."

עוֹד. Temporal adverb restricting the habitual sense of the negated *yiqtol* verb (see 2:18).

בִּשְׁמָם. PP with בְּ indicating the instrument of the passive verb יִזָּכְרוּ. Once he removes the names of the Ba'als from her mouth, those names can no longer activate her memory and lead her astray. It may be significant that שֵׁם is singular in contrast to the previous clause.

2:20

a וְכָרַתִּ֨י לָהֶ֤ם בְּרִית֙ בַּיּ֣וֹם הַה֔וּא
b עִם־חַיַּ֤ת הַשָּׂדֶה֙ וְעִם־ע֣וֹף הַשָּׁמַ֔יִם וְרֶ֖מֶשׂ הָאֲדָמָ֑ה
c וְקֶ֨שֶׁת וְחֶ֤רֶב וּמִלְחָמָה֙ אֶשְׁבּ֣וֹר מִן־הָאָ֔רֶץ
d וְהִשְׁכַּבְתִּ֖ים לָבֶֽטַח׃

Lines a-b and c-d are two bicola distinguishable by content. Lines a-b comprise one long clause which announces a new covenant. The lines are marked by *Zaqeph parvum* and *'Atnaḥ*. Lines c-d describe peace and security and are marked by *Zaqeph parvum* and *Silluq*.

Hosea 2:20

וְכָרַתִּי לָהֶם בְּרִית בַּיּוֹם הַהוּא. *Line a*. Independent clause.

וְכָרַתִּי. Qal *qatal* (irrealis) 1cs √כרת. The irrealis *qatal* signals a prophetic prediction.

לָהֶם. PP with לְ of interest. The nearest antecedent for the 3mp suffix is the Ba'als in the previous verse (2:19), but it cannot mean that. The prophet has been referring to Israel as "she" or "her" (2:16, 17, 19) and "you" (2:18), but here he uses the plural to refer to the people of Israel. The use of √כרת + לְ usually has the nuance of *granting* an agreement (HALOT 500). Here, YHWH is mediating a covenant *for* Israel or on their behalf. The covenant itself is between Israel and the animals (cf. line b).

בְּרִית. Acc compl of וְכָרַתִּי. The word בְּרִית occurs four other times in Hosea. The others are retrospective, referring either to YHWH's previous covenants with Israel (6:7; 8:1) or their attempted agreements with other peoples (10:4; 12:2).

בַּיּוֹם הַהוּא. PP with בְּ indicating that the temporal setting for the following clause is the eschatological future (see 1:5; 2:18).

עִם־חַיַּת הַשָּׂדֶה וְעִם־עוֹף הַשָּׁמַיִם וְרֶמֶשׂ הָאֲדָמָה. *Line b*. These PPs indicate the other party in covenant with Israel. In 2:14 the wild animals of the field were to devour her vines and fig trees. This promise reverses that judgment, stating that Israel will live in peace with the animal kingdom. There will be a reordering of nature itself. These three nouns in this order (רֶמֶשׂ > עוֹף > חַיָּה) occur in two significant clusters in Genesis: in the creation narrative (Gen 1:28, 30) and in the flood narrative (6:20; 7:14, 21; 8:17, 19; 9:2). This covenant in Hos 2:20 recalls YHWH's covenant after the flood narrative that was with humanity as well as "every living creature" (כָּל־נֶפֶשׁ חַיָּה) (Gen 9:12).

וְקֶשֶׁת וְחֶרֶב וּמִלְחָמָה אֶשְׁבּוֹר מִן־הָאָרֶץ. *Line c*. Independent clause.

וְקֶשֶׁת וְחֶרֶב וּמִלְחָמָה. Acc compls of אֶשְׁבּוֹר. They are fronted in the word order for topicalization. These three nouns in this order (קֶשֶׁת > מִלְחָמָה > חֶרֶב) occur in 1:7, where YHWH says he will *not* save them by these things. However, now he states that in "that day" (i.e., the eschatological future), he will abolish these weapons of war.

אֶשְׁבּוֹר מִן־הָאָרֶץ. Qal *yiqtol* 1cs √שבר. The PP with מִן has an ablative sense which would seem to require a verb of motion rather than

√שבר. This is a "pregnant construction" (*constructio praegnans*) because there is a different assumed verb which has not been expressed (GKC §119ee-ff; but see Jer 30:8; Nah 1:13). The use of √שבר is motivated by wordplay with 1:5. There, YHWH said he would break (√שבר) Israel's קֶשֶׁת ("bow") in judgment. In the future spoken of here, YHWH will break *all* weapons and will bring peace to the land. Thus, Israel will experience freedom from harm both from animals (lines a-b) and from humans (lines c-d) (Stuart 1987:58).

וְהִשְׁכַּבְתִּים לָבֶטַח. *Line d*. Independent clause.

וְהִשְׁכַּבְתִּים. Hiph *qatal* (irrealis) 1cs √שכב with a 3mp acc suffix. The antecedent of the suffix is the people of Israel (see 2:20, line a). The covenant with creation means that the land and people will have rest from war.

לָבֶטַח. PP with לְ specifying the manner of the verbal action; the sense is often best translated with an adverb in English (WO §11.2.10d).

2:21 a וְאֵרַשְׂתִּיךְ לִי לְעוֹלָם
b וְאֵרַשְׂתִּיךְ לִי בְּצֶדֶק וּבְמִשְׁפָּט וּבְחֶסֶד וּבְרַחֲמִים׃

2:22 a וְאֵרַשְׂתִּיךְ לִי בֶּאֱמוּנָה
b וְיָדַעַתְּ אֶת־יְהוָה׃ ס

Lines 2:21a-b and 2:22a-b are a quatrain. The first three lines contain obvious parallelism with the repetition of וְאֵרַשְׂתִּיךְ לִי. The fourth line is distinct and concludes the poetic verse. Each of the four lines is marked by a disjunctive *'Atnaḥ* or *Silluq*.

וְאֵרַשְׂתִּיךְ לִי לְעוֹלָם. *Line 2:21a*. Independent clause.

וְאֵרַשְׂתִּיךְ. Piel *qatal* (irrealis) 1cs √ארש with a 2fs acc suffix. The II-guttural consonant does not double, triggering compensatory lengthening of the *hireq* to a *tsere*. The verb √ארש refers to the formal marriage engagement, preceding the act of consummation (cf. Deut 20:7; 22:23).

לִי. Adjunct PP with לְ indicating the person for whom the action is directed. The antecedent of the 1cs suffix is the speaker, YHWH.

לְעוֹלָם. PP with temporal לְ indicating the period of time of the betrothal.

וְאֵרַשְׂתִּיךְ לִי בְּצֶדֶק וּבְמִשְׁפָּט וּבְחֶסֶד וּבְרַחֲמִים. *Line 2:21b*. Independent clause.

וְאֵרַשְׂתִּיךְ לִי. See line 2:21a.

בְּצֶדֶק וּבְמִשְׁפָּט וּבְחֶסֶד וּבְרַחֲמִים. There are four coordinated PPs in this line and one more in line 2:22a. What is the sense of the בְּ prep? The best view in light of the context is that these qualities are gifts to Israel. She will reflect YHWH's character in contrast to her previous idolatry and unfaithfulness (cf. AF 283; Macintosh 2014:84). The noun צֶדֶק refers to right actions as compared to a standard (in this case, the character of YHWH). מִשְׁפָּט refers to "justice" or the application of right actions in every setting so that right is done. חֶסֶד includes a variety of senses such as benevolence, faithfulness, loyalty, generosity, and kindness. This is how YHWH acts toward his people in light of his covenant relationship with them. He also expects his people (covenant members) to treat each other with חֶסֶד. רַחֲמִים is a term of emotion, denoting compassion and the willingness to grant what others do not deserve.

וְאֵרַשְׂתִּיךְ לִי בֶּאֱמוּנָה. *Line 2:22a*. Independent clause.

וְאֵרַשְׂתִּיךְ לִי. See line 2:21a.

בֶּאֱמוּנָה. PP with בְּ indicating what YHWH will grant to Israel (see line 2:21b above). אֱמוּנָה refers to the fidelity and faithfulness that YHWH shows to his people and that he expects from them in return.

וְיָדַעַתְּ אֶת־יְהוָה. *Line 2:22b*. Independent clause.

וְיָדַעַתְּ. Qal *qatal* (irrealis) 2fs √ידע.

אֶת־יְהוָה. Acc compl of וְיָדַעַתְּ. This is similar to a common formula of identification: וִידַעְתֶּם כִּי אֲנִי יְהוָה ("You will know that I am YHWH"). By contrast, the expression here does not speak to the identity of YHWH but rather to intimate knowledge and a relationship with him. For example, in 1 Sam 2:12 the wicked sons of Eli certainly know who YHWH is, but the text says, לֹא יָדְעוּ אֶת־יְהוָה. This phrase is also characteristic of the "new" covenant in Jer 31:34 where all covenant members will be in relationship with YHWH. This is a reversal of 2:15, which says "she forgot me." Hosea has at least somewhat maintained the imagery of his wife and family throughout this chapter, although the referent (Israel, YHWH) has been obvious. Now he relinquishes the imagery completely and uses the name YHWH within the oracle itself.

2:23 a וְהָיָה | בַּיּוֹם הַהוּא
b אֶעֱנֶה נְאֻם־יְהוָה
c אֶעֱנֶה אֶת־הַשָּׁמָיִם
d וְהֵם יַעֲנוּ אֶת־הָאָרֶץ:

2:24 a וְהָאָרֶץ תַּעֲנֶה אֶת־הַדָּגָן וְאֶת־הַתִּירוֹשׁ וְאֶת־הַיִּצְהָר
b וְהֵם יַעֲנוּ אֶת־יִזְרְעֶאל:

The lineation of 2:23a-d and 2:24a-b is difficult to determine. The repetition of the verb √ענה indicates that they are all one unit. There is a kind of staircase parallelism in lines b-c in which the clause begins in line b, is interrupted by the editorial comment נְאֻם־יְהוָה, and then concludes in line c. This would indicate that lines b-c are in one poetic verse. But that leaves lines a and d as orphans. It is more likely that 2:23c-d and 2:24a-b are bicola because of the noun/pronoun grammatical parallelism. The noun הַשָּׁמַיִם in line c corresponds to the pronoun הֵם in line d. Likewise the nouns in line 2:24a correspond to the pronoun הֵם in line 2:24b. Therefore, it is best to analyze lines a-b, c-d, and 2:24a-b as three bicola and all six lines as a tightly integrated strophe.

וְהָיָה | בַּיּוֹם הַהוּא. *Line 2:23a*. Independent clause. The verb is a Qal *qatal* (irrealis) 3ms √היה. It does not have an explicit subject and instead provides the temporal setting for the next main clause (line b), indicated by the PP (see 1:5; 2:18, 20). The temporal setting continues to be an indeterminate eschatological future.

אֶעֱנֶה נְאֻם־יְהוָה. *Line 2:23b*. Independent clause.

אֶעֱנֶה. Qal *yiqtol* 1cs √ענה. There is a wordplay with the use of √ענה in 2:17 (see the discussion there). She has gone to other lovers for what she wants most: fertility, produce, and wealth (2:4, 7). YHWH will respond by stopping up her agriculture and removing her wealth (2:11). But when he makes a fresh start with her and coaxes her back into a relationship, she will "answer" (√ענה) and respond positively to him (2:17). In this verse YHWH will in turn "answer" (√ענה). He will answer the heavens which will in turn begin a chain reaction of fertility from heavens to land to produce in vv. 23-24. Thus, he is using "answer" with a special sense of "rejuvenate" or "restore" (see 14:9b). To "answer" means to "activate" the heavens so that they work correctly.

The וְ conjunctions, the staircase parallelism in v. 23, and the repetition of the root עִנה√ in these verses illustrates this cascading effect. Ironically, YHWH was the one who had provided her with fertility, wealth, and blessing all along. Now she will finally have what she wants when she is properly related to him.

נְאֻם־יְהוָה. Editorial formula that identifies YHWH as the source of the following passage (cf. 2:15, 18).

אֶעֱנֶה אֶת־הַשָּׁמָיִם. *Line 2:23c*. Independent clause.

אֶעֱנֶה. Qal *yiqtol* 1cs ענה√.

אֶת־הַשָּׁמָיִם. Acc compl of אֶעֱנֶה.

וְהֵם יַעֲנוּ אֶת־הָאָרֶץ. *Line 2:23d*. Independent clause.

הֵם. Independent 3mp pronoun and subject of יַעֲנוּ. Its antecedent is הַשָּׁמַיִם ("heavens") in the previous line. As the prophet describes the chain reaction when YHWH restarts nature's fertility, he uses two pleonastic pronouns to link the various elements together and to provide an explicit subject for each verb: YHWH > heavens (23c); they > land (23d); land > products (24a); they > Jezreel.

יַעֲנוּ. Qal *yiqtol* 3mp ענה√. The subject of this verb is the pleonastic pronoun הֵם, which in turn refers to הַשָּׁמַיִם.

אֶת־הָאָרֶץ. Acc compl of יַעֲנוּ.

וְהָאָרֶץ תַּעֲנֶה אֶת־הַדָּגָן וְאֶת־הַתִּירוֹשׁ וְאֶת־הַיִּצְהָר. *Line 2:24a*. Independent clause.

וְהָאָרֶץ. Subject of the following verb תַּעֲנֶה. This is a repetition of, and has the same referent as, הָאָרֶץ in line d.

תַּעֲנֶה. Qal *yiqtol* 3fs ענה√.

אֶת־הַדָּגָן וְאֶת־הַתִּירוֹשׁ וְאֶת־הַיִּצְהָר. Acc compls of תַּעֲנֶה. Israel previously gave the credit for these things (in this same order) to her lovers. Now she will get them from YHWH, who was in fact the giver all along (cf. 2:10).

וְהֵם יַעֲנוּ אֶת־יִזְרְעֶאל. *Line 2:24b*. Independent clause.

וְהֵם. Independent 3mp pronoun, subject of יַעֲנוּ. See the discussion in line d.

יַעֲנוּ. Qal *yiqtol* 3mp ענה√.

אֶת־יִזְרְעֶאל. Acc compl of יַעֲנוּ. This promise reverses the significance of the name of Hosea's son's in 1:4-5. Bloodshed and defeat will give way to life and blessing.

2:25 a וּזְרַעְתִּיהָ לִּי בָּאָרֶץ
b וְרִחַמְתִּי אֶת־לֹא רֻחָמָה
c וְאָמַרְתִּי לְלֹא־עַמִּי עַמִּי־אַתָּה
d וְהוּא יֹאמַר אֱלֹהָי: פ

Lines a-d are a quatrain. All four lines are parallel and there are no features that would suggest breaking them into bicola. The lines are marked by *Zaqep parvum*, *'Atnaḥ*, *Zaqep parvum*, and *Silluq*.

וּזְרַעְתִּיהָ לִּי בָּאָרֶץ. *Line a*. Independent clause.

וּזְרַעְתִּיהָ. Qal *qatal* (irrealis) 1cs √זרע with a 3fs acc suffix. The suffix is feminine so the antecedent cannot be Jezreel (2:24), though some scholars have suggested emending it. Rather, it refers again to the "mother" (cf. 2:4-19, 21f) which is an image for Israel (Wolff 1974:54). The verb √זרע ("to sow") is the basis for the name יִזְרְעֶאל ("God sows"). This verse continues the reversal of the name in 1:4-5. The name had represented bloodshed, but it will be reversed when YHWH sows Israel in the land, resulting in repopulation and flourishing (cf. Jer 31:27).

לִּי. PP with an ל of interest (GKC §119s), indicating that YHWH will sow her in the land for his own benefit. This represents the completion of his purposes.

בָּאָרֶץ. PP with בְּ specifying the location of the action.

וְרִחַמְתִּי אֶת־לֹא רֻחָמָה. *Line b*. Independent clause.

וְרִחַמְתִּי. Piel *qatal* (irrealis) 1cs √רחם.

אֶת־לֹא רֻחָמָה. Acc compl of וְרִחַמְתִּי, consisting of לֹא (negative particle) and רֻחָמָה, a Pual *qatal* 3fs √רחם. This reverses the significance of the name of Hosea's daughter in 1:6. YHWH had said, "Call her name 'Not Pitied' for I will no longer pity the house of Israel." Now he says, "I will pity."

וְאָמַרְתִּי לְלֹא־עַמִּי. *Line c*. Independent clause.

וְאָמַרְתִּי. Qal *qatal* (irrealis) 1cs √אמר.

לְלֹא־עַמִּי. PP with ל indicating the addressee of וְאָמַרְתִּי. This is the name of Hosea's third child (cf. 1:9). The name consists of the negative particle לֹא and the noun עַם with a 1cs pronominal suffix. לֹא usually negates verbal clauses except in the case of single words or compounds (GKC §152a, n. 1).

עַמִּי־אָתָּה. *Line c.* Independent clause; direct speech. This verbless clause has predicate-subject word order. The predicate עַמִּי is fronted for focus, to draw attention to their renewed status as the people of God in contrast to how they had been identified previously. This statement, and the next line, reverse 1:9 in which YHWH had said, "… you are not my people, and I am not your God." In 1:9 he uses the second person plural (אַתֶּם לֹא עַמִּי) because he is addressing the nation which the name "Not My People" represents. Here in 2:25 he uses the second person singular because he is returning to his child as a sign-act. He speaks to the child and cancels his name.

וְהוּא יֹאמַר. *Line d.* Independent clause.

וְהוּא. Independent 3ms pronoun. The antecedent of the pronoun is technically the child named לֹא־עַמִּי who represents the people of Israel referred to here. The verbs in the preceding three lines are all irrealis *qatal* verbs, but in this final line the author uses an independent pronoun and a *yiqtol*. This pleonastic pronoun draws attention to the contrast with the speaker of the preceding line: YHWH will announce his new status, and *he* (i.e., Israel) will respond in kind.

יֹאמַר. Qal *yiqtol* 3ms √אמר.

אֱלֹהָי. *Line d.* This is direct speech introduced by יֹאמַר. The 1cs suffix has the same antecedent as the pronoun הוּא. There is, therefore, a reversal of all three children's names. Lines 24f-25a reverse 1:4-5, line 25b reverses 1:6, and lines 25c-d reverse 1:9. Unlike 2:1-3, here the names are reversed in the same order that they appear in chapter 1.

3:1-5: Two "Wives" Awaiting Full Restoration

Chapter 3 is very short, but it is a distinct unit. It is written in the first person from the prophet's perspective and concludes the introduction to the book in which Hosea's family is a sign-act. Following the command to love a woman in v. 1, in vv. 2 and 3 he hires her, brings her into his house, and then abstains from sexual intercourse. Verses 4 and 5 conclude the unit with an explanation of the symbolism: Israel too will experience a temporary estrangement from YHWH followed by a full renewal of that relationship in the eschaton.

In spite of its brevity, the chapter contains several interpretive difficulties. First, is this Hosea's wife Gomer from chapter 1 or a different woman? While YHWH's command to love "a woman" leaves open the possibility that this is someone new, this is not likely. The use of the word עוֹד ("again") in 3:1 encourages us to read this chapter in connection with chapter 1. Also, 3:1 states that this woman commits adultery (מְנָאָפֶת), which means that she must be married. Finally, it is difficult to make any sense of the parallel between Hosea's marriage and YHWH's relationship with Israel, if Hosea is to give up on his promiscuous wife and love someone new.

A second related question is whether chapter 3 retells the events of chapter 1 from a different perspective or relates new events subsequent to chapter 1. The prophet's use of first person here, in contrast to the third-person report in chapter 1, might suggest that he is recapping his initial pursuit of Gomer in order to conclude the discussion of his marriage as a sign-act. However, the use of עוֹד implies that this is a second episode in the prophet's dealings with Gomer. In 1:2 Hosea was told to *acquire* a wife of fornication (אֵשֶׁת זְנוּנִים), but in 3:1 he is told to *love* a woman who commits adultery (מְנָאָפֶת). This suggests a development in their relationship. In chapter 1 the sign-act focuses on Hosea marrying a promiscuous woman which symbolizes YHWH's love and Israel's unfaithfulness generally. In chapter 3 the prophet takes her back but remains temporarily estranged. This symbolizes YHWH's determination to keep Israel as his people even though restoration will be temporarily preceded by judgment.

¹YHWH said to me again, "Go, love a woman who is loved by another and commits adultery, as YHWH loves the Israelites, though they turn to other gods and are lovers of raisin cakes." ²And I hired her for myself with fifteen pieces of silver and a homer of barley and a letek of barley. ³I said to her, "You will stay with me many days; you will not fornicate and you will not belong to a man and also I will be (so) toward you." ⁴For the Israelites will live many days without king and without prince and without sacrifice and without pillar and without ephod or teraphim. ⁵Afterwards, the Israelites will again seek YHWH their God and David their king. And they will be in dread of YHWH and his goodness in the latter days.

3:1 וַיֹּאמֶר יְהוָה אֵלַי עוֹד לֵךְ אֱהַב־אִשָּׁה אֲהֻבַת רֵעַ
וּמְנָאָפֶת כְּאַהֲבַת יְהוָה אֶת־בְּנֵי יִשְׂרָאֵל וְהֵם פֹּנִים אֶל־
אֱלֹהִים אֲחֵרִים וְאֹהֲבֵי אֲשִׁישֵׁי עֲנָבִים:

וַיֹּאמֶר יְהוָה אֵלַי עוֹד. Independent clause, main narrative line.

וַיֹּאמֶר. Qal *wayyiqtol* 3ms √אמר.

יְהוָה. Subject of וַיֹּאמֶר.

אֵלַי. Adjunct PP with a 1cs suffix indicating the addressee of the verb of speaking. In chapter 1, when YHWH spoke to Hosea, the references were in the third person (cf. 1:2, 4). Here, Hosea narrates in the first person.

עוֹד. This adverb might modify the preceding verb וַיֹּאמֶר ("said *again*") or it might be understood to modify the following verb לֵךְ ("go *again*"). There are parallels for either translation. In Exod 4:6 עוֹד clearly modifies the preceding verb; in Zech 11:15 it modifies the following verb. The masoretic accents do not influence us either way. There is a disjunctive *Rᵉbîaʿ* accent on אֵלַי, which would suggest that the adverb belongs with the following phrase, but a disjunctive *Jetib* accent on עוֹד, which suggests that the phrase ends at that point. AF (294) argue that עוֹד usually follows the verb it modifies. If the author meant "Go again" he would have written לֵךְ עוֹד. Even though עוֹד does not directly follow וַיֹּאמֶר, it modifies that verb. All things considered, this is probably the better understanding. The prophet's point is that this is a second, similar conversation between YHWH and Hosea related to the sign-act. However, the alternate view that Hosea should "go again" would have much the same meaning.

לֵךְ. Independent clause, direct speech. The verb is a Qal impv ms √הלך. This verb initiates and intensifies the following imperative (cf. 1:2).

אֱהַב־אִשָּׁה אֲהֻבַת רֵעַ וּמְנָאָפֶת. Independent clause, direct speech.

אֱהַב. Qal impv ms √אהב.

אֲהֻבַת רֵעַ. The verb is a Qal pass ptc fs √אהב in a construct relationship with רֵעַ ("loved of a companion"), and it modifies אִשָּׁה. The versions interpret their unvocalized Hebrew source texts as אֹהֶבֶת ("who loves"), an active participle which amplifies her guilt (see BHS note ᵃ). Either of the vocalization traditions might be correct. The word רֵעַ is used of lovers in Jer 3:1 and Song 5:16.

Hosea 3:1

וּמְנָאָפֶת. A second attributive participle also modifying אִשָּׁה. It is a Piel ptc fs √נאף. This is the first use of this verb (which means, "commit adultery") in the book (cf. 4:2, 13, 14; 7:4).

כְּאַהֲבַת יְהוָה אֶת־בְּנֵי יִשְׂרָאֵל. Subordinate comparative clause. This is the protasis, consisting of כְּ and an infinitive (cf. WO §38.5). Normally, the protasis precedes the apodosis or main clause, but here it follows.

כְּאַהֲבַת. Prep כְּ on a Qal inf constr √אהב. The infinitive of √אהב is typically spelled אַהֲבָה, but there are five occurrences with ת (cf. 1 Kgs 10:9; 2 Chr 2:10; 9:8; Mic 6:8).

יְהוָה. Subject of the infinitive.

אֶת־בְּנֵי יִשְׂרָאֵל. Acc compl of the infinitive.

וְהֵם פֹּנִים אֶל־אֱלֹהִים אֲחֵרִים. Unmarked concessive clause presenting a causal contrast with the preceding clause (cf. JM §171f). Therefore, the preceding comparative clause is subordinate to the main clause, and this concessive clause is subordinate to the comparative clause. One would think that Israel's turning after other gods would lead to YHWH's *not* loving her, but the concessive clause denies this.

פֹּנִים. Qal act ptc mp √פנה used predicatively.

אֶל־אֱלֹהִים אֲחֵרִים. PP with אֶל indicating the object of turning.

וְאֹהֲבֵי אֲשִׁישֵׁי עֲנָבִים. One might analyze this as a second predicate of the previous clause (i.e., "they turn to other gods and love raisin cakes"; cf. AF 298). However, unlike the previous clause, the participle here is substantival. We should therefore understand it as the predicate of a new verbless clause which assumes the subject הֵם ("[they are] lovers of cakes of raisins"). It is not the other gods who love cakes of raisins, but the Israelites who turn to those gods. Because it is coordinated with the preceding clause, it also functions as an unmarked concessive clause referring to YHWH's love for Israel.

וְאֹהֲבֵי. Qal act ptc mp √אהב functioning as a substantive and the predicate of the verbless clause. It is a construct form, governing a chain of genitives.

אֲשִׁישֵׁי. This is the first genitive in the chain. In its other three occurrences in the Hebrew Bible, the noun means "raisin" (1 Chr 16:3; Song 2:5) or "raisin cake" (2 Sam 6:19). Here it is in a construct relationship with עֲנָבִים ("grapes"), creating some uncertainty as to the intended meaning. The word אֲשִׁישָׁה (m: אָשִׁישׁ) is usually used in the context of cultic worship. Thus, here the Israelites are said to be enjoying the fruits of their "adulterous" idol worship.

3:2 וָאֶכְּרֶ֣הָ לִּ֗י בַּחֲמִשָּׁ֥ה עָשָׂ֛ר כָּ֖סֶף וְחֹ֣מֶר שְׂעֹרִ֑ים וְלֵ֖תֶךְ שְׂעֹרִֽים׃

וָאֶכְּרֶ֣הָ לִּ֗י בַּחֲמִשָּׁ֥ה עָשָׂ֛ר כָּ֖סֶף וְחֹ֣מֶר שְׂעֹרִ֑ים וְלֵ֖תֶךְ שְׂעֹרִֽים. Independent clause, main narrative line.

וָאֶכְּרֶ֣הָ. Qal *wayyiqtol* 1cs √כרה with a 3fs acc suffix. The morphology suggests that this is a Qal from √נכר, with the *dagesh* indicating the assimilated נ. However, √נכר ("to disguise, be foreign"?) does not occur elsewhere as a Qal, and it does not fit the context here. The root √כרה ("to purchase, buy") makes better sense. GKC understands the *dagesh* as a *dagesh dirimens*, which strengthens the כ to make the *shewa* more audible (§20h; but see AF [298] for potential problems with this). The III-ה of the root is lost before the accusative suffix. Job 6:27 and 40:30 both use √כרה for bartering over a person.

לִּ֗י. PP with ל of interest indicating the person for whom the action is directed (WO §11.2.10d).

בַּחֲמִשָּׁ֥ה עָשָׂ֛ר כָּ֖סֶף. PP with בְּ indicating the instrument or means by which he hired her. The numeral "15" consists of the feminine חֲמִשָּׁה ("five") and עָשָׂר ("ten"). Morphologically feminine numerals concord with masculine nouns, as is the case with כֶּסֶף here (JM §100d). The noun כֶּסֶף is collective and refers to money or pieces of silver (cf. Gen 20:16).

וְחֹ֣מֶר שְׂעֹרִ֑ים. PP logically governed by the בְּ prep in the previous phrase with the same meaning. Prepositions are not always repeated on each noun in a list (JM §132g). A חֹמֶר is a common measurement of dry agricultural produce such as wheat (Ezek 45:13), barley (Num 11:32), or generic seed (Lev 27:16). It consisted of 394 liters (HALOT 330).

וְלֵ֖תֶךְ שְׂעֹרִֽים. This PP, also governed by the בְּ in the first PP, describes the third item that Hosea used to hire his wife. This is the only occurrence of לֵתֶךְ in the Hebrew Bible, but it is known as a unit of measurement from other Semitic texts. As BHS note a-a indicates, G has καὶ νεβελ οἴνου ("a vessel of wine") for this phrase in the MT. Elsewhere, the Greek word νεβελ translates the Hebrew noun נֵבֶל ("jar") (cf. 1 Sam 1:24; 2 Sam 16:1). There is no convincing explanation for the origin of

G (but cf. Macintosh 2014:102–3). We can explain the repetition of שְׂעֹרִים in the MT as an accidental repetition. Perhaps G contains the better, original reading.

3:3 וָאֹמַר אֵלֶיהָ יָמִים רַבִּים תֵּשְׁבִי לִי לֹא תִזְנִי וְלֹא תִהְיִי לְאִישׁ וְגַם־אֲנִי אֵלָיִךְ:

וָאֹמַר אֵלֶיהָ. Independent clause, main narrative line.

וָאֹמַר. Qal *wayyiqtol* 1cs √אמר.

אֵלֶיהָ. PP with אֶל indicating the addressee of the direct speech.

יָמִים רַבִּים תֵּשְׁבִי לִי. Independent clause, direct speech.

יָמִים רַבִּים. An adverbial accusative, consisting of the noun יָמִים and the attributive adjective רַבִּים, which gives the duration of the action (cf. WO §10.2.2c).

תֵּשְׁבִי לִי. Qal *yiqtol* 2fs √ישב. The verb is used as a volative to express a command (cf. WO §31.5). The prep לְ is frequently used with √ישב to indicate the location of staying or dwelling (cf. Gen 21:16; Prov 9:14).

לֹא תִזְנִי. Independent clause, direct speech.

תִזְנִי. Qal *yiqtol* 2fs √זנה. *Yiqtol* verbs negated with לֹא are stronger prohibitions than negated jussives. Waltke and O'Connor (§31.5) suggest that volatives such as imperative and jussive express the will of the speaker, but *yiqtols* emphasize the action forbidden. Here Hosea forbids his wife from continuing her characteristic behavior of illicit sexual activity.

וְלֹא תִהְיִי לְאִישׁ. Independent clause, direct speech.

תִהְיִי לְאִישׁ. The verb is a Qal *yiqtol* 2fs √היה. With the לְ PP, it indicates possession, which is here a euphemism for a sexual relationship. The noun אִישׁ does not have an article. There is no specific man that Hosea has in mind; rather she should refrain from sexual relationships with *any* man.

וְגַם־אֲנִי אֵלָיִךְ. Independent clause, direct speech.

וְגַם. This key conjunction associates this clause with the previous one and emphasizes an additional element. The question is whether the relationship is one of contrast or continuity. If the גַּם is adversative ("yet"), then Hosea is telling his wife that she will not have sexual relations with any other man, yet he will belong to her sexually. This would represent the restoration of YHWH's love for Israel. However, the parallel between Hosea's relationship with Gomer and YHWH's relationship with Israel in 3:4-5 suggests a different approach. It is more likely that גַּם emphasizes continuity: just as she is forbidden from sexual relations from any man, Hosea will also behave in the same manner toward her and will abstain from any sexual relationship for "many days." We might assume an elliptical element such as לֹא אָבוֹא ("I will not come in to you") as a sexual euphemism (cf. BHS note ᵃ). Another possibility is that the negative לֹא is carried forward: just as she will not belong to any man, he will not be for her. Hosea's marriage is a sign for Israel, who will also be separated from YHWH for a time (3:4) before a final restoration (3:5).

אֲנִי. Subject of the verbless clause.

אֵלַיִךְ. PP with a 2fs suffix indicating Hosea's wife as the recipient of his behavior.

3:4 כִּי| יָמִים רַבִּים יֵשְׁבוּ בְּנֵי יִשְׂרָאֵל אֵין מֶלֶךְ וְאֵין שָׂר וְאֵין זֶבַח וְאֵין מַצֵּבָה וְאֵין אֵפוֹד וּתְרָפִים:

This entire verse is a subordinate causal clause with כִּי giving the reason for Hosea's prophetic act, that is, his refraining from sexual activity with his wife (3:3). Verses 4-5 are neither narrative nor direct speech to Gomer. They are prophetic oracles which provide the interpretation of Hosea's sign-act related in 3:1-3.

יָמִים רַבִּים. Adverbial accusative which gives the duration of the action (cf. WO §10.2.2c; cf. 3:3).

יֵשְׁבוּ. Qal *yiqtol* 3mp √ישב.

בְּנֵי יִשְׂרָאֵל. Subject of יֵשְׁבוּ.

אֵין מֶלֶךְ וְאֵין שָׂר וְאֵין זֶבַח וְאֵין מַצֵּבָה וְאֵין אֵפוֹד וּתְרָפִים. These are six circumstantial clauses (GKC §156a), all introduced by אֵין except for the last one. Typically, circumstantial clauses with אֵין are connected to the main clause with a וְ (cf. GKC §152l; JM §159d), but the conjunction is not present in the first clause אֵין מֶלֶךְ here. These six items which will not be available to Israel are grouped in three pairs: king and prince, sacrifice and pillar, and ephod and teraphim. In the last two pairs, זֶבַח is part of the orthodox worship of YHWH and therefore legitimate, while מַצֵּבָה is not (see discussion on Hos 10:1), and אֵפוֹד is usually orthodox (cf. Exod 28:6) while תְּרָפִים is not (cf. 2 Kgs 23:24). Therefore, just as

Gomer must cease from all illegitimate *and* legitimate sexual activity, all religious activity—both legitimate and illegitimate—will cease for Israel. In her syncretistic worship, she had combined orthodox and pagan forms of worship, now it will all be removed for a time.

3:5 אַחַ֣ר יָשֻׁ֗בוּ בְּנֵ֣י יִשְׂרָאֵ֔ל וּבִקְשׁוּ֙ אֶת־יְהוָ֣ה אֱלֹהֵיהֶ֔ם וְאֵ֖ת דָּוִ֣ד מַלְכָּ֑ם וּפָחֲד֧וּ אֶל־יְהוָ֛ה וְאֶל־טוּב֖וֹ בְּאַחֲרִ֥ית הַיָּמִֽים׃ פ

אַחַ֣ר יָשֻׁ֗בוּ בְּנֵ֣י יִשְׂרָאֵ֔ל וּבִקְשׁוּ֙ אֶת־יְהוָ֣ה אֱלֹהֵיהֶ֔ם וְאֵ֖ת דָּוִ֣ד מַלְכָּ֑ם. Independent clause.

אַחַ֣ר. Temporal preposition which specifies the time of the verbal action in 3:5 relative to the action in 3:4.

יָשֻׁ֗בוּ. Qal *yiqtol* 3mp √שׁוב. When √שׁוב is followed by a second verb, even when it is separated from that verb by a constituent such as a subject (cf. Gen 26:18), it often functions as an auxiliary meaning "again" (HALOT 1430; JM §177b). Here √שׁוב is used to modify the following verb √בקשׁ. The Israelites had sought YHWH in the past (cf. 2:15). In the future, after they have rebelled and been separated from him, they will seek him once again.

בְּנֵ֣י יִשְׂרָאֵ֔ל. Subject of יָשֻׁ֗בוּ. This is also the referent of the subject of וּבִקְשׁוּ֙ which follows.

וּבִקְשׁוּ֙. Piel *qatal* (irrealis) 3cp √בקשׁ. The *dagesh* is omitted because the ק is followed by a vocal *shewa* (cf. JM §18m).

אֶת־יְהוָ֣ה אֱלֹהֵיהֶ֔ם. Acc compl of וּבִקְשׁוּ֙. The word אֱלֹהֵיהֶ֔ם, which has a 3mp poss suffix, is in apposition to יְהוָ֣ה and further identifies him.

וְאֵ֖ת דָּוִ֣ד מַלְכָּ֑ם. Second acc compl of וּבִקְשׁוּ֙. Similar to the previous phrase, the word מַלְכָּ֑ם with a 3mp poss suffix, is in apposition to דָּוִ֣ד and further identifies him.

וּפָחֲד֧וּ אֶל־יְהוָ֛ה וְאֶל־טוּב֖וֹ בְּאַחֲרִ֥ית הַיָּמִֽים. Independent clause.

וּפָחֲד֧וּ. Qal *qatal* (irrealis) 3cp √פחד.

אֶל־יְהוָ֛ה וְאֶל־טוּב֖וֹ. These two phrases are adjuncts of וּפָחֲד֧וּ. When the verb √פחד means "be afraid," it often does not have an accusative (Deut 28:66), but it can take an accusative either without a preposition (Job 3:25) or with מִן (Job 23:15) to specify the object of fear. In certain contexts √פחד also refers to positive excitement or trembling in response to restoration. In Isa 60:5 it is used in combination with √רהב to speak of a joyful heart. In Jer 33:9 it is used with רגז√ to describe joy and praise. This is the intended meaning here in Hos 3:5, when the Israelites experience YHWH's goodness once again. Therefore, we should understand the use of the prep אֶל in light of this sense. The Israelites are not in fear *of* (מִן) YHWH, rather they are trembling *toward* (אֶל) him. This explains how the Israelites can אֶל־טוּבוֹ ... וּפָחֲדוּ. They are not afraid of his goodness but are coming in excitement toward it, experiencing his good gifts once again.

בְּאַחֲרִית הַיָּמִים. PP with בְּ used temporally to indicate the time that the Israelites will seek YHWH and tremble toward him. The construct phrase אַחֲרִית הַיָּמִים is a common technical expression for an unspecified eschatological future when YHWH will fulfill his promises, judge the nations, and restore his people.

Part 2: YHWH's First Case Against Israel (4:1–11:11)

The prophetic sign-act of Hosea's family and its application to Israel in chapters 1–3 vividly introduce the book and set up the structural pattern. In chapters 4–14 the prophet further explores these phases in two cycles of oracles. He makes YHWH's case first in 4:1–11:11 and then a second time in 12:1–14:9.

In the first case, he begins with Accusation in 4:1–8:14, describing Israel's sin and the failure of that sin to produce its intended effect. The second move, Temporary Judgment, comes in 9:1–10:15 as the prophet describes the consequences of their infidelity. In a tragic irony, YHWH will destroy their food, children, and even the nation itself. Not only will their unfaithfulness fail to produce blessing, it will result in devastation!

Finally, in 11:1-11 the prophet announces that YHWH's resolve to restore is greater than Israel's resolve to rebel. Just as he led them out of captivity in Egypt, he will once again deliver them to himself. There will be Ultimate Reconciliation between YHWH and his people.

4:1–8:14 Accusation: Idols, Political Schemes, and Manipulative Worship

The prophet introduces his case in 4:1-3 before a series of subunits that describe Israel's infidelity. In 4:4–7:2 he condemns Israel's idolatrous and unorthodox worship within the land. The people had hoped that the worship of other gods would make them flourish and give them a rich and vigorous society, but it has brought only lies and shame. In 7:3–8:3

he moves his attention to Israel's schemes directed outside of the land. Israel has refused to trust YHWH for her security and has gone to other nations for help. This constitutes another kind of idolatry and, rather than leading to safety and protection, it will lead to exile and death. The accusation concludes with a summation of the case in 8:4-14 which reviews the evidence of Israel's unfaithfulness.

Introduction to YHWH's case (4:1-3)

These first three verses of chapter 4 are a brief, distinct unit that introduces the first major section (4:4–7:2) of this second part of the book. In contrast to chapter 3, it is poetry. Furthermore, whereas chapter 3 was primarily YHWH's word to Hosea and Hosea's word to Gomer, here the prophet addresses his audience directly in a conventional prophetic formula. YHWH has a formal case (רִיב) against Israel. They have committed sins of omission (v. 1) and sins of comission (v. 2). Therefore, he will devastate the land in response (v. 3).

> ¹*Hear the word of YHWH, Israelites,*
> *for YHWH has a case with the inhabitants of the land*
> *for there is no truth and no covenant love and no knowledge of God in the land.*
>
> ²*Cursing and lying and murder and theft and adultery: they have broken out,*
> *and bloodshed prompts more bloodshed.*
>
> ³*Therefore the land dries up and everything that lives in it languishes;*
> *with the animal of the field and the birds of the sky,*
> *and along with the fish of the sea they perish.*

4:1 a שִׁמְעוּ דְבַר־יְהוָה בְּנֵי יִשְׂרָאֵל
b כִּי רִיב לַיהוָה עִם־יוֹשְׁבֵי הָאָרֶץ
c כִּי אֵין־אֱמֶת וְאֵין־חֶסֶד וְאֵין־דַּעַת אֱלֹהִים בָּאָרֶץ׃

Lines a-c are a tricolon. Line b is a subordinate clause which must be related to line a, and line c is syntactically subordinate to line b. The lines are marked by *'Atnaḥ*, *Zaqep parvum*, and *Silluq*.

שִׁמְעוּ דְבַר־יְהוָה בְּנֵי יִשְׂרָאֵל. *Line a.* Independent clause. This is a conventional prophetic messenger formula, calling the prophet's audience to attention.

שִׁמְעוּ. Qal impv mp √שמע.

דְבַר־יְהוָה. Acc compl of שִׁמְעוּ. The only other occurrence of this phrase in the book occurs in the superscription in 1:1. At the beginning of this new section, the prophet reminds the reader that the following oracles have a divine origin and should therefore be trusted and obeyed.

בְּנֵי יִשְׂרָאֵל. Vocative, indicating that the implied reader is the people of Israel. The construct phrase is a gentilic which refers to the "Israelites" generally; it is not restricted to the sons or men only.

כִּי רִיב לַיהוָה עִם־יוֹשְׁבֵי הָאָרֶץ. *Line b.* Causal, verbless, clause which is subordinate to line a and provides the reason that the Israelites should listen to the word of YHWH.

רִיב לַיהוָה. The root √ריב can refer either to an informal quarrel or to an official case before authorities. In 2:4 the verb form is used for an informal, family quarrel as the metaphorical children are supposed to plead with their mother. Here in 4:1 and again in 12:3, the noun form refers to a formal case that YHWH has against his people. The genitive, or possessive, relationship ("YHWH has a case") is formed with a לְ prep rather than the construct because רִיב is nondefinite (JM §130b). רִיב is the subject of the verbless clause, and לַיהוָה is the predicate.

עִם־יוֹשְׁבֵי הָאָרֶץ. This adjunct PP with עִם marks the personal complement of the verbless clause with רִיב (cf. WO §11.2.14) and specifes the defendant in the case. The substantive יוֹשְׁבֵי is a Qal ptc mp constr √ישׁב. This is the party with whom YHWH has a problem. The oracle is addressed to the Israelites (4:1a) who must also be these inhabitants (4:1b). Therefore, the Israelites are both the jury and defendant in the case (Garrett 1997:108). Garrett notes the significance of this reference: because they are "not my people" (1:9), he refers to them here only as "the inhabitants of the land" (109).

כִּי אֵין־אֱמֶת וְאֵין־חֶסֶד וְאֵין־דַּעַת אֱלֹהִים בָּאָרֶץ. *Line c.* Verbless causal clause subordinate to line b, which provides the reason that YHWH has a רִיב with his people.

אֵין־אֱמֶת וְאֵין־חֶסֶד וְאֵין־דַּעַת אֱלֹהִים. The compound subject of the verbless clause includes the adverb אֵין which adds to the copulative notion the idea of nonexistence (JM §154k). אֱמֶת refers to what is true, and therefore, fidelity and loyalty. On חֶסֶד, see 2:21b. Because YHWH is in a covenant relationship with his people, he acts in אֱמֶת and חֶסֶד toward them, and he expects them to respond in these ways toward each other and toward him in return. The noun דַּעַת is a common wisdom term and contributes to a wisdom theme in the book (cf. 4:6, 14, 18; 5:10; 7:9; 9:7; 10:3; 12:7; 13:13; 14:10). The people have broken covenant (thus the רִיב), and these covenant obligations are absent from their life and society.

בָּאָרֶץ. This PP is the predicate of the verbless clause in line c. The בְּ prep is locative.

4:2 a אָלֹה וְכַחֵשׁ וְרָצֹחַ וְגָנֹב וְנָאֹף פָּרָצוּ
b וְדָמִים בְּדָמִים נָגָעוּ׃

Lines a-b are a bicolon. Line a is marked with a disjunctive *Zaqep magnum*. The Masoretes conclude line a with וְנָאֹף (note the disjunctive *'Atnaḥ*). However, this would leave no verb in line a and two verbs in line b. It makes better sense to read against the usual *'Atnaḥ* line marker and end the line after פָּרָצוּ.

אָלֹה וְכַחֵשׁ וְרָצֹחַ וְגָנֹב וְנָאֹף פָּרָצוּ. *Line a*. Independent clause.

אָלֹה וְכַחֵשׁ וְרָצֹחַ וְגָנֹב וְנָאֹף. The five subjects of the verb פָּרָצוּ are infinitives absolute used as nominals. As a nominal, the infinitive absolute in BH most often serves as an absolute or adverbial complement (e.g., to intensify or nuance a finite verb of the same root). Rarely, they are also used in other grammatical roles, such as the subject of a verbal clause (as here), the complement of a preposition, or as an accusative (WO §35.5.5a-b). אָלֹה is a Qal inf abs √אלה. כַחֵשׁ is a Piel inf abs √כחש. רָצֹחַ is a Qal inf abs √רצח. גָנֹב is a Qal inf abs √גנב. נָאֹף is a Qal inf abs √נאף.

פָּרָצוּ. Qal *qatal* 3cp √פרץ. This verb often conveys breaking something or breaking through something, such as a city wall (e.g., 2 Kgs 14:13). When extended metaphorically, it can convey breaking out of confines, such as wine overflowing its container (Prov 3:10) or a baby coming out of the womb (Gen 38:29). When extended further, it speaks of something which is uncontained, spreading rapidly with nothing to restrict it. Examples include population (Exod 1:12), wealth (Gen

30:30), or a command (2 Chr 31:5). Here, it is wicked actions that multiply when unchecked.

וְדָמִים בְּדָמִים נָגָעוּ. *Line b.* Independent clause.

וְדָמִים. Subject of נָגָעוּ. The word דָּם is used in both the singular and plural forms to denote blood shed violently (HALOT, 224–25). Here, it refers to murder.

בְּדָמִים. Oblique compl of נָגָעוּ. This is the culmination of the list of sins mentioned in the verse.

נָגָעוּ. Qal *qatal* 3cp √נגע. Rashi (1951) understands the clause "bloodshed touches bloodshed" to mean that the extent of bloodshed is so great that the blood of one victim literally touches the blood of the next. It is more likely that the verb here intends a meaning like "prompts" in that one act of murder leads to the next, and so on (cf. Macintosh 2014:130). It conveys a systemic problem parallel to the verb √פרץ ("broken out") in the previous clause.

4:3 a עַל־כֵּן ׀ תֶּאֱבַל הָאָרֶץ וְאֻמְלַל כָּל־יוֹשֵׁב בָּהּ
b בְּחַיַּת הַשָּׂדֶה וּבְעוֹף הַשָּׁמָיִם
c וְגַם־דְּגֵי הַיָּם יֵאָסֵפוּ׃

Lines a-c are a tricolon, with lines marked with *Zaqep parvum*, *'Atnaḥ*, and *Silluq*. The verse addresses a topic distinct from vv. 2 and 4.

עַל־כֵּן תֶּאֱבַל הָאָרֶץ. *Line a.* Independent clause.

עַל־כֵּן. Conjunctive adverb consisting of the prep עַל and the adverb כֵּן. This verse describes the consequences of the rebellion against YHWH in 4:1-2.

תֶּאֱבַל. Qal *yiqtol* 3fs √אבל. BDB gives only the meaning "mourn" for this root (5), and that is a typical translation in this verse (cf. NRSV). However, parallels with √יבש ("dry up") in Jer 12:4; 23:10, and Amos 1:2 indicate that there is a second meaning of the root which means "to dry up" (cf. HALOT 7). In addition, √אבל is parallel in this verse with √אמל ("to dwindle"), and in Joel 1:10 √אבל is used in association with both √יבש and √אמל. The *yiqtol* verb might signify either a present drought or a threat for the future. Israel's sin has brought or will bring a severe drought upon them along with consequent agricultural failure (cf. 2:3, 9, 12).

הָאָרֶץ. Subject of תֶּאֱבַל.

וְאֻמְלַל כָּל־יוֹשֵׁב בָּהּ. *Line a.* Independent clause.

וְאֻמְלַל. Pual *qatal* 3ms √אמל. In the Hebrew Bible, this verb has no active forms and it does not occur as as *yiqtol*. It refers to various kinds of failure and dilapidation: whether in procreation (1 Sam 2:5), fishing (Isa 19:8), the condition of city gates (Jer 14:2), or, as here, the state of the land.

כָּל־. Subject of וְאֻמְלַל.

יוֹשֵׁב. Qal ptc ms √ישב. This participle is a genitive which modifies the noun כֹּל; thus, it is embedded within the clause rather than forming the predicate of a new one.

בָּהּ. Adjunct PP with locative בְּ. The antecedent of the 3fs suffix is הָאָרֶץ in the previous clause.

בְּחַיַּת הַשָּׂדֶה וּבְעוֹף הַשָּׁמַיִם וְגַם־דְּגֵי הַיָּם יֵאָסֵפוּ. *Lines b-c.* Independent clause.

בְּחַיַּת הַשָּׂדֶה וּבְעוֹף הַשָּׁמַיִם וְגַם־דְּגֵי הַיָּם. Three coordinated PPs with בְּ (the third is unmarked and is governed by the preceding prepositions). One might understand the preposition as a בְּ of specification (cf. WO §11.2.5e) meaning, "everything that lives in it, *that is* the animals of the field, the birds of the sky, and the fish of the sea." However, this would preclude humans who live in the land, and the prophet has already primarily defined the inhabitants (יֹשְׁבֵי הָאָרֶץ) as the Israelites in 3:1 (Wolff 1974:65). It is better to understand the בְּ as expressing the idea of accompaniment (cf. JM §133c). In this sense, not only will the inhabitants of the land perish (4:3b), the animals will die as well (4:3c).

יֵאָסֵפוּ. Niph *yiqtol* 3mp √אסף. The root √אסף fundamentally means "to gather," but in the Niphal it is frequently used to refer to dying. The connection probably comes from an idiom in which a person is "gathered" to his or her ancestors in a grave or being taken to join those who have died previously.

The Wicked Priest and the Illegitimate Cult (4:4-19)

Hosea begins his critique of Israel's idolatrous worship with a description of the unorthodox cult and a particular condemnation of its leaders. In 4:4-11 he denounces a wicked priest who has led the people astray. This passage is marked by a pattern in which the prophet alternates between accusation and the corresponding judgment from YHWH (see Garrett 1997:114–15). The structure is as follows: guilt (4:4), punishment (4:5a-b), punishment (4:5c), guilt (4:6a), guilt (4:6b), punishment (4:6c), guilt (4:6d), punishment (4:6e), guilt (4:7a), punishment (4:7b), guilt (4:8), punishment (4:9), punishment (4:10a-b), guilt (4:10c-11a).

In 4:12-19 Hosea describes their illegitimate worship practices and surveys the psychology and motivation behind their spiritual "adultery." The word רוּחַ, which describes a *Zeitgeist* or "spirit of the age," forms an inclusio around this unit in vv. 12 and 19. The people may believe that they are honoring YHWH, or at least including him in their worship, but they are stubborn and their true object of love is really themselves, manifested in their evil practices.

⁴Surely, let a man not contend,
and let a man not accuse,
but my contention is with you, O priest.

⁵You will stumble by day,
and the prophet also will stumble with you by night,

I will destroy your mother—
⁶my people will be destroyed without knowledge.

Because you have rejected knowledge,
I reject you from being a priest to me.

You forgot the law of your God;
I also will forget your children.

⁷When they multiplied, thus they sinned against me.
I will exchange their glory for shame.

⁸They devour the sin offering of my people,
and they desire their guilt offering.

⁹As the people, so will be the priest,
and I will punish him for his ways,
and repay his deeds.

¹⁰And they will eat and not be satisfied;
they will have fornicated but will not increase,

for they have abandoned YHWH in favor of [11]fornication,
and wine and new wine take the heart.

[12]My people consult by their stick,
and their rod declares to them.

For a spirit of fornication has led astray,
And they fornicated away from their God.

[13]They sacrifice on the tops of mountains,
and they make offerings on the hills,
under oak, storax, and terebinth,
for its shade is good.

Therefore, your daughters fornicate,
and your daughters-in-law commit adultery.

[14]I will not punish your daughters when they fornicate,
or your daughters-in-law when they commit adultery,

for they go aside with the prostitutes,
and they sacrifice with the cult women,
and a people who does not understand will come to ruin.

[15]Though you fornicate, O Israel,
let not Judah be guilty.

And do not enter Gilgal,
and do not go up to Beth Aven,
and do not swear, "As YHWH lives!"

[16]Like a stubborn cow, Israel has become stubborn.
Now, will YHWH shepherd them like a lamb in the pasture?

[17]Joined to idols is Ephraim—
leave him alone.

[18]If their drink comes to an end
they fornicate wildly;
they love the dishonor of her shields.

[19]A spirit has wrapped her in its wings,
and they will be ashamed of their altars.

4:4 a אַךְ אִישׁ אַל־יָרֵב
b וְאַל־יוֹכַח אִישׁ
c וְעַמְּךָ כִּמְרִיבֵי כֹהֵן:

Lines a-c are a tricolon. The first two lines are formally parallel, with each containing a prohibition (אַל + juss) as well as an impersonal explicit subject. Line c contains a vocative with an addressee distinct from that in 4:1-3. The lines are marked with disjunctive *Ṭipḥa*, *'Atnaḥ*, and *Silluq*.

אַךְ אִישׁ אַל־יָרֵב. *Line a*. Independent clause.

אַךְ. This adverb occurs frequently at the beginning of a new speech (Wolff 1974:76). It can function as an asseverative particle emphasizing what follows or as an introduction to a restrictive or antithetic statement in relation to what preceded. Because this begins a new unit with a change in topic from 4:1-3, the particle has an asseverative sense here.

אִישׁ. Explicit, impersonal subject of the following jussive יָרֵב. Normally an irrealis jussive verb would trigger VS word order in the clause (as in line b). Therefore, this constituent is fronted for focus and emphasizes the comprehensive scope of the prohibition: "let *no one* contend."

אַל־יָרֵב. Qal juss 3ms √ריב. This root can refer to either an informal quarrel or a formal case against someone (see 2:4). In 4:1 and 12:3 it is used to describe formal proceedings when YHWH brings a case against Israel. In 2:4 and in this verse, it refers to a more general argument or accusation. The prophet is highlighting *his* problem with the illegitimate priest (line c). Others should not quarrel generally, but he certainly has an accusation to make against the priest.

וְאַל־יוֹכַח אִישׁ. *Line b*. Independent clause.

אַל־יוֹכַח. Hiph juss 3ms √יכח.

אִישׁ. Impersonal subject of יוֹכַח.

וְעַמְּךָ כִּמְרִיבֵי כֹהֵן. *Line c*. Independent clause. This is a challenging (and possibly corrupted) clause with several possible interpretations. Three of these are as follows:

(1) "Your people are like those who attack a priest." This translation follows the vocalization of the MT. The word וְעַמְּךָ is the subject of a verbless clause, and the predicate is a PP. מְרִיבֵי is a Hiph ptc mp √ריב in a construct relationship with an objective genitive. One could understand this as a third statement about the problem of quarreling. Hosea is

not saying that the people *are* attacking a priest, rather he is describing the character of their quarreling. The problem with this solution is the 2ms suffix on עַמְּךָ, a reference which continues in vv. 5 and 6. To whom would it refer? In addition, in 4:6 it sounds like there is an actual priest being addressed. It is strange that the priest should be a victim in v. 4 but condemned in v. 6.

(2) "Your people are like a priest's quarrels." This translation also follows the vocalization of the MT. Again וְעַמְּךָ is the subject of a verbless clause with a PP as predicate. In this approach, מְרִיבֵי is a noun (a by-form of מְרִיבָה) in construct with a subjective genitive. However, what would this translation mean? How are people like quarreling?

(3) "My contention is with you, O priest" (וְעִמְּךָ כְּמֹ רִיבִי כֹּהֵן). This third approach makes the best sense within the context. The attention is on the priest addressed in vv. 5-6 rather than the people (who are not in view). Furthermore, the verse initiates an accusation against the priest, who is the subject of vv. 5-6. The translation does not emend the consonants in MT but assumes a different vocalization. (See BHS note a-a.) First, we read עמך as עִמְּךָ ("with you"), a PP which is the predicate of a verbless clause. The priest being addressed in the vocative is the antecedent of the 2ms suffix. Second, the subject of the verbless clause כמריבי can be understood several ways: (1) It is the noun מְרִיבָה with with a 1cs poss suffix. The כ is an emphatic כִּי or a dittography of the כ at the end of the previous word; (2) It is the noun רִיב with a 1cs suffix. The כ is an emphatic כִּי with an enclitic מ (Stuart 1987:72; Kuhnigk 1974:30–31). The noun כֹהֵן is a vocative rather than a genitive.

4:5 a   וְכָשַׁלְתָּ הַיּוֹם
      b   וְכָשַׁל גַּם־נָבִיא עִמְּךָ לָיְלָה
      c   וְדָמִיתִי אִמֶּךָ׃

4:6 a   נִדְמוּ עַמִּי מִבְּלִי הַדָּעַת

Lines 4:5a-b are a bicolon. The lines begin with √כשל and conclude with the לַיְלָה//יוֹם word pair. The disjunctive accents marking the lines are once again *Zaqep parvum* and *'Atnaḥ*. Lines 4:5c-6a are also a bicolon, marked by *Silluq* and *'Atnaḥ*. Even though this colon crosses the verse boundary there are two reasons for analyzing it in this way. First, the lines share the root √דמה and exhibit active//passive (Qal//Niph) grammatical parallelism. Second, in the context, the prophet alternates between the priest's failure or rebellion and YHWH's corresponding response. In this bicolon, YHWH will ruin the "mother" or institutions which house the priest because the priest has ruined the people. In 4:6 b-c the priest has rejected knowledge, so YHWH will reject the priest. In 4:6 d-e the priest forgot the law, so YHWH will forget his children. This is more plausible than understanding 4:5 and the first half of 4:6 as two tricola.

וְכָשַׁלְתָּ הַיּוֹם. *Line 4:5a.* Independent clause.

וְכָשַׁלְתָּ. Qal *qatal* (irrealis) 2ms √כשל. The subject of the 2ms verb is the priest addressed in 4:4. The verb √כשל has a sense of tripping over something or tottering. It is also used metaphorically to describe sin or to describe someone's ruin (cf. NIDOTTE 2:734). In light of the threats in line c and in v. 6, the latter sense is probably intended here. The irreal use describes consequences yet to come and the time references לַיְלָה/יוֹם suggest an ongoing or prospective situation. Both 4:5 and 4:6 (וְאֶמְאָסְךָ and אֶשְׁכַּח), describe warnings of the priest's impending downfall.

הַיּוֹם. Adverbial use of יוֹם ("by day") modifying וְכָשַׁלְתָּ (cf. Rudolph 1966:95–96).

וְכָשַׁל גַּם־נָבִיא עִמְּךָ לָיְלָה. *Line 4:5b.* Independent clause.

וְכָשַׁל. Qal *qatal* (irrealis) 3ms √כשל.

גַּם. Conjunction linking the נָבִיא to the 2ms addressee in the previous clause. Whereas a וְ conjunction would simply connect the two clauses, גַּם draws attention to the fact that a second individual will share the same fate.

נָבִיא. Subject of וְכָשַׁל. This apparently refers to a prophet who joins the priesthood in leading Israel astray.

עִמְּךָ. PP with עִם indicating accompaniment with a 2ms suffix. The antecedent of the suffix is the priest, the same referent as the 2ms verb וְכָשַׁלְתָּ in the previous clause (line a).

לָיְלָה. Adverbial use of לַיְלָה ("by night") modifying וְכָשַׁל. For other examples of this construction, see Exod 12:31 and Neh 2:13. Unlike הַיּוֹם in the preceding line, this noun does not have the article. However, there is no difference in meaning; לַיְלָה receives the article less commonly (AF 351).

Hosea 4:6

וְדָמִ֖יתִי אִמֶּֽךָ. *Line 4:5c.* Independent clause.

וְדָמִ֖יתִי. Qal *qatal* (irrealis) 1cs √דמה. HALOT (225–26) lists three different meanings for √דמה. (I) in the Qal ("I will be like your mother") makes no sense in the context, especially as spoken by the prophet/YHWH. (II) in the Qal ("be silent, still") is not possible because it is intransitive and אִמֶּֽךָ must be the accusative complement here. Perhaps if we vocalize the verb as a Piel וְדִמִּ֖יתִי, it would make sense as "make silent" → "I will bring your mother to an end" (cf. similar solutions in BHS note ᶜ⁻ᶜ), although the Piel is not attested elsewhere in the Hebrew Bible. (III) means "be destroyed" in the Niphal. It is well attested, even in the next verse (4:6; cf. also 10:7, 15). Although the Qal of this root (III) is unattested elsewhere, this is the best solution and it does not require any revocalization. The verb here is active, giving the sense "I will destroy your mother."

אִמֶּֽךָ. Acc compl of וְדָמִ֖יתִי. Garrett argues that the mother represents institutional Israel which corrupts the "children" or ordinary people (cf. 2:4). This is a reference to overthrowing those institutions (1997:117).

נִדְמ֥וּ עַמִּ֖י מִבְּלִ֣י הַדָּ֑עַת. *Line 4:6a.* Independent clause.

נִדְמ֥וּ. Niph *qatal* (irrealis) 3cp √דמה. This is the same root with the same meaning—but passive— as in the previous clause. Even though the *qatal* is not preceded by וְ, the VS word order indicates that it is irrealis and refers to a prediction. Thus, √כשל occurs as irrealis *qatal* in successive lines (4:5a-b), and √דמה occurs as irrealis *qatal* in successive lines (4:5c-6a).

עַמִּ֖י. Subject of נִדְמ֥וּ. The poss 1cs suffix refers to the speaker YHWH, presented by the prophet.

מִבְּלִ֣י הַדָּ֑עַת. The prep מִן and the adverb בְּלִי ("without") form a compound which modifies נִדְמ֥וּ. The sense is that it is a lack of knowledge which makes the ruination of YHWH's people complete. In Lam 1:4 the same construction is used when Zion mourns *without* (מִבְּלִי) people to come to the festival. It is not common for the noun דַּעַת to have the definite article (7/90 occurrences in the Hebrew Bible). Here, the article emphasizes that the word has a particular referent (WO §13.5.1d). It is not general knowledge that the people lack, but specifically the knowledge of God (דַּעַת אֱלֹהִים) discussed in 4:1 (cf. 4:6b).

4:6 b כִּי־אַתָּה הַדַּעַת מָאַסְתָּ
c וְאֶמְאָסְאךָ֙ מִכַּהֵן לִי
d וַתִּשְׁכַּח תּוֹרַת אֱלֹהֶיךָ
e אֶשְׁכַּח בָּנֶיךָ גַּם־אָנִי:

Lines b-c and d-e are bicola. As noted above in 4:5, each of the two bicola alternates between the guilt and punishment of the priest. Lines b-c consist of a subordinate clause and its main clause, marked by disjunctive accents *R^ebi^a'* and *Zaqep parvum*. Lines d-e exhibit grammatical parallelism contrasting conjugation and tense (*wayyiqtol // yiqtol*) of the same root √שׁכח. The lines are marked with *Zaqep parvum* and *Silluq*.

כִּי־אַתָּה הַדַּעַת מָאַסְתָּ. *Line b*. Causal clause subordinate to the following main clause. The reason that YHWH will reject the priest (line c) is that the priest has rejected knowledge (line b).

אַתָּה. This pleonastic 2ms independent pronoun is fronted in the clause for focus. There is a contrast between "you" (the priest) in line b and the speaker (YHWH) in line c.

הַדַּעַת. Acc compl of מָאַסְתָּ. The article on דַּעַת emphasizes that it has a particular referent. The problem is not that the priest has rejected knowledge in general, but that he has rejected the knowledge of God (דַּעַת אֱלֹהִים) mentioned in 4:1 (cf. 4:6a).

מָאַסְתָּ. Qal *qatal* 2ms √מאס.

וְאֶמְאָסְאךָ מִכַּהֵן לִי. *Line c*. Independent clause.

וְאֶמְאָסְאךָ. Qal *yiqtol* 1cs √מאס with a 2ms acc suffix. The final א in the verb is unusual. Earlier scholars thought that it might be a vestige of a voluntative form. It is more likely that it is a copyist's error. BHS note ^b states that many medieval manuscripts have ואמאסך, an apparent later correction.

מִכַּהֵן. Prep מִן on a Piel inf constr √כהן. The root √כהן occurs only in the Piel. It is intransitive and means "to act as a priest" (HALOT 462). In connection with the infinitive, the מִן prep has a consecutive meaning that preserves its ablative nuance (cf. JM 133e). It means, "... so that [you are] far from being a priest." This suggests not just rejection *as* a priest but removal from the priesthood.

לִי. PP with a לְ of interest or advantage. The antecedent of the 1cs suffix is YHWH, the speaker.

וַתִּשְׁכַּח תּוֹרַת אֱלֹהֶיךָ. *Line d.* Independent clause. In the context the clause is semantically subordinate, providing the reason for YHWH's action in line d.

וַתִּשְׁכַּח. Qal *wayyiqtol* 2ms √שכח.

תּוֹרַת אֱלֹהֶיךָ. Constr noun תּוֹרַת as acc compl of וַתִּשְׁכַּח. The word תּוֹרָה occurs only three times in Hosea (cf. 8:1, 12). Here it is related to the knowledge (דַּעַת) of God (4:1, 6a, 6b). The passage emphasizes the priest's failure in promulgating the truth of YHWH, therefore the people are languishing. The antecedent of the 2ms poss suffix on אֱלֹהֶיךָ is the priest, addressed in 4:4-6.

אֶשְׁכַּח בָּנֶיךָ גַּם־אָנִי. *Line e.* Independent clause.

אֶשְׁכַּח. Qal *yiqtol* 1cs √שכח.

בָּנֶיךָ. Acc compl of אֶשְׁכַּח. Hosea seems to be using "children" to refer to a broader group than the priest's biological children. Earlier in the book, בָּנִים represents those ordinary citizens who depend upon the priest for truth and leadership in contrast to the "mother" who represents the institutions, including the priesthood (cf. 2:4; 4:5). Here, the antecedent of the 2ms poss suffix is the priest—they are *his* children. Thus, "children" here may refer to the priesthood in general.

גַּם־אָנִי. גַּם is a conjunction which intensifies the pleonastic independent pronoun אָנִי. The conjunction גַּם, the use of the pronoun אָנִי to reinforce the subject of אֶשְׁכַּח, and the position of these two words at the end of the clause all bring attention to the contrast between the two parties. The priest has forgotten the law, so YHWH (yes, YHWH!) will forget his progeny.

4:7 a כְּרֻבָּם כֵּן חָטְאוּ־לִי
b כְּבוֹדָם בְּקָלוֹן אָמִיר׃

Lines a-b are a bicolon with lines marked with disjunctive *'Atnaḥ* and *Silluq*.

כְּרֻבָּם. *Line a.* This כְּ prep and infinitive form a comparative clause subordinate to the main clause which follows. The verb is a Qal inf constr √רבב with a 3mp suffix as the subject. The antecedent of the suffix is the בָּנִים ("children") of the priest referred to in 4:6.

כֵּן חָטְאוּ־לִי. *Line a*. Independent clause. This is the apodosis, marked by כֵּן, of the preceding comparative clause. The construction logically links the two actions and indicates that multiplying (כְּרֻבָּם) and sinning (חָטְאוּ) correspond in proportion.

חָטְאוּ. Qal *qatal* 3cp √חטא.

כְּבוֹדָם בְּקָלוֹן אָמִיר. *Line b*. Independent clause.

כְּבוֹדָם. This noun כָּבוֹד with a 3mp poss suffix is the first accusative of אָמִיר. This is the element that is taken or exchanged in favor of something else. The "glory" here is likely the privilege and status of the priesthood (Garrett 1997:119).

בְּקָלוֹן. Prep בְּ on the noun קָלוֹן. The verb √מור in the Hiphil marks its second accusative—that which something is exchanged *for*—with a בְּ prep (cf. Lev 27:10; Ps 106:20). Here, the speaker (YHWH) will take away their כָּבוֹד ("glory") and replace it with קָלוֹן ("shame").

אָמִיר. Hiph *yiqtol* 1cs √מור. With one exception (Jer 48:11), this verb occurs only in the Hiphil in the MT.

4:8 a   חַטַּאת עַמִּי יֹאכֵלוּ
     b   וְאֶל־עֲוֺנָם יִשְׂאוּ נַפְשׁוֹ׃

Lines a-b are a bicolon with lines marked with disjunctive *'Atnaḥ* and *Silluq*.

חַטַּאת עַמִּי יֹאכֵלוּ. *Line a*. Independent clause.

חַטַּאת עַמִּי. Noun חַטַּאת is the acc compl of יֹאכֵלוּ. It can refer both to sin and to the sin offering which atones for it. For example, Lev 4:3 uses the word in both ways, "... he shall offer for his sin (חַטָּאתוֹ) which he has committed a bull from the herd without blemish to YHWH for a sin offering (חַטָּאת)." Leviticus 6:19 and Ezek 42:13 refer to the priest eating (√אכל) the חַטָּאת as a part of his responsibility and provision. Here, in Hos 4:8 the prophet is denouncing the priesthood (still in view from 4:6e-7) for improperly taking and eating the offerings (cf. Lev 10:17). The construct relationship indicates possession: the people (עַם) bring their sin offering, and the priests devour it.

יֹאכֵלוּ. Qal *yiqtol* 3mp √אכל. The plural subject of this verb is the priesthood (see 4:6e). The *yiqtol* verbs in this verse represent habitual actions (cf. WO §31.3). This continues Hosea's critique of the group in 4:7, 8, and 10-11.

וְאֶל־עֲוֺנָם יִשְׂאוּ נַפְשׁוֹ. *Line b.* Independent clause.

וְאֶל־עֲוֺנָם. Adjunct PP with אֶל indicating the object of their desire, as is common with the idiom נשׂא נפשׁ ("desire"; see below) (cf. Deut 24:15; Ps 143:8; Prov 19:18). The parallelism suggests that the antecedent of the 3mp suffix on עֲוֺנָם is the people (עַמִּי) in line a. This means that the priests (the subject of the following verb יִשְׂאוּ) desire the iniquity of the people. Unlike חַטָּאת, the noun עָוֺן never refers to a type of offering. Nevertheless, it probably serves as a metonymy for the entire cult apparatus—the more the people sinned the greater the benefit to the priests.

יִשְׂאוּ נַפְשׁוֹ. The verb is a Qal *yiqtol* 3mp √נשׂא. The I-נ has assimilated to the שׂ but the *dagesh* is not written because it is followed by a vocal *shewa*. The idiom נשׂא נפשׁ occurs eight times in the Hebrew Bible and means to desire strongly.

4:9 a וְהָיָה כָעָם כַּכֹּהֵן
b וּפָקַדְתִּי עָלָיו דְּרָכָיו
c וּמַעֲלָלָיו אָשִׁיב לוֹ:

Lines a-c are a tricolon. Line a introduces the verse, while lines b-c are parallel and arranged chiastically. The lines exhibit three pairs of words with semantic correspondence: עָלָיו//לוֹ, √פקד//√שׁוב, and דֶּרֶךְ//מַעֲלָל. The lines are marked with disjunctive accents *'Atnaḥ*, *Zaqep parvum*, and *Silluq*.

וְהָיָה כָעָם כַּכֹּהֵן. *Line a.* Independent clause.

וְהָיָה. Qal *qatal* (irrealis) 3ms √היה.

כָעָם כַּכֹּהֵן. The כְּ prep on these two nouns introduce a comparison. According to GKC (§161c), the construction allows for either the first or second noun to be the topic while the other noun is the thing to which it is compared. For example, the first noun is the topic in Gen 18:25; Deut 1:17; and 1 Kgs 22:4 while the second noun is the topic in Lev 7:7; Judg 8:18; and Isa 24:2. In the present passage, if עָם is the topic, we would translate this line, "the people will be as the priest." This would mean that just as the priest is being condemned in the context, the people will also share a similar fate. However, there are several reasons to understand the priest as the focal point, translating, "as the people, so will be the priest." The surrounding verses (4:4-11) concern the priest and his colleagues. Furthermore, lines b-c contain four singular suffixes that must have the singular כֹּהֵן as their antecedent. Finally, the punishment of the priest is described in lines b-c. The prophet has already spoken about the judgment that awaits the people of Israel. Now he says that this wicked priest will share in their fate.

וּפָקַדְתִּי עָלָיו דְּרָכָיו. *Line b.* Independent clause. Lines b-c in this verse are repeated almost verbatim in Hos 12:3.

וּפָקַדְתִּי עָלָיו. Qal *qatal* (irrealis) 1cs √פקד. In this idiom, the complement PP עָלָיו specifies the recipient of the punishment described by the verb √פקד. The antecedent of the 3ms suffix is the priest mentioned in 4:4-6 and in the first line of this colon.

דְּרָכָיו. Second compl of וּפָקַדְתִּי. This specifies the reason for the punishment (see 1:4 and 2:15). The noun דֶּרֶךְ is a key metaphor in wisdom literature for the character and culmination of one's life choices (see 4:9).

וּמַעֲלָלָיו אָשִׁיב לֹו. *Line c.* Independent clause.

וּמַעֲלָלָיו. Acc compl of אָשִׁיב. The antecedent of the 3ms suffix is the priest described in lines a-b. The nouns דֶּרֶךְ ("way") and מַעֲלָל ("deed") are a common word pair, especially in Jeremiah where they occur together eleven times.

אָשִׁיב. Hiph *yiqtol* 1cs √שוב. In the Qal, √שוב frequently means to repent of actions or change one's mind about something (see 2:9). In the Hiphil it refers to bringing someone or something back, such as bringing an exile back to the land (Isa 49:6) or returning an item to someone (Exod 22:25). In this verse it means that YHWH will return the priest's wicked deeds (מַעֲלָלִים) to him. Because the priest's deeds are repugnant, this is a way that YHWH wreaks vengeance.

לֹו. This PP is a second complement of אָשִׁיב with לְ indicating the person to whom the deeds are returned (i.e., the priest).

4:10 a וְאָכְלוּ וְלֹא יִשְׂבָּ֫עוּ
       b הִזְנוּ וְלֹא יִפְרֹ֫צוּ

4:10-11 c כִּי־אֶת־יְהוָה עָזְבוּ לִשְׁמֹר׃ זְנוּת

4:11 a יַ֫יִן וְתִירוֹשׁ יִקַּח־לֵב׃

Lines 4:10a-b are a bicolon. Each line has a verb followed by a report that the verb did not accomplish what it intended. The lines are marked with *Zarqep parvum* and *'Atnaḥ* disjunctive accents. Reading against the MT accents, lines 4:10c (including the first word of v. 11) and 4:11a are a second bicolon. The first word of 4:11 (זְנוּת) is the complement of the last word in 4:10 (שמר√) and should be read with that previous sentence (see discussion below). Both lines in this second bicolon describe untamed behavior and debauchery.

וְאָכְלוּ. *Line 4:10a.* Independent clause. The verb is a Qal *qatal* (irrealis) 3cp √אכל. The plural subject is the priesthood (the "children" of the priest) criticized in 4:6-8 and 4:10-11.

וְלֹא יִשְׂבָּעוּ. *Line 4:10a.* Independent clause. The verb is a Qal *yiqtol* 3mp √שבע.

הִזְנוּ. *Line 4:10b.* Independent clause. The verb is a Hiph *qatal* (irrealis) 3cp √זנה. Irrealis *qatal* does not have to be preceded with וְ if it is clause-initial. The verb √זנה usually occurs as a Qal, meaning "to commit fornication." Occurrences in the Hiphil outside of Hosea refer to encouraging someone else to commit fornication, always with an explicit accusative complement (Lev 19:29; 2 Chr 21:11, 13; Exod 34:16). The three occurrences of the Hiphil in the book of Hosea are intransitive, without an accusative complement (4:10, 18; 5:3). Macintosh (2014:147) argues that the Hiphil here expresses "an action in some particular direction" (cf. GKC §53f). He cites the medieval Jewish commentator ibn Janaḥ who views this verb as reflecting the abundance or expansiveness of their fornication.

וְלֹא יִפְרֹצוּ. *Line 4:10b.* Independent clause. The verb is a Qal *yiqtol* 3mp √פרץ. The verb √פרץ refers to breaking out of confines, often with the sense of rapidly gaining possessions (Gen 30:30, 43) or increasing in population (e.g., Gen 28:14; Exod 1:12; Isa 54:3). Garrett (1997:120) thinks that the former sense is in view: the fornicating (הִזְנוּ) connected to cultic activity will not result in an increase in wealth. More likely, this is another assault on illegitimate attempts at fertility. Just as eating will not produce its expected outcome of a full stomach, sexual relations will not produce their expected outcome of an increase in progeny.

כִּי־אֶת־יְהוָה עָזְבוּ. *Line 4:10-11c*. Subordinate causal clause providing the reason for the judgment in lines 4:10a-b. This is the final colon relating the priests' guilt in the alternating structure of 4:4-11.

אֶת־יְהוָה. Acc compl of עָזְבוּ. It is fronted in the clause for focus, emphasizing the contrast with the previous lines: they pursue food and fertility, but YHWH they abandon.

עָזְבוּ. Qal *qatal* 3cp √עזב.

לִשְׁמֹר זְנוּת. *Line 4:10-11c*. Subordinate final (or purpose) clause indicating their intention in abandoning (עָזְבוּ) YHWH.

לִשְׁמֹר. Qal inf constr √שמר. Although not a common meaning, the verb √שמר can refer to devoting oneself to something (cf. Ps 31:7; Prov 27:18). Here the verb denotes devotion to fornication rather than true worship of YHWH.

זְנוּת. Acc compl of inf לִשְׁמֹר. As it stands, the MT is difficult because the verb √שמר requires an accusative, and yet there is a disjunctive *Silluq* accent marking the end of the sentence at that point. There have been a number of suggested solutions. Some interpret the last two verbs in 4:10 עָזְבוּ לִשְׁמֹר as a compound verb with יְהוָה as the complement (cf. AF 364). The translation would be, "they have stopped worshiping [YHWH]." A second approach involves taking the first two words of v. 11 (זְנוּת וְיַיִן) as the the complement of לִשְׁמֹר at end of v. 10. For several reasons, Wolff (1974:72) emends the text and combines the two words to the more common זְנוּנִים. Third, the solution adopted here is to take only זְנוּת from v. 11 as the complement. The advantage of this is that the first line in the bicolon deals with fornication and the second line deals with drink. This is also the understanding reflected in G and S.

וְיַיִן וְתִירוֹשׁ יִקַּח־לֵב. *Line 4:11a*. Independent clause.

וְיַיִן וְתִירוֹשׁ. Subjects of יִקַּח. The verb is singular because these two nouns are taken as a single concept (JM §150p). תִּירוֹשׁ occurs earlier in 2:10, 11, and 24 as one of the blessings of agriculture which seduced Israel away from YHWH.

יִקַּח. Qal *yiqtol* 3ms √לקח.

לֵב. Acc compl of יָקַח√. This refers to the reason or the conscience of the people (cf. a similar construction in Gen 31:20). It has been deadened and diminished by their licentiousness. This is the only occurrence of לֵב as the complement of לקח√. There are a few occurrences where לֵב is its subject (e.g., Job 15:12; Prov 10:8).

4:12 a עַמִּי בְּעֵצוֹ יִשְׁאָל
b וּמַקְלוֹ יַגִּיד לוֹ
c כִּי רוּחַ זְנוּנִים הִתְעָה
d וַיִּזְנוּ מִתַּחַת אֱלֹהֵיהֶם:

Lines a-b and c-d are bicola. The first bicolon is identified by word pairs (מַקֵּל//עֵץ and שׁאל√//נגד√) as well as grammatical parallelism (noun עַם//pronoun לוֹ). The lines are marked by *Zaqep parvum* and *'Atnaḥ*. The second bicolon has a form of זנה√ (noun//verb) in each line and the lines are marked with *Zaqep parvum* and *Silluq*.

עַמִּי בְּעֵצוֹ יִשְׁאָל. *Line a.* Independent clause. This verse marks a transition from the prophet's critique of the priest and priesthood in vv. 4-11 to the illegitimate worship of the people and the motivations behind their rebellion in vv. 12-19. It may be the priests who conduct these rituals, but the prophet addresses the guilt of the people as a whole.

עַמִּי. Subject of יִשְׁאָל. The rest of the verbs and pronouns in the following verses which refer to the people are *plural*. Therefore, some have suggested that עַמִּי is a genitive and goes with the preceding verse or it is a *casus pendens*. In that case the subject of the 3ms verbs in lines b and c is still the priest from the preceding section (cf. AF 364). However, the parallel line (וּמַקְלוֹ יַגִּיד לוֹ) would suggest that עַם is the subject of the singular verbs. The words עַמִּי in line a and לוֹ in line b correspond. In line a, the people consult, and in line b the stick/staff responds. Furthermore, there is another occurrence of עַם in 4:14, which is clearly the subject of singular verbs. These two uses of עַם form an inclusio around this short section (vv. 12-14), which describes specific behaviors in the unorthodox cult. The word עַם is collective and perhaps the singular verbs are drawing particular attention to that word. The antecedent of the 1cs poss suffix is YHWH, who frequently speaks of his people as his special possession (2:3, 23; 4:6, 8).

בְּעֵצוֹ. PP with instrumental בְּ indicating the means by which the people attempt to gain knowledge (cf. WO §11.2.5d). The PP is fronted in the clause (it would normally follow the verb). This draws attention to the focal point of the sin. They are attempting to get knowledge through divination, an activity viewed by YHWH's prophets as manipulative and in competition with God's revealed word (1 Sam 15:23; 2 Kgs 17:17; Jer 14:14).

יִשְׁאָל. Qal *yiqtol* 3ms √שאל. The *yiqtol* indicates habitual action.

וּמַקְלוֹ יַגִּיד לוֹ. *Line b*. Independent clause.

וּמַקְלוֹ. Subject of יַגִּיד. The antecedent of the 3ms pronoun is the people (עַם), which is the antecedent of all three pronouns in this bicolon. The noun מַקֵּל usually refers to a branch or a staff. It is used only here as a means of divination.

יַגִּיד. Hiph *yiqtol* 3ms √נגד. This verb occurs only in the Hiphil and Hophal. It refers to the action of announcing or informing.

לוֹ. PP with לְ indicating the addressee of the verb יַגִּיד.

כִּי רוּחַ זְנוּנִים הִתְעָה. *Line c*. Subordinate causal clause giving the reason the people practice divination. They have been led away by a "spirit of fornication." Here Hosea addresses the underlying motivations for their behavior. These are not isolated, independent actions. Rather, their actions arise in a culture of apostasy. Hosea uses the word רוּחַ to refer to a *Zeitgeist* which powerfully influences them. It is used again in 4:19 (the close of the inclusio surrounding this unit) and in 5:4 in this same way.

רוּחַ זְנוּנִים. This construct phrase (and specifically the word רוּחַ) is the subject of the verb הִתְעָה. The noun רוּחַ is usually feminine but there are some verses where it concords with masculine adjectives and verbs (e.g., Exod 10:13; Ps 51:12) as it does here.

הִתְעָה. Hiph *qatal* 3ms √תעה. In the Qal, תעה means "to wander or go astray." In the Hiphil it is causative, meaning "to lead astray." While the Hiphil usually has an explicit complement, it is not obligatory (cf. Prov 10:17; Isa 30:28).

וַיִּזְנוּ מִתַּחַת אֱלֹהֵיהֶם. *Line d*. Independent clause.

וַיִּזְנוּ. Qal *wayyiqtol* 3mp √זנה. In 4:4-11 Hosea used the third person plural to refer to the false priests. This verse begins a new unit, however, in which he addresses the people broadly, describing how the priests' influence has led to their apostasy. He begins with ms references (lines a-b) because he calls them עַמִּי ("my people"), but in this clause he refers to them with the more general plural once again.

מִתַּחַת אֱלֹהֵיהֶם. It is common for the verb √זנה to be followed by a PP describing what people are attracted *to* in their unfaithfulness. For example, in Exod 4:15 the Israelites are warned against adopting Canaanite practices lest they וְזָנוּ אַחֲרֵי אֱלֹהֵיהֶם ("fornicate after their gods"). The use of the prep מִן here indicates that fornication is not so much a move toward a lover, but a move *away from* YHWH, the rightful "spouse." Wolff (1974:85) argues that if Hosea had used מֵאַחֲרֵי (cf. 1:2), he would have simply signaled a break in formal relationship. By contrast, the compound prep מִתַּחַת expresses a nuance of refusal to submit in obedience to an obligatory relationship. The מִן has a privative sense (WO §11.2.11e). The antecedent of the 3mp poss suffix on אֱלֹהֵיהֶם is the Israelite people, the same referent as the subject of the verb וַיִּזְנוּ.

4:13 a עַל־רָאשֵׁי הֶהָרִים יְזַבֵּחוּ
b וְעַל־הַגְּבָעוֹת יְקַטֵּרוּ
c תַּחַת אַלּוֹן וְלִבְנֶה וְאֵלָה
d כִּי טוֹב צִלָּהּ
e עַל־כֵּן תִּזְנֶינָה בְּנוֹתֵיכֶם
f וְכַלּוֹתֵיכֶם תְּנָאַפְנָה:

Lines a-d are a quatrain in which line d summarizes the action in lines a-c. The disjunctive accents marking the lines are *R^ebi^aʿ*, *Zaqep parvum*, *Tipḥa*, and *ʾAtnaḥ*. Lines e-f are a bicolon indicated by the word pairs √זנה//√נאף and בַּת//כַּלָּה as well as chiastic word order. The lines are marked with *Zaqep parvum* and *Silluq*;

עַל־רָאשֵׁי הֶהָרִים יְזַבֵּחוּ. *Line a.* Independent clause.

עַל־רָאשֵׁי הֶהָרִים. PP with עַל indicating the location of the verbal action: the tops of the mountains. The PP is fronted for topicalization: it is the location of their sacrifices that indicates their illegitimacy.

יְזַבֵּחוּ. Piel *yiqtol* 3mp √זבח. This is the first occurrence of the verb √זבח in Hosea. In the Qal (122 times in the OT), this verb has the basic meaning "to slaughter," although it usually refers to sacred slaughter or sacrifice. In the Piel, as here, nineteen out of twenty-two occurrences refer to *illegitimate* sacrifice. This includes both unorthodox worship of YHWH (e.g., 1 Kgs 12:32) and idolatrous worship (e.g., 2 Chr 33:22). Hosea has already mentioned the worship of Ba'al (2:10, 15, 19), and the metaphor in the second half of this verse is that of adultery. It seems that the worship was primarily directed toward Canaanite deities. The *yiqtol* verbs in this verse denote habitual, ongoing activity.

וְעַל־הַגְּבָעוֹת יְקַטֵּרוּ. *Line b*. Independent clause.

וְעַל־הַגְּבָעוֹת. PP with עַל indicating the location of the verbal action. As in the previous clause (line a), this phrase is fronted. It is common for הַר ("mountain") and גִּבְעָה ("hill") to occur together as a word pair in poetry to describe the surrounding countryside (cf. Ps 72:3; Song 2:8). These terms are used in connection with the "high places" (בָּמוֹת), where Israelites were known to practice syncretistic and idolatrous worship. A few passages also mention a connection with green trees (עֵץ רַעֲנָן) (cf. Deut 12:2; Ezek 6:13). In the next line (c), Hosea describes specific trees at these locations.

יְקַטֵּרוּ. Piel *yiqtol* 3mp √קטר. In a priestly context, the verb √קטר can refer to burning incense (e.g., Exod 30:7), but in other contexts it is often a general synonym for sacrifice used in parallel with √זבח as it is here (cf. Hos 11:2).

תַּחַת אַלּוֹן וְלִבְנֶה וְאֵלָה. *Line c*. PP with תַּחַת indicating the location of the sacrifices (as in lines a and b). An אַלּוֹן is a large tree (Rebekah's nurse was buried under one; Gen 35:8), known to be strong (Amos 2:9). A לִבְנֶה or "storax tree" has a white color, while אֵלָה usually refers to a large evergreen tree. This latter type is elsewhere connected with cultic ritual (e.g., Ezek 6:13).

כִּי טוֹב צִלָּהּ. *Line d*. Subordinate causal clause giving the reason that they sacrifice under the trees.

צִלָּהּ. The word צֵל refers to shade, shelter, or protection, here referring to the shade of the trees. The antecedent of the 3fs poss suffix is אֵלָה (fs), which is the last type of tree mentioned in the previous line.

עַל־כֵּן תִּזְנֶינָה בְּנוֹתֵיכֶם. *Line e*. Independent clause which begins a new bicolon.

עַל־כֵּן. The prep עַל ("upon") combined with the adverb כֵּן ("thus") is idiomatic for "for this reason" or "therefore." It expresses the logical consequence of the preceding quatrain. In this case, Israel's idolatrous sacrifices have led to the corruption of their daughters and daughters-in-law. It is the connection with the preceding that makes the following statements more of a lament than an accusation (cf. Wolff 1974:87).

תִּזְנֶינָה. Qal *yiqtol* 3fp √זנה. This verb ("fornicate") occurs twelve times in the book. The prophet uses it to summarize and describe Israel's actions as unfaithful in the sign-act in 1:2, 2:7, and 3:3. It is an effective image not only because it refers to a broken relationship, but also because Caananite religion mixed ritual with sexual acts (cf. Num 25:1-2; Isa 57:5; Ezek 18:6, 11; 22:9). Here in chapter 4, in the midst of this discussion concerning sacrifice, there is a cluster of seven more occurrences of the verb √זנה (4:10, 12, 13, 14 [2×], 15, 18). The idea, continued in the next verse, is that as Israel entangles sexual activity with idolatry, their daughters become victims.

בְּנוֹתֵיכֶם. Subject of תִּזְנֶינָה. The 2mp poss suffix refers to the prophet's audience (now the readers of the book) addressed in 4:1 ("Here the word of YHWH, Israelites"). Since that introduction, the prophet has addressed the idolatrous priest in the second person singular (4:4-11) and the people of Israel in the third person plural (4:12-13a). Now he pivots and addresses the people directly once again.

וְכַלּוֹתֵיכֶם תְּנָאַפְנָה. *Line f.* Independent clause.

וְכַלּוֹתֵיכֶם. Subject of תְּנָאַפְנָה. The noun כַּלָּה can refer to a bride or a daughter-in-law. Parallel lines in Hebrew often feature semantic intensification or amplification from a word in one line to its corresponding word in the second line (see the introduction). Here, the tragedy of the victimization of the women is heightened from line e to line f. Not only do their "daughters" fornicate in this environment (line e), but their "brides" or "daughters-in-law" are made to commit adultery (line f). The sexual activity is all the more deviant because it involves married women as well.

תְּנָאַפְנָה. Piel *yiqtol* 3fp √נאף. The use of the Piel of this verb also heightens the sense of tragedy. According to Jenni (1968:161), in the Qal, √נאף refers to a clearly defined act of adultery. In the Piel it refers to habitual behavior with multiple partners.

Hosea 4:14

4:14 a לֹא־אֶפְק֞וֹד עַל־בְּנוֹתֵיכֶ֗ם כִּ֣י תִזְנֶ֔ינָה
b וְעַל־כַּלּֽוֹתֵיכֶם֙ כִּ֣י תְנָאַ֔פְנָה
c כִּי־הֵם֙ עִם־הַזֹּנ֣וֹת יְפָרֵ֔דוּ
d וְעִם־הַקְּדֵשׁ֖וֹת יְזַבֵּ֑חוּ
e וְעָ֥ם לֹֽא־יָבִ֖ין יִלָּבֵֽט׃

Lines a-b are a bicolon, identified by ellipsis of the verb √פקד, word pairs (בַּת//כַּלָּה and √נאף//√זנה), and identical syntax: עַל + compl + כִּי (temporal clause) + verb. The lines are marked with *Rᵉbîaʿ* and *Zaqep parvum*. Lines c-e are a tricolon. The first two lines, c-d, are parallel with word pairs (זֹנָה//קְדֵשָׁה and √פרד//זבח) and similarities in syntax (i.e., fronted PP). Line e concludes the tricolon with a summary statement. The lines are marked by *Zaqep parvum*, *'Atnaḥ*, and *Silluq*.

לֹא־אֶפְקוֹד עַל־בְּנוֹתֵיכֶם. *Line a.* Independent clause.

לֹא־אֶפְקוֹד. Qal *yiqtol* 1cs √פקד. Some scholars suggest that this is a rhetorical question, and thus YHWH intends to punish the women for fornication and adultery (cf. Nyberg 1935:29; Stuart 1987:83). YHWH makes clear statements to that effect elsewhere (cf. 2:15; 4:10, 12). However, 4:13b-14 concerns a particular issue: the victimization of the women of Israel by the sexualized cult. Later in v. 14, YHWH places the blame on the *men* (note the 3mp pleonastic pronoun) for creating a system which uses women. Thus, it makes the best sense here that YHWH is saying he will *not* punish them. This is first of all because they are victims. Second, although in actuality the women will likely be swept up in the conquest by Assyria, the statement has the rhetorical goal of amplifying the guilt of the men. Garrett notes that the people of the ancient Near East often applied a double standard and judged women more harshly for sexual offenses. But here, "YHWH is in effect saying: 'Why should I be outraged when young women commit adultery? They only learned it from their husbands'!" (1997:124).

עַל־בְּנוֹתֵיכֶם. On the collocation of √פקד and the prep עַל, see 1:4; 2:15; 4:9. The PP עַל specifies the recipient of punishment. As in the previous verse (4:13), the prophet addresses his audience/reader directly with the 2mp poss suffix.

כִּי תִזְנֶינָה. *Line a.* Subordinate temporal clause. The particle כִּי is used when the situations of the subordinate clause and the main clause are contemporary (WO §38.7a). The verb is a Qal *yiqtol* 3fp √זנה. The verb √פקד frequently takes a second accusative complement specifying the actions which are deserving of punishment. Similarly, in this verse Hosea *could have* said: לֹא־אֶפְקוֹד עַל־בְּנוֹתֵיכֶם אֶת זְנוּנֵיהֶן ("I will not punish your daughters for their fornication"). Instead, the prophet relates the actions which would normally call for punishment with temporal clauses (see also line b below). The particular nuance is that *whenever* the women fornicate or commit adultery they will not be punished. There is an emphasis on their illicit activity, which in turn amplifies YHWH's refusal to punish it.

וְעַל־כַּלּוֹתֵיכֶם. *Line b*. Independent clause. The negated verb לֹא־אֶפְקוֹד is elided and must be assumed from the previous line. The PP with עַל is the first complement of the assumed verb √פקד and indicates the recipient of the punishment (which in this case will not occur). The antecedent of the 2mp poss suffix continues to be the audience/reader.

כִּי תְנָאַפְנָה. *Line b*. Subordinate temporal clause. The particle כִּי indicates that the actions of the main clause and the temporal clause are contemporary. The verb is a Piel *yiqtol* 3fp √נאף. On the Piel of √נאף, see 4:13.

כִּי־הֵם עִם־הַזֹּנוֹת יְפָרֵדוּ. *Line c*. Subordinate causal clause giving the reason that YHWH will not punish the daughters and daughters-in-law when they fornicate and commit adultery.

הֵם. This 3mp pleonastic pronoun refers to the same subject—the men of Israel—as the following finite verb יְפָרֵדוּ. Its presence and its location (it is dislocated from the verb by the PP) highlights a contrast with the subject of the previous clauses (cf. WO §16.3.2d). YHWH will not punish the women because it is the *men* who go aside with prostitutes and participate in the sexualized ritual.

עִם־הַזֹּנוֹת. PP with עִם indicating accompaniment, that is, additional participants in the action. The noun זֹנָה is common in the OT (34×), but this is the only occurrence in Hosea. While the verb √זנה can broadly refer to illicit sex or to prostitution, the noun always refers to prostitution (i.e., sex for hire) (NIDOTTE 1:1123). Therefore, although the prophet has used the verb √זנה in the book to refer to unfaithful, illicit sexual relations (though not necessarily prostitution), here the reference is to prostitutes who are part of the cultic apparatus.

יְפָרֵדוּ. Piel *yiqtol* 3mp √פרד. The verb √פרד most commonly occurs in the Niphal (12×), meaning "to separate" or "spread out" (both intransitive). The Hiphil (7×) is transitive and means "to separate" or "keep apart." This is the only occurrence of the Piel of √פרד in the OT. In this context, it must mean "to go aside with a prostitute" (HALOT 962). The corresponding word in the parallel line (d) is √זבח ("to sacrifice"). This does not mean that the two words are synonymous, but it does suggest that both verbs refer to the men engaging in sexual cultic activities.

וְעִם־הַקְּדֵשׁוֹת יְזַבֵּחוּ. *Line d.* Unmarked causal clause giving a second reason that YHWH will not punish the women. Because of the parallel relationship with line c, the force of the כִּי in that line carries to this one.

וְעִם־הַקְּדֵשׁוֹת. PP with עִם indicating accompanying participants in the action. The noun קָדֵשׁ (f: קְדֵשָׁה) is known from Semitic and Egyptian cognate literature, as well as passages in the OT to refer to male and female members of the cult personnel (HALOT 1075). Several passages in the Bible suggest that sexual activity was part of the role of a קָדֵשׁ. In Gen 38:21 Judah refers to Tamar as a קְדֵשָׁה at a shrine after he had engaged in sexual intercourse with her. Deuteronomy 23:18-19 links the lexemes קָדֵשׁ and זֹנָה (along with wages). First Kings 14:24 states that the actions of קְדֵשִׁים are תּוֹעֲבוֹת ("abominations"). There is debate among scholars over whether cult prostitution was practiced in ancient Israel, and thus whether this word refers to cult prostitutes who actually participated in sexual acts as a part of the ritual worship. For arguments that cult prostitution was *not* practiced in ancient Israel, see Fisher 1976, Gruber 1986, Lipinski 2014. For the view that cult prostitution was practiced, see Yamauchi 1973, Wolff 1974:86–88, Stuart 1987:83. The latter position is more convincing. As argued above, the metaphor of sexual fornication for idolatry is doubly appropriate because it refers both to unfaithfulness and to the particular expressions of worship found in Canaanite cult. Hosea's concern in 4:13-14 is meaningful only if the daughters of Israel are doing something *more than* worshiping idols. Rather, they are engaged in sexual activity in this context which makes them victims as well as participants in the cult.

יְזַבֵּחוּ. Piel *yiqtol* 3mp √זבח. When this verb occurs in the Piel, it refers to illegitimate sacrifice (see 4:13).

וְעָם לֹא־יָבִין יִלָּבֵט. *Line e.* This last line of the tricolon consists of a main clause (עָם ... יִלָּבֵט) and an embedded unmarked relative clause לֹא־יָבִין

meaning, "and a people [who] does not understand will come to ruin" (see Holmstedt 2016:145).

וְעָם. Subject of the main clause and head of the relative clause. The noun עָם is pointed with a *qamets* as though it had the definite article (הָעָם) (cf. JM §35d). Each time YHWH has spoken about the people to this point, he has called them עַמִּי ("my people") (1:9; 2:1, 3, 25; 4:6, 8, 12). Now he forgoes the 1cs poss suffix. The sense is that he is stating a truism: *any* people who does not behave in a wise way or consider consequences will eventually come to ruin.

לֹא־יָבִין. Qal *yiqtol* 3ms √בין. This is a common wisdom word which refers to discernment, insight, and the ability to act according to a correct perspective. In this situation, the people of Israel are not practicing wise discernment. Their foolish behavior is shortsighted and will lead to nothing but harm to themselves.

יִלָּבֵט. Niph *yiqtol* 3ms √לבט. This is an uncommon verb (only here, Prov 10:8, 10) that occurs only in the Niphal. The sense of destruction or ruination is evident in Semitic cognates (HALOT 517).

4:15 a אִם־זֹנֶה אַתָּה יִשְׂרָאֵל
b אַל־יֶאְשַׁם יְהוּדָה
c וְאַל־תָּבֹאוּ הַגִּלְגָּל
d וְאַל־תַּעֲלוּ בֵּית אָוֶן
e וְאַל־תִּשָּׁבְעוּ חַי־יְהוָה:

Lines a-b are a bicolon, as indicated by the word pair יְהוּדָה//יִשְׂרָאֵל. The two lines are syntactically related as the clause in line a is subordinate to the main clause in line b; they are marked with disjunctive *Zaqep parvum* and *'Atnaḥ*. Lines c-e are a tricolon: each begins with a negated 2mp juss. The lines conclude with disjunctive *Rᵉbiaʿ*, *Zaqep parvum*, and *Silluq*.

אִם־זֹנֶה אַתָּה יִשְׂרָאֵל. *Line a*. Subordinate concessive clause. A concessive clause introduces a contrast with the main clause combined with the notion of causality (JM §171a). The sense is that one would expect Israel's sin to influence Judah and cause it to sin as well. Hosea warns that *even though* Israel sins, Judah should not participate.

זֹנֶה אַתָּה. The verb is a Qal ptc ms √זנה used predicatively. Usual word order in participial clauses is subject-participle. In this clause the participle is fronted before the subject pronoun אַתָּה for focus in order to contrast it with Judah's potential innocence. Israel is *fornicating*, but Judah should not do so.

יִשְׂרָאֵל. Vocative. This specifies that the addressee of the preceding 2ms independent subject pronoun is Hosea's audience, the nation of Israel.

אַל־יֶאְשַׁם יְהוּדָה. *Line b*. Independent clause.

אַל־יֶאְשַׁם. Qal juss 3ms √אשם negated with אַל. The verb √אשם refers to the guilt or responsibility that a person must bear for an offense, including consequent punishment. This is a warning that Judah must disassociate itself from Israel and its activities lest it be seduced by that bad example (cf. Rudolph 1966:107).

יְהוּדָה. Subject of יֶאְשַׁם.

וְאַל־תָּבֹאוּ הַגִּלְגָּל. *Line c*. Independent clause.

אַל־תָּבֹאוּ. Qal juss 2mp √בוא negated by אַל. Hebrew imperatives cannot be negated; prohibitions are formulated with negated second-person jussives or *yiqtols*. It is difficult to identify the addressee of this 2mp verb and the ones which follow. In line a, Hosea addresses Israel with a 2ms. However, he inconsistently uses singular and plural to refer to Israel in this section. On the other hand, he may be rhetorically addressing the people of Judah and warning them away from the unorthodox cult.

הַגִּלְגָּל. Compl of תָּבֹאוּ, specifying the destination of the verbal action. The verb √בוא usually takes oblique complements with preps אֶל or בְּ indicating destination or מִן indicating origin, but these are not obligatory (Holmstedt 2010:61). This verb also has a complement without a preposition in 9:4 and 9:10. Sometimes the complement is implicit (see 7:1; 9:7). Gilgal was Joshua's base of operations and the site of the twelve memorial stones (Jos 4:20) and the circumcision of the wilderness generation (5:9). In Hosea's day it has apparently become a place of illegitimate sacrifice (cf. also 9:15 and 12:12).

וְאַל־תַּעֲלוּ בֵּית אָוֶן. *Line d*. Independent clause.

אַל־תַּעֲלוּ. Qal juss 2mp √עלה negated with אַל.

בֵּית אָוֶן. Acc compl of תַּעֲלוּ indicating destination. Like the verb √בוא, √עלה takes oblique complements with a אֶל or עַל prep indicating destination or a מִן prep indicating origin. However, it often takes an accusative complement without the preposition as here (see also 8:9). The name בֵּית אָוֶן ("House of Wickedness") is probably a pejorative name for בֵּית־אֵל ("Bethel"), a well-known location that means "House of God" (see the parallel in Amos 5:5). Bethel was the place where Jacob had seen the vision of the staircase to heaven and built a memorial pillar (Gen 35:15). Because of this history, Jeroboam I (930–909 BCE) had chosen Bethel, along with Dan in the north, to serve as alternate sites where the people were to worship instead of going to Jerusalem. The word אָוֶן means "nothingness" or "wickedness" and is a common prophetic term for idols.

וְאַל־תִּשָּׁבְעוּ חַי־יְהוָה. *Line e*. Independent clause.

אַל־תִּשָּׁבְעוּ. Niph juss 2mp √שבע negated with אַל.

חַי־יְהוָה. This invoking of the name "YHWH" with חַי is a very common oath formula in the OT (Conklin 2011:27–30). It is not condemned elsewhere in the OT (cf. Deut 6:13), so the prohibition here must be related to its use in syncretistic worship.

4:16 a כִּי כְּפָרָה סֹרֵרָה סָרַר יִשְׂרָאֵל
b עַתָּה יִרְעֵם יְהוָה כְּכֶבֶשׂ בַּמֶּרְחָב׃

Lines a-b are a bicolon structured chiastically. PPs featuring the image of domestic livestock open and close the verse (כְּכֶבֶשׂ//כְּפָרָה) while the internal elements of the chiasm consist of the subject and verb of each line (יִרְעֵם יְהוָה//סָרַר יִשְׂרָאֵל). The chiasm may iconically reinforce the idea of reversal: Israel the stubborn cow will be treated like a sheep. The lines are marked with *'Atnaḥ* and *Silluq*.

כִּי כְּפָרָה סֹרֵרָה סָרַר יִשְׂרָאֵל. *Line a*. Independent clause. It does not make sense to understand the כִּי as introducing a subordinate causal clause. That would imply that in 4:15 Israel (the addressee) should not go up to Gilgal, Beth-Awen, etc. *because* Israel is stubborn (4:16a). Rather, this כִּי is asseverative, reinforcing the affirmation.

כְּפָרָה סֹרֵרָה. PP with כְּ indicating agreement in manner. Israel is stubborn just as a cow is stubborn (note the repetition of √סרר). The participle סֹרֵרָה is a Qal fs √סרר modifying פָּרָה. The verb √סרר refers to a refusal to obey or to submit to authorities. Hosea uses it again to describe the princes in 9:15.

סָרַר. Qal *qatal* 3ms √סרר. Israel's stubbornness is the occasion for YHWH's actions in the next line.

יִשְׂרָאֵל. Subject of סָרַר.

עַתָּה יִרְעֵם יְהוָה כְּכֶבֶשׂ בַּמֶּרְחָב. *Line b*. Independent clause. AF (377) suggest that the usual precative function of עַתָּה would seem to rule out a question, and therefore they understand the verb √רעה as negative and a reference to harsh treatment. In Mic 5:5 YHWH says that he will "shepherd" Assyria with a sword (implying destruction), and in Jer 2:16 it refers to "shaving" the crown of one's head, suggesting devastation. AF (377) argue that Hosea is using the verb here similarly, with a sinister connotation. However, though otherwise unmarked, the VS word order in this clause indicates that it is intended as an interrogative. Questions need not be introduced by a special interrogative pronoun or adverb (see GKC §150a). Therefore, it is better to understand the verb √רעה in the usual, positive sense, "to feed" as part of a rhetorical question. "Israel is stubborn" (line a), therefore, (line b) "Will YHWH feed them like a lamb ... ?" The implied answer is, "No, he will not feed them."

עַתָּה. Adverb; here it introduces the conclusion drawn from what has been stated (BDB 773).

יִרְעֵם. Qal *yiqtol* 3ms √רעה with a 3mp acc suffix. The antecedent of the 3mp acc suffix is "Israel" in the previous line, an example of grammatical parallelism. In that line יִשְׂרָאֵל concorded with a singular verb, but here Hosea refers to them with a plural pronoun.

יְהוָה. Subject of יִרְעֵם.

כְּכֶבֶשׂ בַּמֶּרְחָב. These two PPs further describe the manner (כְּ) and the location (בְּ) of the verbal action (√רעה).

4:17 a חֲבוּר עֲצַבִּים אֶפְרָיִם
b הַנַּח־לוֹ:

Lines a-b are a bicolon. Noun//pronoun grammatical parallelism (אֶפְרַיִם//לוֹ) indicates that the lines form a unit. The lines conclude with disjunctive *Tipḥa* and *Silluq*.

חֲבוּר עֲצַבִּים אֶפְרָיִם. *Line a*. Independent, verbless clause.

חֲבוּר עֲצַבִּים. The predicate of the verbless clause consists of a Qal pass ptc ms √חבר in a construct phrase with עֲצַבִּים ("idols"). According to AF (378), the *nomen rectum* (or genitive) of a passive participle in the construct state is usually the subject of the verb. This verse seems to be an exception, as עֲצַבִּים is functioning as the complement of the verb, "joined *to* idols." In the Qal, √חבר means "to ally oneself with" or to touch something physically (HALOT 287). The former is the sense here. Genesis 14:3 uses √חבר to describe kings in a military alliance and Ps 94:20 asks whether YHWH can ever be √חבר (allied with) wicked rulers. Here, Hosea condemns Ephraim for depending upon, and making a pact with, idols.

אֶפְרָיִם. Subject of the verbless clause. This is the first of thirty-seven times that Hosea refers to "Ephraim" as a synecdoche for the northern kingdom of Israel. Ephraim was a south-central region, which included prominent cities such as Gilgal, Shiloh, and Bethel. It was thus an important administrative area and a hub of idolatry, thereby drawing Hosea's particular condemnation.

הַנַּח־לוֹ. *Line b*. Independent clause. The verb is a Hiph impv ms √נוח. This verb takes accusative complements as well as oblique complements with prepositions such as עַל, בְּ, or לְ. With לְ it frequently means "to give rest" (cf. Jos 21:44; 2 Sam 7:11). In a few occurrences with לְ, as here, there is the sense of leaving someone alone or letting them do what they intend to do (e.g., Exod 32:10; 2 Sam 16:11).

4:18 a סָר סָבְאָם
b הַזְנֵה הִזְנוּ
c אָהֲבוּ הֵבוּ קָלוֹן מָגִנֶּיהָ:

This verse is difficult, perhaps because it has been somewhat corrupted. There is not space here for a full discussion of the problems and options; for these, see Wolff 1974 and Macintosh 2014. The following discussion represents an attempt to make the best sense of the MT, which is basically supported by the ancient versions. Lines a-c are a tricolon, indicated by common content (drink and fornication). The colon markers are disjunctive accents *'Atnaḥ*, *Zaqep parvum* and *Silluq*.

סָר סָבְאָם. *Line a*. Unmarked conditional clause.

סָר. Qal *qatal* (irrealis) 3ms √סור. This verb frequently means "to turn aside" or "to depart" but this is sometimes extended to mean "come to an end" (cf. Isa 6:7; 11:13; Amos 6:7). The subject of this verb is the following סָבְאָם ("their drink"). The VS word order indicates that the *qatal* is irrealis and indicates contingency, which in turn means that line a is an unmarked conditional clause, "If their drink comes to an end. ..."

סָבְאָם. Subject of סָר. This root occurs frequently as a participle, referring pejoratively to drunkards (cf. Deut 21:20; Prov 23:21). The antecedent of the 3mp poss pronoun is Israel. The prophet refers to them with both singular and plural forms in this section.

הַזְנֵה הִזְנוּ. *Line b*. Independent clause.

הַזְנֵה. Hiph inf abs √זנה. Infinitives absolute have a variety of functions in relationship to the main verb that can only be determined in each context. The sense does not seem to be that of affirmation ("they *surely* fornicate"). Callaham (2010:120) classifies it has "habitual" ("they act like prostitutes"). Perhaps the best option, even though it is rare with infinitives in the prepositive position (WO §35.3.1i), is to understand it as intensifying the activity of the main verb הִזְנוּ ("they fornicate *wildly*"). The prophet is painting a picture in this verse of debauchery arising from their attachment to idols (4:17) as they are swept away by the prevailing thought of their day (4:19).

הִזְנוּ. Hiph *qatal* 3cp √זנה. On the Hiphil of √זנה, see 4:10.

אָהֲבוּ הֵבוּ קָלוֹן מָגִנֶּיהָ. *Line c*. Independent clause.

אָהֲבוּ הֵבוּ. Qal *qatal* 3cp √אהב. The three consonants הֵבוּ require some explanation. Wolff (1974:73) suggests that the second word is an error; perhaps it is the misreading of an infinitive absolute אָהֹב in the postpositive position. Alternatively, it could be an accidental dittography in which the last three letters of אהבו were written a second time (see BHS note ᵈ⁻ᵈ).

קָלוֹן מָגִנֶּיהָ. It is possible to understand the plural מָגִנֶּיהָ as the subject of אָהֲבוּ, and קָלוֹן as the complement giving the sense, "her shields love dishonor." However, it makes better sense—and the parallelism is maintained—if we slightly revocalize קָלוֹן to קְלוֹן. It is then in a construct relationship with מָגִנֶּיהָ and serves as the accusative complement of אָהֲבוּ. Garrett (1997:139) suggests that the "shields" (מָגֵן) are decorative or cult objects associated with the worship of other gods. In spite of the difficulties in the verse, the sense is that they are engaging in the debauchery of drunkenness and sexual licentiousness. The antecedent of the 3fs poss suffix is difficult to identify. Hosea has been using ms and mp forms to refer to Israel, which is the expected referent here. Wolff (1974:73) suggests that perhaps the feminine imagery of Israel as a פָּרָה ("cow") has carried forward and influenced the pronoun here and in 4:19 (אוֹתָהּ).

4:19 a צָרַר רוּחַ אוֹתָהּ בִּכְנָפֶיהָ
b וְיֵבֹשׁוּ מִזִּבְחוֹתָם: ס

Lines a-b form a bicolon. The next verse begins a new unit. The disjunctive accents which mark the lines are *'Atnaḥ* and *Silluq*.

צָרַר רוּחַ אוֹתָהּ בִּכְנָפֶיהָ. *Line a*. Independent clause.

צָרַר. Qal *qatal* 3ms √צרר. This verb an be intransitive, meaning "to be cramped or depressed," or transitive (as here) meaning "to wrap (up) or envelop" (HALOT 1058).

רוּחַ. Subject of צָרַר. The word order is VS; the verb has been fronted for topicalization due to the change in subject from Israel's sin to judgment. The noun רוּחַ is feminine (see the suffix on בִּכְנָפֶיהָ), but concords with a masculine verb as is sometimes the case (cf. GKC §145o). This רוּחַ refers to a *Zeitgeist* or dominant way of thinking that has deeply influenced them (see 4:12). This use of רוּחַ forms an inclusio around 4:12-19, which describes the results of the teaching of the evil priesthood (4:4-11).

אוֹתָהּ. Acc compl of צָרַר. For the uncertain antecedent of the 3fs pronominal suffix, see 4:18. Presumably it refers to Israel because of the parallel "they will be ashamed of their sacrifices" in the next line.

בִּכְנָפֶיהָ. PP with בְּ indicating location. The wind is said to have "wings" in 2 Sam 22:11/Ps 18:11 and Ps 104:3. The antecedent of the 3fs poss suffix is the feminine רוּחַ.

וְיֵבֹשׁוּ מִזִּבְחוֹתָם. *Line b*. Independent clause.

וְיֵבֹשׁוּ. Qal *yiqtol* 3mp √בוש.

מִזִּבְחוֹתָם. An adjunct PP with מִן specifying the source of shame (בוש). A difficulty here is that the word זֶבַח is elsewhere always masculine. Thus we would expect the form: מִזִּבְחֵיהֶם ("of their sacrifices"). A better explanation is that the intended noun is מִזְבְּחוֹת ("altars"). This would make sense of the feminine morphology, but if the מ in the text is a preposition, then the initial מ of the noun must have been lost due to haplography. The correct, original reading would have been מִמִּזְבְּוֹתָם ("of their altars") (see BHS note ᵇ). This reading is supported by the major ancient versions (G, S, T) and is more convincing.

Israel Does Not Truly Seek YHWH (5:1-15)

In this section the prophet addresses the leadership of Israel more broadly and critiques them for the ways that they have led the nation away from fidelity to the covenant with YHWH. There are two subunits. In vv. 1-7, the prophet addresses his audience in the second person and describes their behavior in the third person. The influence of their leaders and a "spirit" of self-dependence has made Israel incapable of repenting (v. 4). They do not "seek" (√בקש) YHWH, for they have been taught an approach to worship that is manipulative (v. 6). It has the appearance of faithful loyalty, but it is treacherous and deceptive (v. 7). Verses 8-15 constitute a second subunit describing the results of this false worship. The first-person voice is predominant, as YHWH announces how he will devastate them. Their religious practices *should* foster a better relationship with YHWH, but instead it provokes his wrath and now nothing will save them from his judgment. Only when they are broken and realize the futility of their pursuits will they truly "seek" (√בקש) YHWH as they should (v. 15).

> ¹*Hear this, priests,*
> *and pay attention, house of Israel*
> *and house of the king, listen*
> *because the verdict is for you.*
>
> *You have become a trap at Mizpah,*
> *and a net spread out over Tabor.*
>
> ²*And the rebels have intensified the slaughter,*
> *but I am fetters for all of them.*
>
> ³*I know Ephraim,*
> *and Israel is not hidden from me.*
>
> *For now you have fornicated, Ephraim;*
> *Israel is defiled.*

⁴*Their deeds do not permit them to return to their God,*
for a spirit of fornication is in their midst,
and they do not know YHWH.

⁵*And the pride of Israel will testify against him,*
and Israel and Ephraim will stumble in their iniquity;
Judah also will stumble with them.

⁶*With their flock and their cattle they go to seek YHWH,*
but they do not find him. He has withdrawn from them.

⁷*They have dealt treacherously with YHWH; they have given birth to illegitimate children.*
Now the New Moon will devour them with their portions.

⁸*Sound the Shophar in Gibeah;*
the trumpet in Ramah.

Raise a shout in Beth Aven;
after you, Benjamin!

⁹*Ephraim, you will be a desolation on the day of rebuke;*
among the tribes of Israel I make known what is sure.

¹⁰*The princes of Judah will be like those who displace a boundary marker;*
on them I will pour out my wrath like the waters.

¹¹*Oppressed will be Ephraim—crushed by judgment;*
for he was persistent in going after what is worthless.

¹²*And I am like disease to Ephraim,*
and like decay to the house of Judah.

¹³*And Ephraim saw his sickness,*
and Judah his sore.

Ephraim went to Assyria,
and sent to the great king.

But he is not able to heal you,
and he will not cure you from the sore.

¹⁴*For I am like the lion to Ephraim,*
and like the young lion to the house of Judah.

I, yes I, will tear and I will go;
I will carry off and no one can deliver.

¹⁵I will go back to my place;
until they are guilty and they seek my face.
In their distress they will seek me.

5:1 a שִׁמְעוּ־זֹאת הַכֹּהֲנִים
b וְהַקְשִׁיבוּ ׀ בֵּית יִשְׂרָאֵל
c וּבֵית הַמֶּלֶךְ הַאֲזִינוּ
d כִּי לָכֶם הַמִּשְׁפָּט
e כִּי־פַח הֱיִיתֶם לְמִצְפָּה
f וְרֶשֶׁת פְּרוּשָׂה עַל־תָּבוֹר:

Lines a–d are a quatrain. A trio of semantically related imperatives (שמע//קשב//אזן) links the first three lines, and the fourth line is a conclusion. Lines b and c are arranged chiastically (verb > vocative//vocative > verb) with similar construct phrases (בֵּית הַמֶּלֶךְ//בֵּית יִשְׂרָאֵל). Quatrains are not common in Hebrew poetry; when they occur they often signal a transition or a new unit. The lines are marked by conjunctive *Gereš*, and disjunctive *R^ebî'*, *Zaqep parvum*, and *'Atnaḥ*. Lines e–f are a bicolon, indicated by word pairs (פַּח//רֶשֶׁת; תָּבוֹר//מִצְפָּה). The verb √היה from line e is elided in line f. The lines are marked by disjunctive *Zaqep parvum* and *Silluq*.

שִׁמְעוּ־זֹאת הַכֹּהֲנִים. *Line a*. Independent clause.

שִׁמְעוּ. Qal impv mp √שמע. The addressee of this and the following two imperatives is the vocative at the end of the line.

זֹאת. Acc compl of שִׁמְעוּ. The antecedent is unspecified. We can assume that the speaker has in mind a feminine noun for "word" or "speech" such as מִלָּה (cf. Job 34:16).

הַכֹּהֲנִים. Vocative and addressee of the imperative שִׁמְעוּ.

וְהַקְשִׁיבוּ ׀ בֵּית יִשְׂרָאֵל. *Line b*. Independent clause.

וְהַקְשִׁיבוּ. Hiph impv mp √קשב. With the exception of one occurrence (Isa 32:3), this verb always appears in the Hiphil. The complement of this verb (what it is that one listens to carefully) is implied.

בֵּית יִשְׂרָאֵל. Vocative and addressee of the imperative וְהַקְשִׁיבוּ. This line probably refers to other leadership in Israel. If that is the case, in this verse the prophet is addressing the leaders of the land: the priests, the leaders of Israel, and the court of the king. Wolff (1974:97) notes that there are three stresses in each of the first three lines and suggests that this might have led to the abbreviation in line b of the longer קְצִינֵי בֵּית יִשְׂרָאֵל ("heads of the house of Israel"; cf. Mic 3:1, 9).

וּבֵית הַמֶּלֶךְ הַאֲזִינוּ. *Line c.* Independent clause.

וּבֵית הַמֶּלֶךְ. The noun בֵּית (in construct) is a vocative and the addressee of the following imperative הַאֲזִינוּ.

הַאֲזִינוּ. Hiph impv mp √אזן. As with the previous verb, the complement specifying what they are to listen to is implied (i.e., the word of the prophet). The three verbs (√שמע, √קשב, √אזן) in these first three lines also occur together in Ps 17:1; Isa 28:23; and 42:23.

כִּי לָכֶם הַמִּשְׁפָּט. *Line d.* Verbless subordinate causal clause giving the reason that Hosea's audience should pay careful attention. The verdict he is about to announce is directed at them; therefore they should consider its contents carefully.

לָכֶם. PP with לְ of interest indicating the party against whom the "verdict" is directed. The antecedent of the 2mp suffix is the three groups mentioned in the preceding lines.

הַמִּשְׁפָּט. Subject of the verbless clause. This legal term is frequently used in prophetic literature to describe both the justice that YHWH expects from his people, as well as his judgment directed toward them for that breach (cf. Hab 1:12; Zeph 3:15; Mal 3:5). The latter sense is intended here as this is an announcement of judgment.

כִּי־פַח הֱיִיתֶם לְמִצְפָּה. *Line e.* Independent clause.

כִּי. This asseverative כִּי is used to reinforce the affirmation; it should be left untranslated (cf. JM §164b).

פַח. Compl of the copular verb הֱיִיתֶם.

הֱיִיתֶם. Qal *qatal* 2mp √היה. The prophet is continuing to address the priests, the leaders of Israel, and the house of the king.

לְמִצְפָּה. PP with לְ of interest indicating that Mizpah was their victim.

וְרֶשֶׁת פְּרוּשָׂה עַל־תָּבוֹר. *Line f.* The copular verb √היה is elided from line e in the parallelism.

וְרֶשֶׁת. Second compl of the verb הֱיִיתֶם.

פְּרוּשָׂה. Qal pass ptc fs √פרשׂ functioning as an attributive modifying רֶשֶׁת.

עַל־תָּבוֹר. PP with עַל indicating the location of the net. This is the usual preposition used with the expression פָּרַשׂ רֶשֶׁת (cf. Hos 7:12).

5:2 a וְשַׁחֲטָה שֵׂטִים הֶעְמִיקוּ
b וַאֲנִי מוּסָר לְכֻלָּם:

Lines a-b are a bicolon. The lines are marked with disjunctive *'Atnaḥ* and *Silluq*.

וְשַׁחֲטָה שֵׂטִים הֶעְמִיקוּ. *Line a.* Independent clause. This words in this line are difficult to identify individually and to relate to each other in a meaningful clause. Scholars have proposed various emendations. Among contemporary commentators, there are two basic camps. First, Wolff (1974), Stuart (1987), and Garrett (1997) understand the MT as corrupted and emend the line to something like וְשַׁחַת הַשִּׁטִּים הֶעְמִיקוּ ("and a pit at Shittim which they dug") (see also BHS note ᵃ⁻ᵃ). In this view, שַׁחֲטָה is a corruption of שַׁחַת ("pit"). The ה at the end of this word belongs on the following word as an article. The word שֵׂטִים should be revocalized as שִׁטִּים ("Shittim") a place name. Second, הֶעְמִיקוּ is an asyndetic relative clause ("which they dug") headed by שַׁחַת ("pit"). Because this line is parallel to lines e and f in 5:1, the verb הֱיִיתֶם is elided. This view is attractive precisely because of its potential parallels with 5:1. Just as there are three groups addressed (priests, leaders, king) in 5:1a-c, they are referred to as three kinds of traps used to catch animals in 5:1e-f and 5:2a. Furthermore, these three traps are located at three places: Mizpah, Tabor, and Shittim. However, there are a number of problems with this approach. First, it requires multiple emendations, none of which find support in the versions. Gelston (2010:59*) states that all the versions seem to presuppose the obscure text of the MT and do the best they can with it. There is no support for the place name "Shittim" in the versions. Second, the verb √עמק in the Hiphil is elsewhere used of intensifying actions (especially deviant ones), but not for digging pits. For that we would expect a verb such as √כרה or √עשׂה. Third, it is curious that

Hosea should choose to refer to Shittim, since that was located east of the Jordan River and was associated with the scandal at Ba'al-Peor in Num 25. It would likely be a historical allusion rather than a location of contemporary unfaithfulness. Finally, the two types of traps (פַּח and רֶשֶׁת) in 5:1 are typically used to catch birds (cf. HALOT 921), making the reference to a pit somewhat obscure. While the emendation is attractive and would create a second quatrain at the beginning of this section, it makes more sense (with AF and Macintosh 2014) to attempt to make sense of the MT as received (see below).

וְשַׁחֲטָה. Acc compl of הֶעְמִיקוּ. This noun is a *hapax*, but it shares a root with the verb √שחט which means "to slaughter," often in connection with cultic worship. Sometimes, the verb is associated with sacrificing humans (e.g., Gen 22:10; Isa 57:5; Ezek 16:21). The prophet has switched from addressing the objects of his critique in the second person plural (5:1) to referring to them in the third person.

שֵׂטִים. Subject of הֶעְמִיקוּ. This noun likely means "rebels" or "corrupt ones" in connection with the verb √שׂוט (Ps 40:5) or √שׂטה (Num 5:12, 19, 20, 29; Prov 4:15; 7:25). The contexts of these verbs indicate that both mean "to go astray." There is also a noun סֵט in Ps 101:3 which describes an action that YHWH hates. Even though Hosea has switched from second person to third person, these "rebels" refer to the three groups of Israel's leadership mentioned in 5:1.

הֶעְמִיקוּ. Hiph *qatal* 3cp √עמק. As mentioned above, the verb √עמק in the Hiphil refers to hiding or intensifying deviant behavior (in this case וְשַׁחֲטָה) (cf. Isa 31:6). Significantly, this is how it is used elsewhere in Hosea as well (9:9).

וַאֲנִי מוּסָר לְכֻלָּם. *Line b*. Independent, verbless clause.

וַאֲנִי. Subject of the verbless clause.

מוּסָר. Some have suggested, partly on the basis of G, that this is a corruption of מְיַסֵּר, a Piel participle. The resulting translation would be, "I discipline all of them" (see BHS note c-c). If one follows the MT (with ו), there are two options. First, the noun מוּסָר usually refers to training or correction ("I am correction for all of them"). However, this may be too gentle of a word given the context and the harsh condemnations of the prophet. The noun מוֹסֵר means "fetters" or "chains" and would require only a slight revocalization. However, there are two passages in which it is vocalized מוּסָר (Job 12:18; Prov 7:22). If this is the correct understanding, it creates a poignant reversal: just as the leaders of Israel are traps (5:1), YHWH will be chains for all of them (5:2).

לְכֻלָּם. PP with לְ of advantage indicating the intended recipients of the מוּסָר ("discipline"). The antecedent of the 3mp suffix is שֵׂטִים, the "rebels" in line a.

5:3 a אֲנִי יָדַעְתִּי אֶפְרַיִם
b וְיִשְׂרָאֵל לֹא־נִכְחַד מִמֶּנִּי
c כִּי עַתָּה הִזְנֵיתָ אֶפְרַיִם
d נִטְמָא יִשְׂרָאֵל:

Lines a-b are a bicolon, indicated by the word pair אֶפְרַיִם//יִשְׂרָאֵל as well as the active//passive verbs יָדַעְתִּי//נִכְחַד. The lines are arranged chiastically (pronoun + verb + PN//PN + verb + pronoun) and are marked by *Zaqep parvum* and *'Atnah*. Lines c-d are also a bicolon with the same features: the word pair אֶפְרַיִם//יִשְׂרָאֵל and active//passive, semantically related, verbs הִזְנֵיתָ//נִטְמָא. The lines are marked by *Zaqep parvum* and *Silluq*.

אֲנִי יָדַעְתִּי אֶפְרַיִם. *Line a*. Independent clause.

אֲנִי. Pleonastic 1cs pronoun; topicalizes YHWH.

יָדַעְתִּי. Qal *qatal* 1cs √ידע. The *qatal* verb presents YHWH's knowledge of Ephraim not as potential but as completed. He has observed their deeds and knows them well.

אֶפְרַיִם. Acc compl of יָדַעְתִּי. Ephraim was an administrative center of the northern kingdom and an influential hub that propogated unorthodox worship practices (see 4:17). Thus, Hosea often uses it as a synechdoche for the entire northern kingdom.

וְיִשְׂרָאֵל לֹא־נִכְחַד מִמֶּנִּי. *Line b*. Independent clause.

וְיִשְׂרָאֵל. Subject of נִכְחַד. There is semantic amplification between the parallel lines. The prophet refers to "Ephraim," the smaller representative, administrative region in line a. In line b the corresponding term is "Israel," the northern kingdom as a whole. This poetic device invites the reader to consider the relationship between the two entities, and the development from one line to the next highlights the expanding, corrupting influence of Ephraim over the rest of the nation. See also 5:9; 6:10, and 11:8.

נִכְחַד. Niphal *qatal* 3ms √כחד. The verb refers to preventing someone from knowing something. In the Niphal it is used of a king, or God, failing to notice something among his subjects. Here, Israel's evil behavior has *not* escaped God's notice.

מִמֶּנִּי. Adjunct PP with מִן indicating the one from whom Israel's actions have (not) been hidden. The antecedent of the 1cs suffix is YHWH, who is speaking.

כִּי עַתָּה הִזְנֵיתָ אֶפְרַיִם. *Line c.* Independent clause. The כִּי is likely asseverative (cf. JM §164b); if it were causal it would be difficult to understand how Ephraim's fornication (line c) is the reason that Israel's behavior is known to YHWH (line b).

עַתָּה. This temporal adverb introduces a shift in the argument (cf. WO §39.3.4f). Its use here is curious since there is no transition from description to command; the entire verse is a description of Israel with *qatal* verbs (cf. AF 390–91).

הִזְנֵיתָ. Hiph *qatal* 2ms √זנה. As noted in 4:10 above, when the verb √זנה occurs in the Hiphil, it usually refers to corrupting someone else and encouraging them to commit fornication, always with an explicit accusative complement (Lev 19:29; 2 Chr 21:11, 13; Exod 34:16). Although none of the three occurrences in Hosea have an explicit accusative complement (4:10, 18; 5:3), here it might be implied in the following parallel line: יִשְׂרָאֵל. The idea is that Ephraim has encouraged Israel to fornicate, and therefore Israel is defiled (line d). This verb √זנה has occurred ten times in the book up to this point, appearing at least once in every chapter. Now, except for one occurrence in 9:1, it ceases to appear.

אֶפְרַיִם. Vocative and referent of the 2ms subject of הִזְנֵיתָ. Hosea had addressed his audience in the second person plural in 5:1, then in the third person in 5:2-3a, and now he addresses Ephraim in the second person singular.

נִטְמָא יִשְׂרָאֵל. *Line d.* Independent clause.

נִטְמָא. Niph *qatal* 3ms √טמא. The Niphal *qatal* usually has a *pataḥ* theme vowel, but here it is a *qamets* because of the III-א weak verb. Therefore, morphologically, this could be a *qatal* or a participle. It makes the best sense to understand it as a *qatal*. Israel is not in the process of being defiled; rather, YHWH states that it has been defiled. It is a summative statement about the consequences of Israel's actions. The verb √טמא is frequently used in ritual contexts in the Pentateuch to describe something that has been defiled and is no longer "clean" (טָהֵר). The defiled person or object is no longer acceptable to God and cannot come into his presence. The prophets expand on this meaning and apply √טמא to spiritual harlotry.

יִשְׂרָאֵל. Subject of נִטְמָא.

5:4 a לֹא יִתְּנוּ מַעַלְלֵיהֶם לָשׁוּב אֶל־אֱלֹהֵיהֶם
b כִּי רוּחַ זְנוּנִים בְּקִרְבָּם
c וְאֶת־יְהוָה לֹא יָדָעוּ׃

Lines a-c are a tricolon. The disjunctive *Zaqep parvum* on מַעַלְלֵיהֶם suggests that the lines should be divided at this point, with לָשׁוּב אֶל־אֱלֹהֵיהֶם as its own line. However, the words לָשׁוּב אֶל־אֱלֹהֵיהֶם are the complement of the verb יִתְּנוּ, and all six words belong together in one clause. Thus, line a is slightly longer than lines b and c. The lines are marked with *'Atnah*, *Zaqep parvum*, and *Silluq*.

לֹא יִתְּנוּ מַעַלְלֵיהֶם לָשׁוּב אֶל־אֱלֹהֵיהֶם. *Line a*. Independent clause.

יִתְּנוּ. Qal *yiqtol* 3mp √נתן. Here the verb means "to permit" or "to allow" (cf. HALOT 734). Its complement is לָשׁוּב. We would also expect a complement indicating *who* was being permitted to return. However, AF (392) note that √נתן does not need an explicit complement when followed by an infinitive.

מַעַלְלֵיהֶם. Subject of יִתְּנוּ. "Their deeds do not permit" means that their actions (and the underlying choices) have made it impossible to repent and turn back to YHWH. The antecedent of the 3mp suffix is the leadership of Israel addressed in 5:1-2.

לָשׁוּב. Qal inf constr √שׁוב.

אֶל־אֱלֹהֵיהֶם. This PP is the complement of לָשׁוּב with אֶל indicating the potential goal. The antecedent of the 3mp suffix is the same as the suffix on מַעַלְלֵיהֶם: the leadership of Israel.

כִּי רוּחַ זְנוּנִים בְּקִרְבָּם. *Line b*. Subordinate causal clause giving the reason that their "deeds do not permit them to repent" (line a). The problem is much deeper than evil actions: they are being driven by an entire mindset and culture that is in rebellion against YHWH. The reason that they cannot repent is not that their deeds are so evil, but that the deeds are symptomatic of a fundamental apostasy.

רוּחַ זְנוּנִים. Subject of the verbless clause. This construct phrase describing a *Zeitgeist* or conventional wisdom appeared in 4:12 and 4:19 as an inclusio around that unit.

בְּקִרְבָּם. Predicate of the verbless clause. A PP with בְּ indicating the location of the רוּחַ. The antecedent of the 3mp suffix continues to be the leadership of Israel.

וְאֶת־יְהוָה לֹא יָדָעוּ. *Line c*. Independent clause.

וְאֶת־יְהוָה. Acc compl of יָדָעוּ. This is fronted in the word order for focus. YHWH knows (√ידע) them (5:3), but they do not know him (5:4).

יָדָעוּ. Qal *qatal* 3cp √ידע. Hosea has used this word to refer to what Israel knows about YHWH (2:10) but also to refer to extensive, personal knowledge of YHWH himself (2:22).

Israel's leaders (including the priests!) were tasked with leading the people to a knowledge of YHWH but instead they had led the people away from him.

5:5 a וְעָנָה גְאוֹן־יִשְׂרָאֵל בְּפָנָיו
b וְיִשְׂרָאֵל וְאֶפְרַיִם יִכָּשְׁלוּ בַּעֲוֹנָם
c כָּשַׁל גַּם־יְהוּדָה עִמָּם:

Lines a-c are a tricolon. Lines b-c are parallel with a repetition of the √כשל and noun//pronoun grammatical parallelism in which יִשְׂרָאֵל וְאֶפְרַיִם in line b corresponds to the 3mp suffix (עִמָּם) in line c. The lines are marked by disjunctive *'Atnaḥ, Zaqep parvum*, and *Silluq*.

וְעָנָה גְאוֹן־יִשְׂרָאֵל בְּפָנָיו. *Line a*. Independent clause. This line is identical to 7:10a.

וְעָנָה. Qal *qatal* (irrealis) 3ms √ענה. The collocation ענה בְּ has a legal sense of "testifying against." The irrealis *qatal* here describes future, potential action; the prophet predicts that the actions of Israel will lead to their demise.

גְאוֹן־יִשְׂרָאֵל. The noun גָאוֹן (in construct) is the subject of וְעָנָה and refers to pride or presumption. Hosea continues to speak against the independence and self-sufficiency of Israel as it refuses to come to YHWH for what it needs.

בְּפָנָיו. The verb √ענה does not require a complement, so this PP is an adjunct specifying the recipient of the testimony. The antecedent of the 3ms suffix is the previous word יִשְׂרָאֵל. Israel is incriminating itself.

וְיִשְׂרָאֵל וְאֶפְרַיִם יִכָּשְׁלוּ בַּעֲוֺנָם. *Line b.* Independent clause.

וְיִשְׂרָאֵל וְאֶפְרַיִם. Compound subject of יִכָּשְׁלוּ. Ephraim is a region within Israel, but the prophet refers to them separately because Ephraim represents the leadership that has corrupted the rest of Israel (see 4:17).

יִכָּשְׁלוּ. Niph *yiqtol* 3mp √כשל. This verb does not have a passive or reflexive sense in the Niphal and has the same meaning as the Qal in line c. √כשל usually occurs in the Qal in the *qatal* conjugation but in the Niphal in the *yiqtol* (WO §23.2.1a).

בַּעֲוֺנָם. Adjunct PP with a בְּ of specification qualifying the realm of the verbal action (cf. WO §11.2.5e). The sense is that it will be their "iniquity" that trips them up and causes them to stumble. The antecedent of the 3mp poss suffix is "Israel" and "Ephraim" from the beginning of the clause.

כָּשַׁל גַּם־יְהוּדָה עִמָּם. *Line c.* Independent clause.

כָּשַׁל. Qal *qatal* (irrealis) 3ms √כשל. This clause has VS word order indicating that the *qatal* is irrealis and predictive. Thus, it is consistent with the irrealis *qatal* and *yiqtol* verbs in lines a and b respectively.

גַּם. This conjunction relates the previous statement (in this case, line b) to this one and invites the reader to consider this as a logical extension of that thought.

יְהוּדָה. Subject of כָּשַׁל.

עִמָּם. PP with עִם indicating the other participants in the verbal action. The antecedent of the 3mp suffix is "Israel" and "Ephraim" in line b.

5:6 a בְּצֹאנָם וּבִבְקָרָם יֵלְכוּ לְבַקֵּשׁ אֶת־יְהוָה
     b וְלֹא יִמְצָאוּ חָלַץ מֵהֶם׃

Lines a-b are a bicolon. "YHWH" in line a is the subject of the verb √חלץ in line b. The lines are marked by disjunctive *Tipḥa* and *Silluq*.

בְּצֹאנָם וּבִבְקָרָם יֵלְכוּ. *Line a.* Independent clause.

Hosea 5:6

בְּצֹאנָם וּבִבְקָרָם. These two coordinated PPs each have a בְּ which indicates that they will be "accompanied by" flocks and cattle (cf. WO §11.2.5d). The antecedent of the 3mp poss suffixes is Israel, Ephraim, and Judah (5:5). Presumably, this is a reference to animals which the Israelites attempt to bring to YHWH for sacrifices. But this is nothing more than manipulation; it is not an action rooted in love of YHWH, but only in the love of what they hope to get from him.

יֵלְכוּ. Qal *yiqtol* 3mp √הלך. The subject of this verb as well as the verb and suffix in line b is Israel, Ephraim, and Judah from 5:5.

לְבַקֵּשׁ אֶת־יְהוָה. *Line a.* Subordinate purpose clause describing that reason that they will "go" (יֵלְכוּ).

לְבַקֵּשׁ. Piel inf constr √בקשׁ. Hosea uses this verb in 2:9 to describe Israel's pursuit of false gods to get what she wants. YHWH wants his people to seek him fully, faithfully, and exclusively (5:15; 7:10). Later, when they are transformed as his people, they will do so (3:5).

אֶת־יְהוָה. Acc compl of לְבַקֵּשׁ.

וְלֹא יִמְצָאוּ. *Line b.* Independent clause.

יִמְצָאוּ. Qal *yiqtol* 3mp √מצא. This verb lacks a complement in the clause indicating what is found; it must be יְהוָה from the end of the previous line. These two clauses in lines a and b are similar to 2:9: וּבִקְשָׁתַם וְלֹא תִמְצָא ("and she will seek [other gods] but will not find."). The tragedy is that in 2:9 Israel is frustrated because competing gods cannot deliver what they seek. Here in 5:6 Israel will be frustrated because YHWH refuses to be found. They do not seek him, only what he can offer; therefore, they will get neither.

חָלַץ מֵהֶם. *Line b.* Independent clause.

חָלַץ. Qal *qatal* 3ms √חלץ. Elsewhere, this verb is transitive and describes the removal of something such as a sandal (Deut 25:10) or, in the Piel, stones from a wall (Lev 14:40, 43). Here, Hosea uses it with the unique intransitive sense of "moving away from." The *qatal* conjugation has a perfective aspect: YHWH's withdrawal is considered to be a finished act. Therefore, when Israel "seeks" him, he is unavailable.

מֵהֶם. This PP is the complement of חָלַץ. The מִן prep has an ablative sense, designating movement away from Israel, Ephraim, and Judah.

5:7 a בַּיהוָה בָּגָדוּ כִּי־בָנִים זָרִים יָלָדוּ
b עַתָּה יֹאכְלֵם חֹדֶשׁ אֶת־חֶלְקֵיהֶם: ס

Lines a-b are a bicolon with lines marked by disjunctive 'Atnaḥ and Silluq.

בַּיהוָה בָּגָדוּ. *Line a*. Independent clause.

בַּיהוָה. This adjunct PP with בְּ specifies the victim of the treacherous behavior indicated by the following verb בָּגָדוּ.

בָּגָדוּ. Qal *qatal* 3cp √בגד. The plural subject of this verb, and the plural verbs and pronouns in the verse, continue to be Israel, Ephraim, and Judah (5:5). The verb describes an action which appears benevolent, when in reality the subject is planning or acting maliciously. Here it again calls to mind the adultery metaphor in the book. In 5:6 the people come to worship YHWH by bringing flocks and herds for sacrifice; they have the outward appearance of faithfulness and piety. But at the same time they are engaged in the fertility cult, worshiping other gods and abusing each other. Thus, they have acted treacherously because their "piety" has been manipulative and nothing more than a ruse to enable their unfaithfulness.

כִּי־בָנִים זָרִים יָלָדוּ. *Line a*. Independent clause with an asseverative כִּי. Translators commonly interpret this כִּי as marking a causal clause, "for they have borne ..." (cf. KJV, NRSV, ESV). However, bearing illegitimate children did not cause the peoples' treachery. Rather, this clause describes the outcome of that treachery.

בָנִים זָרִים. The word בָּנִים ("sons" or more likely "children") is the complement of יָלָדוּ. It is modified by the attributive adjective זָרִים which can refer to something that is "foreign" either in the sense of being from outside of the national or ethnic group or in the sense of being from outside a legitimate family unit. For example, in Prov 7:5 the adulteress is an אִשָּׁה זָרָה because she belongs to another man. Here, the children are "foreign" because they do not belong to YHWH; they have been conceived in adultery. The analogy is that of a husband thinking that his wife is faithful and yet she bears the child of another man.

יָלָדוּ. Qal *qatal* 3cp √ילד.

עַתָּה יֹאכְלֵם חֹדֶשׁ אֶת־חֶלְקֵיהֶם. *Line b*. Independent clause. There have been many different proposed solutions and emendations to make sense of this difficult line. Wolff (1974:95) follows G (ἐρυσίβη) which assumes the Hebrew חסיל ("locust") for חֹדֶשׁ. Stuart (1987:94–95) suggests that there is a missing ע consonant after the second word, and that חֹדֶשׁ should be vocalized חָדָשׁ ("new"). Therefore, the line should read עַתָּה יֹאכַל עַם חָדָשׁ ("Now a new people will eat"). This would be a fulfillment of the covenant curse in Deut 28:33, 51, which says that יֹאכַל עַם אֲשֶׁר לֹא יָדָעְתָּ ("a people who you do not know will eat"). However, one can make sense of the MT as it stands if חֹדֶשׁ ("new moon") is understood as a metonymy for the religious practices of Israel (cf. Garrett 1997:147). Hosea is personifying the Festival of the New Moon in order to portray vividly the corrupt religious practices as the ultimate cause of the destruction of both people and lands (McComiskey 2009:79).

עַתָּה. This temporal adverb introduces the conclusion drawn from what has been stated (BDB 773).

יֹאכְלֵם. Qal *yiqtol* 3ms √אכל with a 3mp acc suffix. The antecedent of the suffix is Israel, Ephraim, and Judah (cf. 5:5) who are acting piously while begetting illegitimate children. Hosea uses the word √אכל to describe destruction again in 7:7, 9, and 11:16.

חֹדֶשׁ. Subject of יֹאכְלֵם. The Festival of the New Moon, or the first day of the month, was a time for specific sacrifices (cf. Num 28:11-15). Here Hosea personifies the festival and states that it (on behalf of all religious practices that have become corrupt) will be the underlying reason for the nation's demise.

אֶת־חֶלְקֵיהֶם. PP with אֶת indicating that their possessions will be devoured along with them (cf. WO §11.2.4a). The word חֵלֶק commonly refers to tracts of land. The antecedent of the possessive suffix is the same as the accusative suffix on יֹאכְלֵם: Israel, Ephraim and Judah.

5:8 a תִּקְעוּ שׁוֹפָר בַּגִּבְעָה
b חֲצֹצְרָה בָּרָמָה
c הָרִיעוּ בֵּית אָוֶן
d אַחֲרֶיךָ בִּנְיָמִין׃

Lines a-b are a bicolon, indicated by ellipsis of the verb תִּקְעוּ in line b as well as the word pairs חֲצֹצְרָה//שׁוֹפָר and רָמָה//גִּבְעָה. The lines are marked with disjunctive *Zaqep parvum* and *'Atnaḥ*. Lines c-d are a bicolon that contains two more place names. The lines are marked with *Zaqep parvum* and *Silluq*.

Hosea 5:8

תִּקְעוּ שׁוֹפָר בַּגִּבְעָה. *Line a*. Independent clause.

תִּקְעוּ. Qal impv mp √תקע. The prophet has been referring to Israel and Ephraim with the third person plural (5:5b-7). Here the plural addressee of this imperative is a general call to prepare for an attack. This is the most common verb in the OT for sounding trumpets (שׁוֹפָר and חֲצֹצְרָה).

שׁוֹפָר. Acc compl of תִּקְעוּ. This horn instrument was not used to make music, but as an audible signal to mark ceremonial occasions, to announce a new king, and to send signals in war (HALOT 1447). Here the prophet is calling for the signal horn to announce the attack of an enemy who brings judgment from YHWH. Usually, the verb √תקע takes an oblique complement with a בְּ prep (i.e., תִּקְעוּ בַּשּׁוֹפָר). The preposition (with article) is omitted here because שׁוֹפָר is indefinite and unspecified. Hosea does not have a particular horn in mind.

בַּגִּבְעָה. PP with בְּ specifying the location where the horn is to be sounded. גִּבְעָה refers here to the town in the territory of Benjamin. In this verse the enemy is envisioned as moving from south to north from Gibeah (3 miles north of Jerusalem) to Ramah (5 miles north of Jerusalem) to Bethel (11 miles north of Jerusalem), and the call to alarm precedes his advance (Wolff 1974:113).

חֲצֹצְרָה בָרָמָה. *Line b*. Independent clause. The verb תִּקְעוּ is elided.

חֲצֹצְרָה. Second compl of תִּקְעוּ (line a). Like a שׁוֹפָר, this horn was used for signals and here announces the attack of an enemy army.

בָרָמָה. PP with בְּ specifying the location where the חֲצֹצְרָה is to be sounded.

הָרִיעוּ בֵּית אָוֶן. *Line c*. Independent clause.

הָרִיעוּ. Hiph impv mp √רוע. This verb describes a loud shout, frequently referring to a war cry in battle. The cry is associated with the blowing of the שׁוֹפָר in Josh 6:5, 20 and in Joel 2:1.

בֵּית אָוֶן. Vocative and addressee of the imperative הָרִיעוּ. This is a pejorative name for "Bethel" (see 4:15), which was located about five miles north of Gibeah and Ramah, just inside the territory of Ephraim.

אַחֲרֶיךָ בִּנְיָמִין. *Line d*. Two analyses are possible. This could be a verbless clause meaning "Benjamin was behind you" (cf. Judg 5:14). Conversely, in the context it makes more sense as a rallying cry, "[We are] behind you, Benjamin!" which is not a complete clause. There is some evidence that Benjamin may have functioned in military leadership (cf. Ps 68:28). Macintosh (2014:193) also mentions the possibility, "Watch your back, Benjamin!" which would be a warning of danger. A rallying or warning cry would be ironic; the prophet is calling the people to a battle that will end in defeat.

אַחֲרֶיךָ. PP with אַחַר. The prep אַחַר can have either a temporal ("after") or spatial ("behind") meaning. The antecedent of the 2ms suffix is the following בִּנְיָמִין.

בִּנְיָמִין. Vocative.

5:9 a אֶפְרַיִם לְשַׁמָּה תִהְיֶה בְּיוֹם תּוֹכֵחָה
    b בְּשִׁבְטֵי יִשְׂרָאֵל הוֹדַעְתִּי נֶאֱמָנָה׃

Lines a-b are a bicolon with the pair אֶפְרַיִם//שִׁבְטֵי יִשְׂרָאֵל. The lines are marked by *'Atnaḥ* and *Silluq*.

אֶפְרַיִם לְשַׁמָּה תִהְיֶה בְּיוֹם תּוֹכֵחָה. *Line a*. Independent clause.

אֶפְרַיִם. Vocative. It is not likely that it is the third-person subject of a following feminine verb תִהְיֶה ("Ephraim will be …") since אֶפְרַיִם concords with masculine verbs and pronouns (cf. Hos 4:17; 5:3, 5). Rather, it is the addressee of תִהְיֶה which is second person masculine. Ephraim is likely a synechdoche, referring to the northern kingdom as a whole.

לְשַׁמָּה. Oblique compl of תִהְיֶה, specifying the new identity or status of the subject אֶפְרַיִם. The noun שַׁמָּה designates something that is ruined or devastated in such a way that it provokes feelings of disgust or horror. It frequently describes land but can also refer to cities or people groups. Significantly, Deut 28:37 uses the same language (וְהָיִיתָ לְשַׁמָּה) to refer to a curse for breaking covenant with YHWH.

תִהְיֶה. Qal *yiqtol* 2ms √היה.

בְּיוֹם תּוֹכֵחָה. PP with בְּ used temporally to mark the time that Ephraim will become a horror. The genitive תּוֹכֵחָה ("rebuke, correction"), derived from the root √יכח, is used in only two other contexts in the OT. In 2 Kgs 19:3 and Isa 37:3 it is used with צָרָה ("distress") and נְאָצָה ("contempt"). In Ps 149:7 it is used in parallel with נְקָמָה ("vengeance"). These occurrences suggest that it is not a gentle correction but a stern and violent reckoning.

בְּשִׁבְטֵי יִשְׂרָאֵל הוֹדַעְתִּי נֶאֱמָנָה. *Line b*. Independent clause.

בְּשִׁבְטֵי יִשְׂרָאֵל. PP with בְּ specifying location amid a domain (cf. WO §11.2.5b). This is where YHWH has "made known what is sure" (see following). This phrase represents amplification in the parallelism. Both "Ephraim" (line a) and "tribes of Israel" (line b) refer to the northern kingdom, but the semantic development from synechoche to literal term and from representative to inclusive group draws attention to the comprehensive scope of the threat: all Israel is under judgment.

הוֹדַעְתִּי. Hiph *qatal* 1cs √ידע. The *qatal* conjugation should be translated with the present tense. Hosea is not saying that he had predicted this situation before. Rather, he is saying (on behalf of YHWH), "I hereby make known what is going to happen." Waltke and O'Connor (§30.5.1d) call this an "instantaneous perfective" which represents a situation occurring at the same time that the expression is uttered. It is common with words of speaking.

נֶאֱמָנָה. Niph ptc fs √אמן. The participle is functioning substantivally as the complement of הוֹדַעְתִּי. It refers to a word that will certainly come to pass (cf. Gen 42:20; 1 Kgs 8:26; Isa 55:3).

5:10 a הָיוּ שָׂרֵי יְהוּדָה כְּמַסִּיגֵי גְּבוּל
b עֲלֵיהֶם אֶשְׁפּוֹךְ כַּמַּיִם עֶבְרָתִי:

Lines a-b are a bicolon with grammatical parallelism. The construct phrase שָׂרֵי יְהוּדָה in line a corresponds to the 3mp pronoun on עֲלֵיהֶם in line b. The lines are marked with *'Atnah* and *Silluq*.

הָיוּ שָׂרֵי יְהוּדָה כְּמַסִּיגֵי גְּבוּל. *Line a*. Independent clause.

הָיוּ. Qal *qatal* (irrealis) 3cp √היה. This verb is usually analyzed as an indicative *qatal* and therefore the clause is understood as a description about Judah's guilt: they are like deceptive thieves who increase their property by moving boundary lines. However, the word order is VS. There is no grammatical word to explain the word order inversion and there is no pragmatic motivation to front the verb √היה. The only reason for the inversion is that the *qatal* verb is irrealis even though it is not preceded by a וְ (cf. 5:5c). This is significant, for it means that Judah *will* be like those who move boundary stones. Is it possible that being like those who move boundary stones refers to consequences rather than guilt? Garrett (1997:152) notes that the moving of boundary stones is too petty and secretive to describe an invasion by Judah of the northern kingdom. In addition, Judah was swept up in the Assyrian onslaught as well. Deuteronomy 27:17 states that anyone who moves boundary stones is under a curse. Therefore, this may be a vivid way of stating that Judah's aristocracy is under judgment. This explanation would make better sense of the continuity and potential parallelism with v. 9, which states that Ephraim *will be* a horror (5:9a), and the tribes of Israel are *about to* experience certain judgment (5:9b).

שָׂרֵי יְהוּדָה. Subject of הָיוּ. Having addressed Ephraim in 5:9a and referred to the tribes of Israel in 5:9b, Hosea again includes Judah in his critique (cf. 4:15; 5:5).

כְּמַסִּיגֵי גְּבוּל. This PP with כְּ is the complement of הָיוּ. The substantive in construct is a Hiph ptc mp √סוג. This activity is forbidden in Deut 19:14 and criticized in Job 24:2.

עֲלֵיהֶם אֶשְׁפּוֹךְ כַּמַּיִם עֶבְרָתִי. *Line b*. Independent clause.

עֲלֵיהֶם. PP with עַל indicating where YHWH will pour his wrath like metaphorical water. The antecedent of the 3mp suffix is שָׂרֵי יְהוּדָה from line a.

אֶשְׁפּוֹךְ. Qal *yiqtol* 1cs √שפך. This is the most common verb for pouring out a liquid. At least twenty-three times the OT speaks of YHWH pouring out his חֵמָה ("anger"), זַעַם ("indignation"), or עֶבְרָה ("wrath").

כַּמַּיִם. PP with כְּ indicating agreement in manner. YHWH's wrath will be poured out like water is poured out.

עֶבְרָתִי. Acc compl of אֶשְׁפּוֹךְ. The antecedent of the 1cs poss suffix is the speaker: either YHWH or the prophet on behalf of YHWH.

5:11 a עָשׁוּק אֶפְרַיִם רְצוּץ מִשְׁפָּט
b כִּי הוֹאִיל הָלַךְ אַחֲרֵי־צָו׃

Lines a-b are a bicolon. אֶפְרַיִם in line a is the subject of the verbs in line b. The clause in line b is subordinate to the main clause in line a. The lines are marked by *'Atnah* and *Silluq*.

עָשׁוּק אֶפְרַיִם רְצוּץ מִשְׁפָּט. *Line a*. Independent verbless clause.

עָשׁוּק. Qal pass ptc ms √עשק, functioning as a predicate adjective (cf. WO §37.4c). The two participles in this line likely have a future orientation because the context refers to YHWH's coming destructive activity (see 9:9) (AF 409).

אֶפְרַיִם. Subject of the verbless clause.

רְצוּץ מִשְׁפָּט. This construct phrase is in apposition to the predicate (עָשׁוּק). רְצוּץ is a Qal pass ptc ms √רצץ, also functioning as a predicate adjective. The construct relationship between the two words is one of "instrument" (cf. WO §9.5.1d). When this occurs, the inanimate genitive is an instrument of the construct form. Here, the crushing (רְצוּץ) is effected by judgment (מִשְׁפָּט).

כִּי הוֹאִיל הָלַךְ אַחֲרֵי־צָו. *Line b*. Subordinate causal clause explaining the reason that Ephraim is oppressed and crushed by judgment.

הוֹאִיל. Hiph *qatal* 3ms √יאל. This verb, which only occurs in the Hiphil, refers to someone doing something even though the circumstances or outcome may not be ideal. Sometimes this takes the form of being "content" to do something (e.g., Josh 7:7) or "to persist" in doing something (e.g., Gen 18:31) or "to accept" something (e.g., Judg 19:6). In this context the sense of persistence or determination is probably intended. No matter what, Israel is determined to be unfaithful and is entrenched in rebellion.

הָלַךְ. Qal *qatal* 3ms √הלך. This verb is the complement of the previous verb הוֹאִיל. Usually, when a verb has its complement in the form of another verbal idea this is done with a complementary infinitive or sometimes an infinitive absolute (cf. GKC §120a). Sometimes, however, the two verbs are simply coordinated, with or without the וְ. It is the second verb that represents the principle idea (GKC §120g; see also JM §177d). Here the translation is, "He was persistent (הוֹאִיל) in going (הָלַךְ) after what is false." Hosea used הלך אַחֲרֵי to describe Israel's pursuit of "lovers" and her trust in what they might provide (2:7; 2:15).

אַחֲרֵי־צָו. PP with אַחַר which has a metaphorical locational sense: to walk after is to behave like (WO §11.2.1a). The word צָו occurs elsewhere only in Isa 28:10, 14, where it apparently functions like "blah blah blah" (צַו לָצָו צַו לָצָו קַו לָקָו קַו לָקָו). In this context צָו refers to worthless political alliances that appear to be helpful, but will fail (cf. 5:13).

5:12 a וַאֲנִי כָעָשׁ לְאֶפְרָיִם
     b וְכָרָקָב לְבֵית יְהוּדָה׃

Lines a-b are a bicolon. The two lines are connected via ellipsis (the subject and implied copula of the verbless clause is elided in line b) as well as parallel PPs with כְּ and word pairs עָשׁ//רָקָב and אֶפְרַיִם//יְהוּדָה. The lines are marked with *'Atnaḥ* and *Silluq*.

וַאֲנִי כָעָשׁ לְאֶפְרָיִם. *Line a*. Independent verbless clause.

וַאֲנִי. Subject of the verbless clause. The speaker is YHWH.

כָעָשׁ. This PP with כְּ is the predicate of the verbless clause. The word עָשׁ (8× in the OT) usually refers to a destructive moth (Isa 50:9; 51:8). In Job 13:28 עָשׁ is used in parallel with רָקָב (as here) in the context of consuming a garment. However, Rudolph (1966:123–24) argues that the meaning "moth" is unsuitable here in Hos 5:12 because moths do not destroy people and because the word pictures in vv. 12-13 concern sickness and the human body. He translates "pus" (cf. Driver 1950:66–67). Macintosh (2014:207) argues that pus is a symptom not a cause of disease. On the basis of Arabic cognates, he prefers "emaciating disease."

לְאֶפְרָיִם. PP with לְ of interest. It is to Ephraim that YHWH will be like disease.

וְכָרָקָב לְבֵית יְהוּדָה. *Line b*. Independent clause. The subject and implied copula of the verbless clause are elided.

וְכָרָקָב. This PP with כְּ is the predicate of the verbless clause. רָקָב refers to rottenness or that which causes decay. It affects the bones in Prov 12:4; 14:30, and Hab 3:16. These are stunning images which YHWH uses of himself; he is opposed to Ephraim and Judah and will ruin them.

לְבֵית יְהוּדָה. PP with לְ of interest.

5:13 a וַיַּרְא אֶפְרַיִם אֶת־חָלְיוֹ
b וִיהוּדָה אֶת־מְזֹרוֹ
c וַיֵּלֶךְ אֶפְרַיִם אֶל־אַשּׁוּר
d וַיִּשְׁלַח אֶל־מֶלֶךְ יָרֵב
e וְהוּא לֹא יוּכַל לִרְפֹּא לָכֶם
f וְלֹא־יִגְהֶה מִכֶּם מָזוֹר׃

This long verse contains three bicola. Lines a-b feature ellipsis of the verb as well as word pairs אֶפְרַיִם//יְהוּדָה and חֳלִי//מָזוֹר. The lines are marked by *Rᵉbîaʿ* and *Zaqep parvum*. Lines c-d feature the word pair

√הלך//√שלח as well as semantic amplification from אַשּׁוּר to מֶלֶךְ יָרֵב. The lines are marked by *Zaqep parvum* and *'Atnaḥ*. Lines e-f feature the word pair גהה√//רפא√ as well as parallelism with 2mp suffixes. The lines are marked by *Zaqep parvum* and *Silluq*.

וַיַּרְא אֶפְרַיִם אֶת־חָלְיוֹ. *Line a*. Independent clause.

וַיַּרְא. Qal *wayyiqtol* 3ms ראה√. This form could be either a Qal or a Hiphil (cf. 2 Kgs 11:4). Here it is a Qal (it has only one complement). Although Hosea has been declaring future disaster for Israel, the *wayyiqtol* narrative past verbs in lines a-d indicate a brief historical review. He describes previous attempts by Israel and Judah to secure help from the king of Assyria.

אֶפְרַיִם. Subject of וַיַּרְא.

אֶת־חָלְיוֹ. Acc compl of וַיַּרְא. חֳלִי is related to the verb חלה√ and describes sickness, disease, or suffering. Here, the context suggests that the word refers to a sickness that will bring further harm and therefore demands a cure.

וִיהוּדָה אֶת־מְזֹרוֹ. *Line b*. Independent clause. The verb וַיַּרְא is elided.

וִיהוּדָה. Subject of the elided verb וַיַּרְא in this clause.

אֶת־מְזֹרוֹ. Acc compl of the elided verb וַיַּרְא in this clause. The word מָזוֹר occurs two times with the meaning "sore" or "boil" in the OT (cf. Jer 30:13). This word is more specific than חֳלִי in line a (amplification).

וַיֵּלֶךְ אֶפְרַיִם אֶל־אַשּׁוּר. *Line c*. Independent clause.

וַיֵּלֶךְ. Qal *wayyiqtol* 3ms הלך√.

אֶפְרַיִם. Subject of וַיֵּלֶךְ.

אֶל־אַשּׁוּר. PP with אֶל indicating movement toward Assyria. This is the first of nine occurrences of אַשּׁוּר ("Assyria") in the book. Hosea speaks of the temptation to look to that mighty empire for the solution to Israel's problems instead of turning back to YHWH (see also 7:11; 8:9; 12:2; 14:4).

וַיִּשְׁלַח אֶל־מֶלֶךְ יָרֵב. *Line d*. Independent clause.

וַיִּשְׁלַח. Qal *wayyiqtol* 3ms שלח√. In the OT the use of שלח√ to describe sending a message to someone is idiomatic in that it usually has an implied complement accusative. It may suggest sending "messengers" (מַלְאָכִים; e.g., Num 21:21) or a "word" (דָּבָר; e.g., Judg 11:28) to someone.

אֶל־מֶלֶךְ יָרֵב. PP with אֶל specifying the recipient of the message. Hoses uses the difficult (and possibly corrupt) phrase מֶלֶךְ יָרֵב to refer to the king of Assyria (cf. also 10:6). There have been several proposed solutions to the meaning of יָרֵב. G treats it as a proper name (Ιαριμ). Rudolph (1966:124) suggests that ירב is a metathesis of √ריב ("to argue"), and that the phrase is a pejorative play on words meaning "King Squabbler." The most convincing solution is that the text is a result of a misdivision of מלכי רב or מלך רב ("great king"). The former spelling is consistent with Hebrew names which have [i] after the first element (AF 414). The latter spelling is known in Ugaritic (*mlk rb*) (Gordon 1965 §19:2297).

וְהוּא לֹא יוּכַל לִרְפֹּא לָכֶם. *Line e*. Independent clause.

וְהוּא. The antecedent of this 3ms pronoun is the king of Assyria (lines c-d). The pleonastic pronoun emphasizes a contrast with the pronoun אֲנִי (YHWH) in v. 12. The prophet is emphasizing that *he* (i.e., the king of Assyria) will not be able to heal Israel but there is another (YHWH) who could do so, if only Ephraim would repent.

יוּכַל. Qal *yiqtol* 3ms √יכל.

לִרְפֹּא. Qal inf constr √רפא. This infinitive phrase is the verbal complement of יוּכַל.

לָכֶם. The verb √רפא takes an oblique complement marked with לְ (as here; cf. 7:1) or an accusative (cf. 6:1; 11:3; 14:5). The 2mp suffix is odd given that references to Ephraim and Judah are third person throughout the context. The antecedent of the plural suffix is the people of Ephraim (cf. lines c-d).

וְלֹא־יִגְהֶה מִכֶּם מָזוֹר. *Line f*. Independent clause.

יִגְהֶה. Qal *yiqtol* 3ms √גהה. This is the only occurrence of the verb √גהה in the OT (there is a noun form of the root in Prov 17:22). If the verb were intransitive ("be healed"), the subject would be מָזוֹר at the end of the line ("and the sore will not depart from you"). However, the parallel with the transitive verb √רפא in line e suggests that this verb is also transitive. Macintosh (2014:210) also argues that the verb is transitive on the basis of the Syriac cognate ܓܗܐ (*gh*). In that case the subject is the king of Assyria and מָזוֹר is the accusative complement: "he will not remove from you [the] sore" (cf. HALOT 181).

מֵהֶם. PP with מִן indicating the recipient of the healing. The preposition has an ablative sense; the hope was that the king could remove the sore (מָזוֹר) *from* them, but he will not.

מָזוֹר. This is the same word "sore" as found in line b.

5:14 a כִּי אָנֹכִי כַשַּׁחַל לְאֶפְרַיִם
      b וְכַכְּפִיר לְבֵית יְהוּדָה
      c אֲנִי אֲנִי אֶטְרֹף וְאֵלֵךְ
      d אֶשָּׂא וְאֵין מַצִּיל׃

Lines a-b are a bicolon, indicated by ellipsis of the subject and copula of the verbless clause in line b, word pairs שַׁחַל//כְּפִיר and אֶפְרַיִם//יְהוּדָה, and parallel PPs. The lines are marked by *Zaqep parvum* and *'Atnaḥ*. Lines c-d are a bicolon containing four verbs in somewhat of a sequence describing YHWH's violent actions against his people. The lines are marked by *Zaqep parvum* and *Silluq*.

כִּי אָנֹכִי כַשַּׁחַל לְאֶפְרַיִם. *Line a*. Subordinate causal clause giving the reason that the king of Assyria will not be able to help Ephraim and Judah (5:13e-f). This is a surprise. The reader might think that the king of Assyria cannot help because he is not as powerful a potential savior as YHWH (contrast the pronoun אֲנִי in v. 12 and הוּא in v. 13). But Hosea goes a step further: the king cannot help because YHWH is the aggressor!

אָנֹכִי. Subject of the verbless clause. The antecedent is YHWH the speaker.

כַשַּׁחַל. This PP with כְּ expressing agreement in kind is the predicate of the verbless clause. The noun שַׁחַל is one of at least seven words for "lion" (cf. אֲרִי, אַרְיֵה, גּוּר, לָבִיא, כְּפִיר, לַיִשׁ) in the OT. It is difficult to make semantic distinctions among them but שַׁחַל (7× in the OT) usually refers to a fierce lion associated with killing (e.g., Prov 26:13). It is used three times in parallel with כְּפִיר (see also Job 4:10; Ps 91:13). Hosea mentions a שַׁחַל as a dangerous animal again in 13:7.

לְאֶפְרַיִם. PP with לְ of interest. This echoes the similar statement in 5:12—וַאֲנִי כָעָשׁ לְאֶפְרַיִם ("I am like disease to Ephraim").

וְכַכְּפִיר לְבֵית יְהוּדָה. *Line b*. Subordinate causal clause. The implied copula of the verbless clause (line a) is elided and the two clauses are coordinated. Therefore, this clause is also subordinate to the main clauses in 5:13e-f. The king of Assyria cannot help (5:13e-f) because YHWH is like a lion (5:14a) and like a young lion (5:14b).

וְכַכְּפִיר. PP with כְּ expressing agreement in kind. This is the predicate of the elided verbless clause. כְּפִיר is often translated "young lion" (cf. HALOT 493). A few passages speak of the כְּפִיר as vulnerable (Ps 34:11) or in parallel with cubs (גּוֹר) (Jer 51:38; Ezek 19:2). Nevertheless, it is often used in the context of a ferocious animal in ambush (e.g., Judg 14:5; Ps 17:12).

לְבֵית יְהוּדָה. PP with לְ of interest. It is toward Judah that YHWH will behave as a young lion.

אֲנִי אֲנִי אֶטְרֹף. *Line c.* Independent clause.

אֲנִי אֲנִי. These pleonastic pronouns continue the emphasis on the contrast between the king of Assyria and YHWH. Hosea's use of the pronouns אֲנִי (YHWH) in 5:12 and הוּא (the king) in 5:13 create an explicit antithesis. In this verse the pronoun is repeated, which heightens the focus even more, to emphasize YHWH's role as a violent aggressor against Ephraim and Judah. Repeated pleonastic pronouns are not common (see Deut 32:39; Isa 48:15; 57:6).

אֶטְרֹף. Qal *yiqtol* 1cs √טרף. This verb is usually used of a wild animal tearing and eating its prey. The sequence in this verse is that he kills the prey violently (√טרף), withdraws (√הלך), takes his prey with him (נשא), and no one can save the prey or snatch it away (√נצל).

וְאֵלֵךְ. *Line c.* Independent clause. The verb is a Qal *yiqtol* 1cs √הלך.

אֶשָּׂא. *Line d.* Independent clause. The verb is a Qal *yiqtol* 1cs √נשא. This verb usually takes an accusative complement which is implied to be Ephraim and Judah because they are the targets of YHWH's violent actions. The meaning is that YHWH will carry them off as an animal would carry its prey somewhere to devour it.

וְאֵין מַצִּיל. *Line d.* Independent verbless clause. The existential particle אֵין is the negative copula ("there is not").

מַצִּיל. Hiph ptc ms √נצל. This substantival participle is the predicate of the verbless clause. The verb √נצל means "to take away" without the holder's permission (cf. 2:11). This clause is an echo of 2:12 where YHWH says, "I will uncover her folly ... and no one will take (נצל) her from my hands" (cf. also the curse in Deut 32:39).

5:15 a אֵלֵךְ אָשׁוּבָה אֶל־מְקוֹמִי
b עַד אֲשֶׁר־יֶאְשְׁמוּ וּבִקְשׁוּ פָנָי
c בַּצַּר לָהֶם יְשַׁחֲרֻנְנִי׃

Lines a-c are a tricolon. Tricola are much less common than bicola and frequently signal the beginning or (as here) the end of a unit. The lines are marked by disjunctive *Zaqep parvum*, *'Atnaḥ*, and *Silluq*.

אֵלֵךְ אָשׁוּבָה אֶל־מְקוֹמִי. *Line a.* Independent clause.

אֵלֵךְ. Qal *yiqtol* 1cs √הלך.

אָשׁוּבָה. Qal juss (cohortative) 1cs √שוב. The coordination of these two verbs without the copula means that the second verb (אָשׁוּבָה) is the principle idea, and its cohortative/volative sense governs both verbs (cf. GKC §120g; 5:11b). YHWH is stating his intention; he says, "I will go back to my place" to wait for Israel to rediscover their need for him.

אֶל־מְקוֹמִי. This PP is the complement of אָשׁוּבָה with אֶל indicating movement toward the place where YHWH will go. The identity of the מָקוֹם is not specified, but the statement is related to the metaphor in 5:14. Like a lion, YHWH has his own "lair" where he will hide away from Israel. When they repent (lines b-c), they will seek him as a deliverer rather than as an enemy.

עַד אֲשֶׁר־יֶאְשְׁמוּ. *Line b.* Subordinate temporal clause introduced by the preposition and relative (עַד אֲשֶׁר) describing a situation subsequent to that of the main clause (line a) (cf. WO §38.7a). The word אֲשֶׁר functions as a general nominalizer and the אֲשֶׁר clause is the complement of the prep עַד (Holmstedt 2016:119, 126).

יֶאְשְׁמוּ. Qal *yiqtol* 3mp √אשם. This verb refers to the guilt or punishment that a person must bear for wrongdoing (cf. 4:15). This statement is not saying that Israel will seek YHWH once they are "guilty" (in a juridical sense); it is saying that they will seek YHWH once they experience the consequences for their sin (described metaphorically in the preceding verses).

וּבִקְשׁוּ פָנָי. *Line b.* Temporal clause subordinate to the main clause in line a. Although it is not introduced by any particles associated with temporal clauses, it is coordinated with the preceding temporal clause and thus both have the same syntactic role in the sentence. This clause is actually logically subsequent to the preceding one. The logic is: YHWH will withdraw → they will experience guilt and consequences → they will seek YHWH. The particles עַד אֲשֶׁר ("until") at the beginning of line b suggest that when they seek him, he will come out of hiding.

וּבִקְשׁוּ. Piel *qatal* (irrealis) 3cp √בקשׁ. The irrealis *qatal* is used because it is coordinated with the preceding *yiqtol*. The theme of seeking and finding or not finding has been important in the book (see 2:9; 3:5; 5:6).

פָנָי. Acc compl of וּבִקְשׁוּ. The antecedent of the 1cs poss suffix is YHWH, the speaker.

בַּצַּר לָהֶם יְשַׁחֲרֻנְנִי. *Line c.* Independent clause.

בַּצַּר לָהֶם. PP with בְּ indicating the circumstances of the action ("in distress"). The phrase לָהֶם expresses possession. The antecedent of the 3mp suffix is the same as the subject of וּבִקְשׁוּ in the previous clause: Ephraim and Judah (5:14).

יְשַׁחֲרֻנְנִי. Piel *yiqtol* 3mp √שחר with a 1cs acc suffix. Note the additional נ in the plural ending of the verb. We would expect the form יְשַׁחֲרֻנִי, but twelve times suffixes are attached to the plural form וּן (see GKC §60e). The verb √שחר indicates a more intense and eager seeking than √בקשׁ in the previous, parallel line.

Call to Return to YHWH (Rejected) (6:1-3)

These three verses in 6:1-3 are a short parenthesis in which the prophet speaks in his own voice and calls Israel to repent. Whereas in the previous section Hosea spoke directly for YHWH in the first person singular, here he refers to YHWH in the third person. Furthermore, Hosea includes himself among his audience. He uses first person plural verbs and accusative suffixes throughout, saying, "Come and let *us* return to YHWH" (6:1) and, "*we* must strive to know YHWH" (6:3). The rhetorical goal of the unit in the context is to show that Israel *refuses* to repent. Although the call itself is straightforward, it is juxtaposed to the previous unit, 5:1-15, in which Hosea states that Israel and Judah do not truly seek YHWH, and the following unit, 6:4–7:2 in which he critiques them for being entrenched in their covenant violations. Thus this unit contributes to the Accusation panel (4:1–8:14) in the macrostructure of the book.

[1]Come and let us return to YHWH,
for he has torn and he will heal us;
he struck, and he will bind us up.

²He will revive us after two days;
on the third day he will raise us up,
and we will live in his presence ³that we might know him.

Let us strive to know YHWH;
his going forth is like the sure dawn.

And he will come to us like rain;
like late rains which water the earth.

6:1 a לְכוּ וְנָשׁוּבָה אֶל־יְהוָה
     b כִּי הוּא טָרָף וְיִרְפָּאֵנוּ
     c יַךְ וְיַחְבְּשֵׁנוּ׃

Lines a-c are a tricolon. Line a introduces the verse, while lines b-c are parallel with word pairs נכה√//טרף√ and רפא√//חבש√. The lines are marked by *Zaqep parvum*, *'Atnaḥ*, and *Silluq*;

לְכוּ. *Line a.* Independent clause. The verb is a Qal impv mp הלך√.

וְנָשׁוּבָה אֶל־יְהוָה. *Line a.* Independent clause.

וְנָשׁוּבָה. Qal juss (cohortative) 1cp שוב√. Hosea states in 5:4 that their deeds do not permit them to return (לָשׁוּב) to YHWH. Now he calls them to return from unorthodox and idolatrous worship.

אֶל־יְהוָה. This PP is the complement of וְנָשׁוּבָה with אֶל indicating the direction that they must return.

כִּי הוּא טָרָף. *Line b.* Subordinate causal clause with כִּי giving the reason that Hosea's audience should return to YHWH.

הוּא. This pleonastic pronoun emphasizes YHWH's role as the one who "tears" (טרף√). It sounds counterintuitive that they should return to the one who has harmed them, but Hosea will go on to say in the next clauses that YHWH is also the one who heals. In actuality, because YHWH is the one who harms, he is the *only* one who can heal.

טָרָף. Qal *qatal* 3ms טרף√. This verb echoes 5:14, where YHWH compares himself to a ferocious lion who rips apart his prey and then carries it off. The *qatal* conjugation indicates a completed action; the context indicates past tense.

וְיִרְפָּאֵנוּ. *Line b.* Subordinate causal clause. This clause is coordinated with the previous one and both are governed by the כִּי. The verb is a

Qal *yiqtol* 3ms √רפא with a 1cp acc suffix. This verb echoes 5:13, where YHWH states that the king of Assyria is unable to cure (לִרְפֹּא) Ephraim and Judah from the wound that YHWH has inflicted. Here Hosea reminds them that YHWH *can* heal that wound, if only they will repent. The antecedent of the 1cp suffix is Hosea and his audience.

יַךְ. *Line c*. Subordinate causal clause. According to the parallelism, this line is related to line a in the same way as line b. The כִּי governs all four clauses in lines b-c. The verb is a Hiphil *yiqtol* 3ms √נכה. BHS note [a] suggests reading it as a *wayyiqtol* וַיַּךְ ("he struck"). The MT reading could have been created if the ו, which is graphically similar to a י, was inadvertently omitted by a scribe. However, a *wayyiqtol* would imply a temporally successive idea (he will heal and *then* he struck), which is not the sense here (Cook 2017). A better explanation is that the shortened form represents an archaic preterite (past) form related to the *wayyiqtol* but without the ו before the prefix (cf. WO §31.1.1d). This would be uncommon, but it would explain the short form (the jussive and preterite are based on the pattern *yaqtul* whereas the *yiqtol* is based on the longer form *yaqtulu*) (see also וְאָט in 11:4c).

וְיַחְבְּשֵׁנוּ. *Line c*. Subordinate causal clause. The verb is a Qal *yiqtol* 3ms √חבש with a 1cp acc suffix. The verb √חבש means "to saddle a donkey" (only in the Pentateuch and Former Prophets), "to tie up," or "to wrap with bandages" (e.g., Isa 1:6). Job 5:18 is very similar to this verse: "he wounds (√כאב), but he binds up (√חבש); he shatters (√מחץ), but his hands heal (√רפא)."

6:2 a יְחַיֵּנוּ מִיֹּמָיִם
b בַּיּוֹם הַשְּׁלִישִׁי יְקִמֵנוּ

6:2-3 c וְנִחְיֶה לְפָנָיו: וְנֵדְעָה

Lines a-c are a tricolon. In this verse, if we follow the disjunctive masoretic accents, we have unusual and fragmentary poetic lines. Line b would end with הַשְּׁלִישִׁי, so that it would not have a verb ("on the third day"). It is better to ignore the *Zaqep parvum* and include יְקִמֵנוּ at the end of line b, thus producing one complete clause in each line. In addition, Stuart (1974:98) and AF (422) follow Gordis (1971:115, 151, n. 36) in moving the first word of 6:3 (וְנֵדְעָה) forward to the end of line c in this verse, ignoring the *Silluq* on לְפָנָיו. The advantages are that now 6:2 ends in two lines of roughly equal length with three stresses in each line, and 6:3a makes better sense without two cohortatives and a repetition of the verb √ידע.

יְחַיֵּנוּ מִיֹּמָיִם. *Line a. Independent clause.*

יְחַיֵּנוּ. Piel *yiqtol* 3ms √חיה with a 1cp acc suffix. In the Qal this verb means "to live," whereas in the Piel it is factitive and means "to preserve alive" or "to bring to life." The latter sense is in view here since this is the potential reversal of the preceding context (cf. 5:14 and 6:1) which describes tearing and killing.

מִיֹּמָיִם. PP with a מִן expressing the temporal sense "after" (cf. WO §11.2.11c; e.g., Ps 73:20; Gen 38:24). The noun יָמִים is a dual, meaning that it specifies two days. It is uncommon for the noun יוֹם to occur in the dual (only 5× in the OT).

בַּיּוֹם הַשְּׁלִישִׁי יְקִמֵנוּ. *Line b. Independent clause.*

בַּיּוֹם הַשְּׁלִישִׁי. PP with בְּ used temporally to define the time of the action (יְקִמֵנוּ). The cardinal number שְׁלִישִׁי ("third") is used attributively to modify יוֹם.

יְקִמֵנוּ. Hiph *yiqtol* 3ms √קום with a 1cp acc suffix. The Qal of √קום means "to arise" and the Hiphil means "to raise up" (causative).

וְנִחְיֶה לְפָנָיו. *Line c. Independent clause.*

וְנִחְיֶה. Qal *yiqtol* 1cp √חיה. Line a has the Piel of √חיה ("he will revive us"); this Qal is an outcome of that action: "we will live."

לְפָנָיו. PP with לִפְנֵי (a combination of לְ and the noun פָּנֶה; see HALOT 941) with the meaning "in the presence of." The antecedent of the 3ms suffix is YHWH, specified in 6:1a. If, as argued above, we include וְנֵדְעָה from the beginning of 6:3 on this line, then that verb expects a complement. AF (422) and Stuart (1987:99) argue that the suffix does double duty. It is the complement of the preposition and also serves as the understood complement of the following verb/clause. The translation is, "in *his* presence, that we might know *him*."

וְנֵדְעָה. *Line c. Independent clause.* The verb is a Qal juss (cohortative) 1cp √ידע. Although this clause is syntactically coordinate to the preceding clause, it is semantically subordinate and has the sense of a purpose clause.

6:3 a נִרְדְּפָה לָדַעַת אֶת־יְהוָה
b כְּשַׁחַר נָכוֹן מוֹצָאוֹ
c וְיָבוֹא כַגֶּשֶׁם לָנוּ
d כְּמַלְקוֹשׁ יוֹרֶה אָרֶץ׃

Lines a-b are a bicolon. The lines are connected via noun//pronoun grammatical parallelism (וֹ//יְהוָה) and are marked with *Zaqep parvum* and *'Atnaḥ*. Lines c-d are also a bicolon, indicated by ellipsis of the verb וְיָבוֹא in line d, as well as by the word pairs מַלְקוֹשׁ//גֶּשֶׁם. The lines are marked by *Zaqep parvum* and *Silluq*.

נִרְדְּפָה. *Line a*. Independent clause. The verb is a Qal juss (cohortative) 1cp √רדף. This verb means "to pursue" or "to aim to secure" (BDB 922). Here it expresses effort and determination to know YHWH.

לָדַעַת אֶת־יְהוָה. *Line a*. Dependent final (purpose) clause indicating the goal of "striving" (נִרְדְּפָה).

לָדַעַת. Qal inf constr √ידע.

אֶת־יְהוָה. Acc compl of לָדַעַת.

כְּשַׁחַר נָכוֹן מוֹצָאוֹ. *Line b*. Independent verbless clause.

כְּשַׁחַר נָכוֹן. PP with כְּ indicating agreement in kind. It introduces the metaphor in which YHWH is compared to the dawn that never ceases to appear each day. This phrase is the subject of the verbless clause. The attributive נָכוֹן is Niph ptc ms √כון modifying שַׁחַר ("dawn"). The verb √כון in the Niphal is used in a variety of ways: "to be true," "to be ready," or "to be fixed." It refers to something that is reliable (e.g., Gen 41:32; Ps 57:8). The purpose of this line is to motivate the people to strive after YHWH; if they seek him, they can be certain of their ability to find him.

מוֹצָאוֹ. Predicate of the verbless clause. The noun מוֹצָא refers to a place of departure or an appearance (HALOT 559). The antecedent of the 3ms suffix is יְהוָה, specified in line a.

וְיָבוֹא כַגֶּשֶׁם לָנוּ. *Line c*. Independent clause.

וְיָבוֹא. Qal *yiqtol* 3ms √בוא.

כַגֶּשֶׁם. Adjunct PP describing the manner of YHWH's coming. The prep כְּ indicates agreement in kind. Agriculture—and life—in ancient Israel was dependent on rain coming at the right time. There are at least eight words for rain in BH, one of which is גֶּשֶׁם (a general term). This prediction that YHWH will cause the land to flourish once again recalls the discussion in 2:5, 21-22.

לָנוּ. PP with לְ indicating the object of the motion ("he will come ... to us").

כְּמַלְקוֹשׁ יוֹרֶה אָרֶץ. *Line d.* Independent clause. The verb וְיָבוֹא (line c) is elided.

כְּמַלְקוֹשׁ. Adjunct PP with כְּ describing the manner of YHWH's coming. The noun מַלְקוֹשׁ, another of the terms in BH's rich vocabulary for rain, refers to late rains which come in the spring (March–May) (Scott 1952:14–15, 23; Brisco 1998:28). These were critical for a bountiful harvest. Thus, there is intensification in the parallelism from גֶּשֶׁם (general) to מַלְקוֹשׁ (specific).

יוֹרֶה אָרֶץ. This is an unmarked relative clause which is headed by מַלְקוֹשׁ (see Holmstedt 2016:145). According to GKC (§155g), this is common with nouns having a preposition of comparison. The verb יוֹרֶה is a Hiph *yiqtol* 3ms √ירה. Elsewhere, √ירה in the Hiphil means "to throw" or "to shoot" or, it is metaphorically extended to mean "to instruct." The sense "to water," unique to Hosea (cf. also 10:12), may also metaphorical extension from "throw." Another possibility is that it may be an alternative form of √רוה ("to water") (cf. Rudolph 1966:132).

It is also possible to analyze line d in another way. If וְיָבוֹא is not elided in the parallelism (see line c), then יוֹרֶה is the main verb in the independent clause. We would translate, "Like late rains he [i.e., YHWH] will water the earth." There would therefore be a chiastic structure in lines c-d: He will come (A) like the rain (B)//Like late rains (B′) he will water (A′).

Israel and Judah Are Entrenched in Covenant Violations (6:4–7:2)

Following his interjection in 6:1-3, Hosea begins speaking on behalf of YHWH again in 6:4. In 6:4-6 YHWH (presented by Hosea) laments that in spite of his warnings from the prophets, Israel continues to observe the cultic stipulations of the covenant while rejecting true faithfulness to it. He begins with a sense of exasperation, wondering what he can possibly do with people who refuse to be loyal. They have rejected prophetic calls for reform, and yet they continue empty sacrifices devoid of fidelity and truth. In 6:7–7:2, he states that they break the ethical stipulations of the covenant. Here he refers again to the wicked priesthood. As a vivid example, he describes a band of priests who ambush and murder on the west-east route through Shechem (6:9), Adam (6:7), and Gilead (6:8). As a result of their leadership, all Ephraim, the rest of Israel, and even Judah has been defiled and is destined for judgment (6:10-11a). They do not realize that YHWH has taken note of every sin.

> [4] *What will I do with you, Ephraim?*
> *What will I do with you, Judah?*
> *Your covenant love is like the morning cloud*
> *and like the dew which disappears early.*
>
> [5] *Therefore, I have hewn [them] by the prophets;*
> *I have killed them with the words of my mouth;*
> *and my justice goes out like light.*
>
> [6] *For I desire covenant love and not sacrifice,*
> *and knowledge of God more than burnt offerings.*
>
> [7] *But they, as [at] Adam, transgressed the covenant;*
> *there they dealt treacherously with me.*
>
> [8] *Gilead is a city of evildoers—*
> *tracked with blood.*
>
> [9] *And as gangs wait for a man,*
> *(a company of priests);*
>
> *they murder on the road to Shechem,*
> *They have committed wickedness.*
>
> [10] *In the house of Israel, I have seen a horrible thing:*
> *there is Ephraim's fornication;*
> *Israel is defiled.*
> [11a] *Also Judah: he appointed a harvest for you.*
>
> [11b] *When I restore the captivities of my people,*
> [7:1] *when I heal Israel,*
>
> *then the iniquity of Ephraim will be revealed,*
> *and the wicked deeds of Samaria,*
> *for they have practiced deception.*

And a thief enters;
a gang has raided outside.

²But they do not consider
that I have remembered all their evil.

Now their deeds have surrounded them;
they are before me.

6:4 a מָה אֶעֱשֶׂה־לְּךָ֣ אֶפְרַ֔יִם
b מָ֥ה אֶֽעֱשֶׂה־לְּךָ֖ יְהוּדָ֑ה
c וְחַסְדְּכֶם֙ כַּעֲנַן־בֹּ֔קֶר
d וְכַטַּ֖ל מַשְׁכִּ֥ים הֹלֵֽךְ׃

Lines a-b are a bicolon with identical lines except for the word pair יְהוּדָה//אֶפְרַיִם. The lines are marked by *Zaqep parvum* and *'Atnaḥ*. Lines c-d are a bicolon featuring verbless clauses including two PPs with כְּ and similar metaphors (cloud//dew). The subject חַסְדְּכֶם and noncopula (line c) are elided in line d. The lines are marked with *Zaqep parvum* and *Silluq*.

מָה אֶעֱשֶׂה־לְּךָ אֶפְרַיִם. *Line a.* Independent clause.

מָה. Interr particle and acc compl of אֶעֱשֶׂה.

אֶעֱשֶׂה. Qal *yiqtol* 1cs √עשׂה.

לְּךָ. PP with לְ of interest. The antecedent of the 2ms suffix is Ephraim. Hosea addresses Ephraim (line a) and Judah (line b) with singular suffixes and then addresses both in line c with a plural suffix (וְחַסְדְּכֶם).

אֶפְרַיִם. Vocative and antecedent of the preceding 2ms suffix.

מָה אֶעֱשֶׂה־לְּךָ יְהוּדָה. *Line b.* Independent clause. This line is identical to line a with the exception of the vocative יְהוּדָה.

וְחַסְדְּכֶם כַּעֲנַן־בֹּקֶר. *Line c.* Independent verbless clause. Lines cβ-d are repeated verbatim in 13:3.

וְחַסְדְּכֶם. Subject of the verbless clause. חֶסֶד (benevolence, faithfulness, loyalty, generosity, kindness) is a synechdoche for the character that YHWH's people were to demonstrate toward each other and toward him as members of a covenant relationship with him (see 2:22; 4:1). The antecedents of the 2mp suffix are Ephraim and Judah, whom YHWH addresses in lines a-b.

כַּעֲנַן־בֹּקֶר. This PP with כְּ indicating agreement in kind is the predicate of the verbless clause. The first metaphor used to describe their חֶסֶד is a "morning cloud." בֹּקֶר is an adjectival genitive (cf. WO §9.5.3) modifying עָנָן. Here, YHWH complains that their חֶסֶד is ephemeral: it may look substantive at first, but it is flimsy and quickly evaporates, just as a morning mist disappears when the sun rises (see Scott 1952:21–22, 24).

וְכַטַּל מַשְׁכִּים הֹלֵךְ. *Line d.* Independent verbless clause. The subject חַסְדְּכֶם and the noncopula are elided.

וְכַטַּל. PP with כְּ indicating agreement in kind.

מַשְׁכִּים. Hiph ptc ms √שׁכם. Hosea has shown a tendency to relate two verbs asyndetically (cf. 5:11, 15; 9:9) and he does so again here. This participle cannot modify טַל ("dew") attributively (i.e., "like the *early* dew") because they do not agree in definiteness (cf. WO §37.5a-b). (If that were the case, one would expect the participle to have the article; i.e., הַמַּשְׁכִּים). Rather, the asyndetic construction means that מַשְׁכִּים modifies the following participle הֹלֵךְ adverbially. It is this second verb, הֹלֵךְ, that expresses the principle idea (cf. GKC §120g; JM §177g; Wernberg-Møller 1959:65). The translation is "it disappears (הֹלֵךְ) early." This understanding is supported by them accents. There is a disjunctive *Ṭipḥa* on וְכַטַּל indicating a minor break after that word, while מַשְׁכִּים has a conjunctive *Mereka* accent, which groups it with הֹלֵךְ.

הֹלֵךְ. Qal ptc ms √הלך. This participle form is a relative clause, headed by and modifying כַטַּל, even though it does not have an article (see WO §19.7b). Thus, in the poetic parallelism, line c supplies the subject (and thus the noncopula), while the ellipsis in line d allows for further elaboration of the טַל (i.e., it disappears early), which is also characteristic of the כַּעֲנַן־בֹּקֶר in line c.

6:5 a עַל־כֵּן חָצַבְתִּי בַּנְּבִיאִים
b הֲרַגְתִּים בְּאִמְרֵי־פִי
c וּמִשְׁפָּטֶיךָ אוֹר יֵצֵא:

Lines a-c are a tricolon. The first two lines are parallel with word pairs √הרג//√חצב as well as corresponding PPs with בְּ. The third line is a conclusion. The lines are marked by *Zaqep parvum*, *'Atnaḥ* and *Silluq*.

Hosea 6:5

עַל־כֵּן חָצַבְתִּי בַּנְּבִיאִים. *Line a*. Independent clause.

עַל־כֵּן. Conjunctive adverb ("therefore") introducing the consequence or the result of the preceding statement. This verse describes the consequences of the situation in 6:4.

חָצַבְתִּי. Qal *qatal* 1cs √חצב. The verb requires an accusative complement, which is implied in this line but identified in line b with the 3mp acc suffix on הֲרַגְתִּים. The verb √חצב refers to hewing rock, such as making cisterns or cutting rocks for building material. In this context, with people as the implied object, it portrays violence (cf. Amos 1:3, where violence is committed with agricultural implements).

בַּנְּבִיאִים. PP with בְּ. G and S understand this phrase as the oblique complement of the preceding verb √חצב, "I have hewn the prophets." However, √חצב takes accusative complements elsewhere. Furthermore, in line b the PP with בְּ must be instrumental, and the parallelism suggests that it is instrumental in this line as well. As noted above, the accusative complement of √חצב is identified in line b with a 3mp suffix on הֲרַגְתִּים. Therefore, the translation is, "I have hewn [them—i.e., my people] *by* the prophets." The hewing is metaphorical: it is the words of YHWH's prophets that have announced disaster.

הֲרַגְתִּים בְּאִמְרֵי־פִי. *Line b*. Independent clause.

הֲרַגְתִּים. Qal *qatal* 1cs √הרג with a 3mp acc suffix. The antecedents of the suffix are Ephraim and Judah (6:4).

בְּאִמְרֵי־פִי. PP with instrumental בְּ indicating the means by which he will kill Ephraim and Judah. The construct phrase "words of my mouth" is a semantic amplification in the parallelism. Line a contains the vehicle or means of revelation (the prophets) > line b refers to the words of YHWH which they spoke on his behalf. This connection between YHWH's word and the consequences he will bring upon them is a warning: history is about to repeat itself because they have not learned their lesson.

וּמִשְׁפָּטֶיךָ אוֹר יֵצֵא. *Line c*. Independent clause. This reading in the MT is difficult. First because Hosea switches back to a 2ms suffix in this line even though he refers to both Ephraim and Judah with plural suffixes in 6:4c and 6:7a. Second, the possessive suffix on "judgments" is difficult to understand. Is it an objective genitive (i.e., judgments *against* Ephraim and Judah)? Third, there is no בְּ prep on אוֹר even though it appears to be a simile. Finally, the plural וּמִשְׁפָּטֶיךָ must be the subject of the singular

יֵצֵא, but it does not agree in number. The major ancient versions G, S, and T all represent a different division of the consonants: וּמִשְׁפָּטִי כָּאוֹר יֵצֵא ("and my judgment like light goes out"). This reading, in which the 2ms suffix כ is a preposition on the following word אוֹר (see BHS note e-e), is superior to that of the MT. The subject of יֵצֵא is now singular, the obvious simile is introduced by כְּ, the 1cs suffix on מִשְׁפָּט is possessive, and there is no abrupt change of person (see Gelston 2010:60*). The Hebrew text presented below represents this reading of the versions.

וּמִשְׁפָּטִי. The subject of יֵצֵא. The antecedent of the 1cs poss suffix is YHWH, the speaker.

כָּאוֹר. PP with כְּ indicating agreement in kind. The meaning of the metaphor is uncertain: how is justice like light? Perhaps it means that it is far-reaching or that it reveals what is hidden.

יֵצֵא. Qal *yiqtol* 3ms √יצא.

6:6 a כִּי חֶסֶד חָפַצְתִּי וְלֹא־זָבַח
b וְדַעַת אֱלֹהִים מֵעֹלוֹת׃

Lines a-b are a bicolon featuring ellipsis of the verb חָפַצְתִּי in line b as well as the word pair עֹלוֹת/זֶבַח. The lines are marked by *'Atnaḥ* and *Silluq*.

כִּי חֶסֶד חָפַצְתִּי וְלֹא־זָבַח. *Line a*. Subordinate causal clause with כִּי giving the reason that YHWH has "hewn" (חָצַבְתִּי) and "killed" (הֲרַגְתִּים) them by his words (v. 5).

חֶסֶד. Compl of חָפַצְתִּי, fronted in the word order. This focus strategy highlights the contrast with זֶבַח which follows. YHWH is saying, "It is *covenant love* that I desire, not (manipulative) sacrifice."

חָפַצְתִּי. Qal *qatal* 1cs √חפץ.

וְלֹא־זָבַח. This noun זֶבַח is a second complement of חָפַצְתִּי. The complement is negated rather than the verb because of the contrast of complements: YHWH desires חֶסֶד *not* זֶבַח.

וְדַעַת אֱלֹהִים מֵעֹלוֹת. *Line b*. Independent clause. The verb חָפַצְתִּי is elided.

וְדַעַת אֱלֹהִים. Compl of the elided verb חָפַצְתִּי (from line a). Hosea states in 4:1 that YHWH has a רִיב ("case") against Israel because there is no דַּעַת אֱלֹהִים in the land. In 4:6 he warns that YHWH has rejected the priest who has rejected knowledge (דַּעַת).

מֵעֹלוֹת. PP with מִן. The preposition is not comparative ("rather than"). In view of the parallelism with וְלֹא in line a, the מִן is privative with the idea of substitution ("rather than burnt offerings"; cf. GKC §199w; WO §11.2.11e, n. 99). There is semantic intensification from זֶבַח (line a), which means sacrifices in general, to the corresponding עֹלָה (line b) which is a specific type of sacrifice— wholly consumed, for the atonement of sin. For similar statements in the OT, see 1 Sam 15:22; Pss 40:7; 51:18-19; Isa 1:11-15; 58:3-4; Mal 1:10.

6:7 a וְהֵ֨מָּה כְּאָדָ֖ם עָבְר֣וּ בְרִ֑ית
b שָׁ֖ם בָּ֥גְדוּ בִֽי׃

Lines a-b are a bicolon. The lines are related by the correspondence of שָׁם//אָדָם and the word pair בגד√//עבר√. The lines are marked by *'Atnaḥ* and *Silluq*.

וְהֵמָּה כְּאָדָם עָבְרוּ בְרִית. *Line a*. Independent clause.

וְהֵמָּה. In 6:4-5 Hosea referred to the people of Ephraim and Judah with plural pronouns. Now, this 3mp pleonastic pronoun introduces a change in subject. He does not identify the antecedent of the pronoun until 6:9, where we learn that it is a "company of priests" that has been treacherous and committed murder. Thus, Hosea concludes this major unit (4:4–7:2) just as he began: with a discussion of the corrupt priesthood.

כְּאָדָם. PP with כְּ. There have been a number of proposals on the meaning of אָדָם. We can consider only two very briefly. The traditional approach has been to understand it as either "man" (i.e., "humanity") or as the proper name "Adam" referring to the first created person (cf. Gen 2:20). G (ἄνθρωπος) and S interpret it as the former and translate, "they have transgressed [the] covenant like a man." However, the meaning is obscure and, even more significantly, the adverb שָׁם ("there") in line b indicates that אָדָם is a location. The most convincing view is that אָדָם is a place name. Joshua 3:16 refers to a town called אָדָם ("Adam") located on the banks of the Jordan River north of Jericho. AF (438) suggest that in Hosea's time there may have been a major Jordan crossing at this point that linked Shechem (cf. 6:9) to the Israelite towns in the Transjordan.

We have no other references to Adam or traditions of violence there, so Hosea seems to be alluding to a recent or contemporary event, known to his audience, in which Adam was the location of a spree of ambush and murder. The כְּ is a comparison of manner (cf. WO); a second preposition "at" is implied giving the translation, "And they, as at Adam... ." Hosea is giving the incident at Adam as an example of the kinds of things that the wicked priests practice.

עָבְרוּ. Qal *qatal* 3cp √עבר. This verb is frequently used to describe the breaking of a covenant (cf. also 8:1). AF write, "This is the general indictment; the particular crime of murder at Adam on the way to Shechem provides a vivid illustration" (439).

בְרִית. Acc compl of עָבְרוּ. This word does not have a 1cs poss suffix (referring to YHWH) or an article. Nevertheless, it is YHWH's covenant with Israel which is intended.

שָׁם בָּגְדוּ בִי. *Line b*. Independent clause.

שָׁם. Locative adverb. The referent, as noted above, is the place name אָדָם in line a.

בָּגְדוּ. Qal *qatal* 3cp √בגד. On the meaning of this word, see 5:7.

בִי. This adjunct PP with בְּ specifies the victim of the treacherous behavior (בָּגְדוּ). The antecedent of the 1cs suffix is YHWH, the speaker.

6:8 a גִּלְעָד קִרְיַת פֹּעֲלֵי אָוֶן
b עֲקֻבָּה מִדָּם:

Lines a-b are a bicolon. The lines are marked with *'Atnaḥ* and *Silluq*.

גִּלְעָד קִרְיַת פֹּעֲלֵי אָוֶן. *Line a*. Independent verbless clause.

גִּלְעָד. Subject of the verbless clause. Judges 10:17 apparently refers to a town called Gilead in that region. One potential candidate is *Khirbet Jel'ad*, which was fifteen miles east of the Jordan river and six miles south of Jabbok.

קִרְיַת פֹּעֲלֵי אָוֶן. Constr chain. קִרְיָה, the predicate of the verbless clause, is a synonym of עִיר (the words are interchangeable in Deut 3:4) meaning "town" or "city." The second constituent פֹּעֲלֵי is a Qal ptc mp √פעל used substantivally ("doers of"). אָוֶן is a general term for evil, unethical behavior. It is particularly common in wisdom literature and in Isaiah.

עֲקֻבָּה מִדָּם. *Line b*. These two words are obscure and difficult to interpret. If we keep the vocalization of the MT, then the two words are in apposition to קְרִיָּה in the previous line and do not constitute a new clause. BDB (784) translates "foot-tracked with blood," in which עֲקֻבָּה is an adjective from עָקֵב ("heel," "footprint").

6:9 a וּכְחַכֵּי אִישׁ גְּדוּדִים
b חֶבֶר כֹּהֲנִים
c דֶּרֶךְ יְרַצְּחוּ־שֶׁכְמָה
d כִּי זִמָּה עָשׂוּ׃

Lines a-b are a bicolon in which line a is a comparative clause subordinate to line b. The lines are marked with *Rᵉbiaʿ* and *Zaqep parvum*. Lines c-d are a bicolon as well, featuring two third-person plural verbs (יְרַצְּחוּ//עָשׂוּ) with the same subject. The lines are marked by *Atnaḥ* and *Silluq*. This verse is difficult and probably corrupted as several words appear to be in the wrong order, but not for pragmatic reasons.

וּכְחַכֵּי אִישׁ גְּדוּדִים. *Line a*. Subordinate comparative clause with כְּ comparing this situation to that of the main clause in line b (cf. WO §38.5).

וּכְחַכֵּי. Piel inf constr √חכה. The כְּ prep indicates agreement in kind. It anticipates and describes the act of murder in the following lines (c-d). The verb √חכה means "to wait" or "to be patient," but in this context it has the sense of lying in wait in an ambush. The *yod* ending is unusual; it is an alternate orthography for the expected form כְּחַכֵּה. GKC (§23l; §75aa) states that when ה only marks a final vowel, it sometimes changes to י when that vowel is an *o* or *e* (as here).

אִישׁ. Compl of חַכֵּי. The reference here is general, with an idea like "someone."

גְּדוּדִים. Subject of חַכֵּי. The noun גְּדוּד refers to a "band" or "troop" of warriors. It usually has connotations of lawlessness, describing robbers or raiders, or of a quick raid by an enemy nation. The translation "gangs" is an attempt to convey these negative connotations in English.

חֶבֶר כֹּהֲנִים. *Line b*. This construct phrase is parenthetical, further describing the גְּדוּדִים ("gangs") in the previous line and explicating the 3mp verbal subjects in the next line. The sense is, "As gangs wait for a man [line a] (company of priests) [line b]." We would expect the apodosis of a comparative clause to be introduced by כֵּן, but here it is implied.

חֶבֶר. The noun חֶבֶר refers to an associate or a companion. Here it is collective and means a "band" or a "company," all having the same purpose.

כֹּהֲנִים. This is the fifth and final occurrence of the noun כֹּהֵן in this book (cf. 4:4, 6, 9; 5:1). Hosea began this unit (4:4–7:2) with a discussion of the corrupt, unorthodox priesthood, and now he closes the unit by once again addressing their actions. We now have an identification of the plural pronoun and verbs in 6:7 above.

דֶּרֶךְ יְרַצְּחוּ־שֶׁכְמָה. *Line c.* Independent clause.

שֶׁכְמָה ... דֶּרֶךְ. PP with an implied preposition indicating the location of the action (יְרַצְּחוּ). The construct phrase is considered "broken" because the verb (יְרַצְּחוּ) intervenes between the bound form (דֶּרֶךְ) and the genitive (שֶׁכְמָה). Under normal circumstances, a construct phrase cannot be interrupted by anything except an article. However, there are exceptions where other elements intrude (cf. Freedman 1972; Blommerde 1974; WO §9.3d). Hosea also uses broken construct phrases in 14:3 and 14:8 (and possibly 8:2). Shechem, a town located west of the Jordan River, was apparently linked to Adam and then Gilead via an east-west road that crossed the Jordan. Therefore, in vv. 6-8 Hosea is describing murderous acts by a band of wicked priests that took place along that route.

יְרַצְּחוּ. Piel *yiqtol* 3mp √רצח. The Qal of √רצח refers to illegitimate acts of killing, including murder. The Piel is frequentative, here suggesting that this is not an isolated act, but something the priests do regularly. This is also the sense conveyed by the *yiqtol* conjugation.

כִּי זִמָּה עָשׂוּ. *Line d.* Independent clause. The כִּי is asseverative emphasizing the depth of their wickedness or the deliberate way that they engage in it (so Macintosh 2014:241; cf. JM §164b).

זִמָּה. Acc compl of עָשׂוּ. This noun refers to particularly heinous sins. It often describes sexual deviancy or lewd behavior (cf. Lev 20:14; Judg 20:6). It also describes intentional plans and schemes to do evil (Prov 21:27; 24:9). In the context, the latter sense is in view: the actions of the priests are deliberate and the result of careful planning.

עָשׂוּ. Qal *qatal* 3cp √עשׂה.

6:10 a בְּבֵית יִשְׂרָאֵל רָאִיתִי שַׁעֲרִירִיָּה
b שָׁם זְנוּת לְאֶפְרַיִם
c נִטְמָא יִשְׂרָאֵל:

6:11 a גַּם־יְהוּדָה שָׁת קָצִיר לָךְ

   Lines 6:10a-11a are a quatrain. Line 6:10a is an introduction, referring to the "house of Israel" which is the nation as a whole. The last three lines then mention each of the parts of the nation: Ephraim (6:10b), Israel (the rest of the northern kingdom; 6:10c), and Judah (6:11a). 6:10a-c describe evil behavior and 6:11a serves as a conclusion which announces judgment ("harvest"). The lines are marked by *'Atnaḥ*, *Zaqep parvum*, *Silluq*, and the *'Atnaḥ* at the midpoint of 6:11.

בְּבֵית יִשְׂרָאֵל רָאִיתִי שַׁעֲרִירִיָּה. *Line 6:10a.* Independent clause.

בְּבֵית יִשְׂרָאֵל. PP with locative בְּ. By "house of Israel" the prophet means the whole nation (cf. 5:1 and "tribes of Israel" in 5:9) (AF 442).

רָאִיתִי. Qal *qatal* 1cs √ראה. The speaker is YHWH.

שַׁעֲרִירִיָּה. This a *ketiv/qere* reading in which the consonants of the word represent one form and the vowels another. In this case, the difference is only one of vocalization. The consonants of the *ketiv* assume the vocalization שַׁעֲרִירִיָּה while the vowels of the *qere* represent the form שַׁעֲרוּרִיָּה. The latter form (with ו) is similar to the only other occurrences in Jer 5:30; 18:13; and 23:14. Therefore, it appears that the *qere* represents the usual spelling. The word שַׁעֲרוּרִיָּה refers to a wicked action that represents unfaithfulness and rebellion (cf. Jer 18:12).

שָׁם זְנוּת לְאֶפְרַיִם. *Line 6:10b.* Independent verbless clause.

שָׁם. This adverb modifies the noncopula of the verbless clause and identifies the location of the זְנוּת ("fornication"). The antecedent is "the house of Israel" in line a. Alternately, it could be the area around Shechem, Adam, and Gilead (6:7-9) referred to above.

זְנוּת. Subject of the verbless clause. Hosea uses this word in 4:11 as well. It is related to זְנוּנִים ("fornication") and means "fornication" or "faithlessness."

לְאֶפְרַיִם. This PP with poss לְ is the predicate of the verbless clause (i.e., "fornication is to Ephraim"). In other words, Ephraim's fornication is there in the house of Israel.

נִטְמָא יִשְׂרָאֵל. *Line 6:10c*. Independent clause.

נִטְמָא. Niph *qatal* 3ms √טמא. See the discussion in 5:3.

גַּם־יְהוּדָה שָׁת קָצִיר לָךְ. *Line 6:11a*. Independent clause.

גַּם. This conjunction indicates continuity with the preceding clauses and emphasizes an additional element. Judah is also under judgment along with the northern kingdom.

יְהוּדָה. It does not make sense that this is the subject of the verb שָׁת since the territories in the preceding parallel lines are condemned, and the conjunction גַּם suggests that Judah will share their fate, not appoint a judgment ("harvest") for them. Furthermore, we must identify an antecedent for the 2ms suffix on לָךְ at the end of the line. Therefore, it makes the best sense to identify יְהוּדָה as a vocative with the same referent as the suffix.

שָׁת. Qal *qatal* 3ms √שׁית. If יְהוּדָה is a vocative, then the 3ms subject of this verb must be YHWH. He is the one who appoints a "harvest" for Judah (and Israel). The use of the third person is curious since YHWH otherwise speaks in the first person in this section (cf. 6:7, 10, 11b). Alternatively, this could be read as a passive participle with an impersonal subject. In that case the implied subject would still be YHWH. Stuart (1987:98–99) takes it as an active participle with YHWH as the implied subject.

קָצִיר. Acc compl of שָׁת. The harvest is often a time of celebration and a sign of YHWH's goodness and provision to Israel. However, the prophets sometimes use the image of harvest (קָצִיר) as a metaphor for a day of reckoning (cf. Isa 17:4-5; Jer 51:33; Joel 4:13).

לָךְ. Adjunct PP with לְ indicating the person for whom the action is directed. The antecedent of the 2ms suffix is יְהוּדָה.

6:11 b בְּשׁוּבִי שְׁבוּת עַמִּי: פ

7:1 a כְּרָפְאִי לְיִשְׂרָאֵל
b וְנִגְלָה עֲוֹן אֶפְרַיִם
c וְרָעוֹת שֹׁמְרוֹן
d כִּי פָעֲלוּ שָׁקֶר
e וְגַנָּב יָבוֹא
f פָּשַׁט גְּדוּד בַּחוּץ:

Lines 6:11b-7:1a are a bicolon. Each line contains a temporal infinitive with the word pairs רפא√//שוב√ and עַם//יִשְׂרָאֵל. These correspondences as well as our analysis of 6:11a (above) indicate that the lines form a unit even though this requires that we separate v. 11 between two bicola. The lines are marked by *Silluq* and *R^ebî^aʿ*. Lines 7:1b-d are a tricolon. The first two lines of the tricolon (b-c) are connected via ellipsis of the verb וְנִגְלָה as well as the word pair שֹׁמְרוֹן//אֶפְרַיִם. Line 7:1d is a causal clause which forms the conclusion of the tricolon. The lines are marked by *Pašta*, *Zaqep parvum*, and *ʾAtnaḥ*. Lines 7:1e-f are a bicolon, linked by the word pairs פשט//בוא√ (both terms express a crime) and גְּדוּד//גַנָּב as well as a chiastic structure (SV//VS). The lines are marked by *Zaqep parvum* and *Silluq*.

בְּשׁוּבִי שְׁבוּת עַמִּי. *Line 6:11b*. Temporal clause subordinate to the main clause in 7:1b.

בְּשׁוּבִי. Qal inf constr שוב√ with a בְּ prep and a 1cs suffix. When an infinitive is introduced by בְּ, it denotes temporal proximity to the main clause (cf. WO §36.2.2b). In other words, this action (YHWH returning captives) and the action of the main clause in 7:1b (iniquity of Ephraim revealed) are occurring at the same time. The 1cs suffix is the subject of the infinitive; its antecedent is YHWH who is speaking. The Qal of שוב√ is usually intransitive, but there are a few other instances where it is transitive (corresponding to the Hiphil) (cf. Ps 85:5 and possibly Num 10:36; Isa 52:8; HALOT 1430).

שְׁבוּת עַמִּי. Constr phrase. שְׁבוּת is the acc compl of the inf בְּשׁוּבִי.

כְּרָפְאִי לְיִשְׂרָאֵל. *Line 7:1a*. Temporal clause subordinate to the main clause in 7:1b.

Hosea 7:1

כְּרָפְאִי. Qal inf constr √רפא with a כְּ prep indicating that it is temporal and a 1cs suffix. In contrast to the preceding temporal infinitive which has בְּ, the כְּ prep here indicates that the temporal clause occurs immediately before the main clause (WO §36.2.2b).

לְיִשְׂרָאֵל. Oblique compl of כְּרָפְאִי. The verb √רפא takes oblique complements with לְ (cf. 5:13) or accusative complements (cf. 6:1; 11:3; 14:5).

וְנִגְלָה עֲוֺן אֶפְרַיִם. *Line 7:1b*. Independent clause.

וְנִגְלָה. Niph *qatal* (irrealis) 3ms √גלה. The verb √גלה refers to exposing or uncovering what was concealed (cf. 2:10). For YHWH to heal and restore his people (lines 6:11b–7:1a), it will require that their sins be exposed and that they are honest about what they have done (cf. Garrett 1997:166).

עֲוֺן אֶפְרַיִם. Constr phrase. עֲוֺן is the subject of וְנִגְלָה. The noun עֲוֺן refers to religious and ethical violations as well as the guilt that they incur.

וְרָעוֹת שֹׁמְרוֹן. *Line 7:1c*. Independent clause. The verb וְנִגְלָה is elided (see line 7:1:b). The genitive שֹׁמְרוֹן ("Samaria") in the construct phrase is a synechdoche representing the whole of Israel. Very frequently, corresponding terms in parallel lines exhibit some kind of semantic intensification or amplification. For example, a more general word in the first line is followed by a more specific, vivid, or intense word in the second line. Elsewhere in instances of the עֲוֺן//רָעָה word pair, the word רָעָה occurs in the first line and עֲוֺן in the second, suggesting that עֲוֺן is a stronger word referring to a greater degree of guilt (cf. Job 22:5; Ps 40:13; Isa 13:11). This verse is the only one in which the order is reversed: עֲוֺן occurs in line 7:1b and רָעָה occurs in 7:1c. This may be an intentional twist by Hosea. He first applies the stronger term עֲוֺן to Ephraim, the district which propogated idolatry and led the rest of the nation astray. They have the greater guilt. Then he applies the more general term רָעָה to the rest of Israel which followed Ephraim's lead.

כִּי פָעֲלוּ שָׁקֶר. *Line 7:1d*. Subordinate causal clause with כִּי giving the reason that the guilt of Ephraim and Samaria will be revealed.

פָעֲלוּ. Qal *qatal* 3cp √פעל. The plural subjects are אֶפְרַיִם and שֹׁמְרוֹן from the preceding lines.

שָׁקֶר. Acc compl of פָעֲלוּ. This segolate noun (שֶׁקֶר) is vocalized with a *qamets* because it is in pause due to the strong disjunctive accent.

It is frequently used in the context of false worship (Jer 3:10; 5:31) or of dealing deceitfully with others in the community.

וְגַנָּב יָבוֹא. *Line 7:1e*. Independent clause.

וְגַנָּב. Subject of יָבוֹא.

יָבוֹא. Qal *yiqtol* 3ms √בוא. Because this is an indicative verb, the SV word order in this clause is expected. This verb usually takes an oblique complement; here it is implicit (see 4:15).

פָּשַׁט גְּדוּד בַּחוּץ. *Line 7:1f*. Independent clause.

פָּשַׁט. Qal *qatal* 3ms √פשט. The VS word order in this clause might suggest that this *qatal* verb is irrealis even though it does not begin with ו. However, the word order is inverted in order to create a chiastic (SV// VS) pattern with its parallel line (7:1e). This indicative *qatal* describes the present situation by means of a completed action, just as the *yiqtol* יָבוֹא in the previous line describes the current state of affairs via frequentative or habitual action. The verb √פשט refers to assaulting or stripping victims in war. It has a more violent, personal connotation than √בוא ("to enter" or in this context, "to break in") in the previous line.

גְּדוּד. Subject of פָּשַׁט. This word ("gang") was used in 6:9 in connection with חֶבֶר כֹּהֲנִים ("company of priests") to describe the lawless, murderous behavior of the priests between Shechem and Gilead.

בַּחוּץ. PP with בְּ describing where the gang has raided. The combination of בְּ, the article, and חוּץ ("street") is an idiom meaning "outside."

7:2 a וּבַל־יֹאמְרוּ לִלְבָבָם
b כָּל־רָעָתָם זָכָרְתִּי
c עַתָּה סְבָבוּם מַעַלְלֵיהֶם
d נֶגֶד פָּנַי הָיוּ׃

Lines a-b are a bicolon. Line a is an independent clause which introduces the embedded complement clause in line b. The lines are marked by *Zaqep parvum* and *'Atnaḥ*. Lines c-d are a bicolon as well. The verbs in both lines share the same subject (מַעַלְלֵיהֶם). The lines are marked with *Zaqep parvum* and *Silluq*.

וּבַל־יֹאמְרוּ לִלְבָבָם. *Line a*. Independent clause.

Hosea 7:2

וּבַל־יֹאמְרוּ. בַּל is a negative particle, used mostly in poetic texts. The verb יֹאמְרוּ is a Qal *yiqtol* 3mp √אמר.

לִלְבָבָם. PP with לְ. The common idiom of speaking בִּלְבָב (with בְּ) refers to speaking *in* one's heart or speaking to oneself. This is the only occurrence in the OT of לֵבָב with a לְ prep, but it must have similar sense as the collocation with בְּ. The antecedent of the 3mp suffix, as well as those in the rest of the verse, is the same as the subject of אמר: Israel, Ephraim, and Samaria (cf. 7:1) who have been led astray by the religious leadership.

כָּל־רָעָתָם זָכָרְתִּי. *Line b*. Unmarked complement clause which indicates the contents of Israel's thoughts in the previous line. Complement clauses are often introduced with כִּי, but they can be asyndetic, as this one is (cf. König 1897:§384g; WO §38.8d). Israel has been deceitful and manipulative in their worship of YHWH, and they think they have gotten away with it.

כָּל־רָעָתָם. Constr phrase and acc compl of זָכָרְתִּי. The noun רָעָה is a general term for evil, encompassing all of their various actions (see 7:1).

זָכָרְתִּי. Qal *qatal* 1cs √זכר.

עַתָּה סְבָבוּם מַעַלְלֵיהֶם. *Line c*. Independent clause.

עַתָּה. This temporal adverb introduces the conclusion of what has been said. The first bicolon in this verse states that they have not been honest with YHWH, but he is not deceived and knows their sins. This second bicolon concludes the unit by stating that their deeds have caught up with them and are obvious to YHWH.

סְבָבוּם. Qal *qatal* 3cp √סבב with a 3mp acc suffix.

מַעַלְלֵיהֶם. Subject of סְבָבוּם.

נֶגֶד פָּנַי הָיוּ. *Line d*. Independent clause.

נֶגֶד פָּנַי. PP with נֶגֶד indicating the location of their deeds. The idiom נֶגֶד פָּנֶה ("before the face of") can refer to physical presence (e.g., 1 Sam 26:20), but it also refers to awareness of something (Lam 3:35) or a particular perspective (Isa 5:21). The antecedent of the 1cs poss suffix on פָּנַי is YHWH.

הָיוּ. Qal *qatal* 3cp √היה. The subject of this verb is מַעַלְלֵיהֶם from the previous line.

Israel Is Like an Oven and a Cake (7:3-10)

In the previous subunits, Hosea addressed Israel's unfaithfulness in the religious sphere. Unorthodox worship and idolatry are obvious acts of infidelity: the people are going to other gods in an attempt to get what they need. In spite of YHWH's promises to provide for his people and richly bless them in the context of the covenant relationship, they believe that they can improve their situation by trusting in other deities. This amounts to spiritual adultery.

In the next two subunits, the prophet concentrates on a parallel betrayal. Though YHWH had promised to protect his people if they would trust him, the people of Israel instead place their confidence in political conspiracy and alliances. They are so determined to solve their problems without submitting to YHWH that they turn to foreign enemies for help and comfort. This betrayal takes a very different form than making a sacrifice to Ba'al, but the motivations are the same: self-reliance, autonomy, and a failure to trust YHWH's ability to save.

Hosea begins his attack on Israel's political machinations with related, vivid metaphors. He states that the political leadership, which may include priests (cf. 6:4–7:2) and nobility as well as the king and princes, are like an overheated oven operated by an incompetent baker. Neither of these conditions will create good food. Like a baker who fails to stir the fire or knead the dough (7:4), or an oven which is much too hot and burns its contents (7:6-7), this group produces a "cake" (i.e., Ephraim) that is ruined (7:8). The passage begins with attention to domestic politics: inflamed with sinful passions and the desire to murder, they conspire against their own rulers (7:7). Then, in a desperate attempt to recover, the political class in Ephraim entangles itself with foreign powers, but this will not help the situation either. Those foreign nations turn and "eat" Ephraim which is in a worse condition than before (7:9). Yet, Israel refuses to seek YHWH.

³With their evil they gladden a king;
and with their deceit—officials.

⁴All of them commit adultery;
they are like a burning oven.

A baker stops from stirring,
from kneading the dough until it is leavened.

⁵*By day they inflamed our king,*
officials with the heat of wine.
Its power drew in scoffers.

⁶*They readied their heart like the oven in their ambush.*
All night their baker is asleep;
in the morning it burns like a flame of fire.

⁷*All of them are hot like the oven,*
so they devour their judges.

All of their kings have fallen;
there is no one among them who calls to me.

⁸*Ephraim: with the nations he is mixed;*
Ephraim was a cake not turned.

⁹*Strangers devoured his strength,*
but he did not know;
also, gray hair crept up on him,
but he did not know.

¹⁰*"And the pride of Israel will testify against him,"*
but they did not return to YHWH their God,
and they did not seek him in all this.

7:3 a בְּרָעָתָם יְשַׂמְּחוּ־מֶלֶךְ
b וּבְכַחֲשֵׁיהֶם שָׂרִים׃

Lines a-b are a bicolon with symmetrical lines each containing PPs with בְּ and two word pairs (כַּחַשׁ/רָעָה and שַׂר/מֶלֶךְ). There is also ellipsis of the verb שׂמח in line b. The lines are marked by *'Atnaḥ* and *Silluq*.

בְּרָעָתָם יְשַׂמְּחוּ־מֶלֶךְ. *Line a.* Independent clause.

בְּרָעָתָם. PP with instrumental בְּ indicating the means by which they make the king glad. The PP is fronted in the clause for topicalization. It is *with their evil* that they make the king glad. The 3mp pronoun, and the plural verbs throughout this section, refer generally to the political class.

יְשַׂמְּחוּ. Piel *yiqtol* 3mp √שׂמח. In the Qal this root means "to be happy"; in the Piel it is factitive and means "to make someone happy." The meaning is somewhat obscure. Perhaps the evil of the priests or nobles is bringing joy to the king (which is a reflection of his bad character). Or, perhaps this is a reference to supplying the king with the means to become inebriated (cf. 7:5). The *yiqtol* denotes action that is frequent or customary.

מֶלֶךְ. Acc compl of יְשַׂמְּחוּ.

וּבְכַחֲשֵׁיהֶם שָׂרִים. *Line b*. Independent clause. The verb יְשַׂמְּחוּ is elided.

וּבְכַחֲשֵׁיהֶם. PP with instrumental בְּ indicating the means by which they make the princes glad. This is the only occurrence of the plural form of the noun כַּחַשׁ in the OT, though in other instances it appears to be a collective. The theme of "deceit" runs throughout the book of Hosea (cf. this root as a noun or verb in 4:2; 9:2; 10:13; 12:1). There is semantic intensification in the parallelism from רָעָה (general) to כַּחַשׁ (specific).

שָׂרִים. Acc compl of the elided verb יְשַׂמְּחוּ.

7:4 a כֻּלָּם מְנָאֲפִים
b כְּמוֹ תַנּוּר בֹּעֵרָה מִן (Word order ≠ MT)
c אֹפֶה יִשְׁבּוֹת מֵעִיר
d מִלּוּשׁ בָּצֵק עַד־חֻמְצָתוֹ׃

This verse is very difficult and possibly corrupt. It seems we must ignore some of the disjunctive accents as line markers (i.e., the *Zaqep parvum* on תַנּוּר in line b and the *'Atnaḥ* on מֵאֹפֶה in line c) in order to make sense of the poetic lines. Lines a-b are a bicolon that contains one clause; line b is an adjunct PP. The lines are marked by *Zaqep parvum* and *Ṭipḥa*. Lines c-d are a bicolon indicated by ellipsis of the verb יִשְׁבּוֹת and parallel PPs with מִן. The lines are marked by *Zaqep parvum* and *Silluq*.

כֻּלָּם מְנָאֲפִים. *Line a*. Independent verbless clause.

כֻּלָּם. Subject of the verbless clause. The 3mp pronoun refers to the political class, including the king and princes (7:3).

מְנָאֲפִים. Piel ptc mp √נאף used as the predicate of the verbless clause.

כְּמוֹ תַנּוּר בֹּעֵרָה. *Line b*. Independent verbless clause. An error in word division likely created two difficulties in this verse. First, the noun תַנּוּר ("oven") in this line is masculine and elsewhere always concords with masculine verbs (Lev 11:35; Mal 3:19) and numerals (Lev 26:26). Yet here the participle בֹּעֵרָה is feminine. Second, the word for "baker" at the beginning of line c is the participle אֹפֶה, but the sense of the מִן

prep is obscure. However, both problems are solved if the ה at the end of בֹּעֵרָה (line b) and the מ at the beginning of מֵאֹפֶה (line c) form the independent 3mp pronoun הֵם, which belongs at the end of line b as the subject of the verbless clause. Line b then reads: כְּמוֹ תַנּוּר בֹּעֵר הֵם ("Like a burning oven are they"). And line d reads אֹפֶה יִשְׁבּוֹת מֵעִיר ("a baker stops from stirring").

כְּמוֹ תַנּוּר. PP with כְּמוֹ, a pleonastic form of כְּ normally used with suffixes (cf. BDB 455). Here it indicates agreement in kind and introduces a simile. Their adulterous and debaucherous passions are likened to the heat produced by an oven.

בֹּעֵרָה. As emended to בֹּעֵר (see above), this is a Qal ptc ms √בער. It is used like an attributive adjective to modify תַנּוּר (cf. WO §37.4b).

מֵאֹפֶה יִשְׁבּוֹת מֵעִיר. *Line c.* Independent clause.

מֵאֹפֶה. As emended to אֹפֶה (see above), this is a Qal ptc ms √אפה. It is a *nomen agentis* ("baker"), serving as the subject of יִשְׁבּוֹת (cf. WO §37.2). While the תַנּוּר ("oven") is explicitly a simile (כְּמוֹ), the baker is not. However, there is no article here, suggesting that a specific baker is not in view.

יִשְׁבּוֹת. Qal *yiqtol* 3ms √שבת. The ו in the theme vowel is a *plene* spelling.

מֵעִיר. Hiph ptc ms √עור. This participle is an adjunct indicating what the baker has ceased (יִשְׁבּוֹת) to do. A more common construction is שבת + מִן + infinitive (see line d), which is an idiom meaning "to stop doing something" (cf. Jer 31:36; Ezek 34:10). This construction with a participle and no preposition is the only instance in the Hebrew Bible, but it has essentially the same meaning. The verb √עור, in both the Qal and Hiphil, can mean "to stir" or "to be awake, alert" (cf. HALOT 802–3).

מִלּוּשׁ בָּצֵק. *Line d.* Independent clause. The verb יִשְׁבּוֹת is elided.

מִלּוּשׁ. Adjunct PP with מִן indicating what has ceased (√שבת). The complement of the preposition is a Qal inf constr √לוש ("to knead").

בָּצֵק. Acc compl of לוש (cf. Jer 7:18).

עַד־חֻמְצָתוֹ. *Line d.* Subordinate temporal clause. The prep עַד introduces a temporal clause referring to a later situation than the main clause (cf. WO §38.7a). חֻמְצָתוֹ is a Qal inf constr √חמץ with a 3ms suffix. The suffix is the subject of the infinitive and its antecedent is בָּצֵק ("dough").

7:5 a יוֹם מַלְכֵּנוּ הֶחֱלוּ
b שָׂרִים חֲמַת מִיָּיִן
c מָשַׁךְ יָדוֹ אֶת־לֹצְצִים׃

Lines a-c are a tricolon. The first two lines are connected via ellipsis of the transitive verb הֶחֱלוּ in line b as well as the word pair שָׂרִים//מֶלֶךְ. This analysis is supported by the similarity with 7:3, which also features מֶלֶךְ and שָׂרִים in parallel lines with an elided verb (AF 458). Line c contains a 3ms verb and 3ms pronoun (יָדוֹ) referring to מַלְכֵּנוּ in line a. Admittedly, on this reading the first line ends with a conjunctive accent *Mereka* (הֶחֱלוּ) rather than the *Zaqep parvum* (מַלְכֵּנוּ). Lines b and c are marked by *'Atnaḥ* and *Silluq* respectively.

יוֹם מַלְכֵּנוּ הֶחֱלוּ. *Line a*. Independent clause.

יוֹם. There may be an implied or missing prep בְּ here ("on the day …"). It seems that here יוֹם refers to a general time and has an adverbial sense similar to the form יוֹמָם ("by day"). It is followed by a reference to night (לַיְלָה) and morning (בֹּקֶר, also without a prep) in the next verse.

מַלְכֵּנוּ. Acc compl of הֶחֱלוּ. The antecedent of the 1cp suffix is the northern kingdom, which includes Hosea the speaker.

הֶחֱלוּ. Hiph *qatal* 3cp √חלה. Some commentators (e.g., Stuart 1987:116; Macintosh 2014:259) and reference grammars (GKC §53d; WO §28.2d) argue that this is an internal or intransitive Hiphil ("they became sick"). However, the verb √חלה occurs three other times, all of which are unambiguously transitive (Prov 13:12; Isa 53:10; Mic 6:13). If my analysis of the parallelism (and the analogy with 7:3) is correct, then this verb must be transitive as well since the singular מַלְכֵּנוּ could not be its subject. Rather, the subject is apparently the leadership of the northern kingdom and the nobility. Just as they "gladdened" the king in 7:3, here they inflame him with wine.

שָׂרִים חֲמַת מִיָּיִן. *Line b*. Independent clause. The verb הֶחֱלוּ is elided.

שָׂרִים. Acc compl of the elided verb הֶחֱלוּ.

חֲמַת מִיָּיִן. PP with an implied preposition describing the means by which they "inflamed" the officials. In 7:4 the imagery of "heat" came from an oven; here it (חֵמָה) is the inebriating effect of the wine. Just as the verb הֶחֱלוּ is elided in line b, this implied PP explains the instrument for line a. For the מִן prep in the midst of a construct phrase, see GKC §130a; JM §129n.

מָשַׁךְ יָדוֹ אֶת־לֹצְצִים. *Line c.* Independent clause.

מָשַׁךְ. Qal *qatal* 3ms √משׁך. Despite many translations which render this verb "stretch out" (cf. KJV, NIV, ESV, NRSV), it actually means the opposite. It is used of drawing in, or dragging, or drawing up. It refers to the action of bringing something toward the subject. Therefore, rather than taking יָדוֹ as the accusative and אֶת־לֹצְצִים as a PP (i.e., "he stretched out his hand with mockers"), the semantics of the verb require that יָדוֹ is the subject (referring to the wine in the previous line) and אֶת־לֹצְצִים is the accusative ("its power drew in scoffers") (cf. Wolff 1974:107).

יָדוֹ. Subject of מָשַׁךְ with a 3ms poss suffix. The antecedent of the suffix is יַיִן in line b. The noun יָד usually means "hand" but it can, by metonymy, also mean "power." Here it is the power of the wine which attracts scoffers. The overall picture is one of debauchery.

אֶת־לֹצְצִים. Polel ptc mp √ליץ. Acc compl of מָשַׁךְ. The one who "scoffs" is the antithesis of the wise (Prov 9:12) or upright (Prov 14:9). The noun לֵץ ("scoffer") is closely related.

7:6 a כִּי־קֵרְבוּ כַתַּנּוּר לִבָּם בְּאָרְבָּם
b כָּל־הַלַּיְלָה יָשֵׁן אֹפֵהֶם
c בֹּקֶר הוּא בֹעֵר כְּאֵשׁ לֶהָבָה׃

Lines a-c are a tricolon. Lines a and c are grammatically parallel with the noun תַּנּוּר (line a) corresponding to the independent pronoun הוּא (line c). The lines are marked by *'Atnaḥ*, *Zaqep parvum*, and *Silluq*.

כִּי־קֵרְבוּ כַתַּנּוּר לִבָּם בְּאָרְבָּם. *Line a.* Independent clause with an asseverative כִּי. Alternatively, it could introduce a temporal clause contemporary with that of the following main clause (cf. WO §38.7a).

קֵרְבוּ. Piel *qatal* 3cp √קרב. While the Qal of √קרב is intransitive, the Piel is transitive in six out of the seven other occurrences in the OT (the exception is Ezek 36:8). Here, the accusative complement is לִבָּם ("their heart") following the PP which is inserted between the verb and accusative (Hosea uses similar constructions in 4:12 and 6:9). In this context √קרב must have the nuance of "to make ready" or "to prepare" because it is compared to an oven which dies down and then is stoked again. In addition, it describes the preparations for an ambush (אָרַב). The sense is that they are "stoking" their hearts or intentions in preparation for the murder they are about to commit. The subject of the verb is the political leadership who are engaged in debauchery.

כְתַנּוּר. PP with כְּ indicating agreement in kind. This is the second occurrence of the imagery of the תַנּוּר (cf. 7:4), which has the underlying metaphor: sin is heat.

לִבָּם. Acc compl of קֵרְבוּ. The antecedent of the 3mp poss suffix is the political leadership.

בְּאָרְבָּם. PP with בְּ of specification indicating the realm in which their heart is like an oven. The "ambush" referred to by אָרַב describes conspiracies and schemes in the court (see 7:7). The antecedent of the 3mp poss suffix continues to be the nobility and ruling class.

כָּל־הַלַּיְלָה יָשֵׁן אֹפֵהֶם. *Line b*. Independent verbless clause.

כָּל־הַלַּיְלָה. This adverbial phrase specifies when the baker is asleep (cf. יוֹם in 7:5a; בֹּקֶר in 7:6c).

יָשֵׁן. Predicate adjective (cf. WO §14.3.2) meaning "asleep" (HALOT 448).

אֹפֵהֶם. Subject of the verbless clause. A number of commentators, following S and T, revocalize this word to אַפֵּהֶם or אַפֵּהֶם (a dual form) meaning, "their anger" with a 3mp poss suffix. This is then taken as the antecedent of the pronoun הוּא in the next line. In other words, their anger sleeps at night but is then rekindled in the morning. However, the vocalization in the MT which reads "baker" makes better sense as that is one of the images in a context which concerns conspiracy and assassination. The suffix makes the noun look plural when it is in fact singular (cf. JM §95e). The sense is that the baker sleeps at night, but in the morning the oven is stoked, and it becomes hot once more (see Macintosh 2014:262–64). Thus the metaphors of the baker and the oven are (naturally) combined in order to present the "flames" of their depravity as constantly renewed.

בֹּקֶר הוּא בֹעֵר כְּאֵשׁ לֶהָבָה. *Line c*. Independent clause.

בֹּקֶר. Adverbial phrase specifying the time of the action (cf. יוֹם in 7:5a).

הוּא. Subject of בֹעֵר. The antecedent is תַנּוּר ("oven") in line a. It cannot be אֹפֵהֶם ("their baker"; line b) who burns, so this pronoun resumes the imagery of the oven (line a).

בֹּעֵר. Qal ptc ms √בער. The participle has a progressive aspect; the action is ongoing and the subject is in the midst of the activity.

כְּאֵשׁ לֶהָבָה. PP with כְּ indicating agreement in kind. The construct phrase אֵשׁ לֶהָבָה is an adjectival genitive (cf. WO §9.5.3a). The literal translation "fire of flame" means "flaming fire" (cf. Isa 4:5; Lam 2:3).

7:7 a כֻּלָּם יֵחַמּוּ כַּתַּנּוּר
b וְאָכְלוּ אֶת־שֹׁפְטֵיהֶם
c כָּל־מַלְכֵיהֶם נָפָלוּ
d אֵין־קֹרֵא בָהֶם אֵלָי:

Lines a-b are a bicolon with lines marked by *Zaqep parvum* and *'Atnaḥ*. Lines c-d are also a bicolon with lines marked by *Zaqep parvum* and *Silluq*.

כֻּלָּם יֵחַמּוּ כַּתַּנּוּר. *Line a*. Independent clause.

כֻּלָּם. Subject of יֵחַמּוּ. The 3mp suffix continues the reference to the nobility and ruling class.

יֵחַמּוּ. Qal *yiqtol* 3mp √חמם. This Qal of √חמם is intransitive and refers to becoming "warm" or "hot" like an oven. This continues the metaphor sin is heat in the context.

כַּתַּנּוּר. Adjunct PP with כְּ indicating agreement in kind. This is the third and final instance of תַּנּוּר in the book. Once the image is introduced without the article in 7:4, it occurs with the article in 7:6 and 7:7 because there is now a particular (metaphorical) oven in view.

וְאָכְלוּ אֶת־שֹׁפְטֵיהֶם. *Line b*. Independent clause.

וְאָכְלוּ. Qal *qatal* (irrealis) 3cp √אכל. The irrealis *qatal* here expresses an action which is the temporal or logical consequence of the *yiqtol* יֵחַמּוּ in line a (cf. WO §32.2.1c). The clause is syntactically coordinate but semantically subordinate. The sense is that once they are all "heated up" and ready for sin (cf. 7:6), they will "devour" their judges. The verb √אכל in this context means "to destroy" or "to assassinate." This is supported by the next line, "all of their kings have fallen."

אֶת־שֹׁפְטֵיהֶם. Acc compl of וְאָכְלוּ. The noun שֹׁפֵט not only refers to officials in legal contexts but also to rulers and administrators in a general sense (see the analogous use of the verb √שפט in 1 Sam 8:5-6 and Prov 29:14).

כָּל־מַלְכֵיהֶם נָפָלוּ. *Line c*. Independent clause.

כָּל־מַלְכֵיהֶם. Subject of נָפָלוּ.

נָפָלוּ. Qal *qatal* 3cp √נפל. This verb is commonly used to refer to dying (cf. Judg 8:10). This may be an abbreviated form of the expression נפל בַּחֶרֶב ("fall by the sword") (cf. 7:16).

אֵין־קֹרֵא בָהֶם אֵלָי. *Line d*. Independent verbless clause.

אֵין־קֹרֵא. The particle אֵין indicates nonexistence. The substantive is a Qal ptc ms √קרא.

בָהֶם. PP with בְּ indicating a location amid a domain ("among them") (cf. WO §11.2.5b). This phrase interrupts the usual juxtaposition of √קרא and the addressee indicated by אֶל and draws attention to it. Perhaps elsewhere there are those who call upon YHWH, but there is no one *among them*. Once again, the antecedent is the leadership in the northern kingdom who, by their rebellion against YHWH, are ruining the nation.

אֵלָי. PP with אֶל indicating the addressee of קרא. The antecedent of the 1cs suffix is YHWH, the speaker.

7:8 a אֶפְרַיִם בָּעַמִּים הוּא יִתְבּוֹלָל
b אֶפְרַיִם הָיָה עֻגָה בְּלִי הֲפוּכָה׃

Lines a-b are a bicolon linked by the repetition of אֶפְרַיִם. The lines are marked by *'Atnaḥ* and *Silluq*.

אֶפְרַיִם בָּעַמִּים הוּא יִתְבּוֹלָל. *Line a*. Independent clause.

אֶפְרַיִם. A *casus pendens*: a noun or pronoun that is "often placed at the head of a clause in such a way as to stand aloof from what follows, and then *resumed* by means of a retrospective pronoun" (JM §156a). Here, it signals a transition from a general description of Israel's administration and ruling class to that of Ephraim specifically. Note that third-person plural forms (7:3–7) are now replaced by third-person singular forms that refer to Ephraim.

בָּעַמִּים. PP with בְּ indicating a location among a domain ("among the peoples"). The "peoples" refer to the surrounding foreign nations to which Ephraim went for help instead of trusting YHWH.

הוּא. Retrospective pronoun which refers back to the *casus pendens* אֶפְרַיִם and functions as the explicit subject of יִתְבּוֹלָל.

יִתְבּוֹלָל. Hithpoʻel *yiqtol* 3ms √בלל. All other occurrences of this verb (42×) in the OT are transitive and occur in the Qal, meaning "to mix" (Gen 11:7, 9), or in ritual texts, "to add oil to an offering" (e.g., Lev 2:4), thus mixing oil with grain. This is the only occurrence in the Hithpoʻel. If the instance here means "to mix" as well, then the Hithpoʻel is reflexive and refers to Ephraim mixing himself up with the nations in alliances and political schemes, just as oil is mixed with flour. This would make sense in light of the imagery of baking a cake (see line b).

אֶפְרַיִם הָיָה עֻגָה בְּלִי הֲפוּכָה. *Line b*. Independent clause.

אֶפְרַיִם. Subject of הָיָה.

הָיָה. Qal *qatal* 3ms √היה.

עֻגָה. Compl of √היה. An עֻגָה is a cake of bread made of flour (e.g., Gen 18:6) or barley (Ezek 4:12) and baked.

בְּלִי הֲפוּכָה. The word הֲפוּכָה is a Qal pass ptc fs √הפך. It functions in this clause as an attributive adjective modifying the feminine noun עֻגָה. Here it is negated by בְּלִי, an uncommon negative particle primarily used in poetry (JM §160m). Ephraim is a cake *not* turned. In other words, rather than baking evenly, it burns on one side and is raw on the other. The metaphor depicts an incompetent baker and an overheated oven, which have together ruined the cake. In the same way, the overheated passions, conspiracies, murder, and general debauchery of the leadership in the northern kingdom have ruined Ephraim.

7:9 a אָכְלוּ זָרִים כֹּחוֹ
b וְהוּא לֹא יָדָע
c גַּם־שֵׂיבָה זָרְקָה בּוֹ
d וְהוּא לֹא יָדָע׃

Lines a-b are a quatrain. The first and third line describe damage done to Ephraim, while the second and fourth lines repeat the statement "but he did not know." The lines are marked by *Zaqep parvum*, *ʾAtnaḥ*, *Zaqep parvum*, and *Silluq*.

אָכְלוּ זָרִים כֹּחוֹ. *Line a*. Independent clause.

אָכְלוּ. Qal *qatal* 3cp √אכל.

זָרִים. Subject of אָכְלוּ. These "strangers" refer to foreign nations which have devoured Ephraim as a result of its weakened status and attempted political schemes.

כֹּחוֹ. Acc compl of אָכְלוּ. The noun כֹּחַ usually refers to "strength" or "power" in terms of capability or might, but in some contexts it refers to "wealth" (e.g., Job 6:22; Prov 5:10) or the "produce" of the land (Job 31:39). There is likely a play on words here. The foreign nations are devouring Ephraim's wealth or produce. But Ephraim is also pictured as an old man (see line c) losing his strength.

וְהוּא לֹא יָדָע. *Line b*. Independent clause.

וְהוּא. Subject of יָדָע. The antecedent is Ephraim (cf. 7:8).

יָדָע. Qal *qatal* 3ms √ידע. What Israel does *not* know is a theme that runs throughout the book. In 2:10 Israel does not know that YHWH had given her the grain, wine, and oil. In 5:4 they do not know YHWH himself. In this verse Ephraim does not know that foreign nations had taken these things away. In 11:3 YHWH's people do not know that he had healed them. Finally, in 13:4 they do not know any god but YHWH, a beautiful statement of renewal and redemption.

גַּם־שֵׂיבָה זָרְקָה בּוֹ. *Line c*. Independent clause.

גַּם. This conjunction associates this clause with the previous one and emphasizes an additional element. Not only is Ephraim's strength being devoured by strangers, he is *also* becoming feeble and weak, like an old man.

שֵׂיבָה. Subject of זָרְקָה. The noun refers to grey hair (e.g., Gen 42:38) or, by metonymy, to old age (Ps 71:18; Isa 46:4). In most occurrences it is used in the context of the age of one's death (though that is often honorable). Here it is parallel with line a and refers to feebleness.

זָרְקָה בּוֹ. Qal *qatal* 3fs √זרק. This verb occurs thirty-five times in the OT, and twenty-nine of those are in cultic contexts where it refers to throwing blood or water (e.g., Lev 8:19). It is transitive (except for a few passive forms; cf. Num 19:13, 20), taking a complement which indicates the item thrown and usually an adjunct PP with עַל specifying against what it is thrown. The occurrence here may be an exceptional use as an intransitive Qal with a unique prep בְּ. If so, the subject is שֵׂיבָה and it means, "grey hair sprinkled on him." Perhaps a better approach is that this is a different root √זרק that occurs only here in the OT. Blau

(1955:341) argues that on the basis of a cognate root *zrq* in Arabic it means "to creep secretly" so that the translation is, "old age crept up on him" (cf. Rudolph 1966:151). In either case the image is one of old age and death coming upon Ephraim slowly and inexorably, even as he struggles to ward it off through political strategies.

וְהוּא לֹא יָדָע. *Line d*. Independent clause.

וְהוּא. Subject of יָדָע. The antecedent is Ephraim (cf. 7:8).

יָדָע. Qal *qatal* 3ms √ידע.

7:10 a וְעָנָה גְאוֹן־יִשְׂרָאֵל בְּפָנָיו
b וְלֹא־שָׁבוּ אֶל־יְהוָה אֱלֹהֵיהֶם
c וְלֹא בִקְשֻׁהוּ בְּכָל־זֹאת:

Lines a-c are a tricolon. The second and third lines are parallel, exhibiting noun//pronoun grammatical parallelism (הוּ/יְהוָה) and the word pair בקש√//שׁוּב√. The lines are marked by *'Atnaḥ*, *Zaqep parvum*, and *Silluq*.

וְעָנָה גְאוֹן־יִשְׂרָאֵל בְּפָנָיו. *Line a*. Independent clause. This line is identical to 5:5a.

וְעָנָה. Qal *qatal* (irrealis) 3ms √ענה. The collocation ענה√ + בְּ has a legal sense of "testifying against." The irrealis *qatal* here describes future, potential action. In 5:5a, where this line appears verbatim, the reference to Israel and Judah's future demise continues in the following lines, which contain *yiqtol* verbs. In this verse, however, this line does not correspond well with the context because 7:10b and c contain indicative *qatal* verbs, suggesting completed action probably in the past. For this reason BHS note ᵃ suggests that either the line or the entire verse was added later. A better explanation is that the repetition and the discontinuity is intentional, signaling an intertextual allusion to 5:5. The point is this: in the same way that 5:5 speaks of the destruction of the nation because of the *cultic* sins of Israel's leadership, this verse (and context) speaks of the destruction of the nation because of their *political* sins.

גְאוֹן־יִשְׂרָאֵל. Constr phrase. גְאוֹן is the subject of וְעָנָה.

בְּפָנָיו. The verb ענה√ does not require a complement. This PP is an adjunct specifying the recipient of the testimony. The antecedent of the 3ms suffix is the previous word יִשְׂרָאֵל. Israel is incriminating itself.

וְלֹא־שָׁבוּ אֶל־יְהוָה אֱלֹהֵיהֶם. *Line b.* Independent clause.

שָׁבוּ. Qal *qatal* 3cp √שׁוב. The references to Ephraim have been singular (7:8-9), but now in this verse that concludes the unit, the people of YHWH are referred to in the plural.

אֶל־יְהוָה אֱלֹהֵיהֶם. This PP is the complement of שָׁבוּ with אֶל indicating the person (here, YHWH) to whom they will (not) return. The antecedent of the 3mp poss suffix is יִשְׂרָאֵל in the previous line.

וְלֹא בִקְשֻׁהוּ בְּכָל־זֹאת. *Line c.* Independent clause.

בִקְשֻׁהוּ. Piel *qatal* 3cp √בקש with a 3ms acc suffix. The antecedent of the 3ms suffix is YHWH in line b.

בְּכָל־זֹאת. PP with בְּ of specification indicating the realm of the verbal action. The demonstrative זֹאת is used generally to refer to the preceding context. According to JM, the neuter (or unspecified) gender is expressed by the feminine (cf. §152a). Although Ephraim's rebellion has led to his being like a spoiled cake (7:8) or an old, weak body with no strength (7:9), he will not seek YHWH.

Israel Is Like a Dove and a Bow (7:11-16)

In the previous section, Hosea compared Israel to an overheated oven and a ruined cake. Now, he uses two new images. First, they are like a fickle, wandering dove that flits from place to place without any sense or intentionality (v. 11). YHWH's response is fitting: he will trap them like birds (v. 12). The second image is that of a slack bow, unable to hit its target (v. 16b). In this case Israel does not *want* to aim at the right thing. Though YHWH would help them if asked (vv. 13c-15b), they are determined to seek help from anyone except him. This weapon imagery also has a fitting end: their leaders will be killed (v. 16c). The passage comes full circle with a second mention of Egypt. Like a dove, Israel had turned from Egypt and trusted in Assyria (v. 11). Now when Assyria turns on Israel, Egypt will mock them (v. 16d).

> *11 And Ephraim was like a dove—*
> *simple; without sense.*
> *To Egypt they called;*
> *to Assyria they went.*
>
> *12 As they go,*
> *I will spread out my net upon them.*

Like the birds of the sky I will bring them down;
I will chastise them according to the report of their meetings.

¹³Woe to them for they have wandered from me.
Destruction is theirs for they have transgressed against me.

And I would redeem them,
but they have spoken lies against me.

¹⁴And they did not cry out to me in their hearts,
but they lament on their beds.

Over grain and wine they cut themselves;
they rebel against me.

¹⁵And I taught—
I strengthened their arms,
but they plot evil against me.

¹⁶They return to "Not-above";
they have become like a slack bow.

Their princes will fall by the sword because of the rage at their tongue.
This is their mocking in the land of Egypt.

7:11 a וַיְהִ֣י אֶפְרַ֔יִם כְּיוֹנָ֖ה
b פוֹתָ֣ה אֵ֣ין לֵ֑ב
c מִצְרַ֣יִם קָרָ֔אוּ
d אַשּׁ֖וּר הָלָֽכוּ׃

Lines a-b are a bicolon. Line b contains a participle and a verbless clause in apposition to יוֹנָה in line a. The lines are marked by *Merᵉka* and *'Atnaḥ*. Lines c-d are a bicolon as well, with two word pairs קרא√/הלך√ and אַשּׁוּר/מִצְרַיִם describing where Ephraim went for help. The lines are marked by *Ṭipḥa*, and *Silluq*.

וַיְהִ֣י אֶפְרַ֔יִם כְּיוֹנָ֖ה. *Line a.* Independent clause.

וַיְהִי. Qal *wayyiqtol* 3ms √היה. The *wayyiqtol* of this verb is frequently used to introduce a new narrative unit and/or to set the scene. Although this is not narrative literature, it serves the same purpose here. YHWH is rehearsing Ephraim's past actions of unfaithfulness. The verb √היה takes a nominative or an oblique complement, here supplied by the PP כְּיוֹנָה.

אֶפְרַיִם. Subject of וַיְהִי.

כְיוֹנָה. This PP with כְּ indicating agreement in kind is the complement of וַיְהִי. Hosea also refers to a יוֹנָה ("dove") in 11:11. It was a common bird in Israel, associated with flying here and there (cf. Gen 8:9; Ps 55:7).

פּוֹתָה אֵין לֵב. *Line b.* This is a continuation of the clause in line a.

פּוֹתָה. Qal ptc fs √פתה. This participle is in apposition to the fs noun יוֹנָה. This analysis is based on the poetic structure, although it could also be functioning like an attributive adjective ("a simple dove"). In the Qal, √פתה means "to be simple" or "gullible" (HALOT 984). In Deut 11:6 a heart that is √פתה is deceived and can be turned to other gods. In Job 5:2 the simpleton (פֹּתֶה) is compared to a fool (אֱוִיל). Here, the יוֹנָה is simple because it does not given any thought to where it is going. It only flies from place to place.

אֵין לֵב. The negative אֵין followed by the noun לֵב forms a phrase that is in apposition to יוֹנָה in line a (cf. JM §160o; GKC §152u). The negative has the sense of "without," and לֵב refers to "sense" or the ability to discern.

מִצְרַיִם קָרָאוּ. *Line c.* Independent clause.

מִצְרַיִם. This PP with implied לְ or אֶל indicating the recipient of Ephraim's call is the complement of קָרָאוּ. Hosea refers to Egypt in three different times relative to his own. In 2:17, 11:1, 12:10, 14, and 13:4, it is a past reference—a historical allusion to YHWH's deliverance from captivity. Here and in 12:2, it is a present reference to the contemporary nation to which Ephraim appeals for help in a time of trouble. It is a symbol of future captivity and oppression in 7:16, 8:13, 9:3, 6, 11:5, and 11:11.

קָרָאוּ. Qal *qatal* 3cp √קרא. The idea is that of summoning Egypt and requesting assistance. The plural subject refers to Ephraim. Hosea again shows some inconsistency in number; in 7:8-9 he used the singular to refer to Ephraim.

אַשּׁוּר הָלָכוּ. *Line d.* Independent clause.

אַשּׁוּר. Adjunct PP with implied אֶל indicating the goal of Ephraim's travel.

הָלָכוּ. Qal *qatal* 3cp √הלך. There is semantic intensification of the corresponding words in lines c and d: from מִצְרַיִם to אַשּׁוּר (a more dangerous nation) and from √קרא (call to a nation for help) to √הלך (travel to a nation for help).

7:12 a כַּאֲשֶׁר יֵלֵכוּ
b אֶפְרוֹשׂ עֲלֵיהֶם רִשְׁתִּי
c כְּעוֹף הַשָּׁמַיִם אוֹרִידֵם
d אַיְסִרֵם כְּשֵׁמַע לַעֲדָתָם׃ ס

Lines a-b are a bicolon consisting of a subordinate clause (line a) and the main clause (line b). The lines are marked by *R^ebiaʿ* and *Zaqep parvum*. Lines c and d are a bicolon featuring the corresponding expressions אוֹרִידֵם ("I will bring them down")//אַיְסִרֵם ("I will discipline them"). The lines are marked by *'Atnaḥ* and *Silluq*.

כַּאֲשֶׁר יֵלֵכוּ. *Line a.* Subordinate temporal clause. The כְּ prep indicates an action contemporary to that of the main clause in line b; The word אֲשֶׁר is a nominalizer and the אֲשֶׁר clause is the complement of the preposition (Holmstedt 2016:119, 124).

יֵלֵכוּ. Qal *yiqtol* 3mp √הלך.

אֶפְרוֹשׂ עֲלֵיהֶם רִשְׁתִּי. *Line b.* Independent clause.

אֶפְרוֹשׂ. Qal *yiqtol* 1cs √פרשׂ. This is the usual verb associated with spreading out a net as a trap (9× in the OT; cf. Hos 5:1). The verb √פרשׂ takes an accusative complement specifying what is spread (i.e., a net, wings, a cloth, etc.) and *usually* has an adjunct PP indicating where it is spread.

עֲלֵיהֶם. Adjunct PP with עַל indicating the location where YHWH will spread his net. The antecedent of the 3mp suffix is Ephraim (cf. 7:11).

רִשְׁתִּי. Acc compl of אֶפְרוֹשׂ. This image of a net as a trap for birds follows and continues the image of Ephraim as a simple dove (7:11). The antecedent of the 1cs poss suffix is YHWH, the speaker.

כְּעוֹף הַשָּׁמַיִם אוֹרִידֵם. *Line c.* Independent clause.

כְּעוֹף הַשָּׁמַיִם. Adjunct PP with כְּ indicating agreement in kind. Ephraim is again compared to birds. In 7:11 it was the haphazard, apparently unintentional flight of a dove, going here and there. In this verse the simile refers to the vulnerability of birds to being trapped and destroyed. Because the genitive (הַשָּׁמַיִם) of the construct phrase is definite, עוֹף must be definite as well. Therefore, it is best understood as a collective: "the birds of the sky."

אוֹרִידֵם. Hiph *yiqtol* 1cs √ירד with a 3mp acc suffix. The antecedent of the 3mp suffix is Ephraim.

אֲיַסְרֵם כְּשֵׁמַע לַעֲדָתָם. *Line d*. Independent clause.

אֲיַסְרֵם. As vocalized in the MT, this verb is a Hiph *yiqtol* 1cs √יסר with a 3mp acc suffix. However, √יסר does not occur in the Hiphil elsewhere, but the Piel ("to chastise") is common. Two other factors weigh against a Hiphil here. First, we would expect a י vowel letter representing the theme vowel, but the spelling is defective (cf. AF 471). Second, in the Hiphil we would expect the י of the first root letter to contract with the a-vowel under the א prefix to ֵ (*tsere*) but it has not done so (cf. GKC §24f, n. 3). Therefore, it is plausible that the word has been incorrectly vocalized as a Hiphil, perhaps under the influence of the Hiphil verb אוֹרִידֵם in the previous line. We should vocalize this verb as אֲיַסְּרֵם, a Piel *yiqtol* 1cs with a 3mp acc suffix.

כְּשֵׁמַע. PP with כְּ indicating agreement in manner. YHWH's discipline (אֲיַסְרֵם) will be commensurate with the report that he hears of Ephraim's scheming.

לַעֲדָתָם. PP with a poss לְ. There have been a number of suggestions to make sense of this phrase. G translates τῆς θλίψεως αὐτῶν ("of their tribulation"), which may represent לְרָעָתָם (metathesis and a ר/ד change) meaning "their evil" (cf. Wolff 1974:107; Stuart 1987:116; BHS note ᵇ). A better explanation is that of Macintosh (2014:276), who suggests that because MT's עֵדָה ("their congregation," from √יעד) refers to a company assembled together by appointment (cf. BDB 417), it is a reference to diplomatic meetings between the Ephraimites and the Egyptians and Assyrians. Therefore, YHWH is saying that when he hears the report that they have met with foreign nations to secure an alliance, he will chastise them accordingly.

7:13 a אוֹי לָהֶם כִּי־נָדְדוּ מִמֶּנִּי
b שֹׁד לָהֶם כִּי־פָשְׁעוּ בִי
c וְאָנֹכִי אֶפְדֵּם
d וְהֵמָּה דִּבְּרוּ עָלַי כְּזָבִים׃

Lines a-b are a bicolon in which both lines contain the same pattern (PP + causal clause + 3cp *qatal* + 1cs suffix). The lines are marked by *Zaqep parvum* and *'Atnaḥ*. Lines c-d are also a bicolon, with lines marked by *Zaqep parvum* and *Silluq*.

אוֹי לָהֶם. *Line a*. Independent verbless clause.

אוֹי. An interjection, common in prophetic literature when the prophet uses this "impassioned expression of grief and despair" (BDB 17) to announce doom and judgment. In Hosea, it is not common, occurring elsewhere only in 9:12.

לָהֶם. This PP with לְ of interest or (dis)advantage is the predicate of the verbless clause. It specifies that the אוֹי ("woe") is directed at Ephraim, the antecedent of the 3mp suffix.

כִּי־נָדְדוּ מִמֶּנִּי. *Line a*. Subordinate causal clause with כִּי giving the reason that woe is upon Ephraim.

נָדְדוּ. Qal *qatal* 3cp √נדד. Hosea continues the metaphor of Ephraim as a wandering bird with the verb √נדד, which is used elsewhere to describe birds that stray from their nest (Prov 27:8) or flee in time of trouble (Jer 4:25).

מִמֶּנִּי. PP with a locational abl מִן. Ephraim has fled *away from* YHWH, the antecedent of the 1cs suffix.

שֹׁד לָהֶם. *Line b*. Independent verbless clause.

שֹׁד. Subject of the verbless clause. This noun, which refers to destruction, represents an amplification in the parallelism. In line a, the prophet announces unspecified אוֹי ("woe"), but in line b that woe is identified as שֹׁד.

לָהֶם. The predicate of the verbless clause is a PP with לְ of interest or (dis)advantage (cf. line a). The destruction is intended for Ephraim, the antecedent of the 3mp suffix.

כִּי־פָשְׁעוּ בִי. *Line b*. Subordinate causal clause with כִּי giving the reason that destruction is intended for Ephraim.

פָשְׁעוּ. Qal *qatal* 3cp √פשע. The verb √פשע is a common term for "sin," but it has the specific nuance of a willful violation by an inferior against a superior (NIDOTTE 3:706). It refers to brazen rebellion against YHWH's will. Thus, this term represents intensification in the parallelism. The corresponding term √נדד in line a refers to abandoning YHWH, but √פשע is a stronger, active defiance.

בִֽי. Oblique compl of פָּשְׁעוּ. The verb √פשע can occur in an absolute sense "to behave as a criminal" (HALOT 981), but with the sense "rebel against," it takes a complement with either a בְּ or עַל prep. The antecedent of the 1cs suffix is YHWH.

וְאָנֹכִי אֶפְדֵּם. *Line c*. Independent clause.

וְאָנֹכִי. This pleonastic 1cs pronoun refers to YHWH, the speaker. It is fronted for focus and highlights the contrast between YHWH's actions (אָנֹכִי; here) and Ephraim's actions (הֵמָּה; line d). Ironically, YHWH stands ready to deliver Ephraim from his troubles, even as he goes everywhere else to look for help! Yet, Ephraim responds by insulting YHWH with lies and deceit.

אֶפְדֵּם. Qal *yiqtol* (irrealis) 1cs √פדה with a 3mp acc suffix. The verb √פדה refers to buying back or rescuing someone who is designated for something, trapped in slavery, or experiencing oppression. Here, the *yiqtol* indicates contingent modality: YHWH says, "I *would* redeem them." We would expect an irreal use of the *yiqtol* to trigger VS word order (cf. Cook 2012:244), yet here the verb is preceded by the pleonastic pronoun אָנֹכִי. The context requires that this verb be understood as irreal; therefore the pronoun is fronted for pragmatic reasons. The possibility of YHWH's redeeming Israel is prevented by the contrast in line d.

וְהֵמָּה דִּבְּרוּ עָלַי כְּזָבִים. *Line d*. Independent clause.

וְהֵמָּה. Pleonastic 3mp pronoun which creates an antithesis with וְאָנֹכִי in the previous line. Ephraim is the antecedent.

דִּבְּרוּ. Piel *qatal* 3cp √דבר.

עָלַי. Adjunct PP with עַל marking the object of disadvantage. The lies (כְּזָבִים) will be *against* YHWH, the antecedent of the 1cs suffix.

כְּזָבִים. Acc compl of דִּבְּרוּ. This noun refers to the ideas (perhaps that YHWH is unable to save?) and competing claims that have influenced Ephraim to look elsewhere for the solutions to their problems, rather than to YHWH.

7:14 a וְלֹא־זָעֲקוּ אֵלַי בְּלִבָּם
b כִּי יְיֵלִילוּ עַל־מִשְׁכְּבוֹתָם
c עַל־דָּגָן וְתִירוֹשׁ יִתְגּוֹרָרוּ
d יָסוּרוּ בִי׃

Lines a-b are a bicolon consisting of the word pair √זעק//√ילל and the contrasting PPs בְּלִבָּם ("in their hearts") and עַל־מִשְׁכְּבוֹתָם ("on their beds"). The lines are marked with *Zaqep parvum* and *'Atnaḥ*. Lines c-d are a bicolon, marked with *Ṭipḥa* and *Silluq*.

וְלֹא־זָעֲקוּ אֵלַי בְּלִבָּם. *Line a*. Independent clause.

זָעֲקוּ. Qal *qatal* 3cp √זעק. This verb expresses a cry for help in a time of need.

אֵלַי. Adjunct PP with אֶל indicating the (potential) addressee of the cry for help. The antecedent of the 1cs suffix is YHWH.

בְּלִבָּם. Adjunct PP with בְּ specifying the location of the cry (√זעק). The antecedent of the 3mp suffix is Ephraim. The idiom לֵב + בְּ refers to one's private thoughts or saying something to oneself. YHWH is suggesting that the bar is quite low. The people of Ephraim need only cry out in their thoughts, and YHWH will respond. Instead, they expend energy lamenting (√ילל) on their beds (line b). The actions look the same, but the first expresses trust in YHWH, and the second expresses only despair.

כִּי יְיֵלִילוּ עַל־מִשְׁכְּבוֹתָם. *Line b*. Independent clause. The כִּי introduces a contrast ("on the contrary") following the negative clause in line a (cf. HALOT 470).

יְיֵלִילוּ. Hiph *yiqtol* 3mp √ילל. This form is unusual since the י prefix has been added to the beginning of the contracted form. (We would expect that the contracted vowel would appear under the prefix and the first root letter would be represented as a vowel letter; e.g., יֵילִילוּ). However, there are several words that behave this way in the Hiphil, and the MT form should be preserved (cf. GKC §70d). The verb √ילל is probably an onomatopoeia for howling or wailing (NIDOTTE 1:976). It always occurs in the Hiphil in the OT and describes a response to pain and judgment.

עַל־מִשְׁכְּבוֹתָם. Adjunct PP describing the location of the people's wailing as their beds. This dramatic, outward lament is contrasted with the appropriate response: internal trust in YHWH's ability to deliver them (line a).

עַל־דָּגָן וְתִירוֹשׁ יִתְגּוֹרָרוּ. *Line c*. Independent clause.

עַל־דָּגָן וְתִירוֹשׁ. PP with עַל indicating the object of interest (cf. WO §11.2.13c). Authors in BH typically repeat the preposition before each item in a list (cf. 1:7; 2:21), so we might expect עַל־דָּגָן וְעַל־תִּירוֹשׁ.

However, in poetry the preposition is sometimes understood before the second of two members (JM §132g). In 2:11 YHWH says that he will take back his דָּגָן ("grain") and his תִּירוֹשׁ ("new wine") because she did not know that they were gifts from him (2:10). Here in 7:14, the people of Ephraim mourn over the loss of these things.

יִתְגּוֹרָרוּ. The form in the MT is a Hithpolel *yiqtol* 3mp √גור. There are several √גור roots in BH: (I) ("they made themselves foreigners"); (II) ("they quarrel"); (III) ("they are afraid"). Yet none of these makes good sense as a response to grain and new wine (except perhaps quarrelling if there is a lack). G has κατετέμνοντο ("they cut themselves") which translates √גדד in 1 Kgs 18:28. If the reading of G is original, the MT reading could easily have been created through the common confusion of ד and ר. This verse should therefore probably be understood as a Hithpo'el *yiqtol* 3mp √גדד. The sense is that they are cutting themselves in mourning (cf. line b) over the loss of grain and wine.

יָסוּרוּ בִי. *Line d*. Independent clause. As vocalized, the verb יָסוּרוּ is a Qal *yiqtol* 3mp √סור ("to turn aside"). However, the PP with בְּ is peculiar and difficult. The verb √סור usually takes adjuncts with locational prepositions such as מִן ("to turn *from*"; cf. Hos 2:14, 19) or אֶל ("to turn *toward*"). (It does occur with עַל in 1 Kgs 22:32 with the meaning "turn against.") S and T represent the vocalization יָסֹרוּ (from the geminate root √סרר), and this is possibly supported by G (see BHS note d). Gelston (2010:62*) argues that this reading is almost required by the prep בְּ. A few recensions of G (σ' and ε') support MT, but then they are compelled to change the preposition to מִן. On balance, this verb should probably be vocalized as יָסֹרוּ, a Qal *yiqtol* 3mp √סרר meaning "they rebel."

7:15 a וַאֲנִי יִסַּרְתִּי
b חִזַּקְתִּי זְרוֹעֹתָם
c וְאֵלַי יְחַשְּׁבוּ־רָע׃

Lines a-c are a tricolon. The first two lines describe YHWH's actions with 1cs *qatal* verbs, while line c forms a conclusion describing the people's response. The lines are marked by *Zaqep parvum*, *'Atnaḥ*, and *Silluq*.

וַאֲנִי יִסַּרְתִּי. *Line a*. Independent clause.

וַאֲנִי. This pleonastic, independent 1cs pronoun highlights the antithesis between YHWH's actions and the actions of Ephraim. This is similar to the pleonastic אָנֹכִי in v. 13c and sets up a relationship between vv. 13 and 15. In 7:13 YHWH's redemption is potential (*yiqtol*) but impossible because of Ephraim's past behavior (*qatal*). In this verse YHWH's benevolence is past (*qatal*), and Ephraim's rebellion is present (*yiqtol*). The chiastic arrangement and temporal contrasts show the futility of YHWH's kindness toward his people: they are determined to rebel no matter what he does.

יִסַּרְתִּי. Piel *qatal* 1cs √יסר. This verb is transitive in the Piel and expects a complement specifying the one taught or disciplined. Here the complement is implied; it is identified by the 3mp poss suffix in line b which refers to Ephraim. Macintosh (2014:283) notices that there is wordplay with יָסוּרוּ in the preceding line (7:14d).

חִזַּקְתִּי זְרוֹעֹתָם. *Line b*. Independent clause.

חִזַּקְתִּי. Piel *qatal* 1cs √חזק. The idiom "strengthen the arm" (with זְרוֹעַ) or "strengthen the hand" (with יָד) refers to encouraging someone (e.g., 1 Sam 23:16) or equipping someone with what they need in order to do a task (e.g., Ezra 1:6; Ezek 30:24-25).

זְרוֹעֹתָם. Compl of חִזַּקְתִּי. The antecedent of the 3mp pronoun is Ephraim (since 7:11). The noun refers to the forearm, and it is used metaphorically to describe one's power or ability.

וְאֵלַי יְחַשְּׁבוּ־רָע. *Line c*. Independent clause.

וְאֵלַי. Adjunct PP with אֶל indicating an ethical dative of (dis)advantage. The phrase is fronted in the word order for focus in order to contrast Ephraim's actions (line c) with YHWH's actions (line b). In spite of his goodness to them, it is against *him* that they scheme.

יְחַשְּׁבוּ. Piel *yiqtol* 3mp √חשב. The verb means "to think" or "to reckon," but in certain contexts it refers to scheming and plotting.

רָע. Compl of יְחַשְּׁבוּ.

7:16 a יָשׁוּבוּ ׀ לֹא עָל
b הָיוּ כְּקֶשֶׁת רְמִיָּה
c יִפְּלוּ בַחֶרֶב שָׂרֵיהֶם מִזַּעַם לְשׁוֹנָם
d זוֹ לַעְגָּם בְּאֶרֶץ מִצְרָיִם׃

Lines a-b are a bicolon with lines marked by *R^ebî^a* and *Zaqep parvum*. Lines c-d are also a bicolon with lines marked by *'Atnaḥ* and *Silluq*.

יָשׁוּבוּ לֹא עָל. *Line a*. Independent clause. This is another difficult line that has prompted a number of emendations and interpretations. The verb is straightforward: a Qal *yiqtol* 3mp √שׁוב. The main difficulty is the word עָל. G translates ἀπεστράφησαν εἰς οὐθέν ("they turned to nothing") and S is similar (see BHS note ᵃ⁻ᵃ). This involves a metathesis of לֹא and עָל and reading לֹא as an existential negative particle. These translations may reflect a variant reading, but Gelston (2010:14) thinks they are exegetical. AF (477) understand עָל as a negative divine name: "they returned to a no-god," but this is speculative. The best option, which does not require emendation, is that עָל is meant as a substantive meaning, "what is above." In 11:7 Hosea uses a similar expression אֶל־עָל to describe Ephraim calling upward (toward YHWH). McComiskey (2009:116) points out that this interpretation helps explain the parallel line, "they have become like a slack bow." A slack bow is inaccurate and misses its mark; Ephraim too is aiming at the wrong thing. Hosea is, therefore, once again describing Ephraim's misdirected trust: "they return to 'not-above.'" Rather than turning upward to the higher things of YHWH and his ethic, they remain mired in self-sufficiency and in the trust of idols *below*.

הָיוּ כְּקֶשֶׁת רְמִיָּה. *Line b*. Independent clause.

הָיוּ. Qal *qatal* 3cp √היה.

כְּקֶשֶׁת רְמִיָּה. This PP with כְּ indicating agreement in kind is the complement of the copular verb הָיוּ. The word רְמִיָּה is an attributive adjective referring to incompetence or negligence. This is a "bow" that fails in its primary task: to deliver an arrow accurately.

יִפְּלוּ בַחֶרֶב שָׂרֵיהֶם מִזַּעַם לְשׁוֹנָם. *Line c*. Independent clause.

יִפְּלוּ. Qal *yiqtol* 3mp √נפל. See 7:7.

בַחֶרֶב. Adjunct PP with instrumental בְּ. The word order in this clause is unusual because the PP comes before the subject of the verb

(שָׂרֵיהֶם). This is probably because the expression נָפַל בַּחֶרֶב is a common idiom and the two words are kept together.

שָׂרֵיהֶם. Subject of יִפְּלוּ. The שָׂרִים ("princes") are mentioned alongside the king in 7:3, 5 as those political leaders who are refusing to turn to YHWH for help. In an ironic twist, they will be killed even as they search for a way to save themselves and their nation. The antecedent of the 3mp poss pronoun is Ephraim (cf. 7:11).

מִזַּעַם לְשׁוֹנָם. PP with מִן expressing the cause of the princes' fall (cf. WO §11.2.11d). The noun זַעַם refers to "indignation" or "wrath" and is used excusively in the OT of YHWH's anger directed toward those who deserve judgment (e.g., Nah 1:6; Zeph 3:8). Here זַעַם is in a construct relationship with לְשׁוֹנָם ("their tongue"). If this were a subjective genitive, it would mean that their tongue expresses wrath. But then who would be the object of their anger? YHWH? This makes little sense in the context of attempting to secure alliances. Israel may be forsaking YHWH, but there has been no mention of anger toward him. It seems more likely that the construct phrase is an objective genitive (cf. WO §9.5.2e). The זַעַם is YHWH's (as usual), directed toward "their tongue," which is a metonymy for the official political discussions. This explains how the phrase functions (with מִן) to give the reason that the princes are killed. We could translate the clause, "Their princes will fall by the sword because of YHWH's anger at their speech."

זוֹ לַעְגָּם בְּאֶרֶץ מִצְרָיִם. *Line d.* Independent clause.

זוֹ. This is a rare, shortened form of the demonstrative pronoun זֹאת (GKC §34b, n. 3). The antecedent is the situation in the previous line. When the leadership in Ephraim turned away from Egypt and went to Assyria for help (cf. v. 11), Assyria turned on them. Now Egypt laughs at Israel's demise and the results of their fickle alliances.

לַעְגָּם. The noun לַעַג is used of being taunted and mocked by neighbors (Ps 44:14; 79:4) and other nations (Ezek 36:4). The antecedent of the 3mp poss pronoun continues to be Ephraim (since 7:11).

בְּאֶרֶץ מִצְרָיִם. PP with בְּ indicating the location of the action.

Israel Has Rejected the Good (8:1-3)

The subunit found in 8:1-3 has traditionally been understood as a call to arms and the announcement of an enemy attack (cf. 5:8). YHWH announces judgment on Israel by urging them to prepare for an enemy onslaught. This is their doing; it is the result of their rebellion and the breaking of the covenant (v. 1). Though they may call to him in desperation, it is too late (v. 2). They have rejected his help ("the good"), and now they will be pursued by an enemy (v. 3). In a twist of poetic justice, they have rejected YHWH and instead have attempted to get help from foreign nations; now foreign nations will come and destroy them. For an alternative view, see Emmerson 1975. She argues that the passage has a cultic, rather than military, setting and is a summons to confrontation with YHWH for breach of covenant (704). In either case, these verses are a continuation of YHWH's accusation against his people in 4:1–8:14.

> ¹*To your mouth—the trumpet!*
> *—like an eagle over the house of YHWH,*
>
> *because they have transgressed my covenant,*
> *and against my instruction they have rebelled.*
>
> ²*To me they cry,*
> *"My God ... We have known you ... Israel!"*
>
> ³*The Good One will reject Israel,*
> *an enemy will pursue him.*

8:1 a אֶל־חִכְּךָ שֹׁפָר
b כַּנֶּשֶׁר עַל־בֵּית יְהוָה
c יַעַן עָבְרוּ בְרִיתִי
d וְעַל־תּוֹרָתִי פָּשָׁעוּ׃

Lines a-b are a bicolon that does not contain a verb. The lines appear to be fragmentary exclamations. Verse 8:2b, below, also contains several terse statements and protestations. It may be that this section is written to emulate the chaotic shouts when soldiers first realize that they are under attack (see Mauchline 1956:644). The lines are marked by *Zaqep parvum* and *'Atnaḥ*. Lines c-d are also a bicolon, indicated by the chiastic pattern (verb > acc//acc > verb) containing two word pairs (פשע√/עבר√; תּוֹרָה//בְּרִית). The lines are marked with *Zaqep parvum* and *Silluq*.

אֶל־חִכְּךָ שֹׁפָר. *Line a*. Exclamation. This is hypothetical reported speech, envisioned as one soldier shouting to another that the enemy is on the way. The statement assumes a verb such as "lift" or "put," though there are no analogous statements in the OT.

אֶל־חִכְּךָ. PP with אֶל indicating the location where the שׁוֹפָר is sounded. Usually, the noun חֵךְ refers to the inside of the mouth which tastes food (Job 34:3; Ps 119:103) or where the tongue sticks when one cannot talk (Job 29:10; Ps 137:6). In this context it must refer to the mouth generally. (It is used as a metonymy for speech in Prov 5:3; 8:7). The antecedent of the 2ms poss suffix does not refer to anyone in particular; it is a general call to sound the alarm.

שֹׁפָר. Acc of an implied verb. This is a defective spelling of the usual שׁוֹפָר. This word was used as an audible signal to call others to worship, to listen to an announcement, or to attack or retreat in battle (see 5:8).

כַּנֶּשֶׁר עַל־בֵּית יְהוָה. *Line b.* Sentence fragment (Deut 28:49 may contain the fuller expression).

כַּנֶּשֶׁר. PP with כְּ indicating agreement in kind. The difficulty here is that the prophet does not specify what is being compared to an eagle or in what way. The eagle is a common image in the OT, used as an example of endurance (e.g., Exod 19:4), speed (e.g., 2 Sam 1:23), inaccessibility (e.g., Prov 23:5), and of a fearsome predator that swoops upon its prey (e.g., Deut 28:49; Job 9:26). In the context of a call to battle, the latter sense must be meant here. The approaching enemy is compared to an eagle, which is strong and swift. It is "over the house of YHWH" because it is threatening Israel.

עַל־בֵּית יְהוָה. PP with עַל indicating the location of the נֶשֶׁר ("eagle"). The phrase בֵּית יְהוָה in the OT usually refers to the temple. However, Hosea is in the northern kingdom where there is no temple. This is likely a reference to the whole land which belongs to YHWH. Wolff (1974:137) cites similar expressions from Egyptian lists of Asian countries that use the expression "house of … ".

יַעַן עָבְרוּ בְרִיתִי. *Line c.* Subordinate causal clause with יַעַן giving the reason that Israel is under threat (cf. WO §38.4). AF (487–88) argue that the main difference between כִּי and יַעַן is that יַעַן usually (more than 70×) introduces a subordinate causal clause that *precedes* the main clause. The implication is that this clause (and the coordinated clause which follows in line d) is actually giving the reason for 8:2 rather than 8:1a-b. However, there are approximately a hundred occurrences of יַעַן in the OT, so that would mean the subordinate clause *follows* the main clause in many instances (e.g., Lev 26:43; Jos 14:14; 1 Kgs 14:13). In this context it makes much more sense that the main clause is 8:1a-b. Israel's rebellion (8:1c-d) is the reason for the attack (8:1a-b), not their cry to YHWH (8:2).

עָבְרוּ. Qal *qatal* 3cp √עבר. This verb is used frequently to describe the breaking of a covenant (בְּרִית) (cf. 6:7). The *qatal* describes completed action in the past.

בְּרִיתִי. Acc compl of עָבְרוּ. The antecedent of the 1cs poss suffix is YHWH, the speaker.

וְעַל־תּוֹרָתִי פָּשָׁעוּ. *Line d*. Independent clause. This clause is coordinated to the causal clause in line c and is therefore semantically subordinate to lines a-b. The conjunction יַעַן, unlike other conjunctions such as כִּי, is not repeated before subsequent coordinated clauses (AF 488). In the parallelism, this line gives a second reason that Israel is under threat.

וְעַל־תּוֹרָתִי. Oblique compl of פָּשָׁעוּ. The verb √פשע means "to rebel against" (see 7:13 where it takes its complement with the more common בְּ prep). The antecedent of the 1cs poss suffix on תּוֹרָה is YHWH. This phrase is fronted because of the chiasm in the parallelism (see line c).

פָּשָׁעוּ. Qal *qatal* 3cp √פשע.

8:2 a לִי יִזְעָקוּ
b אֱלֹהַי יְדַעֲנוּךָ יִשְׂרָאֵל׃

Lines a-b are a brief bicolon. Line a introduces the reported speech in line b. The lines are marked by *'Atnaḥ* and *Silluq*.

לִי יִזְעָקוּ. *Line a*. Independent clause.

לִי. PP with לְ specifying the addressee of Israel's cry. In nineteen similar occurrences elsewhere in the OT, the addressee of the verb √זעק is introduced with the prep אֶל, including in Hos 7:14. However, the prep לְ introduces the addressee of √זעק in 1 Chr 5:20 and, as Macintosh (2014:294) notes, לְ is used with so many verbs of speech it is best not to place too much emphasis on it. The PP is fronted in the clause for focus to contrast with what precedes in 8:1. There, YHWH states that Israel has rebelled against the covenant and his instruction. Nevertheless, in 8:2 he says that they do call *to him*, but only for relief from his judgment.

יִזְעָקוּ. Qal *yiqtol* 3mp √זעק. The *yiqtol* indicates a frequentative nuance. Crying out for help, even in the context of rebellion, is characteristic of them.

אֱלֹהַי יְדַעֲנוּךָ יִשְׂרָאֵל. *Line b*. Fragmentary exclamations in reported speech. The challenge in this line is to discern how the three words relate to one another. The first word אֱלֹהַי ("*my* God") has a 1cs suffix, but the second word, a Qal *qatal* with a 2ms acc suffix, is 1cp ("*we* have known you"). Also, what is the role of יִשְׂרָאֵל in the syntax? BHS note [b] attempts to resolve the difficulties by revocalizing אֱלֹהַי to אֱלֹהֵי (const form) and suggesting that the verb יְדַעֲנוּךָ (a Qal *qatal* 1cp √ידע with a 2ms acc suffix) interrupts the construct phrase אֱלֹהֵי יִשְׂרָאֵל so that the sense is: "We have known you, O God of Israel." Stuart, who supports this reading, suggests that the construct phrase was split for metrical reasons and notes, "composite names and other stereotyped phrases are especially subject to such splitting in the OT" (1987:128; cf. Freedman 1972:536). Wolff (1974:131) interprets the line without emending by understanding יִשְׂרָאֵל to be in apposition to the subject of יְדַעֲנוּךָ, translating, "My God!—We [Israel] know you!" Yet this does not resolve the awkwardness of the transition from first person singular to plural. Alternatively, we can explain all three words as random, fragmentary exclamations: "My God! ... We have known you! ... [We are] Israel!" (for a similar view, see Garrett 1997:181). The form of reported speech conveys turmoil and disorder in their responses (similar to the call to arms in 8:1a-b). This characterizes them as frantic and unsure. Their cries for help are actually manipulative protestations that, although this is judgment, YHWH should help them because they are his people.

8:3 a זָנַח יִשְׂרָאֵל טוֹב
b אוֹיֵב יִרְדְּפוֹ׃

Lines a-b are a bicolon with lines connected via noun/pronoun grammatical parallelism (וֹ//יִשְׂרָאֵל). The lines are marked by *'Atnaḥ* and *Silluq*.

זָנַח יִשְׂרָאֵל טוֹב. *Line a*. Independent clause.

זָנַח. Qal *qatal* (irrealis) 3ms √זנח. There are two potential difficulties in this line. First, the subject of זָנַח is ambiguous as it could be either of the following two words. If יִשְׂרָאֵל is the subject, then it means, "Israel rejects the good," referring to the breaking of covenant or the rejection of YHWH's leadership. By contrast, if טוֹב is the subject, then it means, "The good one (YHWH?) has rejected Israel." The verb √זנח occurs nineteen times in the OT. In fifteen out of eighteen of these occurrences (excluding the present verse), YHWH is the subject and he is rejecting (or may reject) Israel (except in Hos 8:5, where YHWH rejects an idol). In two more occurrences, the subject is a king of Israel who is rejecting Levites (2 Chr 11:14) or utensils (2 Chr 29:19). Because √זנח is used of a ruler rejecting his subjects in seventeen out of eighteen occurrences, it is highly likely that טוֹב (referring to YHWH) is the subject here. The inverted VS word order suggests that the verb is irrealis, referring to something that could or would take place rather than a past completed event. If so, it would be meaningless to say, "Israel will reject the good" since they have clearly already rejected YHWH and his purposes. But to say, "the Good One will reject Israel" is a statement of coming judgment, parallel with line b and consistent with the preceding context in 8:1-2. This analysis is supported by the parallelism with line b. If √זנח is irrealis then it makes a better parallel with the *yiqtol* יִרְדְּפוֹ. Furthermore, the grammatical parallelism of the noun (יִשְׂרָאֵל) and the pronominal suffix on יִרְדְּפוֹ both function as the accusatives of the respective verbs.

אוֹיֵב יִרְדְּפוֹ. *Line b.* Independent clause.

אוֹיֵב. Subject of יִרְדְּפוֹ. This "enemy" is not identified, but it relates to the attacking enemy in 8:1-2.

יִרְדְּפוֹ. Qal *yiqtol* 3ms √רדף with a 3ms acc suffix. The antecedent of the suffix is יִשְׂרָאֵל in the previous line. We would expect this form to be יִרְדְּפֵהוּ since prefixing verbs generally have i-class linking vowels before the suffix. However, there are a number of cases where a prefix verb has an a-class connecting vowel (GKC §60d).

Summation: Idols, Political Schemes, and Manipulative Worship (8:4-14)

In 8:4 the pleonastic pronoun הֵם and the topical shift to "kings" and "princes" signals a transition to a new unit. This conclusion to 4:4–8:14 is the prophet's summation of his case. Like a prosecuting attorney reviews the evidence that he has just presented to a jury, Hosea reviews the three ways that Israel has demonstrated a refusal to submit to YHWH: idolatry, political schemes, and a fastidious concern with sacrifices devoid of actual faith. For some problems they go to other deities for help, for other problems they go to neighboring kings—even kings of enemy nations which pose an existential threat. Even though on the surface the worship of other gods looks very different than requests made to Assyria, they are both motivated by idolatry and a refusal to submit to YHWH. At the same time, they continue their formal worship of YHWH, which he refuses to accept.

YHWH is the speaker throughout this unit. Note the use of the first person in 8:4, 10, 12, 13, and 14. However, the prophet interjects here and there as well, referring to YHWH in the third person (vv. 5, 13). YHWH's speech alternates between two broad categories: political schemes (v. 4a-b), religious worship (vv. 4c-6), political schemes (vv. 7-10), religious worship (vv. 11-13). The alternating structure ties the two topics together and encourages the reader to see how both come from the same motivation and both end in destruction (v. 14).

> *⁴They set up kings, but not from me.*
> *They installed princes, but I did not know.*
>
> *Their silver and their gold they made into idols for themselves,*
> *with the result that he will be cut off.*
>
> *⁵(He has rejected your calf, Samaria!)*
> *My anger burned against them.*
> *How long will they not be capable of innocence?*
>
> *⁶Surely it is from Israel;*
> *a craftsman made it.*
> *And it is not God;*
> *surely the calf of Samaria will be pieces.*
>
> *⁷Indeed they will sow a wind*
> *but will harvest a storm.*
>
> *As for the standing grain—it does not have heads;*
> *it will not make flour;*
> *even if it does, strangers would devour it.*
>
> *⁸Israel will be swallowed up;*
> *now they are among the nations,*
> *like a vessel which no one desires.*

⁹*For they have gone up to Assyria;*
a wild ass alone by himself is Ephraim.
They have paid for lovers.

¹⁰*Even though they hire among the nations;*
now I will gather them.

And they will writhe for a time,
under the burden of the king of princes.

¹¹*When Ephraim multiplied altars for sinning,*
they became to him altars for sinning.

¹²*If I were to write for him 10,000 of my instructions,*
as a strange thing they would be considered.

¹³*They were making sacrifices of my gifts,*
and they ate flesh.
YHWH has not accepted them.

Now he will remember their iniquity,
and he will punish their sins.
They will return to Egypt.

¹⁴*And Israel forgot his maker,*
and he built palaces,
and Judah multiplied fortified cities.

But I will send a fire on his cities,
and it will devour its citadels.

8:4 a הֵ֤ם הִמְלִ֙יכוּ֙ וְלֹ֣א מִמֶּ֔נִּי
b הֵשִׂ֖ירוּ וְלֹ֣א יָדָ֑עְתִּי
c כַּסְפָּ֣ם וּזְהָבָ֗ם עָשׂ֤וּ לָהֶם֙ עֲצַבִּ֔ים
d לְמַ֖עַן יִכָּרֵֽת׃

Lines a-b are a bicolon, identified by the word pair שׁיר√//מלך√ and the related idea at the end of each line. The lines are marked by *Zaqep parvum* and *'Atnaḥ*. Lines c-d are also a bicolon. Line c is the main clause and line d is a subordinate purpose clause. The lines are marked by *Zaqep parvum* and *Silluq*.

Hosea 8:4

הֵם הִמְלִיכוּ. *Line a*. Independent clause.

הֵם. Pleonastic independent pronoun. It signals a new literary unit and topicalizes Israel as the subject of the rebellious actions in lines a and b.

הִמְלִיכוּ. Hiph *qatal* 3cp √מלך. In the Qal this verb means "to reign" or "to be king [or queen]." In the Hiphil, it refers to putting someone on the throne and making them king or queen. This verb requires an accusative complement which is implied here (see also הֵשִׂירוּ in line b).

וְלֹא מִמֶּנִּי. *Line a*. This is either an adverbial phrase modifying הִמְלִיכוּ (i.e., "I did not authorize them to set up kings") or a verbless clause of which the subject is the implied complement of הִמְלִיכוּ: "kings" (i.e., "the kings were not from me"; they were illegitimate). The latter analysis is supported by the presence of the ו conjunction, which suggests a division from הִמְלִיכוּ and the beginning of a new clause.

מִמֶּנִּי. PP with מִן indicating authority (cf. WO §11.2.11d). YHWH is saying that they installed kings, but not kings that he desired.

הֵשִׂירוּ. *Line b*. Independent clause. The verb is a Hiph *qatal* 3cp √שׂרר. With a geminate (II=III) root, we expect the Hiphil to have ֵ (*tsere*) for a theme vowel (e.g., הֵשֵׂרוּ; cf. הֵפֵרוּ from √פרר). The *hireq-yod* here probably comes from contamination with II-ו verbs (JM §82n). This is the only occurrence of the verb √שׂרר in the Hiphil. Because the Qal means "to rule" or "to have oversight," a causative Hiphil would presumably mean "to install someone as ruler." With the Hiphil we expect an accusative complement, but it must be implied (cf. הִמְלִיכוּ in line a). Some scholars understand this verb to be a biform of √סור (thus explaining the *hireq-yod*) which would mean "they deposed [rulers]." Or, perhaps there is a double entrendre between √שׂרר and √סור playing on Israel's propensity both to set up and remove rulers, all without YHWH's approval (cf. Kuhnigk 1974:105).

וְלֹא יָדָעְתִּי. *Line b*. Independent clause. The verb is a Qal *qatal* 1cs √ידע. The expression "I did not know" probably means that YHWH did not accept or acknowledge these kings that were put on the throne (AF 492).

כַּסְפָּם וּזְהָבָם עָשׂוּ לָהֶם עֲצַבִּים. *Line c*. Independent clause.

כַּסְפָּם וּזְהָבָם. When the verb √עשׂה means "to make X into Y" it takes two complements. The first complement (here: כַּסְפָּם וּזְהָבָם) describes the materials from which something is made and the second

עָשׂוּ. Qal *qatal* 3cp √עשׂה.

לָהֶם. Adjunct PP with לְ of advantage, indicating for whom the idols were made. The antecedent of the 3mp suffix is Israel: they made the idols for themselves.

עֲצַבִּים. This is the second complement of עָשׂוּ, which specifies what they have made from their silver and gold. This is the second time Hosea mentions Israel's dependence upon עֲצַבִּים ("idols") (see 4:17).

לְמַעַן יִכָּרֵת. *Line d.* Subordinate consecutive clause. Although לְמַעַן frequently introduces purpose clauses (i.e., "in order that") (cf. JM §169g), here it introduces the effect of the preceding main clause. The sense is, "they made idols (line c) … *with the result that* he will be cut off (line d)."

יִכָּרֵת. Niph *yiqtol* 3ms √כרת. In the Niphal this verb usually refers to being exterminated or destroyed (HALOT 501). The singular subject is not explicit. It might refer back to "Israel" in 8:3. In other words, the people (3mp) make idols, and this results in the destruction of their nation (3ms). Alternatively, it might refer to the עֵגֶל ("calf") in the next line (8:5a).

8:5 a זָנַח עֶגְלֵךְ שֹׁמְרוֹן
b חָרָה אַפִּי בָּם
c עַד־מָתַי לֹא יוּכְלוּ נִקָּיֹן׃

Lines a-c are a tricolon. Line a is a temporary aside by the prophet. Throughout this section, Hosea is speaking directly for YHWH, but here he interjects. Lines b-c refer to Israel with 3mp forms. The lines are marked by *Zaqep parvum*, *'Atnaḥ*, and *Silluq*.

זָנַח עֶגְלֵךְ שֹׁמְרוֹן. *Line a.* Independent clause.

זָנַח. Qal *qatal* 3ms √זנח. If the consonants and vocalization of MT are correct, the 3ms subject of this verb has three possible identities. It could be עֶגְלֵךְ ("your calf has rejected Samaria"). This is problematic, for who then would be the referent of the 2ms suffix? Furthermore, it would be odd for him to attribute this action to an idol. A second option is that Samaria is the subject, "Samaria has rejected your calf." But this is historically false. The best option is to understand YHWH as the subject and translate, "He has rejected your calf, Samaria." As noted above in the discussion on 8:3a, YHWH is almost always the subject of √זנח. Although YHWH is the main speaker throughout this section (through Hosea), here the prophet interjects to highlight the calf as the particular object of YHWH's anger. Then, he picks up YHWH's speech again in 8:5b. That YHWH is the subject of √זנח is supported by the next line, where YHWH states that his "anger burned against them."

עֶגְלֵךְ. Acc compl of זָנַח. The antecedent of the 2fs poss suffix is שֹׁמְרוֹן, which follows. The suffix is feminine because "Samaria" is a city (cf. 14:1, where it concords with a feminine verb).

שֹׁמְרוֹן. Vocative.

חָרָה אַפִּי בָּם. *Line b.* Independent clause.

חָרָה. Qal *qatal* 3ms √חרה. The idiom √חרה ("to burn") with אַף means "to be angry."

אַפִּי. Subject of חרה. YHWH, the speaker, is the antecedent of the 1cs poss suffix.

בָּם. Adjunct PP with בְּ indicating the recipient of YHWH's anger. The בְּ prep (here: "against") is usual in this idiom (cf. Gen 30:2; Exod 4:14) but not obligatory (cf. Gen 39:19). The 3mp suffix refers to the people of Israel.

עַד־מָתַי לֹא יוּכְלוּ נִקָּיֹן. *Line c.* Independent clause.

עַד־מָתַי. Used together, the prep עַד ("until") and the interr adverb מָתַי ("when?") form a common idiom that asks how long a present situation will continue. It always describes a negative situation such as disobedience or injustice in which the speaker implies that resolution or change is already overdue.

יוּכְלוּ. Qal *yiqtol* 3mp √יכל. This verb usually takes an infinitive or a *yiqtol* verb as its complement. Here, the following noun נִקָּיֹן has a verbal quality and is the complement (cf. HALOT 411).

נִקָּיֹן. Acc compl of יוּכְלוּ referring to innocence or purity. In Gen 20:5 it is used in parallel with תָם לֵבָב ("integrity of heart").

8:6 a כִּי מִיִּשְׂרָאֵל וְהוּא
b חָרָשׁ עָשָׂהוּ
c וְלֹא אֱלֹהִים הוּא
d כִּי־שְׁבָבִים יִהְיֶה עֵגֶל שֹׁמְרוֹן:

Lines a-d are a quatrain. The first (line a) and fourth (line d) lines each begin with an asseverative כִּי. There is a second correspondence between lines, but its nature depends upon which line contains the third word וְהוּא. Some scholars place וְהוּא at the beginning of line b as an anacoluthon, "and it—a craftsman made it" (AF 481; Garrett 1997:183). This would mean that the subject of the verbless clause in line a is only implied. The placement would create a chiastic structure with the 3ms pronoun הוּא in lines b and c. On the other hand, if we read with the masoretic accents, the *Zaqep parvum* on וְהוּא indicates that the line ends at that point and וְהוּא, though the conjunction וְ is awkward, belongs at the end of line a. The pronoun would then be the subject of the verbless clause in line a (which would be otherwise only implied). In that case, the correspondence would be between lines a and c as both lines contain verbless clauses with הוּא at the end, creating a contrast between what the calf *is* ("from Israel") and is *not* ("God"). Thus, lines a and c speak to the calf's identity and nature, while lines b and d refer to its status as a physical, created thing. Either analysis is possible, but the masoretic accents tip the balance in favor of the second view which keeps וְהוּא with line a. The lines are therefore marked with *Zaqep parvum*, *Zaqep parvum*, *'Atnaḥ*, and *Silluq*.

כִּי מִיִּשְׂרָאֵל וְהוּא. *Line a.* Independent verbless clause with asseverative כִּי (cf. JM §164b).

מִיִּשְׂרָאֵל. This PP is the predicate of the verbless clause. The מִן prep indicates the authority that commissioned and enabled the making of the calf (cf. WO §11.2.11d).

וְהוּא. Subject of the verbless clause. As noted above, the advantage in reading this word at the end of line a is that it provides an explicit subject for the verbless clause and creates symmetry with line c. The difficulty, however, is the וְ, which apparently interrupts the clause. On the basis of similar occurrences in Ugaritic texts, Pope (1953:96) explains that the וְ is pleonastic. He writes that appearing in an unexpected position it "has the effect of calling special attention to the word to which it is attached" (98). The antecedent of this pronoun, as well as the other 3ms pronouns in the verse, is the עֵגֶל ("calf") in 8:5.

חָרָשׁ עָשָׂהוּ. *Line b*. Independent clause.

חָרָשׁ. Explicit subject of עָשָׂהוּ. The word חָרָשׁ refers to someone skilled in working with metal (2 Chr 24:12), stone (Exod 28:11), wood (2 Kgs 12:12), or other hard materials. This person is also mentioned as the one who fashions an idol (e.g., Deut 27:15; Isa 40:19).

עָשָׂהוּ. Qal *qatal* 3ms √עשה with a 3ms acc suffix. The antecedent of the suffix is the עֵגֶל in 8:5.

וְלֹא אֱלֹהִים הוּא. *Line c*. Independent verbless clause.

אֱלֹהִים. The predicate of the verbless clause, fronted for focus to contrast the common view of the idol (a god) with its true nature (not God).

הוּא. Subject of the verbless clause. The antecedent is עֵגֶל in 8:5.

כִּי־שְׁבָבִים יִהְיֶה עֵגֶל שֹׁמְרוֹן. *Line d*. Independent clause with asseverative כִּי (see line a). It is also possible to understand the כִּי as introducing a subordinate causal clause; that is, the fact that the calf will be destroyed (line d) is proof that it is not God (line c).

שְׁבָבִים. Compl of יִהְיֶה, specifying what the calf will become. This is the only occurrence of שְׁבָבִים in the OT. Some connect it to the later Hebrew word שָׁבַב ("to hew") and to Arabic *sabba* ("to cut") and translate "splinters" (Wolff 1974:142). Alternatively, it may come from Aramaic √שבב ("to burn"; cf. Job 18:5), meaning that the calf will burn up in flames (Stuart 1987:128). In Exod 32:20 Moses both burns the calf-image and grinds it into pieces.

יִהְיֶה. Qal *yiqtol* 3ms √היה.

עֵגֶל שֹׁמְרוֹן. The noun עֵגֶל, in construct, is the subject of יִהְיֶה. The construct relationship with שֹׁמְרוֹן indicates possession.

8:7 a כִּי רוּחַ יִזְרָעוּ
b וְסוּפָתָה יִקְצֹרוּ
c קָמָה אֵין־לוֹ צֶמַח
d בְּלִי יַעֲשֶׂה־קֶּמַח
e אוּלַי יַעֲשֶׂה זָרִים יִבְלָעֻהוּ׃

  Lines a-b are a bicolon indicated by two word pairs: סוּפָה//רוּחַ and √זרע//√קצר. The lines are marked by *Ṭipḥa* and *'Atnaḥ*. Lines c-e are a tricolon which continues the agricultural image of raising and harvesting grain. These lines are difficult and there are two primary ways of understanding them depending on where one places the word צֶמַח. If we read with the accents, the disjunctive *Rᵉbiᵃ'* on לוֹ would seem to indicate that this is the end of line c, giving the translation, "It has no standing grain." In this case the antecedent of the 3ms pronoun presumably refers to the implied seed that is being sown in lines a-b. Alternatively, if we read against the Masoretic accents and place צֶמַח at the end of line c, the line says, "As for standing grain—it does not have heads." There are three advantages to this approach. First, lines c and d are of roughly equal length (three stresses each). Second, the two lines rhyme (קֶמַח//צֶמַח). Third, the 3ms pronominal suffix on לוֹ has a clear antecedent (קָמָה). Line e concludes the tricolon and features a repetition of the verb √עשׂה in line d. The lines of the tricolon are marked by conjunctive *Mahpak* (i.e., reading against the disjunctive accent *Rᵉbiᵃ'*), *Zaqep parvum*, and *Silluq*.

כִּי רוּחַ יִזְרָעוּ. *Line a*. Independent clause with asseverative כִּי (cf. JM §164b).

רוּחַ. Acc compl of יִזְרָעוּ. If they sow "wind" (here a metaphor for attempted political alliances), they should not expect to receive anything substantial in the harvest (cf. 12:2). Instead, the parallel line states that they will get more than they bargained for: a dangerous storm. This idea of harvesting something corresponding to the original seed but multiplied and intensified is a common trope in the OT.

יִזְרָעוּ. Qal *yiqtol* 3mp √זרע.

וְסוּפָתָה יִקְצֹרוּ. *Line b*. Independent clause.

וְסוּפָתָה. Acc compl of יִקְצֹרוּ. Whereas רוּחַ (line a) refers to generic "wind," this term refers to a fierce, destructive storm often associated

Hosea 8:7

with anxiety and fear. Thus it represents semantic intensification in the parallelism (see also Job 21:18; Isa 17:13). The usual form is סוּפָה; here the additional -תָה ending is likely a vestige of an archaic accusative case ending (Wernberg-Møller 1988:161).

יִקְצֹרוּ. Qal *yiqtol* 3mp √קצר.

קָמָה אֵין־לוֹ צֶמַח. *Line c*. Independent clause.

קָמָה. A *casus pendens* (see 7:8a). In lines a-b they sowed and harvested wind (though that was destructive). Now the metaphor, which still concerns agriculture, intensifies to the failure of crops. Their schemes will produce nothing but "empty air" or worse, destruction. קָמָה is a noun derived from the verb √קוּם, which refers to standing grain or the crop growing in the field. The *casus pendens* is resumed by the retrospective 3ms pronominal suffix on לוֹ.

אֵין־לוֹ. The existential particle אֵין is the negative copula ("there is not"). לוֹ is a PP indicating possession: the standing grain (קָמָה) does not have צֶמַח. As noted above, the antecedent of the 3ms pronoun is the feminine noun קָמָה. Lack of gender agreement is known in BH (see GKC §135o; Ratner 1983). Wolff (1974:132) suggests that the 3ms pronoun is used because Israel is the referent of the image.

צֶמַח. This noun, which means "growth" or "sprout," comes from the verb √צמח ("to sprout" or "to spring up"). Here it refers to the heads which contain the kernels of grain. In other words, even though the crops grow in the field (קָמָה), they do not actually produce any grain (צֶמַח).

בְּלִי יַעֲשֶׂה־קֶּמַח. *Line d*. Independent clause.

בְּלִי. This adverb negates the following verb יַעֲשֶׂה. It is an uncommon negative particle primarily used in poetry (JM §160m).

יַעֲשֶׂה. Qal *yiqtol* 3ms √עשׂה.

קֶּמַח. Acc compl of יַעֲשֶׂה. On the *dagesh* in the ק, see JM §18d-h. קֶמַח refers to flour, the food that is made from the grain. This statement reinforces and intensifies line c by describing the implications of having no kernels of grain.

אוּלַי יַעֲשֶׂה. *Line e*. Subordinate conditional clause.

אוּלַי. This adverb usually means "perhaps," but here it functions as the protasis of an irreal conditional clause like לוּ (WO §38.2e). (It is used in a similar way in Gen 18:28-32 with an implied apodosis.) It introduces a pseudosorites. This is a rhetorical device in which the speaker says that something will not happen, but even if it does happen, it will not matter anyway (see O'Connor 1987; Patterson 2010). The crops will not produce grain (line c) and, therefore, there will be no flour (line d). But even if they did produce grain/food, strangers would devour it (line e).

יַעֲשֶׂה. Qal *yiqtol* (irrealis) 3ms √עשׂה. The subject is קָמָה (line c). Because this is a repetition of יַעֲשֶׂה in line d, the implied complement is again קֶמַח (line d).

זָרִים יִבְלָעֻהוּ. *Line e*. Independent clause.

זָרִים. This substantival adjective is subject of יִבְלָעֻהוּ. It refers to those who are outside of Israel (see 5:7). The irony, and poetic justice, is that even as they go outside of Israel to other nations for assistance, those peoples will come and pillage them. Because the following verb is irrealis and refers to a possible situation (see the discussion on אוּלַי above), we expect VS word order. The SV word order in this clause indicates that the subject זָרִים is fronted for topicalization, in order to introduce the idea of exile in the following clauses.

יִבְלָעֻהוּ. Qal *yiqtol* (irrealis) 3mp √בלע with a 3ms acc suffix. The antecedent of the 3ms suffix is the קֶמַח ("flour") in line d (and implied in line e). The overall image is that the crops will fail and produce no food, but even if they did produce food, foreigners would come and hungrily consume it before Israel had a chance to eat anything.

8:8 a נִבְלַע יִשְׂרָאֵל
b עַתָּה הָיוּ בַגּוֹיִם
c כִּכְלִי אֵין־חֵפֶץ בּוֹ׃

Lines a-c are a tricolon. The lines are marked by *'Atnaḥ*, *Zaqep parvum*, and *Silluq*.

נִבְלַע יִשְׂרָאֵל. *Line a*. Independent clause.

נִבְלַע. Niph *qatal* (irrealis) 3ms √בלע. Even though the verb is not preceded by וְ, the irrealis sense is indicated by inverted VS word order. Hosea is not saying that Israel was swallowed up, he's saying that they will be, based on their current trajectory. Note the repetition of √בלע in 8:7. Not only will foreigners devour Israel's crops (if there were any), Israel itself will be consumed by the nations.

יִשְׂרָאֵל. Subject of נִבְלַע.

עַתָּה הָיוּ בַגּוֹיִם. *Line b*. Independent clause.

עַתָּה. Temporal adverb that introduces the logical and chronological result of the previous clause. Because Israel will be swallowed up (line a), they will be scattered among the nations (line b).

הָיוּ. Qal *qatal* 3cp √היה with a present temporal reference.

בַגּוֹיִם. PP with בְּ indicating location amid a domain (WO §11.2.5b). Israel is "among" the nations.

כִּכְלִי אֵין־חֵפֶץ בּוֹ. *Line c*. PP with an embedded unmarked relative clause.

כִּכְלִי. PP with כְּ indicating agreement in kind. כְלִי is a general term for an item that has a particular use including storage, furniture, music, cult, garment, or weapon, among others (see HALOT 479).

אֵין־חֵפֶץ בּוֹ. An unmarked relative clause which is headed by כְלִי. As usual, the head of the relative is resumed by the 3ms pronominal suffix at the end of the clause. חֵפֶץ is usually translated "desire," but in this context it may also have the sense of "usefulness." The idea is that not only is Israel without an identity (among the nations), it is also unwanted and rejected as an unwanted thing.

8:9 a כִּי־הֵמָּה עָלוּ אַשּׁוּר
b פֶּרֶא בּוֹדֵד לוֹ אֶפְרָיִם
c הִתְנוּ אֲהָבִים:

Lines a-c are a tricolon. The *'Atnaḥ* accent on לוֹ in line b would normally indicate the end of that line. But this raises two problems. First, that puts אֶפְרָיִם in line c as the subject of the plural verb הִתְנוּ. Second, the natural referent of the singular פֶּרֶא ("ass") would be Assyria, but it is Ephraim who is pictured as a wild ass in the verse, probably with the same meaning as the "dove" in 7:11, intended to describe his propensity to wander here and there. Therefore it makes more sense to read against the *'Atnaḥ* and to end line b after the disjunctive *Ṭipḥa*, thereby including אֶפְרָיִם in line b as the subject of the verbless clause. This has the benefit of separating the singular and plural constituents in the verse (lines a and c are plural; line b is singular) and strengthens the wordplay between פרא and אפרים. The lines are marked by *Zaqep parvum*, *Ṭipḥa*, and *Silluq*.

כִּי־הֵמָּה עָלוּ אַשּׁוּר. *Line a*. Subordinate causal clause with כִּי giving the reason that Israel is among the nations (8:8b-c).

הֵמָּה. Pleonastic 3mp pronoun referring to the people of Israel, specifically those in leadership. It was *their* plan to go to Assyria, not YHWH's.

עָלוּ. Qal *qatal* 3cp √עלה. Usually one goes "up" *to* Israel, not away from Israel. It is uncertain why the prophet chose this verb; see Macintosh (2014:316) for some possible motivations.

אַשּׁוּר. This is an unmarked PP (assuming אֶל) indicating the goal or termination of עָלוּ.

פֶּרֶא בּוֹדֵד לוֹ אֶפְרָיִם. *Line b*. Independent verbless clause.

פֶּרֶא. Predicate of the verbless clause. A פֶּרֶא is a wild or undomesticated donkey, sometimes used as a vivid metaphor of undisciplined and unrestrained behavior. Here, it refers to Israel going to seek help from Assyria without really considering what they are doing. It is a reckless act, with similarities to another use of פֶּרֶא in Jer 2:24, where Israel is a wild donkey "accustomed to the wilderness, in her heat sniffing the wind. Who can restrain her lust?"

בּוֹדֵד. Qal ptc ms √בדד used as an attributive adjective to modify פֶּרֶא. That Ephraim is "alone" reinforces the idea that he does what he wants with no accountability and no protection.

לוֹ. PP with לְ introducing an ethical dative which emphasizes that the action of the verb has a particular significance for the subject (GKC §119s). Here, the preposition has a reflexive nuance which emphasizes his isolation: the wild donkey is alone "by himself."

אֶפְרָיִם. Subject of the verbless clause.

הִתְנוּ אֲהָבִים. *Line c*. Independent clause.

הִתְנוּ. Hiph *qatal* 3cp √תנה. The meaning of this verb, which also occurs in the following verse, is uncertain. HALOT (1760) suggests several options, including "to recruit" or "to pay a harlot's fee." Either of these related meanings fits 8:10 as well.

אֲהָבִים. Acc compl of הִתְנוּ. This noun, the plural of אַהַב, refers to the lovers that Ephraim is attempting to hire (cf. BDB 13) or to the gifts acquired to recruit those lovers (cf. HALOT 18). If the former is intended, one would expect the Qal participle אֹהֲבִים or the more common Piel participle מְאַהֲבִים (cf. 2:7, 9, 12, 14, 15). In either case Hosea

8:10 a גַּם כִּי־יִתְנוּ בַגּוֹיִם
b עַתָּה אֲקַבְּצֵם
c וַיָּחֵלּוּ מְּעָט
d מִמַּשָּׂא מֶלֶךְ שָׂרִים:

Lines a-b are a bicolon. Line a makes a statement and line b, introduced by עַתָּה, describes its outcome. The lines are marked by *Tipḥa* and *'Atnaḥ*. Lines c-d are also a bicolon consisting of one sentence. The lines are marked by *Zaqep parvum* and *Silluq*.

גַּם כִּי־יִתְנוּ בַגּוֹיִם. *Line a.* Concessive clause subordinate to the main clause in line b. A concessive clause, here marked by גַּם כִּי introduces a modality of the conditional notion (cf. JM §171). The statement in line a would seem to have one outcome, but in fact it will have the opposite outcome (line b). Israel does not realize that her trouble actually comes from YHWH as judgment. Therefore *even though* Israel seeks to ward off trouble by developing alliances among the nations, the people will not be able to stop YHWH's actions against them.

יִתְנוּ. Qal *yiqtol* 3mp √תנה. On this verb, see 8:9c above. The meaning of the verb is unclear, and thus the difference between Hiphil and Qal is uncertain.

בַגּוֹיִם. PP with בְּ indicating location amid a domain (see 8:8b).

עַתָּה אֲקַבְּצֵם. *Line b.* Independent clause. The adverb עַתָּה introduces the conclusion. Ironically, not only will Israel's search for help among the nations fail to stop YHWH's judgment, it will actually increase it, for the search itself is an act of rebellion.

אֲקַבְּצֵם. Piel *yiqtol* 1cs √קבץ with a 3mp acc suffix. The verb √קבץ is used in both positive contexts (e.g., Isa 13:14; Deut 30:3) and in contexts of judgment in which YHWH gathers his enemies into one place to pour out his wrath on them (e.g., Zeph 3:8; Joel 4:2; Mic 4:12; Hos 9:6). The latter sense is in view here. The antecedent of the 3mp suffix is the leaders of Israel, who attempt to make alliances among the nations.

וַיָּחֵלּוּ מְעָט. *Line c.* Independent clause. Wolff (1974:133) calls MT in this half of the verse "absolutely incomprehensible." It seems emendation of some kind is required.

וַיָּחֵלּוּ. Hiph *wayyiqtol* 3mp √חלל. This word is problematic because the *wayyiqtol* conjugation indicates action in the past, but the context is one of future judgment. In addition, the root √חלל ("to begin") expects an infinitival complement, which is missing. Some have supplied the infinitive *ad sensum* (e.g., "begin [to be oppressed]"; Macintosh 2014:320–21) or understood √מעט as an infinitive (Keil and Delitsch 1977:116; Garrett 1997:185). Three other proposed emendations have found adherents among modern commentaries. First, we might emend to וְיֶחֱלוּ, a Hiph *yiqtol* 3mp √חלה, meaning "they will weaken." The problem with this is that the Hiphil is transitive, which makes no sense here (cf. 7:5). Second, we might emend to וְיָחִילוּ, a Hiph *yiqtol* 3mp √חיל, meaning "they will writhe." Wolff (1974:144) notes that this verb is often used to describe those in political danger (e.g., Jer 4:19; 51:29; Ezek 30:16; Mic 4:10). Every option (even MT) requires emendation of some kind. The last option (√חיל) is the best; the *yiqtol* conjugation refers to future judgment and the meaning of √חיל fits well in this context of judgment.

מְעָט. Temporal adverb modifying וַיָּחֵלּוּ (or, as emended, וְיָחִילוּ). It might mean that consequences are coming "soon" (cf. Hos 1:4) or that Israel will be under judgment for a "short while." The latter makes sense in light of Hosea's statements in 3:4-5.

מִמַּשָּׂא מֶלֶךְ שָׂרִים. *Line d.* This PP continues the clause begun in line c. The prep מִן marks the origin of the writhing and pain (if we read וַיָּחֵלּוּ as from √חיל). מַשָּׂא describes a burden such as taxation or oppression. מֶלֶךְ שָׂרִים ("king of princes") is probably a title for the Assyrian monarch who is without equal in power (cf. the title מֶלֶךְ מְלָכִים applied to the king of Babylon in Ezek 26:7).

8:11 a כִּי־הִרְבָּה אֶפְרַיִם מִזְבְּחֹת לַחֲטֹא
b הָיוּ־לוֹ מִזְבְּחוֹת לַחֲטֹא׃

Lines a-b are a bicolon featuring noun//pronoun grammatical parallelism (אֶפְרַיִם//לוֹ). The exact repetition of מִזְבְּחֹת לַחֲטֹא in line b appears to be a dittography. However, all of the ancient versions represent both words, twice, as in MT (Gelston 2010:64*). Therefore, in spite of its awkwardness, the MT should be maintained. The lines are marked by *'Atnaḥ* and *Silluq*.

כִּי־הִרְבָּה אֶפְרַיִם מִזְבְּחֹת לַחֲטֹא. *Line a.* Temporal clause with כִּי subordinate to the main clause in line b. כִּי is similar to כַּאֲשֶׁר in that both can introduce events that take place prior to the main clause (JM §166o). In this verse, line a is subordinate to line b and temporally and logically prior to it.

הִרְבָּה. Hiph *qatal* 3ms √רבה.

אֶפְרַיִם. Subject of הִרְבָּה.

מִזְבְּחֹת. Acc compl of הִרְבָּה. This is the first occurrence of the word מִזְבֵּחַ ("altar") in the book.

לַחֲטֹא. Qal inf constr √חטא. The infinitive construct functions as a gerund that explains the circumstances or nature of the preceding action (WO §36.2.3e).

הָיוּ־לוֹ מִזְבְּחוֹת לַחֲטֹא. *Line b.* Independent clause.

הָיוּ. Qal *qatal* 3cp √היה. The subject of this verb is the first instance of מִזְבְּחֹת in line a.

לוֹ. PP with לְ of interest indicating that the altars became sin *to Ephraim*.

מִזְבְּחוֹת. Compl of הָיוּ. Thus מִזְבְּחֹת is both the subject and the complement of הָיוּ. The repetition seems awkward because "altars for sinning" became "altars for sinning." But that is exactly YHWH's point. They constructed altars to practice unorthodox, illegitimate religion and those altars led to all kinds of sin. Note that the first instance of מִזְבְּחֹת in line a has a defective spelling while the second instance (מִזְבְּחוֹת) in line b is *plene*.

לַחֲטֹא. Qal inf constr √חטא.

8:12 a אֶכְתָּוב־לֹו רֻבֵּי תּוֹרָתִי
b כְּמוֹ־זָר נֶחְשָׁבוּ׃

Lines a-b are a bicolon, with correspondence between נֶחְשָׁבוּ (line b) and its subject רֻבֵּי תּוֹרָתִי (line a). The lines are marked by *'Atnaḥ* and *Silluq*.

אֶכְתָּוב־לֹו רֻבֵּי תּוֹרָתִי. *Line a.* Conditional clause. The *yiqtol* (אֶכְתָּב) marks the protasis and the *qatal* (נֶחְשָׁבוּ) in line b marks the apodosis (see

GKC §159b-c). The idea is that even if YHWH were to write 10,000 instructions, Ephraim would reject them all as strange and inapplicable.

אֶכְתָּוב. Qal *yiqtol* 1cs √כתב. This is a *ketiv/qere*. The *ketiv* assumes the vocalization אֶכְתּוֹב while the vowels of the *qere* represent the form אֶכְתָּב with a short theme vowel due to the *maqqef*. The difference only concerns vocalization.

לוֹ. PP with לְ of interest, marking the person for whom the action is directed. The antecedent of the 3ms suffix is Ephraim (8:11).

רֻבֵּי. A *ketiv/qere*. The *ketiv* רִבּוֹ is a cardinal number referring to an immense number or "ten thousand" (HALOT 1178). The *qere* vocalization represents the form רֻבֵּי, a plural construct form of רֹב, which means "multitude" (HALOT 1173–74). Elsewhere, the plural construct form is רַבֵּי (cf. Job 16:13; Jer 39:13; 41:1). If the *qere* were correct, we would expect that the following genitive תּוֹרָתִי would be plural, "the multitude of my laws." However, because תּוֹרָתִי is singular, the *ketiv* is more likely. When higher cardinal numbers are used, the "enumerated item may follow as a collective singular" (WO §15.2.5a). The notion of writing 10,000 instructions is hyperbole used to show the depth of Ephraim's rebellion. There may be wordplay between 8:11, "Ephraim multiplied (הרבה) altars" and this verse, "10,000 (רבו) of my instructions."

תּוֹרָתִי. Collective singular meaning "my laws" and accusative complement of אֶכְתָּוב. The antecedent of the 1cs poss suffix is YHWH, the speaker in this section.

כְּמוֹ־זָר נֶחְשָׁבוּ. *Line b*. Independent clause.

כְּמוֹ. This is a longer, alternate form of the prep כְּ, which indicates agreement in kind. כְּמוֹ is commonly used with pronominal suffixes, but it is often also used in poetry (JM §103g).

זָר. A substantival adjective referring to something "different" or "peculiar." In other words Ephraim rejects YHWH's instructions and law as odd and therefore irrelevant. The irony is that Israel treats YHWH's laws as if they were foreign in an attempt to justify their worship of foreign gods (cf. Deut 32:16).

נֶחְשָׁבוּ. Niph *qatal* 3cp √חשב. The subject is the collective singular תּוֹרָתִי. The *qatal* is irreal because it marks the apodosis of a conditional sentence introduced by the *yiqtol* in line a.

Hosea 8:13

8:13 a זִבְחֵי הַבְהָבַ֗י יִזְבָּ֔חוּ
b בָּשָׂר֙ וַיֹּאכֵ֔לוּ
c יְהוָ֖ה לֹ֣א רָצָ֑ם
d עַתָּ֞ה יִזְכֹּ֤ר עֲוֺנָם֙
e וְיִפְקֹ֣ד חַטֹּאותָ֔ם
f הֵ֥מָּה מִצְרַ֖יִם יָשֽׁוּבוּ׃

Lines a-c are a tricolon concerned with unorthodox sacrifices. The third word יִזְבָּ֔חוּ must belong with line a in spite of the disjunctive *Rᵉbîaʿ* on הַבְהָבַ֗י. The lines are marked by *Jᵉtib*, *Zaqep parvum*, and *'Atnaḥ*. Lines d-f are also a tricolon. Lines d and e are parallel and feature the word pairs פקד//√זכר and עָוֺן//חַטָּאת, while line f is the conclusion. The lines are marked by *Pašṭa*, *Zaqep parvum*, and *Silluq*.

זִבְחֵי הַבְהָבַי יִזְבָּחוּ. *Line a*. Independent clause.

זִבְחֵי הַבְהָבַי. The noun זִבְחֵי in construct is the acc compl of יִזְבָּחוּ. The genitive הַבְהָבַי is a *hapax* and is usually regarded as corrupt. It may have been formed by duplication of הב and thus probably comes from either √אהב ("to love") or √יהב ("to give"). In support of the former option is G's expanded text which has θυσιαστήρια τὰ ἠγαπημένα ("beloved altars") at the end of the previous verse. This might suggest that G had √אהב in its Hebrew source text (on the other hand, the translator might have been faced with the same problem that we have and simply guessed). A better case can be made for √יהב, without emendation, because of the 1cs poss suffix, which refers to YHWH. The prophet's comments are interspersed throughout YHWH's first-person speech (see 8:1-3, 4-5, 10, 12, 14). The suffix is a subjective genitive (i.e., gifts from YHWH), indicating that they are taking the things that YHWH has given them and sacrificing them to other gods (cf. 2:10).

יִזְבָּחוּ. Piel *yiqtol* 3mp √זבח. The *yiqtol* is past imperfective with a frequentative sense; this is their regular practice. The past tense is indicated by the following *wayyiqtol* (simple past tense) in line b and *qatal* in line c.

בָּשָׂר וַיֹּאכֵלוּ. *Line b*. Independent clause.

בָּשָׂר. Acc complof וַיֹּאכֵלוּ. This is the meat of the sacrifices, which they eat as part of the ritual.

וַיֹּאכֵלוּ. Qal *wayyiqtol* 3mp √אכל. Some argue that the *wayyiqtol* here "represents a consequential or explanatory situation in the same time frame" as the preceding *yiqtol* יִזְבָּחוּ (cf. GKC §111t; WO §33.3.3c; Robar 2015:78–112). Assuming that the *yiqtol* in line a is nonpast, we would translate the present verb with the present tense, "they eat." However, Cook (2012:265) argues that examples of *wayyiqtol* expressing nonpast are all suspect and unconvincing. While it would be rare (or, according to Cook, impossible) for a *wayyiqtol* to express present tense, *yiqtol* verbs frequently refer to imperfective action in the past. Therefore, it makes better sense to translate both lines a and b with the past tense.

יְהוָה לֹא רָצָם. *Line c*. Independent clause. Lines c-e are nearly identical to the second half of Jer 14:10.

יְהוָה. Subject of רָצָם.

רָצָם. Qal *qatal* 3ms √רצה with a 3mp acc suffix. The same verb (negated) is used of rejecting sacrifices in Lev 7:18 and Ps 51:18 (cf. also Mal 1:8). While the antecedent of the 3mp suffix could be the people of Israel, it is more likely the sacrifices which YHWH rejects.

עַתָּה יִזְכֹּר עֲוֹנָם. *Line d*. Independent clause.

עַתָּה. This adverb introduces a transition and the logical conclusion of what precedes. Because YHWH has not accepted their sacrifices (line c), this tricolon (lines d-f) describes the consequences. Lines d-e are repeated (with a few minor differences) in 9:9 below.

יִזְכֹּר. Qal *yiqtol* 3ms √זכר. The idea of remembering in the OT usually refers to the implications that the past has for the present. If something is forgotten it no longer has any effect on the present. Here, YHWH's memory of their sin will result in judgment.

עֲוֹנָם. Acc compl of יִזְכֹּר. The antecedent of the 3mp poss suffix is the people of Israel.

וְיִפְקֹד חַטֹּאותָם. *Line e*. Independent clause. This line represents intensification of the previous line in the parallelism. In line d YHWH refuses to overlook their sin, but in line e he brings punishment.

וְיִפְקֹד. Qal *yiqtol* 3ms √פקד. Hosea used this word in the opening chapters to describe the consequences of unfaithfulness (1:4; 2:15; 4:9, 14).

חַטֹּאותָם. Acc compl of וְיִפְקֹד. The antecedent of the 3mp poss suffix is the people of Israel.

הֵמָּה מִצְרַיִם יָשׁוּבוּ. *Line f.* Independent clause.

הֵמָּה. This pleonastic 3mp pronoun anticipates the verb יָשׁוּבוּ at the end of the clause. It creates an inclusio with the same pronoun in 8:9 above, where הֵמָּה עָלוּ אַשּׁוּר ("they went up to Assyria") to hire lovers. Now, in 8:13 they will return to captivity, symbolized by Egypt. There is a symmetry between Assyria/Egypt and going/returning: the first is an act of rebellion and the second describes the consequences of that rebellion.

מִצְרַיִם. This unmarked PP (assuming לְ or אֶל) is the complement of √שׁוב, indicating its goal. The phrase is focus-fronted: it is to *Egypt* they will return. While historically some Israelites and Judahites did flee to Egypt for refuge in time of conquest and exile, Hosea's tendency to allude to YHWH's past salvation from Egypt (see 7:11) means that here it is probably a metonymy for captivity. This activates the irony that YHWH saved his people from captivity in Egypt and now they are going back.

יָשׁוּבוּ. Qal *yiqtol* 3mp √שׁוב. The *yiqtol* indicates a future reference. This is not a historical allusion to Egypt, but a reference to Egypt as a symbol for future captivity.

8:14 a וַיִּשְׁכַּח יִשְׂרָאֵל אֶת־עֹשֵׂהוּ
b וַיִּבֶן הֵיכָלוֹת
c וִיהוּדָה הִרְבָּה עָרִים בְּצֻרוֹת
d וְשִׁלַּחְתִּי־אֵשׁ בְּעָרָיו
e וְאָכְלָה אַרְמְנֹתֶיהָ: ס

Lines a-c are a tricolon. The first line (a) is introductory, while lines b and c exhibit parallelism with two word pairs (רבה//√בנה and בָּצוּר//הֵיכָל). The lines are marked by *R'bia'*, *Zaqep parvum*, and *'Atnaḥ*. Lines d-e are a bicolon. The noun אֵשׁ ("fire") is the accusative in line d and the subject in line e. In addition, the lines feature the word pair אַרְמוֹן//עִיר. The lines are marked by *Zaqep parvum* and *Silluq*. Lines b-e form a chiastic reversal. They (A) built palaces (הֵיכָל) and (B) cities (עָרִים) but (B') YHWH will burn their cities (עָרִים) and (A') palaces (אַרְמוֹן).

וַיִּשְׁכַּח יִשְׂרָאֵל אֶת־עֹשֵׂהוּ. *Line a.* Independent clause.

וַיִּשְׁכַּח. Qal *wayyiqtol* 3ms √שכח. This verb forms a contrast with √זכר in 8:13d: YHWH remembers their iniquity but they have forgotten (√שכח) him (cf. 2:15; 4:6).

יִשְׂרָאֵל. Subject of וַיִּשְׁכַּח.

אֶת־עֹשֵׂהוּ. Acc compl of וַיִּשְׁכַּח. It is a Qal ptc ms √עשה with a 3ms acc suffix. The antecedent of the suffix is Israel.

וַיִּבֶן הֵיכָלוֹת. *Line b*. Independent clause.

וַיִּבֶן. Qal *wayyiqtol* 3ms √בנה.

הֵיכָלוֹת. Acc compl of וַיִּבֶן. The word הֵיכָל refers to a temple (the dwelling place of a deity; e.g., 1 Sam 1:9) or a palace (the dwelling place of a king; e.g., 1 Kgs 21:1; Prov 30:28). In this context, administrative and royal complexes rather than cult sites are in view.

וִיהוּדָה הִרְבָּה עָרִים בְּצֻרוֹת. *Line c*. Independent clause.

וִיהוּדָה. Subject of הִרְבָּה.

הִרְבָּה. Hiph *qatal* 3ms √רבה. In 8:11 Ephraim "multiplied" (הִרְבָּה) altars for sinning; here Judah is multiplying fortified cities. Both are acts of rebellious independence from YHWH's leadership and protection.

עָרִים בְּצֻרוֹת. The fp noun עָרִים is the acc compl of הִרְבָּה, and it is modified by the attributive adjective בְּצֻרוֹת. The adjective בָּצוּר refers to defensive structures and fortifications such as walls, gates, and bars (cf. Deut 3:5). Deut 28:52 warns against putting one's trust in these fortified cities rather than in YHWH.

וְשִׁלַּחְתִּי־אֵשׁ בְּעָרָיו. *Line d*. Independent clause.

וְשִׁלַּחְתִּי. Piel *qatal* (irrealis) 1cs √שלח. In collocation with אֵשׁ, this verb means "to set fire." It often has humans as its subject (e.g., Judg 1:8; 2 Kgs 8:12) and does not necessarily refer to YHWH sending fire from heaven (but see Ezek 39:6).

אֵשׁ. Acc compl of וְשִׁלַּחְתִּי.

בְּעָרָיו. PP with בְּ indicating the domain of the action. As mentioned above, this is a reversal of line c (עָרִים). The antecedent of the 3ms suffix is Israel (which probably includes Judah).

וְאָכְלָה אַרְמְנֹתֶיהָ. *Line e*. Independent clause.

וְאָכְלָה. Qal *qatal* (irrealis) 3fs √אכל. The subject is the feminine אֵשׁ in the previous line (d).

אַרְמְנֹתֶיהָ. Acc compl of וְאָכְלָה. An אַרְמוֹן is a fortified palace or the citadel or guardroom within a palace. This line is a reversal of line b (הֵיכָל). The 3fs suffix likely refers to the feminine עָרִים and is a collective singular (cf. König 1897:§348g).

9:1–10:15: The Results of Israel's Infidelity

In the previous major unit, 4:1–8:14, Hosea describes Israel's past and present as he prosecutes YHWH's covenant and accuses Israel of having broken it. It was the pursuit of wealth, fertility, and security, combined with a lack of awareness that they had come from YHWH, that led Israel to pursue other means to what they wanted such as idols and foreign alliances.

In the present unit, 9:1–10:15, the prophet moves to the second phase in the structural cycle: Temporary Judgment. He announces, in four subunits, that YHWH will remove all of his good gifts: their food (9:1-9), their offspring (9:10-17), their cult sites (10:1-8), and the nation itself (10:9-15). They had hoped that their schemes would lead to flourishing but instead will lead to their downfall.

YHWH Will Destroy Their Hope: No Food (9:1-9)

The setting is apparently the harvest time, when the people celebrated abundant food and rejoiced in their festivals. But Hosea announces that they should not have joy, for YHWH will take away all of these gifts. Their agriculture was tainted by fertility religion (v. 1) in an attempt to improve the harvest. Instead, it will lead to the ruin of their food (v. 2). When they go into exile, the blessing of food will turn to defilement and mourning (v. 3). They will no longer have agriculture for sacrifices (vv. 4-5), and their carefully cultivated land will become an untended wasteland (v. 6). Apparently, Hosea's unpopular words were met with rejection and scorn. He reports that they called him a "fool" and "insane" (v. 7). In v. 8 he defends himself, stating that he has a responsibility as their "watchman" to tell the truth (v. 8) in spite of their intense corruption (v. 9).

> *¹Do not rejoice, Israel, for joy like the peoples,*
> *because you have committed fornication away from your God.*
> *You have loved the prostitute's fee on all the threshing floors of grain.*

²*Threshing floor and wine vat will not feed them,*
and new wine will fail her.

³*They will not live in the land of YHWH*
and Ephraim will return to Egypt,
and in Assyria they will eat unclean food.

⁴*They will not pour out wine as an offering to YHWH*
and their sacrifices will not be pleasing to him.

Theirs is the bread of mourning,
everyone who eats it will defile themselves.

Their bread is for their appetite,
it will not enter into the house of YHWH.

⁵*What will you do on the day of assembly,*
and on the day of the feast of YHWH?

⁶*For behold, they will have gone from destruction.*
Egypt will gather them,
Memphis will bury them.

As for the delights of their silver—
weeds will inherit them.
Thorns [will be] in their tents.

⁷*The days of punishment will come;*
the days of payment will come.
Let Israel know—

"The prophet is a fool!
The man of the spirit is insane!"

—because the abundance of your iniquity,
and abundant hostility.

⁸*The "watchman of Ephraim" is with my God.*
As for a prophet: a trap of fowlers is in all his ways;
hostility is in the house of his God.

⁹*They have deeply acted corruptly like in the days of Gibeah.*
He will remember their iniquity;
he will punish their sins.

Hosea 9:1

9:1 a אַל־תִּשְׂמַ֨ח יִשְׂרָאֵ֤ל ׀ אֶל־גִּיל֙ כָּֽעַמִּ֔ים
b כִּ֥י זָנִ֖יתָ מֵעַ֣ל אֱלֹהֶ֑יךָ
c אָהַ֣בְתָּ אֶתְנָ֔ן עַ֖ל כָּל־גָּרְנ֥וֹת דָּגָֽן׃

Lines a-c are a tricolon. All three lines address Israel in the second person (there is a change to third person in the next verse), and all three lines contain a verb followed by a PP. The lines are marked by *Zaqep parvum*, *'Atnaḥ*, and *Silluq*.

אַל־תִּשְׂמַח יִשְׂרָאֵל אֶל־גִּיל כָּעַמִּים. *Line a*. Independent clause.

תִּשְׂמַח. Qal juss 2ms √שמח negated with אַל. A time of harvest or a festival would naturally have been a time for rejoicing over plentiful food, but joy is not appropriate for Israel. They have rebelled against YHWH (see line b), and now, rather than an abundance of food, they will suffer agricultural ruin and a lack of food. The second-person verb addresses Israel, indicated by the following vocative יִשְׂרָאֵל.

אֶל־גִּיל. PP with אֶל indicating the purpose or outcome of the verb תִּשְׂמַח. Because the phrase seems awkward and the verbs √שמח and √גיל are often parallel elsewhere, a number of scholars emend and translate גִּיל as a verb ("do not shout") supposing that the major versions (G, T, S, V) represent either אַל־תָּגֵל (Qal juss 2ms √גיל) or אַל־גִּיל (Qal inf abs √גיל) (cf. Wolff 1974:149; AF 514; Stuart 1987:139). However, the infinitive absolute is usually negated with לֹא rather than אַל, and MT's reading is known elsewhere in Job 3:22.

כָּעַמִּים. PP with כְּ indicating agreement in kind. The point is that *other* peoples can celebrate over their bountiful harvest because they are not under judgment as is Israel.

כִּי זָנִיתָ מֵעַל אֱלֹהֶיךָ. *Line b*. Subordinate causal clause introduced by כִּי. This clause gives the preliminary reason that Israel should not rejoice: they have abandoned YHWH to "fornicate" with other gods.

זָנִיתָ. Qal *qatal* 2ms √זנה. It is somewhat strange that the verb is ms when it is usually used of females. However, Hosea is speaking to Israel (line a). This word is used elsewhere only in Hosea in 1:2; 2:7; 3:3; 4:10, 12, 13, 14, 15, 18, and 5:3. Hosea established the metaphor of spiritual unfaithfulness as adultery in the early chapters, and he picks up that theme again here.

מֵעַל אֱלֹהָיִךְ. PP with a compound prep מִן + עַל. The antecedent of the 2ms suffix on אֱלֹהִים is Israel, identified in line a. As mentioned in the discussion on 4:12d, the verb √זנה is frequently followed by a PP indicating what the subject is attracted toward or away from. In each of three occurrences, Hosea uses a different compound preposition. In 1:2 he says, תִזְנֶה הָאָרֶץ מֵאַחֲרֵי יְהוָה ("the land fornicates away from YHWH"—with an emphasis on the break in relationship). In 4:12 he says, וַיִּזְנוּ מִתַּחַת אֱלֹהֵיהֶם ("they fornicated away from their God")—with an emphasis on lack of submission). The compound מֵעַל refers to proximity. This sense might be motivated by the context of going away into captivity (see v. 3). In other words, because they chose to leave YHWH on their terms (in idolatry), now they will be forced to leave him on his terms (in captivity).

אָהַבְתָּ אֶתְנָן עַל כָּל־גָּרְנוֹת דָּגָן. *Line c.* Independent clause.

אָהַבְתָּ. Qal *qatal* 2ms √אהב.

אֶתְנָן. Acc compl of אָהַבְתָּ. The noun occurs nine times in the OT and refers to the pay of a prostitute (it occurs 7× in connection with the root √זנה). Hosea uses a variant form אֶתְנָה to describe the children in 2:14b.

עַל כָּל־גָּרְנוֹת דָּגָן. PP with עַל indicating the location of the action of √אהב. The celebrations at the threshing floor may have included illicit sexual activity. In any case, these events were occasions to credit fertility religion, rather than YHWH, for the successful harvest. In the construct phrase גָּרְנוֹת דָּגָן ("threshing floors of grain"), the genitive דָּגָן functions adjectivally and specifies the type of גָּרְנוֹת.

9:2 a גֹּרֶן וָיֶקֶב לֹא יִרְעֵם
b וְתִירוֹשׁ יְכַחֶשׁ בָּהּ׃

Lines a-b are a bicolon. In line a the verb is negated, and in line b a verb of the opposite sense is not negated, so they make similar statements in opposite ways. The lines are marked by *'Atnaḥ* and *Silluq*.

גֹּרֶן וָיֶקֶב לֹא יִרְעֵם. *Line a.* Independent clause.

גֹּרֶן וָיֶקֶב. The subjects of יִרְעֵם, a verb which is likely singular because גֹּרֶן ("threshing floor") and יֶקֶב ("wine press") are closely related and form a single idea (JM §150p). They both refer to places where a crop is processed by separating out the useable food. In this clause they form a metonymy for the entire agricultural endeavor.

יִרְעֵם. Qal *yiqtol* 3ms √רעה with a 3mp acc suffix. The antecedent of the suffix is the people of Israel (cf. 9:1). As mentioned above, Hosea alternates between second and third person throughout this section.

וְתִירוֹשׁ יְכַחֶשׁ בָּהּ. *Line b*. Independent clause.

וְתִירוֹשׁ. Subject of יְכַחֶשׁ. Hosea's use of תִירוֹשׁ ("new wine") is another link back to earlier chapters of the book. In 2:10 Israel credited Ba'al for the תִירוֹשׁ and as a result, YHWH says he will take it from them (2:11). In 7:14 they mourn over its loss.

יְכַחֶשׁ. Piel *yiqtol* 3ms √כחשׁ. Except for three instances, this verb always occurs in the Piel in the OT. It refers to denial or deception. In this context the "new wine" will deceive Israel because they will expect it, but it will fail to come (see Hab 3:17). We expect the vocalization יְכַחֵשׁ with the accent on the theme vowel. The MT form יְכַחֶשׁ in this verse, with the accent under the first root letter, on a short vowel, is an anomaly (cf. GKC §29g).

בָּהּ. The oblique compl of יְכַחֶשׁ is a 3fs suffix with בְּ. The verb √כחשׁ does not require a complement in all of its uses, but in the sense of "dealing falsely with," the object of deception is marked with בְּ (cf. Lev 5:21; Jos 24:27). Hosea refers to Israel or Ephraim with 3ms pronouns and verbs, or the people with 3mp forms, so the identification of the antecedent of the 3fs suffix here is uncertain. It is possible that the feminine pronoun refers to Israel collectively under the influence of the verb √זנה and the imagery of Israel as a faithless wife in the previous verse (cf. 9:1b-c). Garrett (1997:191) suggests that the antecedent is אֶרֶץ יְהוָה ("the land of YHWH"), which follows in v. 3.

9:3 a לֹא יֵשְׁבוּ בְּאֶרֶץ יְהוָה
b וְשָׁב אֶפְרַיִם מִצְרַיִם
c וּבְאַשּׁוּר טָמֵא יֹאכֵלוּ׃

Lines a-c are a tricolon which refers to Israel's exile from the land and into captivity. Following the primary statement in line a, lines b-c elaborate. They exhibit parallelism in the word pair אַשּׁוּר//מִצְרַיִם as well as semantic intensification from √שׁוב (they will return to captivity) to

√אכל (they will be unclean there). The lines are marked by *'Atnaḥ*, *Zaqep parvum*, and *Silluq*.

לֹא יֵשְׁבוּ בְּאֶרֶץ יְהוָה. *Line a*. Independent clause.

יֵשְׁבוּ. Qal *yiqtol* 3mp √ישב.

בְּאֶרֶץ יְהוָה. PP with locative בְּ. This is the only occurrence of the expression "land of YHWH" in the book. It is a reminder that the land belongs to YHWH (not to the Ba'als or even to Israel) and can be given or taken away. The people will not be able to enjoy the food of the harvest (cf. 9:2) because they will be in exile.

וְשָׁב אֶפְרַיִם מִצְרַיִם. *Line b*. Independent clause.

וְשָׁב. Qal *qatal* (irrealis) 3ms √שוב.

אֶפְרַיִם. Subject of שָׁב.

מִצְרַיִם. Unmarked PP (assuming אֶל), which is the complement of וְשָׁב, indicating the direction and goal of their return. Hosea sometimes omits prepositions (cf. 8:9, 13). How can they return to Egypt (line b) yet eat unclean food in Assyria (line c)? Hosea is again using "Egypt" as a symbol for captivity. While some Israelites might find their way there, the primary captivity will be in Assyria. This statement is similar to 8:13f. where Hosea says הֵמָּה מִצְרַיִם יָשׁוּבוּ ("they will return to Egypt"). See the discussion there and in 7:11.

וּבְאַשּׁוּר טָמֵא יֹאכֵלוּ. *Line c*. Independent clause. The word order is PP > compl > verb. Both the PP and the complement of the verb (טָמֵא) are fronted for focus. Not only will they be *in Assyria* (not the land of YHWH, line a), they will be eating *unclean food*! Hosea is announcing a terrible future and he places the key elements at the front of the clause.

וּבְאַשּׁוּר. PP with בְּ indicating the location where they will eat.

טָמֵא. Acc compl of יֹאכֵלוּ. The word טָמֵא is a substantival adjective. Used with √אכל, it refers to "unclean food." Hosea uses the verb √טמא in 5:3 and 6:10 to describe Israel. There is a certain poetic justice that Israel "defiled herself" with her fornication (√זנה) and now must be defiled in a foreign land.

יֹאכֵלוּ. Qal *yiqtol* 3mp √אכל. The subject is אֶפְרַיִם in the previous line. Although the verb שָׁב was singular in line b, the verb changes to plural (in this line) as the sentence continues because אֶפְרַיִם has a collective sense (GKC §145g). Wolff (1974:150) lists similar occurrences in 6:4; 7:11; 8:5, 8; 9:16.

Hosea 9:4

9:4 a לֹא־יִסְּכוּ לַיהוָה ׀ יַיִן
b וְלֹא יֶעֶרְבוּ־לוֹ זִבְחֵיהֶם
c כְּלֶחֶם אוֹנִים לָהֶם
d כָּל־אֹכְלָיו יִטַּמָּאוּ
e כִּי־לַחְמָם לְנַפְשָׁם
f לֹא יָבוֹא בֵּית יְהוָה׃

This verse contains three bicola. Lines a-b feature grammatical parallelism of noun (יְהוָה)//pronoun (לוֹ) as well as the correspondence of זֶבַח//יַיִן. The lines are marked by *Zarqa* and *R*ᵉ*biaʿ*. Lines c-d also feature grammatical parallelism of noun (לֶחֶם)//pronoun (וֹ) with lines marked by *Zaqep parvum* and *'Atnaḥ*. In lines e-f the noun (לֶחֶם) in line e is the subject of the verb יָבוֹא in line f. The lines are marked by *Zaqep parvum* and *Silluq*.

לֹא־יִסְּכוּ לַיהוָה יַיִן. *Line a*. Independent clause.

יִסְּכוּ. Qal *yiqtol* 3mp √נסך. This verb is used primarily in cultic references to pouring out liquid offerings to a deity including wine (e.g., Exod 29:40) or blood (e.g., Ps 16:4). There are references in the OT to liquid offerings made to YHWH (e.g., Lev 23:13) and to other deities (e.g., Jer 32:29; 44:17). The 3mp subject continues to be the people of Israel (cf. 9:1).

לַיהוָה. Adjunct PP with לְ marking the dative of advantage or the person for whom the action is directed.

יַיִן. Acc compl of יִסְּכוּ, specifying the nature of the liquid offering.

וְלֹא יֶעֶרְבוּ־לוֹ זִבְחֵיהֶם. *Line b*. Independent clause.

יֶעֶרְבוּ. Qal *yiqtol* 3mp √ערב. HALOT (876–77) lists five separate meanings for this root: (I) "to lend support, pawn"; (II) "to be mixed up with"; (III) "to be pleasing"; (IV) "to offer"; and (V) "to turn into evening." Root IV is attractive because of the parallelism with the previous line: "they will not *offer* their sacrifices to him." Both verbs would have the people of Israel as their subject. However, this sense of √ערב would be unique to this verse. The meaning could be root III: "their sacrifices will not *be pleasing* to him," a sense which is attested elsewhere in the OT. This reading, which is supported by G, requires that זִבְחֵיהֶם ("their sacrifices") be the subject.

כִּלְחֶם אוֹנִים לָהֶם. *Line c.* Independent verbless clause.

כִּלְחֶם אוֹנִים. The כְּ prep presents a challenge which has prompted several suggested solutions. First, if it is a comparative כְּ, the verbless clause requires a subject. The subject could be understood as זִבְחֵיהֶם ("their sacrifices") from the previous clause, giving the translation, "Their sacrifices are like bread of mourning to them." This reading is unlikely because זִבְחֵיהֶם (plural) would then be the natural antecedent of the 3ms suffix on אֹכְלָיו in the parallel line (d). A second, better option is to understand the כְּ prep as a כ *veritas*, which means "in every respect like" (cf. GKC §118x). On the basis of analogous instances (e.g., Lev 14:35; Neh 7:2; 1 Sam 20:3), לֶחֶם is the singular subject of the verbless clause (and therefore the antecedent of the 3ms pronoun in the next line), giving the translation, "Bread of mourning is theirs." לֶחֶם is in a construct relationship with אוֹנִים, which is the plural of אוֹנִי ("mourning").

כָּל־אֹכְלָיו יִטַמָּאוּ. *Line d.* Independent clause.

כָּל. Subject of יִטַמָּאוּ.

אֹכְלָיו. Qal ptc mp √אכל with a 3ms acc suffix. The plural participle is attributive and modifies כָּל which has a plural sense. The antecedent of the 3ms suffix is לֶחֶם in the previous line.

יִטַמָּאוּ. Hith *yiqtol* 3mp √טמא. When a Hithpael root begins with ד, ט, or ת (a dental stop), the ת of the Hithpael assimilates. Therefore, the expected form is יִטַמָּאוּ (the *qamets* under the מ is due to pause; cf. Lev 11:24; Ezek 20:7). In the form here, the *dagesh* representing that assimilation has dropped out (see also Ezek 37:23).

כִּי־לַחְמָם לְנַפְשָׁם. *Line e.* Independent verbless clause. The כִּי must be asseverative (see 2:2d).

לַחְמָם. Subject of the verbless clause. The antecedent of the 3mp poss suffix is the people of Israel.

לְנַפְשָׁם. This PP with לְ (of interest or advantage) is the predicate of the verbless clause. The word נֶפֶשׁ has a variety of senses including life, personality, or the self, but it can also refer to the throat. Here, it is a metonymy for their appetite.

לֹא יָבוֹא בֵּית יְהוָה. *Line f.* Independent clause.

יָבוֹא. Qal *yiqtol* 3ms √בוא. The subject is לֶחֶם in the previous line, and the sense is that their defiling food is inappropriate for sacrifices to YHWH (cf. Deut 26:14); it is only for them since they are also in a state of defilement (line d).

בֵּית יְהוָה. Constr phrase. בֵּית is the complement of יָבוֹא, indicating where they will enter. The verb √בוא usually takes an oblique complement with a preposition but not always (see 4:15). The phrase בֵּית יְהוָה usually refers to the temple in the OT. However, that was located in Judah (cf. 8:1b). Here, Hosea probably uses the expression in order to underscore their (future) separation from YHWH.

9:5 a מַה־תַּעֲשׂוּ לְיוֹם מוֹעֵד
b וּלְיוֹם חַג־יְהוָה׃

Lines a-b are a bicolon indicated by ellipsis of the verb תַּעֲשׂוּ. There is also a word pair (חַג//מוֹעֵד). The lines are marked by *'Atnaḥ* and *Silluq*.

מַה־תַּעֲשׂוּ לְיוֹם מוֹעֵד. *Line a*. Independent clause. מַה is the acc compl of תַּעֲשׂוּ. It introduces a rhetorical question that assumes a negative answer. How can they participate in the festivals and celebrations when they are in exile? See the causal clause in the next verse.

תַּעֲשׂוּ. Qal *yiqtol* 2mp √עשה. In this verse Hosea abruptly switches to second person, addressing the people of Israel directly. He switches back to third person plural in the following verse.

לְיוֹם מוֹעֵד. Adjunct PP with temporal לְ indicating the time of the action (cf. WO §11.2.10c). This is a construct phrase in which the adjectival genitive מוֹעֵד specifies the type of יוֹם (cf. WO §9.5.3d-h).

וּלְיוֹם חַג־יְהוָה. *Line b*. Independent clause. The interr מַה־ and the verb תַּעֲשׂוּ are elided. On this PP, see line a above. חַג probably represents semantic intensification in the parallelism. Whereas מוֹעֵד often refers to a general appointed gathering, a חַג is usually a specific feast instituted by YHWH. The construct phrase חַג יְהוָה indicates possession.

a 9:6 כִּי־הִנֵּה הָלְכוּ מִשֹּׁד
b מִצְרַיִם תְּקַבְּצֵם
c מֹף תְּקַבְּרֵם
d מַחְמַד לְכַסְפָּם
e קִמּוֹשׂ יִירָשֵׁם
f חוֹחַ בְּאָהֳלֵיהֶם:

This verse contains two tricola, each with an introductory line followed by two lines in parallel. In the first tricolon (lines a-c), lines b-c are parallel with two word pairs (מֹף//מִצְרַיִם; קבר√//קבץ√). The lines are marked by *Zaqep parvum*, *Ṭipḥa*, and *'Atnaḥ*. In the second tricolon (lines d-f), parallelism is activated by a word pair (חוֹחַ//קִמּוֹשׂ). The lines are marked by *Rᵉbiaʿ*, *Zaqep parvum*, and *Silluq*.

כִּי־הִנֵּה הָלְכוּ מִשֹּׁד. *Line a*. Subordinate causal clause marked with כִּי. This clause gives the reason that they will not be able to participate in the festivals (9:5): they will be captives in foreign lands.

הִנֵּה. Interjection that introduces and emphasizes a new or unsuspecting statement (HALOT 252).

הָלְכוּ. Qal *qatal* 3cp √הלך. In the context of a future threat of judgment, the use of the *qatal* conjugation must be proleptic. It views the action as a completed act in the future. The subject of the third-person plural verbs and pronouns continues to be the people of Israel.

מִשֹּׁד. Adjunct PP with abl מִן, designating movement away. The שֹׁד ("destruction") refers to the land of Israel, which has been devastated (see lines e-f below). They have gone from famine and lack of food in their own land into captivity.

מִצְרַיִם תְּקַבְּצֵם. *Line b*. Independent clause.

מִצְרַיִם. Subject of תְּקַבְּצֵם. Egypt is not just the location of the action, but the subject of the action (the verbs are f). The personification creates a sinister tone (AF 530). Perhaps the people think that they are going to Egypt for refuge, but they will be buried there. In Gen 50:25 Joseph makes his sons promise that they will carry his bones *out* of Egypt. The people of Israel in Hosea's time will not have that option.

תְּקַבְּצֵם. Piel *yiqtol* 3fs √קבץ with a 3mp acc suffix referring to the people of Israel. The verb √קבץ can have positive or negative connotations. In 2:2 it refers to YHWH *gathering* the exiles back together in the eschaton. However, in 8:10 YHWH says that he will *gather* them for punishment in spite of their whoring among the nations. Similarly, in this verse קבץ√ refers to destroying and gathering the dead.

מֹף תְּקַבְּרֵם. *Line c*. Independent clause.

מֹף. Subject of תְּקַבְּרֵם. "Memphis," the capital city of Lower Egypt and likely a synechdoche for the entire nation, is otherwise spelled נֹף in the Hebrew Bible (this is the only occurrence with מ). On the possibility of נ/מ variation in proper nouns, see Macintosh 2014:348.

תְּקַבְּרֵם. Piel *yiqtol* 3fs קבר√ with a 3mp acc suffix.

מַחְמַד לְכַסְפָּם. *Line d*. This construct phrase is a *casus pendens* that is a part of the clause that continues in line e. It is unusual for the construct phrase to be interrupted by the prep לְ, but this does occur elsewhere in the OT (see GKC §130a). The word מַחְמָד denotes something that is desirable and important to someone; it is sometimes used in the collocation מַחְמַד עֵינַיִם ("the delight of the eyes"; cf. 1 Kgs 20:6; Ezek 24:16). Elsewhere in the book, כֶּסֶף is mentioned in connection with making idols (2:10; 8:4; 13:2). That may be suggested here, although it might simply be a reference to their wealth that is destroyed in the ruination of the land.

קִמּוֹשׂ יִירָשֵׁם. *Line e*. Independent clause.

קִמּוֹשׂ. Subject of יִירָשֵׁם. This word for "thistles" or "weeds" is also used in Prov 24:31 and Isa 34:13 to describe abandoned, ruined land. It is a collective singular.

יִירָשֵׁם. Qal *yiqtol* 3ms ירשׁ√ with a 3mp acc suffix referring to the substantive מַחְמָד in the previous line (d). The weeds are personified: they will "inherit" the silver which is precious to the people of Israel.

חוֹחַ בְּאָהֳלֵיהֶם. *Line f*. Independent verbless clause.

חוֹחַ. Subject of the verbless clause. חוֹחַ refers to a "thorn," or by extension, "a hook" (2 Chr 33:11; Job 40:26). It describes a wild, unwanted plant that is often associated with pain. This is a further description of a land that is overrun because its inhabitants are gone.

בְּאָהֳלֵיהֶם. This PP with locative בְּ is the predicate of the verbless clause.

9:7 a בָּאוּ | יְמֵי הַפְּקֻדָּה
b בָּאוּ יְמֵי הַשִׁלֻּם
c יֵדְעוּ יִשְׂרָאֵל
d אֱוִיל הַנָּבִיא
e מְשֻׁגָּע אִישׁ הָרוּחַ
f עַל רֹב עֲוֺנְךָ
g וְרַבָּה מַשְׂטֵמָה:

This verse and v. 8 are among the most difficult in the book. Challenging (corrupt?) syntax as well as a cluster of ambiguities make it difficult to ascertain the meaning. Among the problems are: Who is the נָבִיא ("prophet") in these two verses? Is it Hosea himself or the false prophet mentioned in 4:5? What is the meaning of צֹפֶה in v. 8? What are the antecedents of the 1cs and 3ms suffixes in v. 8? Does נָבִיא in v. 8 belong with the preceding or following clause? In this verse, lines a-c are a tricolon. The first two lines are parallel, with identical repetition of the first two words followed by the correspondence of the word pair פְּקֻדָּה//שִׁלֻּם, and the third line forms a conclusion. The lines are marked by R⁴bi̅a‛, Zaqep parvum, and 'Atnaḥ. Lines d-e are a bicolon, indicated by the word pair מְשֻׁגָּע//אֱוִיל and semantic correspondence of נָבִיא//אִישׁ הָרוּחַ. The lines are marked by R⁴bi̅a‛ and Zaqep parvum. Lines f-g are also a bicolon, with correspondence of מַשְׂטֵמָה//עָוֺן. The lines are marked by Zaqep parvum and Silluq.

בָּאוּ יְמֵי הַפְּקֻדָּה. *Line a*. Independent clause.

בָּאוּ. Qal *qatal* (irrealis) 3cp √בוא. Even though this verb does not begin with a וְ, the VS word order indicates that it is irrealis. The prophet is describing a future judgment based on their present behavior. The complement of this verb (and the repetition in line b) is implicit (see 4:15).

יְמֵי הַפְּקֻדָּה. Constr phrase in which יְמֵי is the subject of בָּאוּ. The genitive פְּקֻדָּה comes from √פקד, a verb that always has YHWH as its subject in the book of Hosea (1:4; 2:15; 4:9, 14; 8:13; 9:9; 12:3). It describes punishment for particular actions.

בָּאוּ יְמֵי הַשִׁלֻּם. *Line b*. Independent clause.

בָּאוּ. Qal *qatal* (irrealis) 3cp √בוא. See above on line a.

יְמֵי הַשִׁלֻּם. Constr phrase in which יְמֵי is the subject of בָּאוּ. The genitive שִׁלֻּם is apparently a substantive derived from a Piel of √שׁלם (cf. HALOT 1511). It occurs two other times in the OT. In Isa 34:8 it is used in parallel with נָקָם ("vengeance") to describe punishment that fits the crime, and in Mic 7:3 it refers to a bribe. The Leningrad Codex (and thus BHS) does not have a *dagesh* in the שׁ with the definite article. This is likely an error (see BHS note a).

יֵדְעוּ יִשְׂרָאֵל. *Line c.* Independent clause.

יֵדְעוּ. Qal juss 3mp √ידע. Note the VS word order which is triggered by the jussive verb. The prophet is directing Israel to make note of the coming consequences (lines a-b).

יִשְׂרָאֵל. Subject of יֵדְעוּ.

אֱוִיל הַנָּבִיא. *Line d.* Independent verbless clause.

אֱוִיל. Predicate of the verbless clause.

הַנָּבִיא. Subject of the verbless clause. In 4:5 Hosea mentioned a prophet who was allied with the corrupt and illegitimate priesthood in leading the people astray. There is no other critique of Israel's leadership in the context here, however, so it seems that in this verse and in v. 8 the נָבִיא is Hosea himself (see also on מְשֻׁגָּע below). He uses the third person because he is quoting the statements that his audience is making against him. The people do not want to hear about coming judgment, so they call him a fool and insane.

מְשֻׁגָּע אִישׁ הָרוּחַ. *Line e.* Independent verbless clause.

מְשֻׁגָּע. Predicate of the verbless clause. מְשֻׁגָּע is a Pual ptc ms √שגע. It is used five times in the OT, always as an adjective which describes insane behavior. Significantly, in two of the four times outside of this verse, it is used in dismissive mocking of a prophet (2 Kgs 9:11; Jer 29:26). This supports the idea that Hosea's audience is mocking him in this verse, and he is reporting it.

אִישׁ הָרוּחַ. Constr phrase in which אִישׁ is the subject of the verbless clause. All of the occurrences of רוּחַ in the book have a negative sense (4:12, 19; 5:4; 8:7; 12:2; 13:15). Here, Hosea's audience is using the label derisively to refer to his role as a prophet.

עַל רֹב עֲוֹנְךָ. *Line f.* PP with עַל introducing a cause (cf. WO §11.2.13e). The accusations against Hosea in the previous two lines (d and e) are a parenthetical interruption in the sentence. Hosea has announced days of judgment (lines a-b), and now he resumes the sentence (in the second person) in lines f and g with the cause: their iniquity. רֹב עֲוֺנְךָ is an adjectival construct phrase in which the construct form רֹב modifies עֲוֺנְךָ (i.e., "the abundance of your iniquity"). This is sometimes called an "epexegetical genitive" (WO §9.5.3c). The antecedent of the 2ms suffix is Israel (cf. 9:1). It is also possible to understand lines f and g as a continuation of the speech quoted by Hosea. In other words, the people are accusing *him* of iniquity and hostility (cf. AF 515).

וְרַבָּה מַשְׂטֵמָה. *Line g*. This line is also governed by the prep עַל in the parallel line (f), therefore it also describes the cause of Hosea's rejection. The attributive adjective רַבָּה is not in construct with the substantive מַשְׂטֵמָה; it is in apposition (GKC §132b). The word מַשְׂטֵמָה only occurs two times in the OT, here and in v. 8 below. It is derived from √שׂטם—a by-form of √שׂטן—which means "to be hostile toward someone" (HALOT 1316).

9:8 a צֹפֶה אֶפְרַיִם עִם־אֱלֹהָי
b נָבִיא פַּח יָקוֹשׁ עַל־כָּל־דְּרָכָיו
c מַשְׂטֵמָה בְּבֵית אֱלֹהָיו:

Lines a-c are a tricolon. Line a introduces the verse while lines b-c exhibit grammatical parallelism of noun (נָבִיא)//pronoun (ו). The lines are marked by *'Atnaḥ*, *Zaqep parvum*, and *Silluq*. In this verse Hosea responds to the attacks directed toward him (reported in v. 7). He first defends himself in line a by stating that he is a watchman over Ephraim, and thus it is his responsibility to tell the truth. He then describes the difficulties of the prophetic office in lines b-c.

צֹפֶה אֶפְרַיִם עִם־אֱלֹהָי. *Line a*. Independent verbless clause.

צֹפֶה אֶפְרַיִם. The substantive צֹפֶה (Qal ptc ms √צפה), in construct with אֶפְרַיִם, refers to Hosea and is the subject of the verbless clause. The construct phrase indicates an objective genitive: he is the "watchman" over Ephraim. Hosea is contending that he says what is unpopular because he has a responsibility to say what is true, for their sake (cf. Ezek 33:2-7).

עִם־אֱלֹהָי. This PP is the predicate of the verbless clause. The prep עִם indicates accompaniment: Hosea joins his God in watching over Ephraim. The antecedent of the 1cs suffix is Hosea himself.

נָבִיא פַּח יָקוֹשׁ עַל־כָּל־דְּרָכָיו. **Line b.** Independent verbless clause.

נָבִיא. *Casus pendens.* The question is whether the prophet is the פַּח (trap) or the victim of the trap. Because the context is one of hostility against the prophet, it seems best to see נָבִיא as the victim as well as the antecedent of the 3ms pronouns in lines b and c.

פַּח יָקוֹשׁ. The noun פַּח (in constr) is the subject of the verbless clause. This construct phrase is used elsewhere (Ps 91:3). יָקוֹשׁ refers to a "fowler" or one who hunts for birds (see Prov 6:5; Jer 5:26).

עַל־כָּל־דְּרָכָיו. This PP with locative עַל is the predicate of the verbless clause. The antecedent of the 3ms pronoun on דְּרָכָיו is the prophet. Hosea is describing the challenges of being a prophet among such a hostile audience. They lay traps for him in whatever he does.

מַשְׂטֵמָה בְּבֵית אֱלֹהָיו. *Line c.* Independent verbless clause.

מַשְׂטֵמָה. Subject of the verbless clause. See 9:7g.

בְּבֵית אֱלֹהָיו. This PP with locative בְּ is the predicate of the verbless clause. The antecedent of the 3ms pronoun on אֱלֹהָיו is the *casus pendens* נָבִיא in the previous line, which in turn refers to Hosea. In line a, Hosea uses a 1cs pronoun to refer to himself. However, in lines b-c he speaks of the prophetic office in a more general sense in order to describe the challenges that he faces and to vindicate himself. If אֱלֹהָיו ("his God") refers to the prophet (i.e., Hosea) and YHWH, then בֵּית must refer to the land rather than to the temple, which was located in Judah (cf. 5:1; 6:10; 8:1; 9:4).

9:9 a הֶעְמִיקוּ־שִׁחֵתוּ כִּימֵי הַגִּבְעָה
b יִזְכּוֹר עֲוֹנָם
c יִפְקוֹד חַטֹּאותָם׃ ס

Lines a-c are a tricolon. Lines b-c are parallel, with corresponding verbs פקד√//זכר√ and the word pair עָוֹן//חַטָּאת. These lines are almost identical to lines 8:13d-e. In 8:13 these lines form a tricolon with a concluding line (f). Here, they form a tricolon with an introductory line (a). The lines are marked in this verse by *'Atnaḥ*, *Zaqep parvum*, and *Silluq*.

הֶעְמִיקוּ־שִׁחֵתוּ כִּימֵי הַגִּבְעָה. *Line a.* Independent clause.

הֶעְמִיקוּ. Hiph *qatal* 3cp עמק√. This verb is in an asyndetic relationship to the following verb שִׁחֵתוּ and modifies it adverbially. In this kind of construction, the second verb represents the principle idea (GKC §120g; JM §177g). The translation is, "They have deeply acted corruptly." See Hos 5:2 which uses √עמק similarly like an adverb; cf. also Isa 31:6 for the same construction.

שִׁחֵתוּ. Piel *qatal* 3cp √שחת. In the Piel this verb is usually transitive and means "to ruin" or "to corrupt." However, in a few occurrences it occurs without a complement and has a reflexive sense, in which the subject is "behaving corruptly" or corrupting itself (e.g., Ezek 32:7; Deut 9:12). This is the sense here as well.

כִּימֵי הַגִּבְעָה. Adjunct PP with כְּ indicating agreement in kind. The construct phrase יְמֵי הַגִּבְעָה is probably an allusion to the story found in Judg 19–21 in which a brutal gang rape led to civil war. In that dark time in Israel's history, rejection of the truth and the abuse of others brought about destruction. Hosea may be thinking of himself as the victim of a similar culture that is also destined for ruin.

יִזְכּוֹר עֲוֹנָם. *Line b*. Independent clause. See 8:13d. In this verse יִזְכּוֹר has a *plene* spelling.

יִפְקוֹד חַטֹּאותָם. *Line c*. Independent clause. See 8:13e. In this verse יִפְקוֹד has a *plene* spelling and no וְ conjunction.

YHWH Will Destroy Their Hope: No Children (9:10-17)

A new subunit begins in 9:10 with a mention of "Israel" (see also 9:1; 10:1) and a transition back to YHWH as speaker (cf. 8:4-14). In the previous section (9:1-9), Hosea declared that although the people had hoped that their fertility religion would increase food, it would instead lead to loss of food. In the present passage, Hosea looks at the situation from a different angle. The people had hoped that fertility religion would increase their offspring; instead it will lead to infertility and the death of their offspring. YHWH begins with an historical allusion to Ba'al Peor (cf. Num 25) which is appropriate given its sexual nature (v. 10). In vv. 11-13 and 16, YHWH declares that they will be unable to conceive and give birth to children, and even if they were to do so, he would kill their offspring. In v. 14 Hosea calls on YHWH to give the people miscarrying wombs and dry breasts.

At the end of the unit a second theme of expulsion and exile emerges. YHWH says in v. 15 that he will drive them out of his "house" (i.e., "land") because of their wickedness. Hosea speaks a second time in the last verse (v. 17), reporting that YHWH will scatter them among the nations. Thus, it is clear that the nation is not simply in the midst of a difficult season. YHWH is working against them—in fulfillment of the covenant curses—and he will ensure that their trust in the fertility cult results in the opposite of what they had hoped. Although the passage begins with a reference to "Israel" (v. 10), a *casus pendens* at the beginning of v. 11 shifts our attention to Ephraim for the remainder of the unit. The people there serve as a synechdoche for the rest of the nation.

> *10Like grapes in the wilderness I have found Israel;*
> *like early figs on a fig tree in its first season I have seen your fathers.*
>
> *They have come to Ba'al-Peor,*
> *and they consecrated themselves to shame,*
> *and they become detestable things like what they loved.*
>
> *11As for Ephraim, their population will fly away like a bird—*
> *without birth and without womb and without conception.*
>
> *12But if they raise their children,*
> *I will bereave them so that not a man is left.*
> *Indeed, woe is also theirs when I turn away from them.*
>
> *13Ephraim, as I saw, has become a palm tree planted in a pleasant place.*
> *And Ephraim is about to bring out his children to the killer.*
>
> *14Give to them, O YHWH—What will you give to them?*
> *Give to them a miscarrying womb and dried up breasts.*
>
> *15All their evil is at Gilgal,*
> *indeed there I hated them.*
>
> *On account of the evil of their deeds,*
> *I will drive them from my house.*
>
> *I will no longer love them;*
> *all their leaders are rebellious.*
>
> *16Ephraim will be stricken.*
> *Their root is dried up,*
> *they will not bear fruit.*
>
> *Even though they give birth,*
> *I will kill the cherished of their womb.*

¹⁷My God will reject them
for they have not listened to him.
And they will be wanderers among the nations.

9:10 a כַּעֲנָבִ֣ים בַּמִּדְבָּ֗ר מָצָ֙אתִי֙ יִשְׂרָאֵ֔ל
b כְּבִכּוּרָ֤ה בִתְאֵנָה֙ בְּרֵ֣אשִׁיתָ֔הּ רָאִ֖יתִי אֲבֽוֹתֵיכֶ֑ם
c הֵ֙מָּה֙ בָּ֣אוּ בַֽעַל־פְּע֔וֹר
d וַיִּנָּזְר֖וּ לַבֹּ֑שֶׁת
e וַיִּהְי֥וּ שִׁקּוּצִ֖ים כְּאָהֳבָֽם׃

Lines a-b are a bicolon with corresponding PPs with כְּ, PPs with בְּ, 1cs verbs (ראה√//מצא√), and complements (אָב//יִשְׂרָאֵל). The lines are marked by *Zaqep parvum* and *'Atnaḥ*. Lines c-e are a tricolon featuring a historical allusion to the incident at Ba'al-Peor. Lines d and e each contain a *wayyiqtol* verb and the corresponding substantives בֹּשֶׁת and שִׁקּוּץ. The lines are marked by *Rᵉbiaʿ*, *Zaqep parvum*, and *Silluq*.

כַּעֲנָבִים בַּמִּדְבָּר מָצָאתִי יִשְׂרָאֵל. *Line a*. Independent clause.

כַּעֲנָבִים. PP with כְּ indicating agreement in kind. Hosea previously used עֲנָבִים ("grapes") in 3:1. The PPs in this line and in line b are fronted for topicalization. Just as finding grapes, or early figs, in a harsh wilderness would be a delightful, wonderful surprise, YHWH found Israel in the wilderness and they were his delight. But joy turned to revulsion when they fornicated and worshiped with the people at Ba'al-Peor (lines c-e).

בַּמִּדְבָּר. PP with locative בְּ specifying the location of the grapes.

מָצָאתִי. Qal *qatal* 1cs מצא√. The subject of this verb is YHWH.

יִשְׂרָאֵל. Acc compl of מָצָאתִי.

כְּבִכּוּרָה בִתְאֵנָה בְּרֵאשִׁיתָהּ רָאִיתִי אֲבוֹתֵיכֶם. *Line b*. Independent clause.

כְּבִכּוּרָה. PP with כְּ indicating agreement in kind. The word בִּכּוּרָה refers to a delicious and desirable fig. In Isa 28:4 one swallows it as soon as he has it in his hand (cf. Jer 24:2; Mic 7:1).

בִתְאֵנָה. PP with locative בְּ specifying the location of the early figs.

בְּרֵאשִׁיתָהּ. PP with בְּ used temporally to specify further the time that the early figs are on the tree. The antecedent of the 3fs suffix is תְּאֵנָה ("fig tree").

רָאִיתִי. Qal *qatal* 1cs √ראה.

אֲבוֹתֵיכֶם. Acc compl of רָאִיתִי. YHWH usually refers to Israel in the third person in this section, but here he addresses them directly with a 2mp poss suffix.

הֵמָּה בָאוּ בַעַל־פְּעוֹר. *Line c.* Independent clause.

הֵמָּה. This 3mp pleonastic pronoun is the subject of בָּאוּ and refers to the people of Israel. It signals a transition from the activity of YHWH (lines a-b) to the activity of Israel (lines c-e).

בָּאוּ. Qal *qatal* 3cp √בוא.

בַעַל־פְּעוֹר. Compl of בָּאוּ. The verb √בוא usually takes oblique complements (see 4:15). This is another occurrence where the preposition is omitted (cf. 9:4). The place name בַעַל־פְּעוֹר is the site of an infamous apostasy in Israel's history (see Num 25:3-5 as well as references in Deut 4:3 and Ps 106:28).

וַיִּנָּזְרוּ לַבֹּשֶׁת. *Line d.* Independent clause.

וַיִּנָּזְרוּ. Niph *wayyiqtol* 3mp √נזר. This verb, in the Niphal and Hiphil, typically refers to abstaining from some substance or activity. For example, in Lev 22:2 the Aaronite priests are to "refrain" from the holy things dedicated to YHWH so that they do not profane his holy name. In Ezek 14:7 the verb describes one who "separates" himself from YHWH in order to pursue idols. Here, however, Hosea uses the verb not of separation but of consecration to something. It is likely a play on words that is highly ironic. A worshiper of YHWH was to abstain from things in order to demonstrate his or her devotion to YHWH, but at Ba'al-Peor the people joined themselves to what he finds abominable (Rudolph 1966:185–86). The sense would be something like, "they abstained *to* shame." The *wayyiqtol* conjugation of the verb indicates simple, narrative past which is appropriate for a historical allusion (see also line e).

לַבֹּשֶׁת. PP with לְ. We would expect the prep מִן with √נזר since it normally means "abstain *from* something." The choice of לְ continues Hosea's wordplay as it indicates the datival goal: that to which they consecrated themselves. The noun בֹּשֶׁת means "shame"; it is frequently used in later texts (possibly influenced by Hosea?) as a disparaging substitute for the name בַּעַל (cf. אֶשְׁבַּעַל in 1 Chr 8:33 rather than אִישׁ־בֹּשֶׁת in 2 Sam 2:8).

וַיִּהְיוּ שִׁקּוּצִים כְּאָהֳבָם. *Line e*. Independent clause.

וַיִּהְיוּ. Qal *wayyiqtol* 3mp √היה. The subject is the people of Israel who were at Ba'al Peor.

שִׁקּוּצִים. Compl of וַיִּהְיוּ. Here √היה means "to become something," therefore it takes a complement which indicates what the subject has become. שִׁקּוּץ means something that is detestable. It is used as a euphemism for excrement in Nah 3:6. In the other twenty-seven (out of 28 total) occurrences in the OT, it used of false gods or the cult objects that represent those gods. Therefore, this is another play on words. The Israelites have become detestable like the thing they worshiped.

כְּאָהֳבָם. PP with כְּ indicating a comparison. The form אָהֳבָם is unusual and it is unclear whether the suffix is objective or subjective. Some revocalize the word as אֹהֲבָם (a noun) and translate "their lover," which would refer to Ba'al. In other words, Israel has become as detestable to YHWH as Ba'al (cf. Stuart 1987:151–52). AF (541) read it as a *nomen agentis* (ptc) with an accusative suffix, "the one who loved them." Another approach is to analyze it as an infinitive construct with a subjective genitive. For example, Garrett (1997:149) translates, "like their love." In his view it is their love itself that is detestable. The problem with this belief is that, although the vowels in MT look like an infinitive, the usual form is אַהֲבָתָם with a ת (see 9:15 below). Therefore, we are left with either emending the vowels or viewing this form as anomalous. The translation above reflects vocalizing it as a noun אֹהַב with a 3mp poss suffix referring to the people of Israel (cf. הֵמָּה in line c). "Love" in this context means religious allegiance, although it may have a further relevance given the sexual nature of the actions at Ba'al-Peor.

9:11 a אֶפְרַיִם כָּעוֹף יִתְעוֹפֵף כְּבוֹדָם
b מִלֵּדָה וּמִבֶּטֶן וּמֵהֵרָיוֹן׃

Lines a and be are therefore a bicolon; line b decodes the metaphor in line a. The lines are marked by *'Atnaḥ* and *Silluq*.

אֶפְרַיִם כָּעוֹף יִתְעוֹפֵף כְּבוֹדָם. *Line a*. Independent clause.

אֶפְרַיִם. *Casus pendens* (see 7:8a where אֶפְרַיִם functions similarly; also 8:7c; 9:6d; 9:8b). This is a focus strategy which redirects the reader's attention to the contemporary situation following the historical allusion in 9:10. אֶפְרַיִם is resumed by the 3mp poss suffix on כְּבוֹדָם (see JM §156). Ephraim will now be the topic of the rest of the passage as a synechdoche for the nation as a whole.

כָּעוֹף. PP with כְּ indicating agreement in kind. Note the article, which is present because the noun is collective and used to make a comparison (GKC §126o).

יִתְעוֹפֵף. Hithpolel *yiqtol* 3ms √עוף. This is the only occurrence of the Hithpolel √עוף in the OT. In the Qal (21×) ths verb is usually used of flying in a particular direction, whereas the Polel (5×) is used of flying about here and there. The reflexive nature of the Hithpolel, in combination with the context here in 9:11, suggests that perhaps it means "to scatter" or "to fly off in different directions" (cf. HALOT 801).

כְּבוֹדָם. Subject of יִתְעוֹפֵף. The noun כָּבוֹד normally refers to "glory" or "riches." In this context it refers to Israel's population and perhaps especially their children who are so valuable to them (cf. Isa 5:13). In spite of their efforts in fertility religion, their "glory" will disappear and be gone. The antecedent of the 3mp suffix is the people of Ephraim.

מִלֵּדָה וּמִבֶּטֶן וּמֵהֵרָיוֹן. *Line b*. This line consists of three PPs which conclude the clause begun in line a. Each phrase is introduced by מִן which is used privatively, meaning "without" (cf. WO §11.2.11d). The verb לֵדָה is a Qal inf constr √ילד meaning "to give birth." The form is rare; we normally expect לֶדֶת with a ת suffix (see GKC §69m; Isa 37:3; Jer 13:21). The second phrase contains the noun בֶּטֶן meaning "belly" or "womb," here referring to gestation or pregnancy. The final noun הֵרָיוֹן is from the verb √הרה and means "conception." Thus, Hosea describes conception, gestation, and birth in reverse chronological order, as though it is being undone by YHWH. According to the logical order it is a pseudosorites (see 8:7e): there will be no conception; but even if there is conception there will be no gestation; and even if there is gestation there will be no birth.

9:12 a כִּי אִם־יְגַדְּלוּ אֶת־בְּנֵיהֶם
b וְשִׁכַּלְתִּים מֵאָדָם
c כִּי־גַם־אוֹי לָהֶם בְּשׂוּרִי מֵהֶם:

Lines a-c are a tricolon. The first two lines form a conditional sentence while line c is a separate independent clause that concludes the verse. The lines are marked by *Zaqep parvum*, *'Atnah*, and *Silluq*.

כִּי אִם־יְגַדְּלוּ אֶת־בְּנֵיהֶם. *Line a*. Subordinate conditional clause. The collocation כִּי אִם is usually exceptive or restrictive. It frequently functions as a strong adversative, "but" or "rather" (cf. WO §38.6; 39.3.5d). Here, however, line a is the protasis in a conditional sentence. Perhaps the כִּי is adversative; אִם is the conditional particle. The context (v. 11) would suggest that line a is another pseudosorites (see 8:7e). YHWH has just said that they will *not* have children (9:11b). Now he says that even if they do (9:12a), he will bereave them (9:12b). If this analysis is correct, we would expect an irreal conditional clause, which is usually introduced by the particle לוּ rather than אִם. However, GKC (§159m) suggests that the distinction between the two particles is not always strictly observed.

יְגַדְּלוּ. Piel *yiqtol* 3mp √גדל. The Qal of √גדל means to "grow" and the Piel means "to raise." It is the latter that is frequently used of raising children to adulthood.

אֶת־בְּנֵיהֶם. Compl of יְגַדְּלוּ. The antecedent of the 3mp poss suffix is the people of Israel/Ephraim (cf. 9:10-11).

וְשִׁכַּלְתִּים מֵאָדָם. *Line b*. Independent clause which is the apodosis of the conditional sentence in lines a-b.

וְשִׁכַּלְתִּים. Piel *qatal* (irrealis) 1cs √שכל with a 3mp acc suffix. The Piel of √שכל is usually transitive and refers to depriving someone of his or her children (i.e., killing them). Intransitive uses refer to miscarriage or the failure to produce offspring in the first place.

מֵאָדָם. PP with privative מִן (see 9:11b). The sense is, "I will bereave them *to a man*!" or "so that not a person is left."

כִּי־גַם־אוֹי לָהֶם. *Line c*. Independent verbless clause. With כִּי and גַם we expect the common expression גַם כִּי, which is usually concessive (e.g., "even though"). Here the words are reversed. כִּי is probably asseverative (although it could be causal) and גַם has the common adverbial sense "also." In other words, in addition to the pain of bereavement (line b), they will experience additional woe (אוֹי) as well.

אוֹי. Subject of the verbless clause. Hosea pronounces אוֹי on Ephraim in 7:13 for straying from YHWH and going to other nations for help. Here, he describes the specifics of that woe.

לָהֶם. The predicate of the verbless clause is a PP with לְ indicating possession. The antecedent of the 3mp suffix is the people of Israel and Ephraim.

בְּשׂוּרִי מֵהֶם. *Line c.* Temporal clause.

בְּשׂוּרִי. Qal inf constr √שׂור with a 1cs subject suffix. √שׂור is an alternate spelling of √סור ("to turn aside"). The בְּ prep indicates that the temporal infinitive describes action that takes place at the same time as the preceding main clause. YHWH is the main speaker in the discourse and the antecedent of the 1cs suffix.

מֵהֶם. PP; מִן has an ablative sense. The antecedent of the 3mp suffix is the people of Israel and Ephraim.

9:13 a אֶפְרַיִם כַּאֲשֶׁר־רָאִיתִי לְצוֹר שְׁתוּלָה בְנָוֶה
b וְאֶפְרַיִם לְהוֹצִיא אֶל־הֹרֵג בָּנָיו׃

Lines a-b are a bicolon featuring a repetition of אֶפְרַיִם at the beginning of each line. The lines are marked by *'Atnaḥ* and *Silluq*.

אֶפְרַיִם כַּאֲשֶׁר־רָאִיתִי לְצוֹר שְׁתוּלָה בְנָוֶה. *Line a.* The line begins with the subject (אֶפְרַיִם) of a clause, continues with a parenthetical temporal clause (כַּאֲשֶׁר־רָאִיתִי), and concludes with the predicate of the clause (לְצוֹר שְׁתוּלָה בְנָוֶה).

כַּאֲשֶׁר־רָאִיתִי. *Line a.* Subordinate temporal clause. The כְּ prep indicates an action contemporary to that of the main clause which precedes. The word אֲשֶׁר is a nominalizer; the אֲשֶׁר clause is the complement of the prep כְּ (Holmstedt 2016:119, 124).

רָאִיתִי. Qal *qatal* 1cs √ראה. YHWH is the speaker.

לְצוֹר שְׁתוּלָה בְנָוֶה. *Line a.* This conclusion of the clause begun with אֶפְרַיִם is difficult and many solutions have been proposed. One possible explanation of MT is as follows:

לְצוֹר. Macintosh (2014:370–71) proposes that this PP with לְ is the oblique complement of an implied verb הָיָה. Hosea has left out the verb due to the elliptical style of the oracle. When the verb √היה means "to become" something, it typically marks its complement with לְ (cf. the first five occurrences of היה in the OT: Gen 1:14, 15, 29; 2:10, 24). The word צוֹר has commonly been read as the place name "Tyre," but that would be a sudden introduction into the context. Furthermore, the following verb שְׁתוּלָה, which modifies צוֹר, is always used of plants or trees. Macintosh (2014:371) suggests that the word refers to a "palm tree" in connection with Arabic *ṣur*.

שְׁתוּלָה. Qal pass ptc fs √שׁתל.

בְנָוֶה. PP with locative בְּ. The word נָוֶה refers to a meadow or a place for grazing. It has positive connotations of being pleasant. The sense of line a on this reading would then be that Ephraim is like a flourishing plant in a pleasant location, yet the following lines states that their children are about to be slaughtered by their enemy. This shocking contrast is similar to the one in 9:10 above.

וְאֶפְרַיִם לְהוֹצִיא אֶל־הֹרֵג בָּנָיו. *Line b*. Independent verbless clause.

וְאֶפְרַיִם. Subject of the verbless clause.

לְהוֹצִיא. This Hiph inf constr √יצא is the predicate of the verbless clause (i.e., "Ephraim [is] to bring out …"). The infinitive in this construction can have the sense of an action that is inescapable (or imperatival) or an action that is immanent (cf. GKC §114h, k; WO §36.2.3g).

אֶל־הֹרֵג. PP with אֶל indicating direction or goal. הֹרֵג is a Qal ptc ms √הרג used as a substantive.

בָּנָיו. Acc compl of לְהוֹצִיא. The antecedent of the 3ms poss suffix is אֶפְרַיִם from the beginning of the line.

9:14 a תֵּן־לָהֶם יְהוָה מַה־תִּתֵּן
b תֵּן־לָהֶם רֶחֶם מַשְׁכִּיל וְשָׁדַיִם צֹמְקִים׃

Lines a-b are a bicolon featuring repetition of תֵּן־לָהֶם as well as a correspondence between the interr מַה and the phrases רֶחֶם מַשְׁכִּיל and וְשָׁדַיִם צֹמְקִים. This verse represents a kind of staircase parallelism, a poetic structure in which a sentence is begun in the first line of a bicolon, interrupted by a vocative (here, יְהוָה), then started again and brought to completion in the second line (cf. Watson 1986:150–56). In this instance

Hosea 9:14

there is an additional question following the vocative in line a. The lines are marked by *'Atnaḥ* and *Silluq*.

תֵּן־לָהֶם יְהוָה. *Line a*. Independent clause.

תֵּן־לָהֶם. Qal impv ms √נתן. This is a trivalent verb taking two complements. The first complement, which indicates the goal or recipient of the action, is the following PP לָהֶם. The second complement (the semantic patient) is omitted in this clause because of the interruption of the vocative יְהוָה in the staircase parallelism. However, the accusative complement is supplied in the context by the interr מָה in the next clause and the complements of √נתן in line b.

מַה־תִּתֵּן. *Line a*. Independent clause.

מָה. This interrogative particle is the accusative complement of the following תִּתֵּן. Its referent is identified, in line b, as רֶחֶם and שָׁדַיִם.

תִּתֵּן. Qal *yiqtol* 2ms √נתן. In contrast to the previous clause, here √נתן has an accusative complement (מָה) but not the second PP complement that indicates the recipient of the action. It is supplied by לָהֶם in the previous clause.

תֵּן־לָהֶם רֶחֶם מַשְׁכִּיל וְשָׁדַיִם צֹמְקִים. *Line b*. Independent clause.

תֵּן־לָהֶם. Qal impv ms √נתן. See the discussion for line a.

רֶחֶם. First of two acc compls of תֵּן in this line.

מַשְׁכִּיל. Hiph ptc ms √שכל. This participle functions as an attributive adjective modifying רֶחֶם. The use of √שכל ("bereave" or "miscarry") does not suggest that the רֶחֶם ("womb") will be unable to conceive. Rather, it means that having conceived, it will miscarry.

וְשָׁדַיִם. Second of two acc compl of תֵּן. Usually nouns are feminine if they are body parts that occur in pairs (e.g., רֶגֶל, עַיִן). However, שַׁד ("breast") is an exception; it is masculine (cf. JM §134j).

צֹמְקִים. Qal ptc mp √צמק. This participle functions as an attributive adjective modifying שָׁדַיִם. It is plural because verbs, adjectives, and pronouns have no dual form (GKC §145n). The verb is a *hapax*, but cognates indicate that it refers to drying up or withering (HALOT 1034). Hosea's call for miscarrying wombs and dry breasts "mocks and cancels the prayers for fecundity that went with the fertility rites" (AF 544).

9:15 a כָּל־רָעָתָם בַּגִּלְגָּל
b כִּי־שָׁם שְׂנֵאתִים
c עַל רֹעַ מַעַלְלֵיהֶם
d מִבֵּיתִי אֲגָרְשֵׁם
e לֹא אוֹסֵף אַהֲבָתָם
f כָּל־שָׂרֵיהֶם סֹרְרִים:

This verse consists of three bicola. Lines a-b are joined through the correspondence of שָׁם/גִּלְגָּל as well as the repetition of the 3mp pronominal suffix ם- in each line. The lines are marked by *Pašta* and *Zaqep parvum*. Lines c-d comprise one sentence: line c is a PP in the clause completed in line d. These lines also repeat the 3mp suffix. The lines are marked by *Zaqep parvum* and *'Atnaḥ*. Lines e-f also have corresponding 3mp pronominal suffixes. The lines of this last bicolon are marked by *Zaqep parvum* and *Silluq*.

כָּל־רָעָתָם בַּגִּלְגָּל. *Line a*. Independent verbless clause.

כָּל־רָעָתָם. Constr phrase. Subject of the verbless clause. The antecedent of the 3mp poss suffix is the people of Ephraim (vv. 13, 16), which serve as a metonymy for Israel as a whole.

בַּגִּלְגָּל. This PP with locative בְּ is the predicate of the verbless clause. Gilgal was a significant site in the history of YHWH's dealings with Israel from the time of Joshua. However, it had become a central place of illegitimate sacrifice and an epicenter of the nation's corruption and rebellion (see 4:15). Because he states, "all their evil is at Gilgal," the site must be a synechdoche for the nation as a whole (Stuart 1987:154).

כִּי־שָׁם שְׂנֵאתִים. *Line b*. Independent clause. The כִּי is asseverative. It would make no sense to analyze it as introducing a causal clause stating that they were evil (line a) because YHWH hated them (line b). YHWH is stating the opposite: he hated them because they were evil.

שָׁם. A locative adverb specifying where YHWH hated them.

שְׂנֵאתִים. Qal *qatal* 1cs √שׂנא with a 3mp acc suffix. YHWH continues to speak in this section (except for vv. 14 and 17) with 1cs forms (cf. 9:10, 12, 13, 16). The verb שָׂנֵא refers to the antithesis of √אהב ("love"). Just as √אהב often refers not to an emotion but to actions that will lead to someone's benefit, שָׂנֵא refers to rejection and actions that bring harm to someone. It is the response to the breaking of the covenant. The *qatal* is inchoative, stating that the events at Gilgal triggered the change in YHWH's attitude toward Israel.

עַל רֹעַ מַעַלְלֵיהֶם. *Line c*. PP with עַל indicating the cause of the action in line d (cf. WO §11.2.13e). The construct phrase is epexegetical (cf. WO §9.5.3c): the noun רֹעַ ("evil" or "corrupt") characterizes the genitive מַעַלְלֵיהֶם ("their deeds").

מִבֵּיתִי אֲגָרְשֵׁם. *Line d*. Independent clause.

מִבֵּיתִי. PP with abl מִן designating movement away from a specified point (WO §11.2.11b). The word בַּיִת refers to the land of Israel, from which YHWH will drive them (cf. 8:1; 9:4, 8). The antecedent of the 1cs poss suffix is YHWH, the speaker in this section.

אֲגָרְשֵׁם. Piel *yiqtol* 1cs √גרש with a 3mp acc suffix. The antecedent of the suffix is the people of Ephraim (see line a).

לֹא אוֹסֵף אַהֲבָתָם. *Line e*. Independent clause.

אוֹסֵף. This verb looks like a Hiph juss 1cs √יסף (the indicative *yiqtol* form would be אוֹסִיף). However, it is negated by לֹא, which is used with indicative verbs. The reference grammars solve this problem in various ways: GKC argues that לֹא is, on occasion, used with jussive forms (§109d). JM, however, argues that the verb is indicative (§114g). They analyze the verb as a Qal *yiqtol* 1cs √יסף, which only resembles the Hiphil jussive (§75f). In any case, the verb is here used as an auxiliary meaning "to do again" with the infinitive אַהֲבָתָם as its complement (see 1:6). The 1cs subject is YHWH.

אַהֲבָתָם. Qal inf constr √אהב with a 3mp acc suffix. This verb √אהב ("love") forms a pair with √שנא ("hate") in line b and also refers to an act of the will rather than to an emotion. YHWH will no longer benefit them and act for their good.

כָּל־שָׂרֵיהֶם סֹרְרִים. *Line f*. Independent verbless clause.

כָּל־שָׂרֵיהֶם. Constr phrase. Subject of the verbless clause. The noun שַׂר is a general term for "leader" or "official." Note that in BHS the word is missing an expected ָ (*qamets*) under the שׂ. BHS note ᵃ states that the vowel is missing in the Leningrad Codex. However, that is incorrect; it is clearly present in the facsimile (Freedman et al. 1998) and is represented correctly in BHQ (18).

סֹרְרִים. Qal ptc mp √סרר. This is the predicate of the verbless clause (cf. WO §37.6a).

9:16 a הֻכָּה אֶפְרַיִם
b שָׁרְשָׁם יָבֵשׁ
c פְּרִי בַלִי־יַעֲשׂוּן
d גַּם כִּי יֵלֵדוּן
e וְהֵמַתִּי מַחֲמַדֵּי בִטְנָם׃ ס

Lines a-c are a tricolon. The general description of Ephraim in line a ("stricken") is explained with the metaphors (פְּרִי//שֹׁרֶשׁ) that correspond in lines b and c. The lines are marked by *Zaqep parvum*, *Tipḥa*, and *ʾAtnaḥ*. Lines d-e are a bicolon. Line d contains a concessive clause subordinate to the main clause in line e. The lines are marked with *Zaqep parvum* and *Silluq*. This verse contains another pseudosorites (cf. 8:7e; 9:11, 12). Hosea states that they will not give birth to children (lines b-c), but *even if they do* (line d), YHWH will kill those children (line e).

הֻכָּה אֶפְרַיִם. *Line a*. Independent clause.

הֻכָּה. Hoph *qatal* (irrealis) 3ms √נכה. The VS word order in this clause indicates that the verb is irrealis and expresses a prophetic prediction. The verb √נכה refers to being beaten, wounded, or killed, depending upon the context. Here the reference to Ephraim is metaphorical: their wound consists of being unable to bear children (cf. lines b-c). The agent of the passive verb is identified in the context as YHWH (cf. 9:12, 14, 15, 16e).

אֶפְרַיִם. Subject of הֻכָּה.

שָׁרְשָׁם יָבֵשׁ. *Line b*. Independent clause.

שָׁרְשָׁם. Subject of יָבֵשׁ. The antecedent of the 3mp poss suffix is the people of Ephraim (cf. line a). The metaphor is that of a sickly plant that is unable to produce offspring. The "root" refers to the nation that is unable to bear children or "fruit" (see line c). It is from a healthy root that a plant grows and produces fruit, but this root is dried up.

יָבֵשׁ. Qal *qatal* 3ms √יבש. The *qatil* vowel pattern indicates that this is a stative verb (see JM §41b). In contrast to fientive or dynamic verbs that describe what the subject *does*, stative verbs describe a circumstance, quality, or state (WO §22.2.1). Therefore, *qatal* stative verbs are typically translated in the present tense. Here the present character of the root ("dried up"; line b) means that it will not bear fruit in the future (line c).

פְּרִי בְלִי־יַעֲשׂוּן. *Line c*. Independent clause.

פְּרִי. Acc compl of יַעֲשׂוּן. The people of YHWH served fertility deities in an attempt to *increase* their offspring. Instead, their actions will result in no offspring at all.

בְלִי. A *ketiv/qere*. The *ketiv* assumes the vocalization בְּלִי. The word בְּלִי usually negates substantives (e.g., "without"), but it can negate finite verbs (cf. 8:7). The *qere* form is בַּל, a negative particle used mostly in poetic texts (cf. HALOT 131). The *ketiv* is probably preferable since Hosea uses it elsewhere in 4:6, 7:8, and 8:7. In addition, it rhymes with the preceding word פְּרִי (Macintosh 2014:378).

יַעֲשׂוּן. Qal *yiqtol* 3mp √עשׂה with a paragogic ן (see WO §31.7.1a-b; JM §44e). When עשׂה has פְּרִי as its complement, it means "to bear" or "to produce" (cf. Ezek 17:23; Amos 9:14).

גַּם כִּי יֵלֵדוּן. *Line d*. Subordinate concessive clause with גַּם כִּי (cf. JM §171c). A concessive clause introduces a contrast with the main clause combined with the notion of causality. One would expect that giving birth would lead to a having a child (line d), but they will not have a child after all (line e). This line is the focal point of the pseudosorites. YHWH has just said that they will not be able to bear children (lines a-c), now he says that even if they do, he will take away their offspring anyway.

יֵלֵדוּן. Qal *yiqtol* 3mp √ילד with a paragogic ן (see line c above).

וְהֵמַתִּי מַחֲמַדֵּי בִטְנָם. *Line e*. Independent clause.

וְהֵמַתִּי. Hiph *qatal* (irrealis) 1cs √מות.

מַחֲמַדֵּי בִטְנָם. Constr phrase. מַחֲמַדֵּי is the acc compl of וְהֵמַתִּי. The genitive relationship of the phrase is possessive, literally, "the precious things [i.e., children] belonging to their womb." The children are precious to their parents and highly valued. The image is startling and uncomfortable as the בֶּטֶן ("belly" or "womb"), which evokes the ideas of maternal care and protection, is the place where YHWH kills. The masculine 3p suffix is strange given the imagery of childbearing; it likely refers to the population as a whole (see AF 546).

9:17 a יִמְאָסֵם אֱלֹהַי
b כִּי לֹא שָׁמְעוּ לוֹ
c וְיִהְיוּ נֹדְדִים בַּגּוֹיִם: ס

Lines a-c are a tricolon that concludes this section. The tricolon features noun (אֱלֹהַי)//pronoun (לוֹ) parallelism in lines a-b. Lines a and c describe Ephraim's fate, while line b specifies the cause. The lines are marked by *Zaqep parvum*, *'Atnaḥ*, and *Silluq*.

יִמְאָסֵם אֱלֹהַי. *Line a.* Independent clause.

יִמְאָסֵם. Qal *yiqtol* 3ms √מאס with a 3mp acc suffix. The antecedent of the suffix is the people of Ephraim. Stuart (1987:149, 154) understands this verb and וְיִהְיוּ in line c as jussives. For him, Hosea is calling down the covenant curses on Israel and urging YHWH to judge them

אֱלֹהַי. Subject of יִמְאָסֵם. YHWH has been the speaker in this section (except for v. 14), using 1cs verb forms. Here, the prophet speaks, referring to YHWH as "my God." In v. 14 Hosea addressed YHWH in a prayer, here he addresses his audience/the reader in a concluding statement.

כִּי לֹא שָׁמְעוּ לוֹ. *Line b.* Subordinate causal clause with כִּי giving the reason that YHWH will reject his people.

שָׁמְעוּ. Qal *qatal* 3cp √שמע.

לוֹ. Oblique compl of שָׁמְעוּ indicating the person listened to. Although Hosea could have used the stronger idiom שמע בְּקוֹל ("to obey"), his use of the PP לוֹ likely refers to Ephraim's failure to heed or submit to YHWH, not simply that they did not hear what he said.

וְיִהְיוּ נֹדְדִים בַּגּוֹיִם. *Line c.* Independent clause.

וְיִהְיוּ. Qal *yiqtol* 3mp √היה.

נֹדְדִים. Qal ptc mp √נדד used substantivally. In a twist, Israel has √נדד ("wandered") from YHWH (7:13), so now they will be wanderers (נֹדְדִים) among the nations.

בַּגּוֹיִם. Adjunct PP with locative בְּ. Hosea concludes the section with another reference to exile. YHWH's wrath is fearsome: not only will he ruin their hope as a nation by destroying their offspring and preventing future generations, he will scatter them in distant lands.

YHWH Will Destroy Their Cult Sites (10:1-8)

Hosea once again begins a new unit with a mention of "Israel" (9:1; 9:10; 10:9; 11:1). This unit is also distinguished from the previous one by topic (cult sites) and primary speaker (Hosea). YHWH was the speaker in 8:4-14, Hosea in 9:1-9, and YHWH in 9:10-17. Now, in 10:1-8 Hosea speaks once again, referring to the people of Israel in the third person except when he quotes them (vv. 3, 5, 8).

The unit is structured so that references to illicit worship practices and items (vv. 1-2, 5-6, 8) are interwoven with Israel's trust in politics (vv. 3-4, 7). The prophet begins by describing how Israel took YHWH's good gifts and used them to rebel against him by creating illicit cult structures. Their worship at ritual high places was intended to secure their future and make their land flourish. Instead, YHWH will destroy their ritual places (vv. 2, 5-6) along with their nation (v. 7). Those who survive will wish for death because of their shame and hopelessness (v. 8).

¹A luxuriant vine is Israel;
he produced fruit for himself.

According to the abundance of his fruit,
he multiplied altars.
According to the good of his land,
they improved pillars.

²Their heart is false—
now they are guilty.

He will break the neck of their altars;
he will devastate their pillars.

³Now they will say,
"We have no king,
for we have not feared YHWH,
and the king—what could he do for us?"

⁴They made promises;
made empty oaths;
made a covenant.

"Justice" sprouts like a poisoned plant
in the furrows of the field.

> ⁵*For the calves of Beth Aven they are afraid,*
> *and for the "resident" of Samaria.*
>
> *Its people will mourn over it,*
> *and its idolatrous priests, over it—*
>
> *who rejoice over its glory—*
> *for it will have gone into exile from them.*
>
> ⁶*Moreover it will be carried to Assyria—*
> *a gift for the great king.*
>
> *Ephraim will receive shame,*
> *and Israel will be ashamed of its decision.*
>
> ⁷*Samaria is destroyed;*
> *its king is like foam on the surface of the water.*
>
> ⁸*The high places of wickedness will be destroyed—the sin of Israel.*
> *Thorn and thistle will go up on their altars.*
>
> *And they will say to the mountains, "Cover us!"*
> *and to the hills, "Fall on us!"*

10:1 a גֶּפֶן בּוֹקֵק יִשְׂרָאֵל
   b פְּרִי יְשַׁוֶּה־לּוֹ
   c כְּרֹב לְפִרְיוֹ
   d הִרְבָּה לַמִּזְבְּחוֹת
   e כְּטוֹב לְאַרְצוֹ
   f הֵיטִיבוּ מַצֵּבוֹת׃

Lines a-b are a bicolon featuring noun (יִשְׂרָאֵל)//pronoun (וֹ) parallelism. The lines are marked by *Zaqep parvum* and *'Atnaḥ*. Lines c-f are a quatrain with an ABA′B′ pattern. Lines c and e feature PPs with כְּ followed by the corresponding terms פְּרִי and אֶרֶץ and a 3ms poss suffix. Lines d and f have Hiphil verbs followed by the corresponding complements מִזְבֵּחַ and מַצֵּבָה. In addition, the lines feature phonological parallelism (*kerov lepiryo*//*ketov le'arṣo*; *lamizbeḥot*//*maṣevot*). The lines are marked by *Zaqep parvum*, *Zaqep parvum*, and *Silluq*.

גֶּפֶן בּוֹקֵק יִשְׂרָאֵל. *Line a*. Independent verbless clause.

גֶּפֶן. Subject of the verbless clause. The noun גֶּפֶן is typically feminine and concords with feminine verbs and pronouns (cf. Judg 9:12; Ps 80:15). However, here it appears to be masculine (note the adjectival ptc בּוֹקֵק), perhaps because it refers to the masculine יִשְׂרָאֵל (WO §6.4.1d). The imagery of Israel as a fruitful vine is abrupt since the preceding sections have detailed how YHWH will stop their fertility and put an end to their food and offspring. However, Hosea's point here is that Israel has been fruitful, but they have used their resources to pursue their rebellion against YHWH. The prophet will continue, in this section, to predict Israel's future ruin.

בּוֹקֵק. Qal ptc ms √בקק. The participle modifies גֶּפֶן as an attributive adjective. The root √בקק occurs in a total of seven verses in the OT. In six passages it means "to empty" or "to lay waste." Nevertheless, that meaning is difficult to relate to line b, which states that the vine is productive and fruitful. Therefore, it is best to understand the occurrence here in Hos 10:1 as a second root (II) which means "to be luxuriant" (cf. Arabic *baqqa*) (cf. HALOT 150). This sense is supported by G which has the participle εὐκληματοῦσα (from εὐκληματέω, "to grow luxuriantly"; cf. also S and V).

פְּרִי יְשַׁוֶּה־לּוֹ. *Line b*. Independent clause.

פְּרִי. Acc compl of יְשַׁוֶּה. The metaphor of "fruit" refers to the wealth and abundance that Israel had procured.

יְשַׁוֶּה. Piel *yiqtol* 3ms √שוה. This verb is listed in BDB and HALOT under two different roots, but each lexicon aligns the occurrences and meanings in different ways. BDB (1000) is more convincing: (I) in the Piel means "to level" or "smooth" something, a sense which does not fit the present context. (II) means "to place" or "establish" (cf. 2 Sam 22:34; Ps 16:8; 89:20) (BDB 1001). The idiom here refers to "fixing" fruit to the vine's branches (McComiskey 2009:159). The sense may be that rather than naturally producing fruit for YHWH, as he intended, they are designating their resources for their own interest (note also the reciprocal לוֹ which follows).

לוֹ. PP with a לְ of interest indicating that the fruit is for Israel himself (rather than for YHWH). On the *dagesh*, see JM §18d-h.

כְּרֹב לְפִרְיוֹ. *Line c*. PP with כְּ expressing comparison. רֹב is a noun from √רבב. The prep לְ expresses possession (not a constr phrase). The antecedent of the 3ms poss suffix on פִּרְיוֹ is "Israel" (see line a).

הִרְבָּה לַמִּזְבְּחוֹת. *Line d.* Independent clause.

הִרְבָּה. Hiph *qatal* 3ms √רבה. This verb in the Hiphil refers to increasing quantity or making something plentiful. The subject is Israel. The more "fruit" (or wealth) Israel attained, the more he applied those resources to increasing his idolatrous practices.

לַמִּזְבְּחוֹת. Acc compl of הִרְבָּה. The ל is anomalous since √רבה does not elsewhere take oblique complements with prepositions.

כְּטוֹב לְאַרְצוֹ. *Line e.* PP with כ expressing comparison. As in line c, this is not a construct phrase. The word טוֹב is a substantival adjective ("the good") and the prep ל indicates possession (i.e., "the good things belonging to his land"). The antecedent of the 3ms poss suffix on אַרְצוֹ is, once again, Israel.

הֵיטִיבוּ מַצֵּבוֹת. *Line f.* Independent clause.

הֵיטִיבוּ. Hiph *qatal* 3cp √יטב. The Hiphil of this verb can be intransitive ("to do good") or transitive ("to act for the benefit of"), taking either oblique or accusative complements. Note the repetition of roots in the substantives and verbs in lines c-d (רבה/√רב) and lines e-f (טוֹב/√יטב). The correspondences heighten Israel's guilt: they took all of their blessings from YHWH and turned them into sinful means of rebellion.

מַצֵּבוֹת. Acc compl of הֵיטִיבוּ. Israel formerly set up these "pillars" as stones of witness or memorials to YHWH, and these were legitimate for the biblical authors (e.g., Gen 28:18; Exod 24:4). But מַצֵּבוֹת were condemned as part of the idolatrous cult apparatus of the Canaanites, and Israel was explicitly instructed to destroy them (Exod 23:24; Deut 7:5). Instead, Israel adopted them and incorporated them into their illegitimate worship. Second Kings 17:10 states that these were one of the causes of Israel's exile.

10:2 a חָלַק לִבָּם
b עַתָּה יֶאְשָׁמוּ
c הוּא יַעֲרֹף מִזְבְּחוֹתָם
d יְשֹׁדֵד מַצֵּבוֹתָם:

Lines a-b are a bicolon with lines connected thematically. Line a describes the people's character; line b describes their guilt. The lines are marked with *Ṭipḥa* and *'Atnaḥ*. Lines c-d are also a bicolon. Apart from the pleonastic pronoun הוּא at the beginning of line c, each line contains corresponding verbs (√ערף//√שדד), corresponding complements (מַצֵּבָה//מִזְבֵּחַ), and 3mp poss suffixes. The lines are marked by *Zaqep parvum* and *Silluq*.

חָלַק לִבָּם. Line a. Independent clause.

חָלַק. Qal *qatal* 3ms √חלק. Often VS word order signals that a *qatal* is irrealis. In this verse, however, the following adverb עַתָּה ("now") introduces an action that follows from this one, suggesting that we should read this as indicative and past tense. The inverted VS word order marks this clause pragmatically for focus, to contrast Israel's current depravity with their promising past. The verb √חלק is listed in HALOT under two roots (322–23). Some scholars understand the use here in 10:2 as (II) which means "to divide" in the sense that their hearts were divided between YHWH and Ba'al. However, in the Qal it is transitive, and there is no complement in this clause (לִבָּם is the subject). Furthermore, it is usually used of dividing land (e.g., Jos 14:5). In this context (I) "to be smooth" (Qal) or "to flatter" (Hiph) makes better sense. This root is intransitive and refers to being false or deceptive (cf. Ps 55:22, where it describes a mouth/פֶּה).

לִבָּם. Subject of חָלַק.

עַתָּה יֶאְשָׁמוּ. Line b. Independent clause.

עַתָּה. This temporal adverb introduces the conclusion drawn from what has been stated (BDB 773; cf. 5:7; 7:2; 8:8, 13).

יֶאְשָׁמוּ. Qal *yiqtol* 3mp √אשם. See 4:15b.

הוּא יַעֲרֹף מִזְבְּחוֹתָם. Line c. Independent clause.

הוּא. This pleonastic 3ms pronoun, referring to YHWH, signals a contrast with the subject of the preceding lines. Lines a-b describe Israel's sin and guilt. Now, lines c-d describe YHWH's reaction.

יַעֲרֹף. Qal *yiqtol* 3ms √ערף. This verb occurs six times in the OT, and in the five occurrences outside of Hosea, it refers to breaking the neck of an animal. It is usually used (except in Isa 66:3) in contexts of sacrifice. Here, Hosea uses the technical term to create an image of violently tearing down the altars, perhaps beginning by breaking off the horns of the altar (Wolff 1974:174; cf. Amos 3:14).

מִזְבְּחוֹתָם. Acc compl of יַעֲרֹף. The antecedent of the 3mp poss suffix is the people of Israel (cf. 10:1).

יְשֹׁדֵד מִזְבְּחוֹתָם. *Line d*. Independent clause.

יְשֹׁדֵד. Poel *yiqtol* 3ms √שדד. This is the only occurrence of the Poel in the OT. The Piel of this root means "to do violence."

מִזְבְּחוֹתָם. Acc compl of יְשֹׁדֵד. The antecedent of the 3mp poss suffix is again the people of Israel. Note the repetition of מִזְבְּחוֹת and מַצֵּבוֹת, in that order, from 10:1. The people have forsaken YHWH to build up these illegimate means of worship, but YHWH will destroy them anyway.

10:3 a כִּי עַתָּה יֹאמְרוּ
b אֵין מֶלֶךְ לָנוּ
c כִּי לֹא יָרֵאנוּ אֶת־יְהוָה
d וְהַמֶּלֶךְ מַה־יַּעֲשֶׂה־לָּנוּ׃

Lines a–d are a quatrain. The lines do not exhibit much parallelism. Line a introduces direct speech which is given in lines b–d. The word מֶלֶךְ is repeated in lines b and d. The lines are marked by *Zaqep parvum*, *'Atnaḥ*, *Zaqep parvum*, and *Silluq*.

כִּי עַתָּה יֹאמְרוּ. *Line a*. Independent clause. The כִּי is not introducing a causal clause ("for") because Hosea is transitioning to a new topic. Neither does an adversative sense ("but") make sense. It is asseverative and left untranslated (cf. JM §164b).

עַתָּה. This temporal adverb introduces the result of the judgment in 10:2. It refers to a "time ideally present" from Hosea's point of view and could be translated "then" (BDB 773).

יֹאמְרוּ. Qal *yiqtol* 3mp √אמר. How we understand the temporal reference of Hosea's statement determines whether we understand this *yiqtol* verb as present or future. One possibility is that the people are saying, in the present, "We have no king" because their current king (Hoshea?) is ineffective in protecting them against the Assyrian threat. That is, they might as well have no king. This would make sense of their statement in line d, "What can the king do for us?" AF (553) argue that Israel is rejecting YHWH as king. A final possibility is that Hosea is predicting or hoping that Israel will say these words in exile when they come to their senses. When they finally recognize their guilt (line c), they will say, quite literally, "We have no king" (line b) because they also have no country! In any of these understandings, we would translate יֹאמְרוּ as present.

אֵין מֶלֶךְ לָנוּ. *Line b.* Independent verbless clause. Direct speech. The adverb אֵין adds to the copulative notion the idea of nonexistence (JM §154k).

מֶלֶךְ. Predicate of the verbless clause.

לָנוּ. PP with לְ indicating possession. The antecedent of the 1cp suffix is the people of Israel who are presented as speaking.

כִּי לֹא יָרֵאנוּ אֶת־יְהוָה. *Line c.* Subordinate causal clause with כִּי giving the reason that they have no king (line b). Their speech is proleptic: Hosea presents Israel in the future, looking back on their past mistakes which have led to exile.

יָרֵאנוּ. Qal *qatal* 1cp √ירא. The past reference of this *qatal* verb supports the notion that Hosea is quoting Israel's potential words in exile. It is unlikely that they are acknowledging their guilt in the present, before the judgment.

אֶת־יְהוָה. Acc compl of יָרֵאנוּ.

וְהַמֶּלֶךְ מַה־יַּעֲשֶׂה־לָּנוּ. *Line d.* Independent clause, direct speech.

וְהַמֶּלֶךְ. A *casus pendens*, which is suspended in the syntax and resumed as the subject of יַעֲשֶׂה (see 7:8a). It is curious that having just said in line b that they "have no king" now they speak as if they do have one. The explanation is that they are presented as speaking in the future in exile (cf. the future *yiqtol* verb in line a). They literally have no king, and as they look back, they see that it was foolish to place their trust in any king. The article may indicate that they have a particular king in mind (perhaps Hoshea, the last king of Israel).

מַה. Interr particle serving as the acc compl of יַעֲשֶׂה.

יַעֲשֶׂה. Qal *yiqtol* 3ms √עשׂה. The *yiqtol* is either past durative ("what did *he ever do* for us?") (JM §113f) or modal in the past ("what could he do for us?") (GKC §107t).

לָּנוּ. PP with לְ of interest indicating that the king's actions were potentially for their benefit. The antecedent of the 1cp suffix is the speaker, the people of Israel.

10:4 a דִּבְּרוּ דְבָרִים
b אָלוֹת שָׁוְא
c כָּרֹת בְּרִית
d וּפָרַח כָּרֹאשׁ מִשְׁפָּט
e עַל תַּלְמֵי שָׂדָי׃

Lines a-c are a tricolon consisting of three actions described in three short lines of two words each. Lines b-c exhibit parallelism with corresponding Qal infinitives absolute. The lines are marked by *Zaqep parvum*, *Ṭipḥa*, and *'Atnaḥ*. Lines d-e are a bicolon comprising one sentence. The lines are marked by *Zaqep parvum* and *Silluq*.

דִּבְּרוּ דְבָרִים. *Line a*. Independent clause.

דִּבְּרוּ. Piel *qatal* 3cp √דבר. Having reported Israel's potential words in 10:3 ("And the king—what could he do for us?"), Hosea now explains why the kings were impotent. He brings the time-frame back to the present and uses a *qatal* verb (past) to begin describing their actions. The verb is likely plural because הַמֶּלֶךְ in 10:3d refers to the kingship as an institution rather than to a particular king (Macintosh 2014:394).

דְבָרִים. Acc compl of דִּבְּרוּ. In the context דָּבָר refers to political promises or treaties.

אָלוֹת שָׁוְא. *Line b*. Independent clause.

אָלוֹת. Qal inf abs √אלה. The usual form is אָלֹה (cf. 4:2). This form, ending in וֹת-, may be due to attraction to or rhyming with the infinitive כָּרֹת in the next line (cf. GKC §75n). The subject and aspect/tense of the infinitive is determined by the preceding finite verb (GKC §113z; ff), in this case דִּבְּרוּ in line a.

שָׁוְא. Acc compl of אָלוֹת. This noun refers to something empty or ineffective. Here it is used of empty oaths or meaningless political agreements made by a corrupt and ineffectual government.

כָּרֹת בְּרִית. *Line c*. Independent clause.

כָּרֹת. Qal inf abs √כרת. On the use of the infinitive absolute, see line b above.

בְּרִית. Acc compl of כָּרֹת. These covenants may be those made between the king and the people of Israel (Wolff 1974:175) or between Israel and Assyria (AF 554). In any case, they did not stop the devastation.

וּפָרַח כָּרֹאשׁ מִשְׁפָּט. *Line d*. Independent clause.

וּפָרַח. Qal *qatal* (irrealis) 3ms √פרח. The irrealis *qatal* expresses habituality: the verse is summative of the typical schemes of Israel's political leadership.

כָּרֹאשׁ. Adjunct PP with כְּ indicating agreement in kind. The noun רֹאשׁ usually refers to "poison" (HALOT 1167). In the context of "furrows of the field" and the verb פָּרַח ("sprout"), it likely refers to a poisonous or noxious plant.

מִשְׁפָּט. Subject of וּפָרַח. At first glance, it is odd that Hosea is comparing מִשְׁפָּט ("justice"), valued so highly in the OT, to a poisonous plant. Wolff (1974:175) suggests that the king is misusing the apparatus of justice for corrupt ends. Hosea may also be using the word sarcastically. The kings' actions, which should be just, are like weeds that overrun and ruin a field. Thus, I put quotation marks around "justice" when translating מִשְׁפָּט.

עַל תַּלְמֵי שָׂדָי. *Line e*. Adjunct PP indicating the location (עַל) where "justice" sprouts. The noun תֶּלֶם ("furrow") is in a construction relationship with the genitive שָׂדָי, expressing possession (see also 12:12). שָׂדָי is an archaic form of the noun שָׂדֶה ("field") which reveals the original ʸunderlying the usually occurring final ה. The ָ under the ד is due to vowel lengthening in pause because of the *Silluq* disjunctive accent.

10:5 a לְעֶגְלוֹת בֵּית אָוֶן יָגוּרוּ
b שְׁכַן שֹׁמְרוֹן
c כִּי־אָבַל עָלָיו עַמּוֹ
d וּכְמָרָיו עָלָיו
e יָגִילוּ עַל־כְּבוֹדוֹ
f כִּי־גָלָה מִמֶּנּוּ׃

Lines a-b are a bicolon. The verb יָגוּרוּ is elided in line b, and the lines of the bicolon are marked with *Tipḥa* and *'Atnaḥ*. Lines c-d are also a bicolon, identified by ellipsis of the verb אָבַל in line d. The lines also repeat the PP עָלָיו and are marked by disjunctive *Rᵉbîaʿ* and a conjunctive *Munaḥ*. Lines e-f are a bicolon consisting of a main clause (line e) and a subordinate causal clause (line f). The lines are marked with disjunctive *Tipḥa* and *Silluq*.

יָגוּרוּ לְעֶגְלוֹת בֵּית אָוֶן. *Line a.* Independent clause.

לְעֶגְלוֹת בֵּית אָוֶן. PP with לְ of specification (WO §11.2.10d). The verb יָגוּרוּ ("to be afraid"; line b) is usually used with preps מִן or מִפְּנֵי ("to be afraid *of*"; HALOT 185). Here, the לְ apparently means "they are afraid *concerning* the calves of Beth Aven." The fp עֶגְלוֹת requires some explanation since we know of only one calf in Bethel (the other one was in Dan), and it is usually refered to by the masculine עֵגֶל (cf. 8:5, 6; 13:2). Furthermore, it is referenced subsequently with 3ms pronouns (see lines c, d, e, and perhaps f) and a 3ms verb (line f). Rudolph (1966:195) argues that the plural ending is an abstract plural because the reference includes the entire calf cult. It is also possible that Hosea begins with both calves in mind (Dan and Bethel) before turning to the valuable calf idol that was taken to Assyria (thus the 3ms pronouns and verb). Hosea uses בֵּית אָוֶן ("House of Wickedness") as a pejorative name for "Bethel" also in 4:15 and 5:8 (see the discussion at 4:15).

יָגוּרוּ. Qal *yiqtol* 3mp √גור. There are three different meanings for √גור: (I) "to dwell as an alien," (II) "to attack," and (III) "to be afraid." The context with √אבל ("mourn"; line c) and √גיל ("wail"; line e) indicate that here root (III) is intended. The people have worshiped these idols and given them their trust. There will be a reversal when the calf is taken to Assyria (line f). Rather than it protecting them, they will be afraid for *its* security.

שְׁכַן שֹׁמְרוֹן. *Line b.* This is an unmarked PP of specification related to the elided verb יָגוּרוּ. In the parallelism, שְׁכֵן corresponds to עֶגְלוֹת ("calves") in the previous line and both are references to the false gods. The idol has become so entrenched in the culture that the prophet sarcastically refers to it as a שְׁכֵן ("resident"). Therefore, I use quotation marks in the translation.

כִּי־אָבַל עָלָיו עַמּוֹ. *Line c.* Independent clause. The כִּי is asseverative and left untranslated (JM §164b).

אָבַל. Qal *qatal* (irrealis) 3ms √אבל. This *qatal* refers to a potential action in the future, in agreement with the *yiqtols* in lines b and e. The verb refers to mourning or lamenting over something lost.

עָלָיו. Adjunct PP with עַל indicating the object of interest (WO §11.2.13c). The verb √אבל does not require a complement that specifies the object of mourning (e.g., Hos 4:3), but when it does have one, it is marked with עַל or (sometimes) אֶל. The antecedent of the 3ms suffix is the calf (עֶגְלוֹת) in line a).

עַמּוֹ. Subject of אָבַל. The antecedent of the 3ms poss suffix is the calf. It is as though the people belong to the calf: they have given themselves over to it.

וּכְמָרָיו עָלָיו. *Line d.* Independent clause. The verb אָבַל is elided.

וּכְמָרָיו. Subject of the elided verb אָבַל. The noun כֹּמֶר occurs three times in the OT. It is a technical word for "priest," reserved for those who serve Ba'al or other idols (cf. 2 Kgs 23:5; Zeph 1:4). Here, the 3ms poss suffix indicates that the priests belong to the calf cult and serve in it.

עָלָיו. See above on line c.

יָגִילוּ עַל־כְּבוֹדוֹ. *Line e.* Asyndetic relative clause.

יָגִילוּ. Qal *yiqtol* 3mp √גיל. This verb occurs forty-eight times in the OT and in forty-seven of them it clearly has the meaning "to rejoice" (cf. HALOT 189). It introduces an asyndetic relative clause headed by עַמּוֹ and כְּמָרָיו in lines c and d above. The causal clause in the following line (f) would then be subordinate to lines c and d. In other words, the people and priests are described as those who typically rejoice over the calf (line e). But now they are in mourning (lines c-d) because it will go into exile (line f).

עַל־כְּבוֹדוֹ. Adjunct PP with עַל indicating the object of rejoicing (יָגִילוּ). Complements of the verb √גיל are usually marked with the prep בְּ and only one other time with עַל (Zeph 3:17). כָּבוֹד may refer to the costly materials from which the idol was made (cf. 2:10; 8:4) or generally to the significance of the idol. Note that כָּבוֹד refers to Israel's offspring in the previous unit in 9:11; once again YHWH will destroy what is most precious to his people. The antecedent of the 3ms suffix is the idol as in lines c and d.

כִּי־גָלָה מִמֶּנּוּ. *Line f.* Causal clause marked by כִּי which is subordinate to the main clauses in lines c and d (i.e., "will mourn over it"). Hosea first tells us that the people will mourn over the lost calf-idol (line c-d), then invites us to compare its supposed glory (line e) with the reason that they are mourning: it is powerless in the face of the enemy (line f).

גָּלָה. Qal *qatal* 3ms √גלה. The implied subject is the calf (introduced as עֶגְלוֹת but subsequently referred to with 3ms pronouns). The context refers to a future time frame and the tense is determined by the preceding *yiqtols* and irrealis *qatal*. Therefore, the translation is "will have gone into exile."

מִמֶּנּוּ. PP with abl מִן indicating the place from which the calf-idol went into exile (גלה). The suffix could be 3ms or 1cp. If it is the latter, Hosea is including himself among the people, "it will go into exile from *us*." More likely, the suffix is 3ms and refers to the people (עַם is singular and the subject of the singular verb אָבַל). Even though the word is singular, in English it should be translated as "them."

10:6 a גַּם־אוֹתוֹ לְאַשּׁוּר יוּבָל
b מִנְחָה לְמֶלֶךְ יָרֵב
c בָּשְׁנָה אֶפְרַיִם יִקָּח
d וְיֵבוֹשׁ יִשְׂרָאֵל מֵעֲצָתוֹ:

Lines a-b are a bicolon. Line b is related to line a via apposition. The lines are marked by *Zaqep parvum* and *'Atnaḥ*. Lines c-d are a bicolon as well, indicated by the word pairs יִשְׂרָאֵל/אֶפְרַיִם and בָּשְׁנָה/√בוש. In addition, the lines exhibit a chiastic order: line a is complement-SV, but line b is VS-complement. The lines are marked by *Zaqep parvum* and *Silluq*.

גַּם־אוֹתוֹ לְאַשּׁוּר יוּבָל. *Line a*. Independent clause.

גַּם. This conjunction links this verse to the preceding (10:5) and emphasizes the thematic continuity. This line is essentially repeating the sense of 10:5f.

אוֹתוֹ. The particle אֵת is most commonly used to mark the accusative in a clause. Although it is a less common function, the particle אֵת sometimes marks the subjects of intransitive and passive verbs (cf. GKC §117i; §121b; JM §125j; Saydon 1964; MacDonald 1964:272). Here it marks the subject of the passive verb יוּבָל, which is the 3ms suffix referring to the calf-idol (cf. 10:5).

לְאַשּׁוּר. PP with locative לְ.

יוּבָל. Hoph *yiqtol* 3ms √יבל. This verb occurs only in the Hiphil and Hophal in the OT.

מִנְחָה לְמֶלֶךְ יָרֵב. *Line b*. This line consists of a noun and modifying PP, which are in apposition to the 3ms suffix and subject of יוּבָל in line a.

מִנְחָה. This noun is in apposition to the 3ms suffix (אוֹתוֹ) in line a which refers to the calf-idol (cf. 10:5). The word מִנְחָה refers to a gift. Thus the idea is not that Assyria has taken the idol in the spoils of victory, but that Israel is taking it to them as tribute (AF 557).

לְמֶלֶךְ יָרֵב. PP with לְ of interest: the idol is *for* the king of Assyria. On מֶלֶךְ יָרֵב, see the discussion in 5:13d.

בָּשְׁנָה אֶפְרַיִם יִקָּח. *Line c.* Independent clause.

בָּשְׁנָה. This feminine noun is a *hapax* which probably means "shame" (see HALOT 165). It is the accusative complement of the verb יִקָּח, and it is fronted in the clause for focus to contrast the expected outcome of the gift (honor) with its actual outcome (shame).

אֶפְרַיִם. Subject of יִקָּח.

יִקָּח. Qal *yiqtol* 3ms √לקח.

וְיֵבוֹשׁ יִשְׂרָאֵל מֵעֲצָתוֹ. *Line d.* Independent clause.

וְיֵבוֹשׁ. Qal *yiqtol* 3ms √בושׁ.

יִשְׂרָאֵל. Subject of יֵבוֹשׁ.

מֵעֲצָתוֹ. Adjunct PP with מִן indicating the object of Israel's shame. The noun עֵצָה might mean "plan" or "scheme," referring either to Israel's religious aspirations (with the preceding context) or political schemes. An intriguing alternative is that עֵצָה is a *nomen unitatis* ("unitary noun") of עֵץ ("wood") (Rudolph 1966:196). This means that whereas עֵץ refers to the material, עֵצָה refers to a particular specimen of the group. If so, Hosea is referring to the idol pejoratively as a mere "wooden stick," perhaps because the precious metals have been stripped away from it (cf. Hos 4:12).

10:7 a נִדְמֶה שֹׁמְרוֹן
b מַלְכָּהּ כְּקֶצֶף עַל־פְּנֵי־מָיִם:

Lines a-b are a bicolon, but the placement of the noun מַלְכָּהּ is a challenge. According to the Masoretic accents (i.e., the disjunctive *'Atnaḥ*), it belongs at the end of line a. If so, how should we translate שֹׁמְרוֹן מַלְכָּהּ? AF (558) render it, "The king of Samaria" (lit. "Samaria, her king") although they admit that there are no examples of this construction elsewhere. We might understand the two words as related asyndetically and the complex subject of נִדְמֶה ("Samaria and her king are destroyed"). Or, we could take שֹׁמְרוֹן as a nominative absolute and מַלְכָּהּ as the subject of the verb ("As for Samaria, her king is destroyed") (see Macintosh 2014:406). Each of these options seems strained, however. A more convincing solution is to divide the lines after the disjunctive *Tipḥa* (שֹׁמְרוֹן) rather than the usual *'Atnaḥ*. Although this gives us two lines of unequal length, if מַלְכָּהּ is in line b, then it and שֹׁמְרוֹן are each the subject of a clause. In the parallelism line b is an expansion on line a. The city will be destroyed, and furthermore its king will be carried away. Thus, the lines are marked by *Tipḥa* and *Silluq*.

נִדְמֶה שֹׁמְרוֹן. *Line a*. Independent clause.

נִדְמֶה. Niph ptc ms √דמה. There are three different roots listed in the lexicon for √דמה. The sense here is (II) "be destroyed" (cf. 4:5, 6; 10:15). Participles have a default SV word order, so the verb here is fronted for focus. The equivalent in English would be, "Destroyed is Samaria!" The participle is probably to be understood as referring to the imminent future (GKC §116p), much the same way an English speaker would say, "*about* to be destroyed."

שֹׁמְרוֹן. Subject of נִדְמֶה.

מַלְכָּהּ כְּקֶצֶף עַל־פְּנֵי־מָיִם. *Line b*. Independent verbless clause.

מַלְכָּהּ. Subject of the verbless clause. The antecedent of the 3fs poss suffix is שֹׁמְרוֹן in the previous clause. It is unusual for the king of a nation to be referenced by his capital city, but there are other examples in the OT (1 Kgs 21:1; 2 Kgs 1:3; Jonah 3:6).

כְּקֶצֶף. This PP with כְּ expressing agreement in kind introduces the predicate of the verbless clause. The noun קֶצֶף is a *hapax*. Some have understood it as a "stick" or "twig" that is helplessly carried away on the water. This is apparently G's view, which has φρύγανον ("stick"). Morely likely, it should be related to the verb √קצף ("to be angry"). The noun would refer to the troubling of the waters or the foam which results. This makes somewhat better sense with the verb √דמה in line a. Just as foam or turmoil on the waters rapidly dissipates, the king will pass away along with the city.

עַל־פְּנֵי־מָיִם. PP with locative עַל.

10:8 a וְנִשְׁמְד֞וּ בָּמ֣וֹת אָ֗וֶן חַטַּאת֙ יִשְׂרָאֵ֔ל
b ק֣וֹץ וְדַרְדַּ֔ר יַעֲלֶ֖ה עַל־מִזְבְּחוֹתָ֑ם

c וְאָמְרוּ לֶהָרִים֙ כַּסּוּנוּ
d וְלַגְּבָעוֹת נִפְלוּ עָלֵינוּ: ס

Lines a-b are a bicolon. The parallelism exhibits amplification as line b explains what is meant by וְנִשְׁמְדוּ ("will be destroyed") in line a. The lines are marked by *Zaqep parvum* and *'Atnaḥ*. Lines c-d are a bicolon identified by ellipsis of the verb וְאָמְרוּ in line d. The two lines also have two corresponding word pairs (הַר//גִּבְעָה and √נפל//√כסה) as well as 1cp pronominal suffixes. The lines are marked *Zaqep parvum* and *Silluq*.

וְנִשְׁמְדוּ בָּמוֹת אָוֶן חַטַּאת יִשְׂרָאֵל. *Line a*. Independent clause.

וְנִשְׁמְדוּ. Niph *qatal* (irrealis) 3cp √שמד.

בָּמוֹת אָוֶן. The noun בָּמָה, in construct with אָוֶן, is the subject of וְנִשְׁמְדוּ. The construct relationship is an attributive genitive, in which אָוֶן ("wickedness") characterizes the בָּמוֹת. In a construct form, we would normally expect reduction of the initial vowel (e.g., בְּמוֹת) but the noun בָּמָה is exceptional (JM §97b). The word בָּמָה in the OT usually refers to an illicit place of worship, often on a "high place" such as a hilltop. Hosea uses the word אָוֶן ("wickedness") as part of a pejorative name for "Bethel" three other times in the book (4:15; 5:8; 10:5). Furthermore, Bethel is mentioned in 10:15, which closes the next unit and speaks of the king (מֶלֶךְ) being destroyed (דמה) similar to 10:7 at the end of this unit. Therefore, the prophet might be using אָוֶן as a short form of "Beth Aven" here. It is also possible that Hosea is speaking more broadly about all of the "high places of wickedness" not just those at Bethel (cf. Wolff 1974:176).

חַטַּאת יִשְׂרָאֵל. This construct phrase (indicating possession) is in apposition to the previous noun בָּמוֹת and further defines it. The high places are "the sin of Israel."

קוֹץ וְדַרְדַּר יַעֲלֶה עַל־מִזְבְּחוֹתָם. *Line b*. Independent clause.

קוֹץ וְדַרְדַּר. These two nouns are the subject of the following verb יַעֲלֶה. It is common, when two nouns are closely related and form a single idea, for the verb to be in the singular (see JM §150p). These nouns form a pair also in Gen 3:18. Hosea uses a different pair of synonyms (קִמּוֹשׂ and חוֹחַ) in 9:6.

יַעֲלֶה. Qal *yiqtol* 3ms √עלה. The thorns and thistles will grow (lit. "go up") because the worship sites will have no more inhabitants or activity due to their destruction.

עַל־מִזְבְּחוֹתָם. PP with locative עַל indicating where the thorns and thistles will grow. The antecedent of the 3mp poss suffix cannot be the בָּמוֹת in line a (i.e., the altars located in the high places) because בָּמוֹת is feminine. Therefore, the suffix must refer to the people of Israel mentioned in line a (see also the verb and pronouns in lines c-d).

וְאָמְרוּ לֶהָרִים. *Line c.* Independent clause.

וְאָמְרוּ. Qal *qatal* (irrealis) 3cp √אמר.

לֶהָרִים. Adjunct PP with לְ indicating the addressee of the speech verb וְאָמְרוּ.

כַּסּוּנוּ. *Line c.* Independent clause. The verb is a Piel impv mp √כסה with a 1cp acc suffix. The antecedent of the suffix is the same as the subject of וְאָמְרוּ: the people of Israel (mentioned in line a).

וְלַגְּבָעוֹת. *Line d.* Independent clause. The verb וְאָמְרוּ is elided (see the previous line). וְלַגְּבָעוֹת is an adjunct PP with לְ indicating the addressee of the speech.

נִפְלוּ עָלֵינוּ. *Line d.* Independent clause.

נִפְלוּ. Qal impv mp √נפל.

עָלֵינוּ. Adjunct PP with locative עַל indicating the place where they wish the hills to fall. The antecedent of the 1cp suffix is again the people of Israel. Apparently, those who survive the great devastation of Israel will no longer wish to live and will call on the mountains and hills to bring about their deaths.

YHWH Will Destroy the Nation Itself (10:9-15)

This last subunit (9:1–10:15) completes the torrent of bad news for Israel. Everything that YHWH's people had hoped to improve through the worship of other deities will be undone. Not only will YHWH destroy their food (9:1-9), bereave them of their children (9:10-17), and destroy their cult sites (10:1-8), Hosea states in this section that YHWH will bring war and an end to the nation itself.

Hosea's uses three historical allusions to depict Israel's sin and the judgment that awaits them. First, he mentions the "days of Gibeah" in which an infamous crime led to a devastating civil war (v. 9). Now, similarly, YHWH will bring nations against them (v. 10). The second historical allusion goes back to the beginnings of the nation when YHWH first elected his people and called them to reflect his character (vv. 11-12).

But they disregarded his expectations and did exactly the opposite (v. 13). Therefore, war will come against them (v. 14a-b). The third allusion is to Shalman's destruction of Beth-Arbe'l (an event which is unknown to us) (v. 14c-d). In the same way, YHWH will destroy Bethel (and, by extension, the nation) in war and the king will be killed (v. 15). The first two allusions connect sin and judgment in the past with Israel's present. The third allusion is a picture of battle that will consume the nation.

> *⁹From the days of Gibeah, you have sinned O Israel.*
> *There they remain.*
>
> *Will not war overtake them in Gibeah—*
> *against the wicked ones?*
>
> *¹⁰In my desire I will rebuke them,*
> *and the peoples will be gathered against them*
> *when they bind (them) for their two iniquities.*
>
> *¹¹Now Ephraim is a trained heifer loving to trample,*
> *and I have passed by her fine neck.*
>
> *I would harness Ephraim,*
> *Judah was to plough,*
> *Jacob was to harrow for himself.*
>
> *¹²Sow for yourselves for righteousness,*
> *harvest for the expression of lovingkindness,*
> *plough for yourself the fallow ground.*
>
> *And it is time to seek YHWH*
> *until he comes and showers righteousness on you.*
>
> *¹³You have ploughed wickedness,*
> *you have harvested injustice,*
> *you have eaten the fruit of deceit.*
>
> *For you trusted in your own way:*
> *in the multitude of your warriors.*
>
> *¹⁴And the tumult will rise against your people,*
> *and all your fortified cities will be devastated,*
>
> *like the devastation of Shalman on Beth Arbel in the day of war:*
> *mothers were shattered with the children.*

¹⁵ Thus he will have done to you, Bethel,
because of your great wickedness.
In the dawn, the king of Israel will have certainly been destroyed.

10:9 a   מִימֵי הַגִּבְעָה חָטָאתָ יִשְׂרָאֵל
     b   שָׁם עָמָדוּ
     c   לֹא־תַשִּׂיגֵם בַּגִּבְעָה מִלְחָמָה
     d   עַל־בְּנֵי עַלְוָה:

Lines a-b are a bicolon. There is a correspondence between שָׁם/גִּבְעָה and, in spite of the change from second person to third person, between יִשְׂרָאֵל and the subject of עָמָדוּ. The lines are marked by *'Atnaḥ* and *Zaqep parvum*. There is also a *Zaqep parvum* on the second word הַגִּבְעָה, and the lines could be divided at that point. However, lines a-d exhibit a pattern of alternating long and short lines. Lines c-d are another bicolon consisting of one sentence. Line d is a PP that concludes the clause begun in line c. The lines are marked by *Ṭipḥa* and *Silluq*.

מִימֵי הַגִּבְעָה חָטָאתָ יִשְׂרָאֵל. *Line a*. Independent clause.

מִימֵי הַגִּבְעָה. PP with temporal מִן expressing the elapsed time since the days of Gibeah (cf. WO §11.2.11c). The construct phrase "days of Gibeah" refers to an infamous, brutal crime that those inhabitants had committed against a Levite's concubine (cf. Judg 19–21). When the other tribes confronted the tribe of Benjamin, they refused to hand over the perpetrators (Judg 20:13), which led to a devastating civil war (see Hos 5:8; 9:9).

חָטָאתָ. Qal *qatal* 2ms √חטא. This line is an introductory address to Israel (note the vocative) before YHWH switches to third person in line 9b and following.

יִשְׂרָאֵל. Vocative and the referent of the 2ms verb חָטָאתָ.

שָׁם עָמָדוּ. *Line b*. Independent clause.

שָׁם. This adverb functions as an oblique complement of the verb עָמָדוּ. The verb √עמד is almost always followed by a PP indicating that the subject stood "upon" (עַל), "outside" (בַּחוּץ), or "before" (לִפְנֵי) something, or stood "there" (שָׁם).

עָמְדוּ. Qal *qatal* 3cp √עמד, which has the sense of "remain." YHWH is stating that Israel committed a terrible sin at Gibeah, which was reflective of their overall character, and they never left! They have continued to sin in similar ways, with rebellious hearts, ever since. The logic of the historical allusion continues in the next two lines (c-d). Just as the events at Gibeah resulted in a destructive war (an existential threat to the people), they should expect war now.

לֹא־תַשִּׂיגֵם בַּגִּבְעָה מִלְחָמָה. *Line c*. Independent clause.

לֹא. Taking this particle as a straightforward negative creates problems. A past statement ("war did not overtake them in Gibeah") is not historically accurate. A future statement ("war will not overtake them in Gibeah") is at odds with Hosea's claims throughout the rest of the book and vv. 14 and 15 in this unit (AF 565). Some read it as an asseverative ("War will surely overtake them") (e.g., Wolff 1974:178). A simpler solution is to understand the sentence as an unmarked rhetorical question assuming a positive answer ("Will not war overtake them?").

תַשִּׂיגֵם. Hiph *yiqtol* 3fs √נשׂג with a 3mp acc suffix. This verb occurs only in the Hiphil in the OT. Its basic sense is that of pursuing someone and catching up to them (e.g., Gen 44:4; 2 Sam 30:8). Here, it evokes the vivid image of Israel attempting to escape from war but being swamped in its destruction. The antecedent of the 3mp suffix is the inhabitants of Israel (cf. lines a-b).

בַּגִּבְעָה. Adjunct PP with locative בְּ specifying where they will be overtaken. Because Israel has remained (√עמד, line b) in the sin of Gibeah, they will be destroyed in war like Gibeah.

מִלְחָמָה. Subject of תַשִּׂיגֵם.

עַל־בְּנֵי עַלְוָה. *Line d*. This PP concludes the clause begun in line c. We could understand the עַל prep as introducing the cause of the preceding clause ("war will overtake them *because of* the wicked ones") (cf. WO §11.2.13e). However, it more likely means "against" and further characterizes those who will be overtaken by the מִלְחָמָה ("war") (Macintosh 2014:412). If so, it is in apposition to the 3mp acc suffix on the verb תַשִּׂיגֵם ("war will overtake them [i.e., the wicked ones]"). The construct phrase בְּנֵי עַלְוָה is idiomatic and means "those characterized by wickedness." The word עַלְוָה is a *hapax* and is likely a corruption (metathesis) of עַוְלָה ("wickedness," "injustice").

10:10　a בְּאַוָּתִי וְאֶסֳּרֵם
　　　b וְאֻסְּפוּ עֲלֵיהֶם עַמִּים
　　　c בְּאָסְרָם לִשְׁתֵּי עֵינֹתָם׃

Lines a-c are a tricolon. The lines are connected topically (YHWH brings the nations against Israel) and via a predominance of 3mp suffixes. The lines are marked with *'Atnaḥ*, *Zaqep parvum*, and *Silluq*.

בְּאַוָּתִי וְאֶסֳּרֵם. *Line a.* Independent clause.

בְּאַוָּתִי. PP with בְּ indicating the circumstance of the main verb which follows (cf. WO §11.2.5d). The noun אַוָּה ("desire") is related to the common verb אוה√, "to desire" (HALOT 21). The antecedent of the 1cs suffix is the speaker, YHWH.

וְאֶסֳּרֵם. Qal *yiqtol* 1cs יסר√ with a 3mp acc suffix. On the *khatef qamets* ֳ following ס, see GKC §60a. The I-י of the verbal root has assimilated to the ס, with doubling indicated by the *dagesh*. This verb apparently acts like a I-צ verb in which the I-י assimilates to the sibilant (cf. GKC §71; JM §77a). The antecedent of the 3mp suffix is the people of Israel (cf. 10:9). The ו preceding the verb is apparently a ו of apodosis, indicating that the action of the verb אֶסֳּרֵם takes place within the sphere of the divine will (בְּאַוָּתִי) (McComiskey 2009:173; see also 11:1 where a ו precedes an independent clause).

וְאֻסְּפוּ עֲלֵיהֶם עַמִּים. *Line b.* Independent clause.

וְאֻסְּפוּ. Pual *qatal* (irrealis) 3cp אסף√. The agent of the passive Pual verb is not identified, but since YHWH states that this is his "desire" (בְּאַוָּתִי, line a), Hosea must have in mind his sovereign control.

עֲלֵיהֶם. PP with עַל indicating that the nations will be gathered "against" the people of Israel, the antecedent of the 3mp suffix.

עַמִּים. The subject of וְאֻסְּפוּ which receives the action of that verb. Hosea uses עַמִּים to refer to the surrounding nations also in 7:8 and 9:1. In those verses Israel is mixing with the peoples and joining them in rebellion; now these nations are YHWH's instruments against Israel.

בְּאָסְרָם לִשְׁתֵּי עֵינֹתָם. *Line c.* Temporal clause subordinate to the main clause in line b.

בְּאָסְרָם. Qal inf constr אסר√ with a 3mp subjective suffix. Only 1cs and 2ms suffixes are morphologically marked as subjective or objective when used with infinitives. The syntactic role of the others must be determined by context (WO §36.1.1e). This 3mp suffix is subjective and refers to the עַמִּים (the surrounding nations). The accusative complement is assumed to be the people of Israel (cf. line b). The בְּ prep marks the infinitive as temporal and indicates that the action occurs in general proximity to that of the main clause (WO §36.2.2b).

לִשְׁתֵּי עֵינֹתָם. Adjunct PP with לְ indicating purpose (WO §11.2.10d). The form עֵינֹתָם is a *ketiv/qere*. The *ketiv* assumes the vocalization עֵינֹתָם ("their eyes"). McComiskey (2009:173) translates the phrase "to their two eyes" as "in their sight," a reference to the nations which are binding Israel. The *qere* makes more sense, representing the form עוֹנֹתָם ("their iniquities"), with the people of Israel as the antecedent of the 3mp suffix. The full PP is, "for their two iniquities." This could be a reference to the two sins at Gibeah mentioned in v. 9 (the crime + the war or the crime + the failure to turn over the criminals) or it could be a way of stating that their sin is extremely severe (Stuart 1987:169). Another option is that it refers to the historical sin at Gibeah (Judg 19–21) and Israel's continuation of that sin (cf. v. 9).

10:11 a וְאֶפְרַיִם עֶגְלָה מְלֻמָּדָה אֹהַבְתִּי לָדוּשׁ
b וַאֲנִי עָבַרְתִּי עַל־טוּב צַוָּארָהּ
c אַרְכִּיב אֶפְרַיִם
d יַחֲרוֹשׁ יְהוּדָה
e יְשַׂדֶּד־לוֹ יַעֲקֹב׃

Lines a-b are a bicolon featuring grammatical parallelism: noun (עֶגְלָה)//pronoun (הּ). The lines are marked by *Zaqep parvum* and *'Atnaḥ*. Lines c-e are a tricolon. Each line contains one verb relating to agriculture (√שׂדד//√חרשׁ//√רכב) and one name for a part of the broader nation of Israel (אֶפְרַיִם//יְהוּדָה//יַעֲקֹב). The lines are marked by *Pašta*, *Zaqep parvum*, and *Silluq*.

וְאֶפְרַיִם עֶגְלָה מְלֻמָּדָה. *Line a*. Independent verbless clause.

וְאֶפְרַיִם. Subject of the verbless clause. The וְ introduces a new rhetorical subunit that uses agricultural imagery (vv. 11-13a).

עֶגְלָה. Predicate of the verbless clause. This is the same word used for the "calf" of Beth Aven (10:5).

מְלֻמָּדָה. Pual ptc fs √למד functioning as an attributive adjective and modifying עֶגְלָה. It refers to being trained for a skill such as singing (1 Chr 25:7) or fighting (Song 3:8). The sense here is that this heifer is domesticated, adding to its value.

אֹהַבְתִּי לָדוּשׁ. *Line a*. Relative clause headed by עֶגְלָה.

אֹהַבְתִּי. Qal ptc fs √אהב, also modifying עֶגְלָה. The usual form would be אֹהֶבֶת. GKC (§901) argues that the final ‍ִי- is the remains of an early case ending. JM (§93n), however, points out that there is no notion of the construct state here at all and the ending is probably there for the rhythm.

לָדוּשׁ. This Qal inf constr √דוש is the complement of אֹהַבְתִּי (cf. WO §36.2.1d). This verb refers to threshing grain by trampling on it (cf. Isa 28:28; 1 Chr 21:20). Deut 25:4 states that animals were to be allowed to eat some of the grain while they threshed. The positive portrayal here is of an animal that likes to work and has a great deal of potential.

וַאֲנִי עָבַרְתִּי עַל־טוּב צַוָּארָהּ. *Line b*. Independent clause.

וַאֲנִי. This independent 1cs pronoun pragmatically marks the speaker (YHWH) as the topic.

עָבַרְתִּי. Qal *qatal* 1cs √עבר. The sense is similar to that of 9:10 when YHWH found Israel as unexpected, pleasing grapes in the wilderness. He passed by this beautiful animal and appreciated its fine neck which has potential for good work.

עַל־טוּב צַוָּארָהּ. PP with locative עַל meaning "beside." The construct phrase טוּב צַוָּארָהּ is an epexegetical genitive in which the genitive צַוָּארָהּ ("her neck") is modified by the construct nouns טוּב ("goodness") (cf. WO §9.5.3c). The sense is, "her fine neck." Some commentators suggest that the verse is missing the noun על ("yoke"), which has been lost by haplography with עַל (note the combination of the two words in 11:4). However, nowhere in the OT does the verb √עבר describe the placing of a yoke on an animal (the expected verb would be √עלה or √נתן).

אַרְכִּיב אֶפְרַיִם. *Line c*. Independent clause.

אַרְכִּיב. Hiph *yiqtol* (irrealis) 1cs √רכב. The Qal of √רכב means "to ride" and the Hiphil refers to placing someone or something in a chariot (Gen 41:43), on a donkey (Exod 4:20), or in a cart (2 Sam 6:3) so that they or it can ride. That cannot be the meaning in the present verse since אֶפְרַיִם (acc compl) is here pictured as a heifer—see line a. This is apparently a unique usage in which Ephraim is being harnassed, perhaps to work the plough with Judah (line d) (AF 567–68). The parallelism of lines c-e encourages us to read them all as a closely connected unit. In lines d and e below, the clauses have VS word order indicating that the *yiqtol* verbs are irrealis; the 1cs verb אַרְכִּיב in this clause should be understood as irrealis as well. The context is that of a historical allusion (lines a-b) as well as disappointed expectations (vv. 12-13). Thus, these irrealis *yiqtol* verbs refer to YHWH's hopes and intentions in the past: "I *would* harness Ephraim" (line c) or "Judah was to plough" (line d).

אֶפְרַיִם. Acc compl of אַרְכִּיב.

יַחֲרוֹשׁ יְהוּדָה. *Line d*. Independent clause.

יַחֲרוֹשׁ. Qal *yiqtol* (irrealis) 3ms √חרשׁ, which refers to breaking up the ground for planting.

יְהוּדָה. Subject of יַחֲרוֹשׁ.

יְשַׂדֶּד־לוֹ יַעֲקֹב. *Line e*. Independent clause.

יְשַׂדֶּד. Piel *yiqtol* (irrealis) 3ms √שׂדד. This verb only occurs three times in the OT, twice in parallel with √חרשׁ (Isa 28:24; Hos 10:11) and once in connection with "valleys" (עֲמָקִים) (Job 39:10). It apparently refers to breaking up the ground and creating rows.

לוֹ. PP with לְ indicating an ethical dative which has a reflexive sense. The action is for the interest of the performer (WO §11.2.10d). The antecedent of the suffix is יַעֲקֹב.

יַעֲקֹב. Subject of יְשַׂדֶּד.

10:12 a זִרְעוּ לָכֶם לִצְדָקָה
b קִצְרוּ לְפִי־חֶסֶד
c נִירוּ לָכֶם נִיר
d וְעֵת לִדְרוֹשׁ אֶת־יְהוָה
e עַד־יָבוֹא וְיֹרֶה צֶדֶק לָכֶם:

Lines a-c are a tricolon. Each line consists of a plural imperative which continues the agricultural metaphor begun in v. 11. Lines a and b contain לְ of purpose or manner; lines a and c bracket the unit with ethical datives (לָכֶם). The lines are marked by *Pašta*, *Zaqep parvum*, and *ʾAtnaḥ*. Lines d and e are a bicolon with correspondence between the subject יְהוָה (line d) and 3ms verbs (line e). The lines are marked by *Zaqep parvum* and *Silluq*.

זִרְעוּ לָכֶם לִצְדָקָה. *Line a*. Independent clause.

זִרְעוּ. Qal impv mp √זרע. The time reference of the three imperatives (lines a-c) and the verbless clause (line d) is indicated by the context. This verse continues the historical allusion began in the previous verse (10:11). Therefore, although these imperatives are addressed to Hosea's contemporary audience, they are located rhetorically in the past and represent the covenant expectations that YHWH had for Israel when he called them to be his people. The verb √זרע first appears in the book in 2:25 as a reference to YHWH placing Israel in the land. In 8:7 it is a metaphor for actions that have a particular result. The following PPs are adjuncts; the complement of this verb describing *what* Israel is to sow is understood to be the actions and ethic that is demanded of them as the people of YHWH.

לָכֶם. PP with ל indicating an ethical dative. The action of sowing (זרע√) is for their own benefit (cf. 10:11e). The antecedent of the 2mp suffix is the people of Israel, addressed directly in this verse.

לִצְדָקָה. PP with ל of purpose ("for") or manner ("according to") (cf. WO §11.2.10d). A ל of purpose would mean that they were to sow (i.e., act) in order to produce righteousness; manner would mean that they were to sow (act) righteously. It is not probable that the ל is a less common accusative marker (cf. Stuart 1987:170; JM §125k); more likely, the use of ל signals that צְדָקָה and פֶה (line b) are *not* the complements of the verbs in these lines.

קִצְרוּ לְפִי־חֶסֶד. *Line b*. Independent clause.

קִצְרוּ. Qal impv mp √קצר. Like זִרְעוּ in the previous line, the complement of this verb is omitted but assumed to refer to the conduct that is expected as a result of Israel's election.

לְפִי־חֶסֶד. PP with ל of purpose or manner (cf. line a). פִי is the construct form of פֶה ("mouth"), which is in turn a metonymy for what comes out of one's mouth, or "expression." Therefore, the translation is, "for the expression of covenant love" (חֶסֶד).

נִירוּ לָכֶם נִיר. *Line c*. Independent clause.

Hosea 10:12

נִירוּ. Qal impv mp √ניר. This verb ("to plough") occurs twice in the OT. Jer 4:3 also has the noun נִיר ("prepared ground") as a cognate accusative like the present verse.

לָכֶם. See line a.

נִיר. Cognate acc of נִירוּ ("fallow ground").

וְעֵת. *Line d.* Independent verbless clause without an explicit subject. We expect a pronoun הוּא, but it is implied.

לִדְרוֹשׁ אֶת־יְהוָה. *Line d.* Modal clause with an infinitive construct subordinate to the previous verbless clause. This kind of clause expresses obligation and is found with verbless clauses (cf. WO §36.2.3f).

לִדְרוֹשׁ. Qal inf constr √דרשׁ.

אֶת־יְהוָה. Acc compl of לִדְרוֹשׁ.

עַד־יָבוֹא. *Line e.* Temporal clause subordinate to the previous clause לִדְרוֹשׁ אֶת־יְהוָה in line d. The conjunction עַד indicates that the situation in this clause is later (i.e., they must seek YHWH *until* he comes) (cf. WO §38.7a). The verb is a Qal *yiqtol* 3ms √בוא.

וְיֹרֶה צֶדֶק לָכֶם. *Line e.* Unmarked temporal clause. The וְ which coordinates this clause to the previous one (עַד־יָבוֹא) indicates that the two clauses are on the same syntactic level and have the same function.

וְיֹרֶה. Hiph *yiqtol* 3ms √ירה. The agricultural imagery in the context here suggests that the sense is "to water" or "cause to rain" (cf. HALOT 436). Hosea apparently uses this same root in 6:3, but the syntax is different. In 6:3 the complement of √ירה is the thing watered (אֶרֶץ), whereas here it is the means of "watering" (צֶדֶק). The solution to the problem is uncertain since the only other probable occurrence of this root is a Hofal in Prov 11:25.

צֶדֶק. Acc compl of וְיֹרֶה.

לָכֶם. PP with לְ of interest. The antecedent of the 2mp suffix continues to be the people of Israel.

a 10:13 חֲרַשְׁתֶּם־רֶשַׁע
b עַוְלָתָה קְצַרְתֶּם
c אֲכַלְתֶּם פְּרִי־כָחַשׁ
d כִּי־בָטַחְתָּ בְדַרְכְּךָ
e בְּרֹב גִּבּוֹרֶיךָ׃

Lines a-c are a tricolon, with each line containing a *qatal* verb and its accusative complement. Lines a and c features standard (verb-compl) word order and enclose line b which has complement-verb word order. The alternation is a kind of chiastic pattern which links the lines together. The lines are marked by *Tᵉbir*, *Ṭipḥa*, and *'Atnaḥ*. Lines d-e are a bicolon indicated by ellipsis of the verb בָטַחְתָּ. Each line concludes with a PP introduced by בְּ and concluding with a 2ms poss suffix. This bicolon is also set apart from the preceding tricolon by a shifts from 2mp to 2ms verbs. The lines are marked by *Ṭipḥa* and *Silluq*.

חֲרַשְׁתֶּם־רֶשַׁע. *Line a*. Independent clause.

חֲרַשְׁתֶּם. Qal *qatal* 2mp √חרשׁ. This 2mp verb is addressed to Hosea's contemporary audience. The *qatal* refers to actions in the past from Hosea's perspective and describes Israel's response to the expectations set forward when they were called (10:11-12). The repetition of √חרשׁ (see 10:11) underscores that although they did "plow" as YHWH had commanded, they produced the very opposite of what he had intended.

רֶשַׁע. The verb √חרשׁ usually refers to breaking up the ground so that it can be planted. It does not normally take an accusative complement; rather it is sometimes followed by a PP that describes the means (e.g., Deut 22:10) or time (e.g., Prov 20:4) of plowing. This verse is one of two cases where √חרשׁ is used as a metonymy for all of the actions involved in planting a field, from preparing the ground to sowing the seed (see also Job 4:8). Therefore, because of the particular semantics of חֲרַשְׁתֶּם in this verse, רֶשַׁע is its accusative. Within the metaphor, it represents the seed that is planted in anticipation of harvest (see line b). Rather than "sowing" (√זרע) righteousness and חֶסֶד ("covenant love") (10:12), they have worked to produce wickedness and evil intent.

עַוְלָתָה קְצַרְתֶּם. *Line b*. Independent clause.

עוֹלָתָה. Acc compl of קְצַרְתֶּם. The noun עוֹלָה refers to "injustice," which is the opposite of חֶסֶד ("covenant love") commanded in 10:12. Israel was called בְּנֵי־עַלְוָה\עוֹלָה (likely an error due to metathesis) in 10:9. Here, the unexpected ת in the form is likely a remnant of an archaic accusative case ending (see 8:7b).

קְצַרְתֶּם. Qal *qatal* 2mp √קצר. This verb refers to harvesting, the expected outcome of the metonymy √חרשׁ in line a.

אֲכַלְתֶּם פְּרִי־כָחַשׁ. *Line c*. Independent clause.

אֲכַלְתֶּם. Qal *qatal* 2mp √אכל.

פְּרִי־כָחַשׁ. Acc compl of אֲכַלְתֶּם. The metaphor has progressed from planting (line a) to harvesting (line b) to the fruits of their labors (פְּרִי). The segolate noun כַּחַשׁ is derived from the verb √כחשׁ, "to deceive" or "to lie."

כִּי־בָטַחְתָּ בְדַרְכְּךָ. *Line d*. Causal clause subordinate to the main clause in line c and, by extension, lines a and b as well. This clause (including line e) explains why they planted wickedness and harvested injustice and deceit.

בָטַחְתָּ. Qal *qatal* 2ms √בטח. After using mp verbs to address the people of Israel in vv. 12-13c, Hosea now shifts to 2ms verbs and suffixes (vv. 13d-14). He last used a 2ms verb in the beginning of this unit in 10:9 (חָטָאתָ), the referent of which is clearly identified by the vocative (יִשְׂרָאֵל). It is possible that he is resuming that address here (cf. AF 569). If so, there is not a significant difference between the singular and plural forms in terms of Hosea's audience (i.e., the nation as opposed to the people of the nation). Alternatively, these 2ms forms in vv. 13d-14 may have a different referent than 10:9, being addressed to the king of Israel who trusted in his military might. Note that מֶלֶךְ יִשְׂרָאֵל is specifically mentioned in v. 15. This explanation is preferable since Hosea ends the unit in 10:15 with 2mp suffixes, concluding with an address to the nation as a whole. In other words, he consistently uses plural forms in his overall address to the nation, while the singular forms indicate an aside to the king.

בְדַרְכְּךָ. This PP with בְּ is the oblique compl of בָטַחְתָּ. When √בטח means "be confident," it has no complement; when it means "to trust in," it takes a complement marked with בְּ or עַל. The word דֶּרֶךְ ("way") is a metaphor that refers to the trajectory and accumulation of one's life choices.

בְּרֹב גִּבּוֹרֶיךָ. *Line e.* Independent clause. This line is a second oblique complement of the verb בָּטַחְתָּ, which is elided. Several English translations (NIV, ESV, HCSB) insert the word "and" before this line. However, the parallelism with the elided verb encourages us to equate Israel's trust in their דֶּרֶךְ ("way") with their trust in גִּבּוֹרִים ("warriors"), similar to an appositional relationship. In other words, Israel does not trust in two things rather than YHWH, they trust in one thing: their ability to make war. The amplification in the parallelism indicates that their "way" (line d) *is* their army.

a 10:14 וְקָאם שָׁאוֹן בְּעַמֶּךָ
b וְכָל־מִבְצָרֶיךָ יוּשַּׁד
c כְּשֹׁד שַׁלְמַן בֵּית אַרְבֵאל בְּיוֹם מִלְחָמָה
d אֵם עַל־בָּנִים רֻטָּשָׁה:

Lines a–d comprise one long sentence and do not demonstrate many features of parallelism. Lines a–b are a bicolon, indicated by the correspondences of יוּשַּׁד//שָׁאוֹן and מִבְצָרֶיךָ//בְּעַמֶּךָ. The lines are marked by *Segolta* and *Zaqep parvum*. Lines c and d are also a bicolon which likens the coming destruction to that of a specific historical allusion. Line c is disproportionately long, and we might divide it after the *Tipha* disjunctive accent on אַרְבֵאל. However, this would leave only a short PP in the following line and there would be less semantic correspondence between the lines. It is best to end the line with the *'Atnah* on מִלְחָמָה. The lines are marked by *'Atnah* and *Silluq*.

וְקָאם שָׁאוֹן בְּעַמֶּךָ. *Line a.* Independent clause.

וְקָאם. Qal *qatal* (irrealis) 3ms √קוּם. The א as a vowel letter for ָ (*qamets*) is unusual and inexplicable but known elsewhere (see GKC §23g; §72p; JM §7b).

שָׁאוֹן. Subject of וְקָאם. This noun refers to the roar of waters (cf. Ps 65:8) or the shouts and clashing of weapons in battle (cf. Isa 13:4). It is a metonymy for war that will arise against the people.

בְּעַמֶּךָ. PP with בְּ indicating movement "against" something (WO §11.2.5d). The noun is singular; usually the vocalization would be עַמְּךָ, but this form is in pause (note the *Segolta* disjunctive accent). The antecedent of the 2ms poss suffix is apparently the king of Israel (see the discussion in 10:13d).

וְכָל־מִבְצָרֶיךָ יוּשַּׁד. *Line b*. Independent clause.

וְכָל־מִבְצָרֶיךָ. Constr phrase. כָל is the subject of the following singular verb יוּשַּׁד. The genitive מִבְצָר refers to fortifications or strongholds. This line is an amplification of line a. Not only will the people be attacked (i.e., the nation in general) (line a), but the attack will succeed as the strongholds are destroyed (line b). The antecedent of the 2ms suffix is once again the king of Israel (see 10:13d).

יוּשַּׁד. Qal pass *yiqtol* 3ms √שדד. The form is pointed like a Hofal; but there is no attested Hiphil for this root, and it is likely a Qal passive (cf. GKC §53u; WO §22.6b, n. 29). The *dagesh* in the שׁ apparently indicates that rather than R2 (ד) and R3 (ד) geminating, R2 (ד) has assimilated to R1 (שׁ), an Aramaizing pattern (cf. JM §82h).

כְּשֹׁד שַׁלְמַן בֵּית אַרְבֵאל בְּיוֹם מִלְחָמָה. *Line c*. Adjunct PP with כְּ indicating agreement in kind and providing a comparison for the destruction of the nation in lines a-b.

שֹׁד שַׁלְמַן בֵּית אַרְבֵאל. Constr chain. שַׁלְמַן is a subjective genitive: it is *Shalman*'s destruction (שֹׁד) against בֵּית אַרְבֵאל. Although the name שַׁלְמַן and his conquest must have been well known to Hosea's audience in order to serve as an illustration, we are unable to identify the referent with any certainty (for the major options, see Macintosh 2014:429ff). Dewrell suggests that it is short for "Shalmaneser V" (שַׁלְמַנְאֶסֶר) who attacked Israel (2 Kgs 17:1-5) (2016:422-3). However, Hosea's allusion here is to the past. If he is looking back on this major destruction, to what future one does he refer? Lemaire (2005:107–8) suggests that שַׁלְמַן is Salamanu of Moab. He argues that the "New Moabite Inscription," which dates to the eight century, belongs to this king who is known from the inscriptions of Tiglath-pileser III. בֵּית אַרְבֵאל is an objective genitive: the "destruction" is *against* that location (see WO §9.5.2b).

בְּיוֹם מִלְחָמָה. PP with temporal בְּ indicating the time of *Shalman*'s destruction. The construct phrase יוֹם מִלְחָמָה represents an adjectival genitive in which יוֹם is characterized by מִלְחָמָה (cf. WO §9.5.3a).

אֵם עַל־בָּנִים רֻטָּשָׁה. *Line d*. Unmarked relative clause headed by יוֹם in line c. This clause gives more information about that day when Shalman destroyed בֵּית אַרְבֵאל.

אֵם. Subject of רֻטָּ֫שָׁה and recipient (patient) of the action. The noun is singular which gives it an indeterminate sense for amplification (GKC §125c).

עַל־בָּנִים. PP with עַל. The context refers to mothers and children being killed together, so we might translate the preposition as "beside" or "along with" or even "upon."

רֻטָּ֫שָׁה. Pual *qatal* 3fs √רטש. The *qatal* verb refers to a past situation within the historical allusion (lines c-d). This verb occurs six times in the OT, always in the context of killing infants in brutal ways, and often alongside mentions of horrific war crimes (2 Kgs 8:12; Isa 13:16). If these things occurred when Shalman attacked Beth-Arbe'l in the past, then Israel should anticipate the same thing when YHWH brings war against them in the future (cf. 10:15a).

10:15 a בָּ֫כָה עָשָׂה לָכֶם בֵּית־אֵל
b מִפְּנֵי רָעַת רָעַתְכֶם
c בַּשַּׁחַר נִדְמֹה נִדְמָה מֶלֶךְ יִשְׂרָאֵל׃

Lines a-c form a tricolon which concludes the unit. Lines a-b are linked syntactically (line b is a PP) and by repetition of the 2mp pronominal suffix. Line c is a concluding line that stands apart. The lines are marked by *Zaqep parvum*, *'Atnaḥ*, and *Silluq*.

בָּ֫כָה עָשָׂה לָכֶם בֵּית־אֵל. *Line a*. Independent clause.

בָּ֫כָה. Adverb serving as the acc compl of עָשָׂה. It introduces a clause which points back to what precedes and indicates its logical conclusion (cf. WO §39.3.4e).

עָשָׂה. Qal *qatal* 3ms √עשׂה. We must identify both the tense and subject of this verb. The *qatal* verb is marked for a perfective aspect and does not necessarily indicate past time. Here, tense is determined by the context and discourse which is future, as the prophet transitions from an historical allusion in 10:14 (Shalman's [שַׁלְמַן] destruction of Beth-Arbe'l), to address his contemporaries (לָכֶם), predicting that they too will be destroyed. We maintain the perfective nuance by translating it as a perfective future, "he will have done to you" (see Cook 2012:212). The subject of the 3ms verb is not certain. AF (571) argue that the subject is שַׁלְמַן from the previous verse. Perhaps his conquest of Beth-Arbe'l was recent, and he will return. A second option is to understand בֵּית־אֵל as the subject. The sense would be that Bethel, which had instigated and been at the epicenter of the nation's idolatry, had brought judgment upon it. Third, the subject may be intentionally ambiguous. Perhaps it refers to YHWH who, though not mentioned, is ensuring Israel's fate (cf. 10:10a). This interpretation may be behind G's translation οὕτως ποιήσω ὑμῖν ("thus I will do to you"). It is likely that G understood the subject of the verb as YHWH and shifted it to first person to make that understanding explicit in the text.

לָכֶם. Adjunct PP with לְ indicating the person for whom the action is directed. The antecedent of the 2mp suffix is specifically the people of Bethel (see below) and by synechdoche the people of Israel more broadly.

בֵּית־אֵל. This vocative is in apposition to the 2mp suffix on לָכֶם and identifies its referent. Bethel had been at the center of Israel's rebellious, idolatrous cult. Now, it is the target of YHWH's judgment and is a synechdoche for the entire nation.

מִפְּנֵי רָעַת רָעַתְכֶם. *Line b.* PP with מִפְּנֵי indicating the cause of the action in line a (cf. WO §11.3.1a).

רָעַת רָעַתְכֶם. This construct phrase (lit. "the wickedness of your wickedness") expresses a superlative (cf. GKC §133i; WO §9.5.3j).

בַּשַּׁחַר נִדְמֹה נִדְמָה מֶלֶךְ יִשְׂרָאֵל. *Line c.* Independent clause.

בַּשַּׁחַר. PP with בְּ used temporally to indicate the time of the action. Perhaps the beginning of the battle, which will kill the king, begins in the new day.

נִדְמֹה. Niph inf abs √דמה used to intensify the cognate finite verb which follows as an absolute complement (WO §35.3.1).

נִדְמָה. Niph qatal (irrealis) 3ms √דמה; For the meaning of this verb, see 4:5c.

מֶלֶךְ יִשְׂרָאֵל. Subject of נִדְמָה.

YHWH's Resolve and Israel's Repentance Will Lead to Relationship (11:1-11)

In the previous major unit (9:1–10:15), Hosea systematically dismantled each aspect of Israel's hope and painted a dreary picture of destruction and loss. The problem with Israel's hope was that it lay in the nation's own resources and in false gods. However, the end of false hope does not mean that there is no hope at all. The answer to Israel's troubles lies in the same place that it always has: with YHWH. The present unit opens with an address from YHWH and begins, once again with a mention of יִשְׂרָאֵל in the first verse. The structure of the passage corresponds to the three-part pattern of Accusation, Temporary Judgment, and Ultimate Reconciliation that structures the major sections of the book in 2:4-25, 4:1–11:11 and 12:1–14:8.

In vv. 1-4 YHWH reviews the past, beginning with an historical allusion all the way back to the beginning of Israel's history, when YHWH called them as his people and rescued them from captivity in Egypt. Israel is pictured as a child that YHWH loved and trained (vv. 1, 3), yet from the very beginning they showed their propensity to stray as they engaged in idol worship at Ba'al-Pe'or (v. 2). In v. 4 the image switches to that of a farm animal that YHWH intended to domesticate so that it could serve him.

In vv. 5-7 YHWH shifts from the past to the present and near future to address judgment. His gentle leadership and expectations of service were rejected by Israel, and he announces consequences in the form of a return to captivity. In v. 5a Hosea uses מִצְרַיִם ("Egypt") a second time in the passage as a metonymy for captivity. He then specifies in v. 5b that this captivity will be in Assyria. It will be a violent end (v. 6), but they are fixed on apostasy (v. 7).

In the last part of the passage, vv. 8-11, YHWH shifts from the near future to the eschatological future to proclaim ultimate reconciliation. He addresses Israel directly (with second-person forms) in vv. 8-9 and portrays himself as internally conflicted and unwilling to allow the judgment to be total (v. 8). He states in v. 9 that he will not destroy them *again* (an indication that the temporal judgment *will* take place even as he has plans for their ultimate restoration). Yet, in the midst of judgment on his enemies (signaled by his "roar"; v. 10), he will return his own people from captivity (v. 11). The prophet concludes with a third use of מִצְרַיִם ("Egypt"), again used as a metonymy for captivity. Thus the passage comes full circle. In the past YHWH brought Israel out of physical captivity in Egypt (v. 1). In the near future they will go back to "Egypt" (i.e., exile in Assyria) (v. 5). In the eschatological future he will bring them out of "Egypt" (i.e., the captivity of ruin) again, once and for all (v. 11).

*¹When Israel was a youth, I loved him,
and from Egypt I called my son.*

*²As they called to them,
thus they went away from me.*

*They kept sacrificing to the Ba'als,
and to the idols they were burning incense.*

*³And I taught Ephraim;
I took them in my arms;
but they did not know that I healed them.*

*⁴With the cords of man I was drawing them—with ropes of love.
And I was to them like those who lift a yoke on their jaws.*

*And I bent down to him
in order that I might domesticate him.*

*⁵He will return to the land of "Egypt,"
and Assyria— it (will be) his king,
for they have refused to return.*

*⁶And the sword will wreak havoc in his cities
and bring to an end his oracle priests,
and it will devour because of their plans.*

*⁷And my people are fixed on apostasy from me.
Though upward they call him,
altogether he will not exalt (them).*

*⁸How will I give you up, Ephraim?
Will I hand you over, Israel?
How will I give you up like Admah?
Will I deal with you like Zebo'im?*

*My heart recoils within me;
my compassions are agitated altogether.*

*⁹I will not execute my burning anger;
I will not again destroy Ephraim.*

*Because I am God and not a man—
the holy one in your midst,
and I will not enter a city.*

¹⁰They will walk after YHWH.
He will roar like a lion.

He will roar,
and children will come trembling from the west.

¹¹They will tremble like a bird from "Egypt,"
and like a dove from the land of Assyria.
And I will settle them in their estates.
A declaration of YHWH.

11:1 a כִּי נַעַר יִשְׂרָאֵל וָאֹהֲבֵהוּ
b וּמִמִּצְרַיִם קָרָאתִי לִבְנִי׃

Lines a-b are a bicolon with a correspondence between יִשְׂרָאֵל and -הוּ in line a and בְּנִי in line b. The lines are marked by *'Atnaḥ* and *Silluq*.

כִּי נַעַר יִשְׂרָאֵל. *Line a*. Subordinate temporal clause with כִּי indicating that the situations of this clause and the following main clause are contemporary (cf. WO §38.7a).

נַעַר. Predicate of the verbless clause. The word נַעַר refers to a "youth" but covers a range of ages. It is used to describe an unborn child (Judg 13:5, 7), an infant (Exod 2:6), a teenager seventeen years old (Gen 37:2), and a full adult (Gen 41:12). It is used here as a metaphor for Israel's earliest beginnings when he was first called and commissed by YHWH.

יִשְׂרָאֵל. Subject of the verbless clause.

וָאֹהֲבֵהוּ. *Line a*. Independent clause. The verb is a Qal wayyiqtol 1cs √אהב with a 3ms acc suffix. In this context the verb √אהב refers to YHWH's election of Israel; it is an adoption metaphor (cf. the opposite in 9:15b).

וּמִמִּצְרַיִם קָרָאתִי לִבְנִי. *Line b*. Independent clause.

וּמִמִּצְרַיִם. PP with מִן. Some have understood the מִן as temporal, meaning "since the time of Egypt" (cf. WO §11.2.11c; see Macintosh 2014:437 for examples). However, elsewhere Hosea uses מִן with מִצְרַיִם in an ablative sense, designating movement away (11:11; 12:14). By contrast, in 10:9 he uses the expression מִימֵי ("since the days of") for an unambiguous temporal reference. Thus his typical language supports interpreting the preposition as ablative here (Wolff 1974:190).

קְרָאתִי. Qal *qatal* 1cs √קרא. With an oblique complement marked by לְ (לְבְנִי) in this context, the verb means "to summon." YHWH called Israel out of Egypt and to a particular covenantal relationship with himself.

לְבְנִי. Oblique compl of קְרָאתִי. The antecedent of the 1cs poss suffix is YHWH, the speaker.

11:2 a קָרְאוּ לָהֶם
b כֵּן הָלְכוּ מִפְּנֵי (word division ≠ MT)
c הֵם לַבְּעָלִים יְזַבֵּחוּ
d וְלַפְּסִלִים יְקַטֵּרוּן:

Lines a-b are a bicolon with each line consisting of a 3cp *qatal* verb and a PP with a 3mp suffix. The lines in MT are marked by *'Atnaḥ* and *Zaqep parvum*. However, the word מִפְּנֵיהֶם (end of line b) is likely an error in MT, which is better analyzed as two words: מפני and הם (the latter belongs at the beginning of line c). Lines c-d are also a bicolon, with each line consisting of a PP with לְ and a 3mp *yiqtol* verb. The lines are marked by *Zaqep parvum* and *Silluq*.

קָרְאוּ לָהֶם. *Line a.* Unmarked comparative clause (see JM §174e).

קָרְאוּ. Qal *qatal* 3cp √קרא. The 3cp subject is a continuation of the historical allusion begun in v. 1 (when YHWH first called Israel) and precedes v. 3 (when he guided Israel's early history). Lexical connections evoke the incident at Ba'al-Pe'or such as √קרא (Num 25:2), √זבח (Num 25:2), and בַּעַל (Num 25:3), and Hosea has previously linked YHWH's initial calling with that incident in 9:10. Therefore, the subject of קָרְאוּ here is most likely the people of Moab who drew the people of Israel away from YHWH.

לָהֶם. Oblique compl of קָרְאוּ. With לְ, the verb √קרא means "to summon" here as it did in 11:1b.

כֵּן הָלְכוּ מִפְּנֵי. *Line b.* Independent clause. In the MT the last word in this line is מִפְּנֵיהֶם ("before them"). However, this makes little sense as the מִן prep is ablative, and it is difficult to identify the referent of the 3mp suffix. As BHS note ᵇ indicates, G and S represent a different and more likely word division of the same consonantal text: מפני הם which is followed here. The word מִפָּנַי ("from me") describes Israel's apostasy away from YHWH. The independent pronoun הֵם is pleonastic and belongs at the beginning of line c, anticipating the subject of יְזַבֵּחוּ.

כֵּן. This adverb introduces a clause which points back to what precedes and expresses its logical conclusion (cf. WO §39.3.4e).

הָלְכוּ. Qal *qatal* 3cp √הלך.

מִפָּנָי. Compound PP with abl מִן and פָּנֶה ("before," "in the presence"). The antecedent of the 1cs suffix is YHWH, the speaker. Thus Israel's apostasy at Ba'al-Pe'or was a reversal of YHWH's initial call. In 11:1b YHWH called (√קרא) his son (לִבְנִי) from (מִן) Egypt. In 11:2 the women of Moab called (√קרא) to Israel (לָהֶם) and they went from (מִן) YHWH.

הֵם לַבְּעָלִים יְזַבֵּחוּ. *Line c*. Independent clause.

הֵם. This pleonastic pronoun (which is a 3mp suffix in MT—see above) anticipates the following subject יְזַבֵּחוּ.

לַבְּעָלִים. PP with לְ of interest indicating to whom the action is directed. On the plural בְּעָלִים, see 2:15a.

יְזַבֵּחוּ. Piel *yiqtol* 3mp √זבח. The context (vv. 1-4) is a historical allusion, and the verbs in lines a-b are past tense. Therefore, this *yiqtol* verb (and the one in line d) is translated as past imperfective (see Cook 2012:218; WO §21.2b). The imperfective aspect communicates an iterative or frequentative action. Israel did not sacrifice to the Ba'als one time but over and over. The Piel of √זבח almost always refers to illegitimate sacrifice (see 4:13a).

וְלַפְּסִלִים יְקַטֵּרוּן. *Line d*. Independent clause.

וְלַפְּסִלִים. PP with לְ of interest indicating to whom the action is directed. This is the only occurrence of פָּסִיל in Hosea. It refers to carved images and idols, usually made out of wood (cf. Deut 7:5).

יְקַטֵּרוּן. Piel *yiqtol* 3mp √קטר with a paragogic ן (cf. WO §31.7.1a-b; JM §44e). On the meaning of this verb, see 2:15; 4:13. The *yiqtol* is a past imperfective (like יְזַבֵּחוּ above).

11:3 a וְאָנֹכִי תִרְגַּלְתִּי לְאֶפְרַיִם
b קָחָם עַל־זְרוֹעֹתָיו
c וְלֹא יָדְעוּ כִּי רְפָאתִים׃

Lines a-c are a tricolon, identified by content (YHWH's actions with Ephraim) as well as the concern with Ephraim (אֶפְרַיִם and 3mp pronominal suffixes) in all three lines. The lines are marked by *Zaqep parvum*, *'Atnaḥ*, and *Silluq*.

וְאָנֹכִי תִרְגַּלְתִּי לְאֶפְרַיִם. *Line a*. Independent clause.

וְאָנֹכִי. Pleonastic independent 1cs pronoun that anticipates the 1cs subject of תִרְגַּלְתִּי. It constrasts with the pronoun הֵם in 11:2c: *they* (Israel) were sacrificing to idols, but *I* (YHWH) tenderly cared for them.

תִרְגַּלְתִּי. A *qatal* 1cs √רגל. The *binyan* of this verb is uncertain and has been the subject of much discussion in the history of interpretation. For a thorough summary and evaluation, see Hutton and Marzouk 2012. Modern scholars often analyze it as an uncommon Tif'el, which may be an error for, or an equivalent of, a Hiphil of √רגל meaning "to teach to walk" (cf. GKC §55h; HALOT 1184). JM (§59e) understands it as a denominal of רֶגֶל ("foot") meaning "to lead." Hutton and Marzouk (2012:37) argue, in an extensive article, that the form is a tG (comparable to a Hithpael but semantically related to the Qal), similar to the Hithpe'el in Aramaic. The loss of the initial ה of the *binyan* is due to the phonetic environment. They are unwilling to propose a meaning for the verb but are confident that it does *not* have a causative sense, so meanings such as "I taught to walk" or "I led" should be abandoned. For now, the translation "taught" will have to do: it is sufficiently general and is in keeping with a context of YHWH's gentle care for Israel.

לְאֶפְרַיִם. Acc compl of תִרְגַּלְתִּי, marked by ל. The prep ל marks the complement of a verb occasionally in Hebrew, which may reflect influence from Aramaic (cf. WO §11.2.10g).

קָחָם עַל־זְרוֹעֹתָיו. *Line b*. Independent clause.

קָחָם. This is another difficult verb. It looks like a Qal impv ms with a 3mp acc suffix (though it should have an i-class linking vowel: קָחֵם). But what would this mean? YHWH is the speaker throughout this unit and has been referring to Israel/Ephraim in the third person. Some have suggested that it is an unusual form of an infinitive absolute with a 3mp acc suffix (cf. AF 580). All of the major versions translate this with a first-person verb (see BHS note [a]). Although it is possible that they are making the best sense they can of the text (as we are), it is also possible that the original text read אֶקָּחֵם. This is a difference of only one letter (א) from MT since the ל in √לקח assimilates in closed syllables. The verb would then have been a Qal *yiqtol* 1cs with a 3mp acc suffix understood as a past imperfective in the context.

עַל־זְרוֹעֹתָיו. PP with locative עַל. YHWH is reminding them how he took them up on his arms to support them. It is very difficult to make sense of the 3ms poss suffix on זְרוֹעֹתָיו. If YHWH is the speaker, to whom would it refer? I follow G, S, and V in understanding the suffix as 1cs (see BHS note b). The MT reading is easily explained as a dittography followed by confusion of י and ו.

וְלֹא יָדְעוּ. *Line c*. Independent clause. The verb is a Qal *qatal* 3cp √ידע. This statement recalls 2:10, where YHWH says that Israel did not know (√ידע) that he was the one who had given her the agricultural blessings and wealth. √ידע probably has the sense of "acknowledge" in both verses.

כִּי רְפָאתִים. *Line c*. Complement clause in an accusative frame which indicates what Israel knew (√ידע) in the previous line. Complement, or constituent noun clauses, are often introduced with כִּי (cf. WO §38.8d). The verb is a Qal *qatal* 1cs √רפא with a 3mp acc suffix. The use of √רפא ("heal") may be a play on the name אֶפְרַיִם. It occurs elsewhere in 5:13; 6:1; 7:1, and 14:5.

11:4 a בְּחַבְלֵי אָדָם אֶמְשְׁכֵם בַּעֲבֹתוֹת אַהֲבָה
b וָאֶהְיֶה לָהֶם כִּמְרִימֵי עֹל עַל לְחֵיהֶם
c וְאַט אֵלָיו

11:4-5 d אוֹכִיל: לֹא

This verse consists of two bicola of very different lengths. The first bicolon, lines a-b, has five words in the first line and six in the second. The lines are linked via the imagery of a domestic animal and 3mp suffixes and are marked by *Zaqep parvum* and *'Atnaḥ*. The second bicolon, lines c-d, is much shorter with only two words in each line. Each line contains a 1cs *yiqtol* verb and a 3ms suffix. The word לֹא (i.e., לוֹ) is brought forward from the beginning of the first line of 11:5 to conclude line d. Although this goes against the Masoretic accents, it solves a syntactic and interpretive problem (see below).

בְּחַבְלֵי אָדָם אֶמְשְׁכֵם בַּעֲבֹתוֹת אַהֲבָה. *Line a*. Independent clause.

Hosea 11:4-5

בְּחַבְלֵי אָדָם. PP with instrumental בְּ indicating the means by which YHWH drew Israel/Ephraim (WO §11.2.5d). The construct phrase חַבְלֵי אָדָם is an adjectival genitive (WO §9.5.3a). אָדָם refers to humanity and thus these are "humane" cords (note the apposition with אַהֲבָה, "love").

אֶמְשְׁכֵם. Qal *yiqtol* 1cs √משׁד with a 3mp acc suffix. The figurative imagery has shifted from that of a young child (vv. 1, 3) to that of a domestic animal, but this is still part of the historical allusion to YHWH's earliest dealings with Israel. That context, including the simple past *wayyiqtol* verb in line b, means that we should translate this *yiqtol* as an imperfective past ("was drawing"). The antecedent of the suffix is the people of Israel/Ephraim (see vv. 1-3).

בַּעֲבֹתוֹת אַהֲבָה. PP with instrumental בְּ in apposition to the previous PP and further describing it. This construct phrase is also an adjectival genitive. The ropes by which YHWH drew Israel were characterized by love.

וָאֶהְיֶה לָהֶם כִּמְרִימֵי עֹל עַל לְחֵיהֶם. *Line b.* Independent clause.

וָאֶהְיֶה. Qal *wayyiqtol* 1cs √היה.

לָהֶם. PP with a לְ of interest. YHWH's attitude and approach (היה) was directed toward the people of Israel and Ephraim, the antecedent of the 3mp suffix.

כִּמְרִימֵי. The prep כְּ indicates agreement in kind and introduces a simile. מְרִימֵי is a Hiph ptc mp √רום. It is a substantival participle, in the construct state, which governs the accusative complement עֹל ("yoke"). The Qal of √רום is intransitive and means "to be high" while the Hiphil is transitive and means "to lift (something) up." Here it could refer to lifting the yoke to place it on the animal, or lifting it up to remove it.

עֹל. Acc compl of מְרִימֵי. Apart from a few literal references to a device which harnesses an animal to a cart or plough (e.g., Num 19:2), the "yoke" (עֹל) is usually used metaphorically of oppression or servitude. A more positive picture is given in Lam 3:27, which suggests that bearing the yoke can be a means of growth, and G's reading of Jer 2:20, which suggests that the yoke sometimes entails submission to God.

עַל לְחֵיהֶם. PP with עַל. Within the metaphor of YHWH's tender treatment of a farm animal, we might understand this action as liberation from oppression (a "yoke"; cf. "Egypt" in 11:1b). YHWH would then be lifting the yoke *off* of the animal (Israel). Kuhnigk (1974:133) understands עַל as having an ablative sense "from." However, the typical meaning of עַל indicates direction *toward* something ("onto"), supporting the idea that YHWH is putting the yoke on the animal. In this case the yoke does not represent oppression but appropriate and expected labor (cf. 10:11). The reference to "their jaws" (לְחֵיהֶם) is difficult since the yoke would primarily have rested on an animal's shoulders. Perhaps the prophet has in mind the part of the device that goes around the animal's head and directs its movement.

וְאַט אֵלָיו. *Line c*. Independent clause.

וְאַט. Hiph (apocopated) *yiqtol* 1cs √נטה. The I-נ has assimilated to the ט, but the *dagesh* is not written because it is the final consonant in the word. The non-apocopated form would be אַטֶּה. Usually, apocopated forms are found in the jussive (אַט) or the *wayyiqtol* (וַיֵּט). This is likely another archaic preterite (past) form related to the *wayyiqtol* but without the וַ before the prefix (see the discussion on יָדְ in 6:1; cf. WO §31.1.1d). The Hiphil of √נטה is normally transitive ("to turn aside," "divert") but there are a few cases where it appears to be intransive and means "to bend down" (cf. Isa 30:11; Job 23:11).

אֵלָיו. PP with אֶל indicating direction toward. The antecedent of the 3ms suffix is Israel/Ephraim as a metaphorical animal. Suffixes in lines a-b are plural, but here perhaps the image of an animal is in Hosea's mind.

אוֹכִיל לֹא. *Line d*. Independent clause.

אוֹכִיל. Commentators often understand this verb as a Hiph *yiqtol* 1cs √אכל meaning "I fed." If so, the I-א is quiescent (cf. אֲבִידָה in Jer 46:8) although in the other three occurrences of √אכל in the Hiphil, the א does not quiesce (cf. Job 6:11; 9:16; Isa 48:9). The main problem with this identification is that √אכל in the Hiphil usually takes two accusatives: one to specify *who* is being fed and one to specify *what* is being fed. In this verse there are either no accusatives or, if we move up לוֹ/לֹא from 11:5, there is only one, and that is introduced with לְ. It is more plausible to understand the verb as from √יכל. It could be a Hiph *yiqtol* 1cs √יכל (though that is not attested in the OT). Or, we could revocalize it to אוּכַל (without the י), a Qal *yiqtol* 1cs √יכל. This is apparently the reading of G (δυνήσομαι αὐτῷ, "I will prevail with him"). In the Qal the verb √יכל in combination with לְ (see below) means "to prevail over" or "subdue" (cf. Gen 32:26; Num 13:30; Judg 16:4; Jer

20:10; 38:22). In this context YHWH may be saying that although he is gentle, it is his intention to "domesticate" Israel and to bring him to heed. This makes sense of the imagery of the cords, ropes, and yoke in lines a–c. Like his statement in 10:11-13, this verse sets up the discrepancy between YHWH's expectations for Israel and his response. The *yiqtol* here has an irrealis nuance and is semantically subordinate to אַט in line c: YHWH bent down *in order that* he might domesticate him.

לֹא. This word, brought forward from the beginning of 11:5, should be read as לוֹ, a לְ with a 3ms suffix. The interchange between לוֹ and לֹא is a common one in the OT. Whether אוֹכִיל is from √אכל or √יכל, it requires a complement and this provides one. The move also avoids the interpretive difficulties of a negative particle at the beginning of 11:5. G supports this reading: it represents לוֹ (αὐτῷ) at the end of 11:4 but does not have לֹא at the beginning of 11:5 (see BHS note d-d).

11:5 a יָשׁוּב֙ אֶל־אֶ֣רֶץ מִצְרַ֔יִם
b וְאַשּׁ֖וּר ה֣וּא מַלְכּ֑וֹ
c כִּ֥י מֵאֲנ֖וּ לָשֽׁוּב׃

Lines a–c are a tricolon. Lines a–b are parallel with corresponding מִצְרַיִם//אַשּׁוּר and the concept of going into captivity. Line c is a subordinate causal clause concluding the verse. The lines are marked with *Zaqep parvum*, '*Atnaḥ*, and *Silluq*.

יָשׁוּב אֶל־אֶרֶץ מִצְרַיִם. *Line a*. Independent clause. In MT the verse begins with the negative particle לֹא (see discussion on previous verse). However, it is difficult to see how this can be correct given that Hosea has repeatedly said that Israel *will* return to Egypt, an image of exile and captivity (cf. 8:13; 9:3, 6; 11:11). We might resolve the problem by understanding the לֹא as an asseverative particle: "they will *certainly* return to Egypt" (see Sivan and Schniedewind 1993:219–26). Alternatively, we could understand it as a rhetorical question (see 10:9c). The best solution is to take it with the end of 11:4, for reasons stated in the discussion there.

יָשׁוּב. Qal *yiqtol* 3ms √שׁוב. The *yiqtol* could refer to the present: Israel is going to Egypt for help, but Assyria is his king (line b) (cf. Wolff 1974:192). In the context, and in light of Hosea's previous use of Egypt as an image of exile, it is better understood as (near) future.

אֶל־אֶרֶץ מִצְרָיִם. PP with אֶל indicating the goal of movement (יָשׁוּב).

וְאַשּׁוּר הוּא מַלְכּוֹ. *Line b.* Independent verbless clause. This is a tripartite verbless clause which includes two nouns and an independent 3ms pronoun. Early analyses of BH argued that the pronoun was the copula of the verbless clause, in which case אַשּׁוּר would the subject and מַלְכּוֹ would be the predicate (cf. WO §16.3.3b). By contrast, some modern scholars would argue that the pronoun does not function as a copula. Rather, it is the subject of the clause, while אַשּׁוּר is a focus constituent, or *casus pendens* (cf. JM §154i-j; WO §16.3.3b; Muraoka 1999:203–4). Recently, Holmstedt and Jones 2014 have argued that 3ms pronouns function both ways in BH.

מַלְכּוֹ. Predicate of the verbless clause. The antecedent of the 3ms poss suffix is Israel/Ephraim (cf. 11:1, 3).

כִּי מֵאֲנוּ לָשׁוּב. Line c. Subordinate causal clause with כִּי giving the reason that Israel will go into captivity (lines a-b).

מֵאֲנוּ. Piel *qatal* 3cp √מאן. Note the singular verbs and pronouns in lines a-b which transition to plural here in line c. We find the same pattern in 11:6.

לָשׁוּב. Qal inf constr √שׁוּב. Compl of מֵאֲנוּ (WO §36.2.1d). √שׁוּב refers to returning to YHWH in the sense of submission and trust. It can also refer to repentance.

11:6 a וְחָלָה חֶרֶב בְּעָרָיו
b וְכִלְּתָה בַדָּיו
c וְאָכֵלָה מִמֹּעֲצוֹתֵיהֶם:

Lines a-c are a tricolon. Each of the three lines begins with an irrealis *qatal* verb. חֶרֶב ("sword") in line a is the subject of all three. The *'Atnaḥ* on וְאָכֵלָה suggests the end of a line. However, it is more plausible that each verb is followed by a complement or a PP. The lines are marked by *Zaqep parvum*, *Ṭipḥa*, and *Silluq*.

וְחָלָה חֶרֶב בְּעָרָיו. *Line a.* Independent clause.

וְחָלָה. Qal *qatal* (irrealis) 3fs √חול. This verb refers to dancing (e.g., Judg 21:21) or twisting (Lam 4:6). In most occurrences, however, it refers to an attack (e.g., 2 Sam 3:29; Jer 23:19). The sense here is of a dangerous sword swinging wildly and killing in the cities. Based on other occurrences, we expect an accusative or oblique complement (with עַל), but it is understood to be the inhabitants of Israel.

חֶרֶב. This feminine noun is the subject of וְחָלָה as well as the verbs in lines b and c. It is used as a metonymy for an enemy attack.

בְּעָרָיו. PP with locative בְּ specifying the area within which the sword will attack. The antecedent of the 3ms poss suffix is Israel/Ephraim.

וְכִלְּתָה בַדָּיו. *Line b.* Independent clause.

וְכִלְּתָה. Piel *qatal* (irrealis) 3fs √כלה. The Piel of √כלה can mean "to bring an end to a task" (i.e., complete it) or to bring an end to someone or something's existence: "to destroy" (HALOT 477). The subject is the feminine noun חֶרֶב (line a).

בַדָּיו. Acc compl of וְכִלְּתָה. There are at least five different roots for בד listed in the lexicon (HALOT 108–9), and it is not certain which is meant here. The best option may be (V) "oracle priests" or "false prophets" (בַּד). This would make sense of the parallel with מוֹעֵצָה ("plans") in line c, if the priests are advising the nation to turn away from YHWH. The antecedent of the 3ms suffix is again Israel/Ephraim.

וְאָכְלָה מִמֹּעֲצוֹתֵיהֶם. *Line c.* Independent clause.

וְאָכְלָה. Qal *qatal* (irrealis) 3fs √אכל. The subject is again the feminine noun חֶרֶב (line a). It is very common in the OT to anthropomorphize the "sword" which devours. Like the verb וְחָלָה in line a, we expect an accusative complement but it is missing. It must be understood as the people of Israel.

מִמֹּעֲצוֹתֵיהֶם. Adjunct PP with causal מִן indicating the reason that the sword is devouring. The noun מוֹעֵצָה can refer to wise advice (e.g., Prov 22:20) but usually refers to rebellious schemes (e.g., Ps 5:11; Ps 81:13; Prov 1:31; Mic 6:16). The antecedent of the 3mp poss suffix is the people of Israel/Ephraim. (Hosea switches from singular to plural in 11:5 as well).

11:7 a וְעַמִּי תְלוּאִים לִמְשׁוּבָתִי
b וְאֶל־עַל֙ יִקְרָאֻ֔הוּ
c יַ֖חַד לֹ֥א יְרוֹמֵֽם׃

Lines a-c are a tricolon, identified by content (apostasy). Lines a-b are marked by *'Atnaḥ* and *Zaqep parvum*. Strangely, although there is a *sof pasuq* after יְרוֹמֵם, the expected *Silluq* accent below the first מ is missing. It is missing in Codex L, which BHS has faithfully reproduced. This verse is very difficult and scholars have proposed a number of emendations as potential solutions. It is possible, however, to make sense of the MT as it stands.

וְעַמִּי תְלוּאִים לִמְשׁוּבָתִי. *Line a*. Independent verbless clause.

וְעַמִּי. Subject of תְלוּאִים. The antecedent of the 1cs suffix is YHWH, the speaker throughout this passage.

תְלוּאִים. Qal pass ptc mp √תלא. This root occurs in only one other passage (Deut 28:66). It is apparently a variant form of √תלה ("to hang"), which is quite common (see GKC §75rr). √תלא/תלה usually refers to being hung on a tree or fixed with nails, but here it has an abstract sense (i.e., to be "stuck" on something) with the idea of being unable or unwilling to change. The verb is plural because the subject וְעַמִּי is a collective singular (see WO §7.2.1b).

לִמְשׁוּבָתִי. PP with לְ of interest. The noun מְשׁוּבָה occurs twelve times in the OT (9× in Jeremiah), including Hos 14:5. It refers to faithlessness or turning away from the rightful object of one's loyalty. The 1cs suffix, which refers to YHWH, must be objective or have an ablative sense, "apostasy *away from* me."

וְאֶל־עַל יִקְרָאֻהוּ. *Line b*. Unmarked subordinate concessive clause. It states that Israel's action might be expected to cause the event in line c (i.e., YHWH exalting them), but in fact does not (cf. WHS §527).

וְאֶל־עַל. PP with אֶל indicating where or to whom they call (√קרא). The word עַל is difficult and has elicited a number of proposed solutions. It seems preferable to interpret עַל in accord with how Hosea used it previously in 7:16, where it contrasts potential trust in what is עַל—"above" (i.e., YHWH) with Israel's own schemes below. If the same meaning is intended in the present verse, עַל + √קרא refers to calling upward to YHWH.

יִקְרָאֻהוּ. Qal *yiqtol* 3mp √קרא with a 3ms acc suffix. The subject of the verb is "my people" (line a), and the 3ms suffix refers to YHWH. If the analysis here is correct, the call to YHWH for help is a form of rebellion. Perhaps the people are disingenuous or use a hypocritical call for help as a cover for their apostasy. Thus, YHWH will not help when they call (line c).

יַחַד לֹא יְרוֹמֵם. *Line c*. Independent clause.

יַחַד. Adverb meaning "altogether." It probably means "the people as a whole" in the sense of thoroughness or completeness. There is a wordplay with יַחַד in v. 8.

יְרוֹמֵם. Polel *yiqtol* 3ms. This verb refers to lifting something physically but is also used metaphorically of exalting people or lifting them out of negative circumstances (e.g., 1 Sam 2:7; 2 Sam 22:49). It takes an accusative complement which is sometimes assumed and omitted (e.g., Job 17:4) as here.

11:8 a אֵיךְ אֶתֶּנְךָ אֶפְרַיִם
b אֲמַגֶּנְךָ יִשְׂרָאֵל
c אֵיךְ אֶתֶּנְךָ כְאַדְמָה
d אֲשִׂימְךָ כִּצְבֹאיִם
e נֶהְפַּךְ עָלַי לִבִּי
f יַחַד נִכְמְרוּ נִחוּמָי׃

Lines a-d are a quatrain with lines linked together via alternating אֵיךְ in the first and third lines, the repeating 2ms acc suffix on each verb, and the corresponding place names: אֶפְרַיִם/יִשְׂרָאֵל and אַדְמָה/צְבֹאיִם. The lines are marked by *R^ebi^{a‘}*, *Zaqep parvum*, *Zaqep parvum*, and *'Atnaḥ*. Lines e-f are a bicolon with corresponding Niphal verbs (נֶהְפַּךְ//נִכְמְרוּ) and corresponding nouns with 1cs suffix (לִבִּי//נִחוּמָי). The lines are marked by *Zaqep parvum* and *Silluq*.

אֵיךְ אֶתֶּנְךָ אֶפְרַיִם. *Line a*. Independent clause.

אֵיךְ. This adverb can function as an interrogative ("How can I give you up?") or can introduce an exclamation ("How I will give you up!") that expresses certainty (e.g., 2 Sam 1:19). The following context (lines e-f; v. 9) indicates the former is intended here. Although YHWH has just announced certain destruction (v. 7), he suddenly presents himself as conflicted. How can he allow this to be the end of them?

אֶתֶּנְךָ. Qal *yiqtol* 1cs √נתן with a 2ms acc suffix. The four *yiqtol* verbs in lines a-d are all irrealis and used to describe potential actions. In this verse the rhetorical questions assume a negative response and the actions will *not* come to pass. YHWH has been referring to Israel/Ephraim in the third person (s and p), but now he addresses them directly with the second person singular in vv. 8-9.

אֶפְרַיִם. Vocative in apposition to the 2ms suffix on אֶתֶּנְךָ.

אֲמַגֶּנְךָ יִשְׂרָאֵל. *Line b*. Independent clause. The two uses of אֵיךְ in lines a and c might be assumed also in lines b and d of the quatrain. Alternatively, we can translate lines b and d as unmarked rhetorical questions (see translation). This is preferable because it preserves the alternating pattern between the lines.

אֲמַגֶּנְךָ. Piel *yiqtol* 1cs √מגן with a 2ms acc suffix. This verb, likely a denominal from the noun מָגֵן, is used only three times in the OT (cf. Gen 14:20; Prov 4:9).

יִשְׂרָאֵל. Vocative in apposition to the 2ms suffix on אֲמַגֶּנְךָ.

אֵיךְ אֶתֶּנְךָ כְאַדְמָה. *Line c*. Independent clause.

אֵיךְ. See line a above.

אֶתֶּנְךָ. See line a above.

כְאַדְמָה. PP with כְּ indicating agreement in kind. The place names אַדְמָה and צְבֹאִים (line d) occur together four other times (Gen 10:19; 14:2, 8; Deut 29:22) and always in connection with the infamous cities of סְדֹם (Sodom) and עֲמֹרָה (Gomorah). These statements raise the possibility of total destruction (via the allusion) and then dismiss it.

אֲשִׂימְךָ כִּצְבֹאִים. *Line d*. Independent clause. This is an unmarked rhetorical question (see line b).

אֲשִׂימְךָ. Qal *yiqtol* 1cs √שׂים with a 2ms acc suffix.

כִּצְבֹאִים. PP with כְּ indicating agreement in kind. צְבֹאִים is a place name (see line c).

נֶהְפַּךְ עָלַי לִבִּי. *Line e*. Independent clause.

נֶהְפַּךְ. Niph *qatal* 3ms √הפך. The *qatal* conjugation (also in line f) refers to a completed event (perfective) in the present. When the subject of √הפך is לֵבָב/לֵב, it means "to change one's mind" (e.g., Exod 14:5; Ps

105:25) or to be remorseful (Lam 1:20). This verb is commonly used to refer to overthrowing cities, perhaps most notably Sodom and Gomorrah (cf. Gen 19:21, 25, 29; Lam 4:6; Amos 4:11). There is likely a wordplay here: in lines c-d YHWH will *not* overthrow Admah and Zeboi'im (cities always linked to Sodom and Gomorrah) because his heart is "overturned" (הפך√).

עָלַי. PP with עַל indicating opposition (WO §11.2.13f). This preposition presents YHWH's will or intentions as having a "mind of their own," and it emphasizes the internal conflict and indecision. The antecedent of the 1cs suffix is YHWH, the speaker.

לִבִּי. Subject of נֶהְפַּךְ. The antecedent of the 1cs poss suffix is YHWH.

יַחַד נִכְמְרוּ נִחוּמָי. *Line f.* Independent clause.

יַחַד. This adverb modifies נִכְמְרוּ and expresses an action that is comprehensive in scope. There is likely an intended wordplay with the same word in v. 7 previously. In line c YHWH says that he will not lift up Israel as a whole (יַחַד)—judgment is certain. In the present verse, YHWH will ensure Israel's ultimate survival because his compassions are all stirred-up together (יַחַד).

נִכְמְרוּ. Niph *qatal* 3cp √כמר. As in line e, the *qatal* here refers to perfective (completed) action in the present. The verb √כמר is not common; it refers to the arousal of deep concern and compassion (cf. Gen 43:30; 1 Kgs 3:26).

נִחוּמָי. This plural noun is the subject of נִכְמְרוּ. It is used elsewhere only in Isa 57:18 and Zech 1:13 of feelings of "comfort" and "consolation." Here it refers to feelings of compassion.

11:9 a לֹא אֶעֱשֶׂה חֲרוֹן אַפִּי
b לֹא אָשׁוּב לְשַׁחֵת אֶפְרָיִם
c כִּי אֵל אָנֹכִי וְלֹא־אִישׁ
d בְּקִרְבְּךָ קָדוֹשׁ
e וְלֹא אָבוֹא בְּעִיר:

Lines a-b are a bicolon. Each line begins with the negative adverb לֹא, and there is amplification from line a (basis: YHWH's anger) to line b (action: destroy Ephraim). The lines are marked with *Zaqep parvum* and *'Atnaḥ*. Lines c-e are a tricolon. Line d is related appositionally to line c. Again, we see amplification in the parallelism from line c (basis: YHWH's nature) to line e (action: enter a city). The lines are marked by *Zaqep parvum*, *Zaqep parvum*, and *Silluq*.

לֹא אֶעֱשֶׂה חֲרוֹן אַפִּי. *Line a*. Independent clause.

אֶעֱשֶׂה. Qal *yiqtol* 1cs √עשׂה.

חֲרוֹן אַפִּי. Constr phrase. חֲרוֹן is the acc compl of אֶעֱשֶׂה. The construct relationship represents an epexegetical genitive: חֲרוֹן ("burning") modifies and characterizes אַף ("anger") (WO §9.5.3c).

לֹא אָשׁוּב לְשַׁחֵת אֶפְרָיִם. *Line b*. Independent clause.

אָשׁוּב. Qal *yiqtol* 1cs √שׁוּב. This verb functions as an auxiliary with the sense "again," modifying the following infinitive construct לְשַׁחֵת like an adverb (cf. 3:5; JM §177b). This is a key word in the verse, for it forms a pivot between vv. 5-7 and vv. 8-11, which at first appear to be contradictory, and explains the relationship between them. When YHWH states that he will not again destroy Ephraim, he is referring back to the temporal judgment announced in vv. 5-7, which involves destruction and captivity by Assyria. But that refusal to "destroy again" also looks forward to the eschatological restoration in vv. 8-11.

לְשַׁחֵת. Piel inf constr √שׁחת. This verb is usually transitive in the Piel, meaning "to ruin" or "destroy" (see 9:9a).

אֶפְרָיִם. Acc compl of לְשַׁחֵת.

כִּי אֵל אָנֹכִי. *Line c*. Verbless subordinate causal clause with כִּי giving the reason that YHWH will not unleash his anger or destroy Ephraim (lines a-b). אֵל is the predicate and אָנֹכִי, a 1cs independent pronoun referring to YHWH, is the subject.

וְלֹא־אִישׁ. *Line c*. Verbless clause in which the subject (אָנֹכִי) is assumed from the previous clause. Because this clause is coordinated with the previous one, it is also to be understood as subordinate (causal) to lines a-b.

בְּקִרְבְּךָ קָדוֹשׁ. *Line d*. קָדוֹשׁ is a substantival adjective ("the holy one") referring to YHWH and in apposition to אָנֹכִי in line c.

בְּקִרְבְּךָ. Adjunct PP with locative בְּ. The noun קֶרֶב means "midst." The antecedent of the 2ms suffix is Israel/Ephraim, which YHWH addresses directly (see 11:8a).

וְלֹא אָבוֹא בְּעִיר. *Line e*. Independent clause.

אָבוֹא. Qal *yiqtol* 1cs √בוא.

בְּעִיר. Oblique compl of אָבוֹא. The verb √בוא usually takes complements with בְ or אֶל (see 4:15c).

11:10 a אַחֲרֵי יְהוָה יֵלְכוּ
b כְּאַרְיֵה יִשְׁאָג
c כִּי־הוּא יִשְׁאַג
d וְיֶחֶרְדוּ בָנִים מִיָּם:

Lines a-b and c-d comprise two bicola that are related to each other in a chiastic structure. There are plural verbs in lines a and d, while the singular verb יִשְׁאָג ("roar") is repeated in lines b and c. In addition, line a ends with the verb (יֵלְכוּ), but line d begins with the verb (וְיֶחֶרְדוּ). The lines of the first bicolon are marked by *Ṭipḥa* and *'Atnaḥ*. The lines of the second bicolon are marked by *Zaqep parvum* and *Silluq*.

אַחֲרֵי יְהוָה יֵלְכוּ. *Line a*. Independent clause.

אַחֲרֵי יְהוָה. PP with אַחֲרֵי used in a locational sense (WO §11.2.1a). The sense is that YHWH will lead his people out of captivity and they will follow *after* him.

יֵלְכוּ. Qal *yiqtol* 3mp √הלך. The *yiqtol* refers to a future time (in this case, eschatological).

כְּאַרְיֵה יִשְׁאָג. *Line b*. Independent clause.

כְּאַרְיֵה. PP with כְ indicating agreement in kind. There are at least seven words for "lion" in the OT (see 5:14). The word אַרְיֵה probably refers to an African lion (NIDOTTE 1:514). YHWH is also compared to a lion in Hos 5:14 (כְּפִיר//שַׁחַל) and 13:7-8 (לָבִיא; שַׁחַל).

יִשְׁאָג. Qal *yiqtol* 3ms √שאג. YHWH "roars" (שאג√) in Amos 1:2; 3:8; Joel 4:16 [3:16]; and Jer 25:30 in order to announce eschatological judgment. In the present passage, the status of YHWH's people will have changed so that even as YHWH brings judgment, his own people will be secure (cf. 11:11). Thus, there is a great contrast between his temporal judgment against Israel (vv. 5-7) and his eschatological salvation of his people in the midst of judgment (vv. 8-11).

כִּי־הוּא יִשְׁאַג. *Line c*. Independent clause. The כִּי is not likely introducing a temporal clause. YHWH's roar (line c) would precede the trembling

(יֶחֱרְדוּ) of this children (line d), yet when כִּי introduces a temporal clause, the actions of the main clause and the subordinate clause are contemporary (cf. WO §38.7a). Therefore, the כִּי should be understood as asseverative (JM §164b).

הוּא. A pleonastic 3ms independent pronoun. This draws attention to the contrast of the action of YHWH (line c) with the action of the בָּנִים ("children") in line d.

יִשְׁאָג. Qal *yiqtol* 3ms √שאג.

וְיֶחֶרְדוּ בָנִים מִיָּם. *Line d.* Independent clause.

וְיֶחֶרְדוּ. Qal *qatal* (irrealis) 3cp √חרד. The irrealis *qatal* is predictive. It follows three *yiqtol* verbs and, like them, refers to a time in the eschatological future. The verb √חרד refers to "trembling," usually in fear of judgment. However, here the בָּנִים react this way in response to the roar of YHWH in a time of restoration (line c). In several passages √חרד serves as a metonymy for walking or moving in a trembling manner (Gen 42:28; 1 Sam 13:7; 16:4; 21:2). This is the sense here as well ("will come trembling") in connection with the abl PP מִיָּם.

בָנִים. Subject of וְיֶחֶרְדוּ.

מִיָּם. PP with abl מִן. The word יָם means "sea," but it is also used to indicate the direction "west." In the context this may be a reference to Egypt; perhaps it is imagery of a new exodus.

a 11:11 יֶחֶרְדוּ כְצִפּוֹר מִמִּצְרַיִם
b   וּכְיוֹנָה מֵאֶרֶץ אַשּׁוּר
c   וְהוֹשַׁבְתִּים עַל־בָּתֵּיהֶם
d   נְאֻם־יְהוָה׃ ס

Lines a-c is a tricolon. Lines a-b are parallel, with ellipsis of the verb יֶחֶרְדוּ in line b as well as corresponding PPs with כְּ and מִן. In addition, there is amplification (increased specificity) of the corresponding terms יוֹנָה//צִפּוֹר. Line c is the conclusion of the tricolon. The lines are marked by *Zaqep parvum*, *'Atnah*, and *Tipha*. Line d is an editorial comment that stands outside of the poetic structure.

יֶחֶרְדוּ כְצִפּוֹר מִמִּצְרַיִם. *Line a.* Independent clause.

יֶחֶרְדוּ. Qal *yiqtol* 3mp √חרד. On the meaning of this verb, see 11:10d above.

כְצִפּוֹר. PP with כְּ indicating agreement in kind.

מִמִּצְרָיִם. PP with abl מִן indicating movement away from. In 11:1 YHWH spoke of bringing Israel out of Egypt in the past. In 11:5 he predicted that Israel would go to "Egypt" (an image of captivity and exile) in the near future (cf. 8:13; 9:3, 6). In the present statement, he predicts that in the eschatological future he will bring Israel out of "Egypt" (i.e., captivity), reversing the judgment and echoing the historical exodus as a pattern of his redemptive action.

וּכְיוֹנָה מֵאֶרֶץ אַשּׁוּר. *Line b.* Independent clause. The verb יֶחֶרְדוּ is elided.

וּכְיוֹנָה. PP with כְּ indicating agreement in kind. Not only will Israel be like a "bird" (צִפּוֹר—line a), they will more specifically be like a "dove" (יוֹנָה). This image recalls 7:11, where Israel is compared to a יוֹנָה that goes to Egypt and Assyria (not to YHWH!) for help. It flits this way and that without direction or purpose, illustrating that Israel is lost in his rebellion against YHWH. In the future that dove—Israel—will return from Egypt and Assyria knowing that he belongs to YHWH.

מֵאֶרֶץ אַשּׁוּר. PP with abl מִן indicating movement away from אַשּׁוּר.

וְהוֹשַׁבְתִּים עַל־בָּתֵּיהֶם. *Line c.* Independent clause.

וְהוֹשַׁבְתִּים. Hiph *qatal* (irrealis) 1cs √ישב with a 3mp acc suffix. The verb √ישב in the Qal means "to dwell" or "to settle." In the Hiphil it is transitive and takes two complements: the first is the accusative indicating who is placed, the second is a PP indicating where they are being placed. G has ἀποκαταστήσω αὐτοὺς ("I will restore them"), which probably reflects the reading וַהֲשִׁיבֹתִים, a Hiph *qatal* (irrealis) 1cs √שוב with a 3mp acc suffix (see BHS note ᶜ). S and T represent √שוב as well. This may be preferable to MT because the verb √שוב is more natural and likely with the prep עַל. (By contrast, the verb √ישב commonly takes adjunct PPs with בְּ).

עַל־בָּתֵּיהֶם. Compl PP with locative עַל. The word בָּתִּים probably has a broader sense than "houses," referring to land and estates (AF 592). The antecedent of the 3mp poss suffix is the people of Ephraim and Israel (cf. 11:9b).

נְאֻם־יְהוָה. *Line d.* This editorial comment marks the end of the unit. It indicates that the passage originates with YHWH and is therefore authoritative.

Part 3: YHWH's Second Case Against Israel (12:1–14:9)

The prophet established the three-part pattern of Accusation, Temporary Judgment, and Ultimate Reconciliation in the introduction to the book in 2:4-25. That same pattern organizes the oracles in 4:1–11:11 as YHWH presents his case against Israel the first time. In that cycle, the Accusation panel is quite long (4:1–8:14) and goes into great detail about Israel's unfaithfulness to YHWH. The Temporary Judgment panel (9:1–10:15) is also lengthy, dwelling upon the reversal of YHWH's generosity and the consequences of breaking covenant. Yet, the cycle ends with a note of hope in 11:1-11. Surprisingly, Israel's reconciliation with YHWH and the return of the blessings will not be at Israel's initiative. It is YHWH's resolve and his own action that will lead to restoration.

In 12:1–14:9, the prophet brings YHWH's second case against Israel, again in the three-part pattern. 12:1-15 is the accusation that Israel is not repenting from their schemes like their father Jacob. The second unit, 13:1–14:1 is the announcement of judgment. Finally, 14:2-9 proclaims future hope. It corresponds to 2:16-25 and 11:1-11 in depicting God's people back in relationship with YHWH and once again enjoying his good gifts. The three units in this final cycle are shorter than the previous one and also more personal and emotionally raw. They serve as a final call to repentance as well as a message of good news.

Accusation: Israel Is Not Like Their Father Jacob (12:1-15)

Chapter 12 is a self-contained unit that condemns Israel's deceitful ways. Lexical and thematic links tie the chapter together and provide coherence. Most notably, vv. 3 and 15 envelop the unit with several correspondences (יָשִׁיב לוֹ//יְשִׁיב לוֹ; אָדוֹן//יְהוָה; הִכְעִיס//רִיב). In v. 1 the prophet states his thesis: Ephraim is deceptive and filled with falsehood, violence, and scheming (v. 2). Hosea anchors the passage with two clusters of allusions to the patriarch Jacob (vv. 4-6; vv. 13-14). Jacob was known as a trickster from birth (v. 4). He schemed, manipulated, and looked for shortcuts to achieve his ends, but then he encountered YHWH (v. 5). This YHWH is the same God who calls to Jacob's descendants (i.e., Hosea's audience) as well (v. 6). Jacob's life was blessed by YHWH and, similarly, his descendants were rescued from slavery in Egypt (vv. 13-14). The logic is simple: if the sin of the patriarch is also characteristic of the nation that bears his name, then the same cure is available to them as well. In the center of the passage (v. 7), Hosea uses directive verbs to call his audience to turn from *their* schemes and deception, which are described further in vv. 8-9 and 12. Unfortunately, although YHWH has continually revealed his word and will through the prophets (v. 11), Ephraim has rejected him. Now, they will face certain judgment (v. 15).

¹Ephraim has surrounded me with deceit,
and the house of Israel with treachery.

But Judah still wanders with God
and with the Holy One is faithful.

²Ephraim shepherds the wind
and pursues the east wind all day;
he multiplies lies and destruction.

They make a covenant with Assyria,
and oil is carried to Egypt.

³And YHWH has a dispute with Judah,
so that he will punish Jacob according to his ways;
according to his deeds he will repay him.

⁴In the womb he (Jacob) tricked his brother,
and in his power he strove with God.

⁵And he strove with an angel and prevailed.
He (Jacob) wept and implored him (Esau).

At Bethel he (God) kept finding him (Jacob),
and there he (God) speaks with us.

⁶YHWH—the God of armies—
YHWH is his memorial.

⁷Now you, return to your God.
Keep covenant love and justice,
and wait for your God continually.

⁸As for Canaan, in his hand are treacherous scales.
He loves to oppress.

288   Hosea 12:1

⁹And Ephraim said,
"Surely I have become rich,
I have found wealth for myself.
All my gains do not incur in me
iniquity, which is sin."

¹⁰But I am YHWH your God from the land of Egypt.
I will again make you live in tents, as in the days of the assembly.

¹¹And I continually spoke to the prophets,
and I multiplied visions
and through the prophets I spoke in parables.

¹²Since Gilead was wicked,
surely they have become deceitful.
In Gilgal they have sacrificed bulls;
furthermore their altars are also like heaps of stones
beside the furrows of my field.

¹³Jacob fled to the country of Aram,
and Israel worked for a wife,
and for a wife he kept (sheep).

¹⁴By a prophet YHWH brought Israel from Egypt,
and by a prophet he was kept.

¹⁵Ephraim has provoked (YHWH) bitterly
and his bloodguilt he will leave upon him.
And his Lord will return his reproach upon him.

12:1 a סְבָבֻ֤נִי בְכַ֙חַשׁ֙ אֶפְרַ֔יִם
     b   וּבְמִרְמָ֖ה בֵּ֣ית יִשְׂרָאֵ֑ל
     c וִֽיהוּדָ֗ה עֹ֥ד רָד֙ עִם־אֵ֔ל
     d   וְעִם־קְדוֹשִׁ֖ים נֶאֱמָֽן׃

Lines a-b are a bicolon, indicated by ellipsis of the verb סְבָבֻ֫נִי and its 1cs acc suffix. There is correspondence of the prepositional phrases and synonyms אֶפְרַיִם//יִשְׂרָאֵל בֵּית and בְּכַחַשׁ//בְּמִרְמָה. The lines are marked by *Zaqep parvum* and *'Atnaḥ*. Lines c-d are a bicolon, with יְהוּדָה serving as the subject of the verbs in both lines. The lines are also structured in a chiasm (verb + PP//PP + verb). They are marked by *Zaqep parvum* and *Silluq*.

סְבָבֻנִי בְכַחַשׁ אֶפְרַיִם. *Line a*. Independent clause.

סְבָבֻנִי. Qal *qatal* 3cp √סבב with a 1cs acc suffix. The word order is V-PP-S for pragmatic reasons: it has been fronted for focus. There is a contrast between Ephraim's actions and those of Judah (line c; see below). The identity of the 1cs suffix is not certain. Hosea is the speaker in most of this passage so this might be a reference to the rejection of his ministry. However, the historical allusions to Jacob and the message of the passage deal with a refusal to submit to YHWH and the need to do so. On balance, this verse is probably spoken by YHWH, and he is the referent of the 1cs suffix.

בְכַחַשׁ. PP with instrumental בְּ indicating the means by which Ephraim has surrounded YHWH. It is as though כַחַשׁ ("deceit") is a weapon used in a siege against him.

אֶפְרַיִם. Subject of סְבָבֻנִי. It is odd that the verb is plural. אֶפְרַיִם is the subject of singular verbs in every other occurrence in the book (14×), including the following verse (12:2). However, it does not make sense to understand it as a vocative, for then we would be left without a subject for the verb. It must be the subject, just as בֵּית יִשְׂרָאֵל is the subject of the (elided) verb in line b.

וּבְמִרְמָה בֵּית יִשְׂרָאֵל. *Line b*. Independent clause. The verb סְבָבֻנִי is elided.

וּבְמִרְמָה. PP with instrumental בְּ. See line a.

בֵּית יִשְׂרָאֵל. Subject of the elided verb סְבָבֻנִי.

וִיהוּדָה עֹד רָד עִם־אֵל. *Line c*. Independent clause. This bicolon (lines c-d) can be understood in two opposite ways. We could interpret the lines as a critique of Judah who worships אֵל, the Canaanite deity, and is faithful to the קְדוֹשִׁים ("holy ones"), perhaps a reference to the Canaanite pantheon. This is an attractive view because two verses later, in 12:3, Hosea states that YHWH has a רִיב (a "dispute," "case") against Judah. A second possible interpretation is that אֵל and קְדוֹשִׁים refer to YHWH. In this view these lines are stating that Judah is not (or not yet) guilty of the same *specific* sin as Israel, which, in the context, involves treacherous political alliances. This view is preferable for several reasons. First, Hosea uses אֵל and קָדוֹשׁ to refer to YHWH (not Canaanite deities) just a few verses earlier in 11:9. Hosea also uses אֵל to refer to YHWH in 2:1 but never to another deity. Second, the וְ at the beginning of line c should be taken as disjunctive, indicating a contrast with Ephraim/Israel in lines a-b. Third, the word עֹד ("still") suggests another contrast: that Judah is still doing something that Ephraim/Israel are not. Fourth, the passage concerns the character of their relationship with YHWH (cf. the allusions to Jacob), not idolatry. In 1:7 and in this verse, Hosea seems to indicate that Judah's status before YHWH is better than Israel's. Nevertheless, they are still under YHWH's judgment (cf. 12:3).

וִיהוּדָה. Subject of רָד.

עֹד. Temporal adverb modifying רָד.

רָד. This form is unique in the OT (see the Mp). It is either a Qal *qatal* 3ms √רוד or a Qal ptc ms √רוד. Either would account for the SV word order, but the adverb עֹד makes a participle more likely. The verb √רוד refers to wandering or roaming freely (HALOT 1194). McComiskey (2009:200) explains the sense of "wandering" as a certain carefree attitude since, for all of Judah's sins, their relationship with YHWH is not encumbered by deceit and treachery

עִם־אֵל. PP with עִם indicating accompaniment.

וְעִם־קְדוֹשִׁים נֶאֱמָן. *Line d.* Independent clause.

וְעִם־קְדוֹשִׁים. PP with עִם indicating accompaniment. If, as argued above, this bicolon refers to Judah's relative innocence of deceit and treachery, we could understand קְדוֹשִׁים as the pious people of YHWH (cf. Ps 34:10) (Wolff 1974:210). A more convincing interpretation is that it refers again to YHWH since it is parallel with אֵל. Hosea called YHWH קָדוֹשׁ (a substantive adjective) in 11:9. GKC (§124h) states that the plural here is perhaps analogous to the plural אֱלֹהִים.

נֶאֱמָן. Niph ptc ms √אמן. It has a progressive or durative aspect, parallel with the participle in the previous line.

12:2 a אֶפְרַיִם רֹעֶה רוּחַ
b וְרֹדֵף קָדִים כָּל־הַיּוֹם
c כָּזָב וָשֹׁד יַרְבֶּה
d וּבְרִית עִם־אַשּׁוּר יִכְרֹתוּ
e וְשֶׁמֶן לְמִצְרַיִם יוּבָל׃

Lines a-c are a tricolon. The first two lines exhibit parallelism with corresponding verbs (רדף√//רעה√) and accusatives (קָדִים//רוּחַ). The explicit subject אֶפְרַיִם in line a is elided in line b, which provides space for the additional phrase כָּל־הַיּוֹם. The lines are marked by *Pašta*, *Šalšelet*, and *'Atnaḥ*. Lines d and e are a bicolon with corresponding מִצְרַיִם//אַשּׁוּר and semantic development from the literal בְּרִית ("covenant") to the metonymy שֶׁמֶן ("oil" = tribute for an agreement). The lines are marked by *Zaqep parvum* and *Silluq*.

אֶפְרַיִם רֹעֶה רוּחַ. *Line a.* Independent clause.

אֶפְרַיִם. Subject of רֹעֶה. The word order is SV as we would expect with a participle.

רֹעֶה. Qal ptc ms √רעה. This metaphor envisions foreign treaties as domesticated animals. Just as a shepherd guides his flock with the hope that it will flourish, Ephraim manages ("shepherds") foreign alliances, hoping that they will bring him security. Yet, even with great effort, they will come to nothing. He will have shepherded only wind (see 8:7, where sowing and harvesting crops is used as a metaphor for foolish political schemes).

רוּחַ. Acc compl of רֹעֶה.

וְרֹדֵף קָדִים כָּל־הַיּוֹם. *Line b.* Independent clause.

וְרֹדֵף. Qal ptc ms √רדף. The subject of the participle is אֶפְרַיִם (see line a).

קָדִים. Acc compl of רֹדֵף. This is a semantic intensification of רוּחַ (line a) in the parallelism. רוּחַ is a general term, but קָדִים refers to a destructive, scorching wind (cf. 13:15). Like the similar metaphor in 8:7, it looks initially as though their effort will bring no result (a failure), but the subsequent parallel line reveals that the result will actually lead to their destruction.

כָּל־הַיּוֹם. This construct phrase functions adverbially to indicate the time of the verbal action (רֹדֵף).

כָּזָב וָשֹׁד יַרְבֶּה. *Line c.* Independent clause. The accusatives of the verb יַרְבֶּה are fronted for focus. Whatever Ephraim *thinks* he has been "shepherding" and pursuing, he has been cultivating lies and destruction. This is probably a reference to self-deception and harm he has brought upon himself.

כָּזָב וָשֹׁד. Acc compls of יַרְבֶּה.

יַרְבֶּה. Hiph *yiqtol* 3ms √רבה. The *yiqtol* has a progressive sense, parallel to the participles in lines a and b. In the Hiphil, this verb is causative: "to multiply."

וּבְרִית עִם־אַשּׁוּר יִכְרֹתוּ. *Line d*. Independent clause.

וּבְרִית. Acc compl of יִכְרֹתוּ. YHWH had made a covenant with Israel with attendant blessings and expectations and they broke it (6:7; 8:1). One of the ways that they did this was by making their own, competing covenant with others (cf. 10:4).

עִם־אַשּׁוּר. PP with עִם indicating the other party of the בְרִית ("covenant").

יִכְרֹתוּ. Qal *yiqtol* 3mp √כרת. The *yiqtol* again indicates a progressive aspect. This is not what Ephraim has done in the past … this is what they *do* (cf. 10:4).

וְשֶׁמֶן לְמִצְרַיִם יוּבָל. *Line e*. Independent clause.

וְשֶׁמֶן. Subject (and patient) of the pass verb יוּבָל.

לְמִצְרַיִם. Adjunct PP with לְ indicating where the שֶׁמֶן will be carried. לְ is the usual preposition for marking the locative goal of √יבל (cf. Hos 10:6).

יוּבָל. Hof *yiqtol* 3ms √יבל. This verb is often used for bringing gifts to a superior (e.g., a king or God) in the context of relationship (e.g., Ps 76:12; Isa 18:7). This is the second occurrence in Hosea (cf. 10:6), and both instances refer to a covenant with foreign powers instead of being faithful to YHWH.

12:3 a וְרִיב לַיהוָה עִם־יְהוּדָה
b וְלִפְקֹד עַל־יַעֲקֹב כִּדְרָכָיו
c כְּמַעֲלָלָיו יָשִׁיב לוֹ׃

Lines a-c are a tricolon. The first line introduces the verse and serves as a transition from Israel's actions (vv. 1-2) to the consequences (v. 3b-c). Lines b-c have corresponding word pairs (שׁוּב√//פקד; מַעֲלָל//דֶּרֶךְ) as well as noun//pronoun parallelism (ו//יַעֲקֹב). Lines b-c are also arranged chiastically (verb > PP with כְּ//PP with כְּ > verb). The lines are marked by 'Atnaḥ, Zaqep parvum, and Silluq.

וְרִיב לַיהוָה עִם־יְהוּדָה. *Line a*. Independent verbless clause.

וְרִיב לַיהוָה. On √רִיב, see 2:4 and 4:1b. In 2:4 the verb √רִיב was used in the context of the family metaphor to refer to an informal case or argument. In 4:1, 4 it referred to YHWH's metaphorical case against Israel over internal sins such as an unorthodox priesthood. Here, the scope of the רִיב is broadened to international affairs (cf. 12:2). The typical construction used to indicate possession is the construct relationship, but a PP with לְ is used in cases where the noun is not definite (JM §130b). רִיב is the subject of the verbless clause, and לַיהוָה is the predicate.

עִם־יְהוּדָה. This adjunct PP with עִם marks the personal complement of the verbless clause with רִיב (cf. WO §11.2.14) and specifes the defendant in the case (see 4:1b).

וְלִפְקֹד עַל־יַעֲקֹב כִּדְרָכָיו. *Line b*. Independent clause. At first glance, we expect the infinitive construct (לִפְקֹד) to introduce a subordinate clause ("in order to punish"), which would mean that the וְ is problematic. However, this construction is known elsewhere. The infinitive continues the idea of the previous clause (here, a רִיב) and virtually has the function of a finite verb (GKC §114p; JM §124p; WO §36.1.2). In order to convey both of these nuances, we translate, "YHWH has a dispute ... *so that* he will punish." The imperfective sense comes from the parallel *yiqtol* (יָשִׁיב) in line c.

וְלִפְקֹד. Qal inf constr √פקד.

עַל־יַעֲקֹב. When the verb √פקד has the sense "to bring punishment for X upon Y," it takes two complements (cf. also 1:4; 2:15; 4:9). This first complement, a PP with עַל, specifies the recipient of the punishment. יַעֲקֹב may refer to the northern kingdom (in contrast to Judah, line a) or to the people of Israel as a whole (including Judah). Because the word triggers another historical allusion, this time to the patriarch Jacob and Israel's earliest origins, the latter is probably in view here. YHWH's רִיב is against the whole people. Line a begins by indicting Judah (i.e., Ephraim in v. 2 is not the only problem). There is then intensification to "Jacob" in line b, which is a reference to both Ephraim and Judah. Intensification from smaller to larger entities is common in parallel lines (cf. Gevirtz 1973:15–24).

כִּדְרָכָיו. PP with כְּ indicating agreement in manner or norm (WO §11.2.9b). We expect the second complement of √פקד to be in the accusative and to indicate the reason for the punishment or the form that the punishment will take. For example, 4:9 has a bicolon almost identical to that of lines b-c in this verse: וּפָקַדְתִּי עָלָיו דְּרָכָיו וּמַעֲלָלָיו אָשִׁיב לוֹ. There, the word דְּרָכָיו is a second complement of √פקד and indicates the reason for the punishment ("I will punish him *for* his ways"). By comparison, כִּדְרָכָיו in this verse is a PP with כְּ. The difference in sense is subtle but important. The כְּ signals that YHWH will punish Jacob *according to* his ways. Although it is certainly Jacob's ways that have led to punishment, the nuance here is one of correspondence and proportion. The antecedent of the 3ms poss suffix is יַעֲקֹב, which in turn refers to the nation (Judah and Ephraim) as a whole.

כְּמַעֲלָלָיו יָשִׁיב לוֹ. *Line c.* Independent clause.

כְּמַעֲלָלָיו. PP with כְּ indicating agreement in manner or norm (see line b). On מַעֲלָל, see 4:9c. The antecedent of the 3ms suffix is again יַעֲקֹב.

יָשִׁיב. Hiph *yiqtol* 3ms √שוב. On the semantics of this verb in the Hiphil, see 4:9c. Here, the accusative complement of √שוב is implied. As with כִּדְרָכָיו in the previous line, מַעֲלָל is not *what* is returned on Jacob as punishment but rather the measure of punishment.

לוֹ. This PP is a second complement of יָשִׁיב with לְ indicating the person to whom punishment is rendered (i.e., יַעֲקֹב).

12:4 a בַּבֶּטֶן עָקַב אֶת־אָחִיו
b וּבְאוֹנוֹ שָׂרָה אֶת־אֱלֹהִים:

Lines a-b are a bicolon. Each line contains a PP with בְּ, a *qatal* verb, and a complement (in line a אֶת־אָחִיו is an acc; in line b אֶת־אֱלֹהִים is a PP). The lines are marked by *'Atnaḥ* and *Silluq*.

בַּבֶּטֶן עָקַב אֶת־אָחִיו. *Line a.* Independent clause. The use of יַעֲקֹב as a metonymy for the people of Israel triggers a historical allusion to the patriarch who was initially characterized by deceit and trickery but learned to submit to YHWH. This first line is an allusion to Jacob's birth (cf. Gen 25:21-26).

בַּבֶּטֶן. PP with locative בְּ. The noun בֶּטֶן usually means "belly," but it can refer to the womb, as it does in Gen 25:23 when YHWH states that two nations (Jacob and Esau) are in Rebekah's בֶּטֶן.

עָקַב. Qal *qatal* 3ms √עקב. The *yiqtol* verbs in 12:2-3 refer to present, ongoing activities or future threats. The *qatal* verbs in this verse (and in v. 5a-b) refer to completed action in the past in connection with Hosea's allusion to Jacob the patriarch. The verb √עקב ("to grasp at the heel") is a denominal of עָקֵב ("heel"). The noun is used in Gen 25:26 when Jacob came out of the womb with his hand grasping the עָקֵב of Esau. The verb only occurs four times in the OT. In Job 37:4 (a Piel) it has its literal sense of holding back. But in the Qal it has a metaphorical sense of "deceive" or "trick" (cf. Jer 9:3) In Gen 27:36 Esau uses a play on words with the name Jacob (יַעֲקֹב) when he states that Jacob is aptly named because he "deceived me" (וַיַּעְקְבֵנִי). In keeping with the allusion, Hosea is using the same wordplay here.

אֶת־אָחִיו. Acc compl of עָקַב. The antecedent of the 3ms poss suffix is again יַעֲקֹב.

וּבְאוֹנוֹ שָׂרָה אֶת־אֱלֹהִים. *Line b.* Independent clause. The second line in the bicolon is an allusion to the events recorded in Gen 32:23-33 when Jacob wrestled with a man later identified as אֱלֹהִים (32:29).

וּבְאוֹנוֹ. PP with circumstantial בְּ indicating Jacob's age and status when he strove (שָׂרָה). The noun אוֹן can refer to "wealth" or "power." It clearly means "wealth" later in this passage in 12:9. However, its correspondence with בֶּטֶן in the parallel line (a) suggests that it means "power" here. In the womb (line a) Jacob tricked, and when he was in his full strength (i.e., an adult), he strove (line b). Thus the two corresponding terms form a hendiadys which describes the whole of Jacob's life: he was always scheming, deceiving, and contending with others to get his way.

שָׂרָה. Qal *qatal* 3ms √שׂרה. This word occurs elsewhere only in 12:5 and in Gen 32:29. In the latter passage, it summarizes Jacob's actions when he wrestled with a man all night. It therefore refers to striving or contending with someone. This is the explanation of Jacob's second name: יִשְׂרָאֵל ("he has striven with God").

אֶת־אֱלֹהִים. This PP with אֶת is the complement of שָׂרָה indicating with whom Jacob strove. In Gen 32:29 we find the similar prep עִם with שָׂרָה instead.

12:5 a וַיָּ֤שַׂר אֶל־מַלְאָךְ֙ וַיֻּכָ֔ל
b בָּכָ֖ה וַיִּתְחַנֶּן־לֹ֑ו
c בֵּֽית־אֵל֙ יִמְצָאֶ֔נּוּ
d וְשָׁ֖ם יְדַבֵּ֥ר עִמָּֽנוּ׃

This verse contains numerous difficulties and ambiguities. Ancient and modern commentators have argued for a wide variety of understandings of its morphology, syntax, and meaning. The following is an attempt to describe the text in a way that makes sense both in this context and in terms of its intertextual relationship with the Jacob narratives in Genesis. Lines a-b are a bicolon, identified by *wayyiqtol* and *qatal* 3ms verbs that continue the allusions began in 12:4. Each line contains two independent clauses. The lines are marked by *Zaqep parvum* and *'Atnaḥ*. Lines c-d are also a bicolon, with lines linked by שָׁם//בֵּית־אֵל as well as contrasting suffixes at the end of each. In addition, these two lines contain *yiqtol* verbs, a contrast from the preceding bicolon. The lines are marked by *Zaqep parvum* and *Silluq*.

וַיָּ֤שַׂר אֶל־מַלְאָךְ. *Line a*. Independent clause.

וַיָּ֤שַׂר. As vocalized in the MT, there are three possible analyses of this verb. First, it could be a Qal *wayyiqtol* 3ms √שׂרר. This is a rare verb (7×) in the OT that means "to rule" (cf. Judg 9:22; Hos 8:4). Understanding the verb in this way, a number of scholars (cf. Nyberg 1935; Wolff 1974; Eslinger 1980; Macintosh 2014) vocalize the following prep אֶל ("against") as אֵל ("God") and take it as the subject of the verb. This creates a wordplay on the name "Israel" (יִשְׂרָאֵל) with the theophoric element intact (cf. Gen 32:29). According to this view, Hosea has reinterpreted and reversed the traditions in Gen 32:23-33 in which Jacob prevailed over the "man"/God (32:25, 29), so that now it is God who prevailed over Jacob (Macintosh 2014:486). There is, therefore, no cause for pride on the part of Hosea's contemporaries who are descendants of Jacob (Eslinger 1980:94). A second possible analysis of וַיָּ֤שַׂר is that it is a Qal *wayyiqtol* 3ms √שׂור. (Normally, a Qal *wayyiqtol* of a II-ו verb would have an o-class theme vowel [e.g., וַיָּ֤שָׁב]; however, the III-ר in √שׂור is a guttural, which "prefers" a preceding a-class vowel; cf. JM §21). Except for Hos 8:4 (where it is a by-form of √שׂרר) and 9:12 (where it is a by-form of √סור), √שׂור occurs elsewhere only in 1 Chr 20:3, where it means "to saw" (HALOT 1313). Therefore, here it may be a by-form of a different root—namely √שרה ("to strive")—which we find in the previous line (12:4b). Third, we could revocalize the verb to וַיָּשַׂר, a Qal *wayyiqtol* 3ms √שרה. The allusion to Jacob's wrestling at the Jabbok (cf. Gen 32:29) and the connection with v. 4 above strongly suggest options two or three: that the verb is √שרה ("to strive"). The subject of this verb (and the other verbs in lines a-b) is Jacob, continuing from v. 4.

אֶל־מַלְאָךְ. This PP with אֶל is the complement of וַיָּשַׂר, indicating with whom Jacob strove. Wolff (1974:212) argues that the prep אֶל with √שרה is one reason that it must be emended to אֵל ("God"), since it is "inexplicable" that Hosea would use אֶת with √שרה in v. 4, but אֶל here. However, the prep אֶל is appropriate here if it means "against," similar to עַל, and we know that various prepositions are possible with √שרה (as noted above, Gen 32:29 has עִם) (Kaiser 1985:40; cf. WHS §303). In addition, Hosea may have chosen an unusual prep אֶל in order to create wordplay with the name יִשְׂרָאֵל at the beginning of this line: ישר אל. Genesis 32 does not speak of a מַלְאָךְ wrestling with Jacob: there he is called an אִישׁ (32:25) who is identified as God (32:29, 31). Nevertheless, God manifests himself as a מַלְאָךְ in a variety of contexts in the OT (Gen 16:13; Judg 13:3). Thus, 12:5a is a restatement of 12:4b which reads שָׂרָה אֶת־אֱלֹהִים ("he strove with God").

וַיֻּכָל. *Line a.* Independent clause. Qal *wayyiqtol* 3ms √יכל. This verb frequently takes an infinitive or a *yiqtol* verb as its complement, which states what one is "able" to do (cf. 5:13; in 8:5 the complement is a noun). Here, without a complement, the verb has the absolute sense, "to prevail." This is the same sense as in Gen 32:26 (the "man" could not prevail against Jacob) and 32:29 (Jacob strove with God and men and prevailed).

בָּכָה. *Line b.* Independent clause. Qal *qatal* 3ms √בכה. There is no report in the Genesis account of Jacob weeping (√בכה) or imploring (√חנן—the next clause) with his opponent at the Jabbok. Rather, it is Jacob who prevails, and it is his opponent who asks Jacob to release him (32:27). Holladay (1966:56–57) has presented a convincing argument that this line alludes to Jacob's later meeting with Esau, described in Gen 33:1-17. The verb √בכה appears in Gen 33:4 when Jacob and Esau weep together. Although the verb √חנן does not appear, the related noun חֵן refers to the favor that Jacob hopes to find (Gen 32:6; 33:8). Holladay argues that vv. 4-5b are chiastically arranged:

v. 4a—Jacob grabbed Esau's heel in the womb
v. 4b—Jacob strove with *God*
v. 5a—Jacob strove with the *angel* (of God)
v. 5b—Jacob wept and implored Esau

The subject of the two verbs in line b is therefore Jacob (1966:55; see also McKenzie 1986:315).

וַיִּתְחַנֶּן־לוֹ. *Line b*. Independent clause.

וַיִּתְחַנֶּן. Hith *wayyiqtol* 3ms √חנן. In the Qal this verb refers to *showing* favor to someone; in the Hithpael it refers to *seeking* favor from someone (HALOT 334–35). It takes an oblique complement with לְ (as here), אֶל, or לִפְנֵי which specifies from whom the subject of the verb is seeking favor. The antecedent of the 3ms suffix on לוֹ is Esau (see comments on בְּכָה above).

בֵּית־אֵל יִמְצָאֶנּוּ. *Line c*. Independent clause. In lines c-d there is a change in place (Bethel), change in subject (YHWH), and a change in verbal conjugation (*yiqtol*). The prophet now applies the allusion to his contemporaries.

בֵּית־אֵל. An "accusative of local determination" that specifies the location of the action of יִמְצָאֶנּוּ (JM §126h cf. also GKC §118g).

יִמְצָאֶנּוּ. Qal *yiqtol* 3ms √מצא with a 3ms energic acc suffix. Although Jacob (12:3b) has been the subject of the verbs in vv.4-5b, the subject of the verbs in lines c-d is likely YHWH. In the book of Genesis, it was he who initiated the encounter with Jacob at Bethel (cf. Gen 35:1, 6, 7). Furthermore, God spoke (√דבר—line d) with Jacob at Bethel (Gen 28:15; 35:15) but Genesis does not say that Jacob spoke with God. The antecedent of the 3ms acc suffix is Jacob. The imperfective *yiqtol* conjugation has a past, frequentative sense: "he *kept* finding." God met Jacob at Bethel two times (Gen 28:10-19; 35:1-15) and maintained his promises to him in spite of his scheming.

וְשָׁם יְדַבֵּר עִמָּנוּ. *Line d*. Independent clause.

וְשָׁם. The antecedent of this locative adverb is בֵּית־אֵל in the previous line (c).

יְדַבֵּר. Piel *yiqtol* 3ms √דבר. The subject of this verb is God (see comments above). The *yiqtol* verb has a frequentative sense, but in this line it shifts to the present tense because of the 1cp suffix on the following עִמָּנוּ (see below).

עִמָּנוּ. This PP with עִם is the oblique complement of יְדַבֵּר and indicates with whom God spoke at Bethel. The suffix in MT is 1cp, "with us." Because vv. 4-5 consist of an allusion to God's interaction with Jacob at Bethel, many modern commentators read the PP as עִמּוֹ ("with him") with G and S (cf. BHS note [b]). The MT 1cp makes sense if Hosea is applying the allusion to himself and his contemporaries (Kaiser 1985:43). It is possible that the form is a deliberate ambiguity in order to link the ancestor (Jacob) with his descendants (Hosea and his audience). If Jacob was a schemer but was found by God at Bethel, the people of Hosea's time can hear from God and submit to him there as well. Thus the verb יְדַבֵּר has a present reference: God keeps speaking with us, Hosea says, and we can choose to listen.

12:6 a וַיהוָה אֱלֹהֵי הַצְּבָאוֹת
b יְהוָה זִכְרוֹ:

Lines a-b are a bicolon featuring staircase parallelism. The verse begins in line a with the divine name יְהוָה, is interrupted by the phrase אֱלֹהֵי הַצְּבָאוֹת in apposition, repeats יְהוָה at the beginning of line b, and then concludes. The lines are marked by *'Atnaḥ* and *Silluq*.

וַיהוָה אֱלֹהֵי הַצְּבָאוֹת. *Line a.* The ו on וַיהוָה is epexegetical, here connecting יְהוָה to the preceding verse and supporting the analysis above that God is the subject of the verbs in 12:5c-d. יְהוָה anticipates the subject of the verbless clause in line b.

אֱלֹהֵי הַצְּבָאוֹת. Constr phrase. אֱלֹהֵי is in apposition to the previous word, יְהוָה, and further describes it. The noun צָבָא ("army") occurs 486 times in the OT and just over half of those (282; 58%) are used as a divine title for YHWH, emphasizing his power and ultimate victory.

יְהוָה זִכְרוֹ. *Line b.* Independent verbless clause with יְהוָה as its subject.

זִכְרוֹ. Predicate of the verbless clause. The antecedent of the 3ms poss suffix is YHWH. That name, יְהוָה, is the name by which he is remembered (√זכר). The God of Jacob, who changed his name to "Israel," is the same YHWH who calls Jacob's descendants to be faithful to him in the covenant.

Hosea 12:7

a וְאַתָּה בֵּאלֹהֶיךָ תָשׁוּב
b חֶסֶד וּמִשְׁפָּט שְׁמֹר
c וְקַוֵּה אֶל־אֱלֹהֶיךָ תָּמִיד:

Lines a-c are a tricolon. In contrast to the indicative verbs in the preceding and following lines, each of these three lines contains a volative verb. Lines a and c bracket the tricolon with the word אֱלֹהִים. Lines b and c are arranged chiastically (compl > impv//impv > compl). The lines are marked by *'Atnaḥ*, *Zaqep parvum*, and *Silluq*.

וְאַתָּה בֵּאלֹהֶיךָ תָשׁוּב. *Line a*. Independent clause.

וְאַתָּה. This pleonastic 2ms independent pronoun anticipates the 2ms verb תָשׁוּב. It is a topicalization strategy that signals a transition from the historical allusion (vv. 4-6) to Hosea's contemporary audience.

בֵּאלֹהֶיךָ. This PP with בְּ is the oblique compl of תָשׁוּב. It is not usual for √שוב to take a complement with בְּ when it has the sense of "return" or "repent" (as here); the preposition is usually אֶל. The בְּ is probably intended as instrumental (cf. WO §11.2.5d). It is not only *to* God that they should return, but *by* him (i.e., with his help) (see the instrumental use of בְּ in 12:14 below).

תָשׁוּב. Qal *yiqtol* 2ms √שוב. In the context (including the imperatives in lines b and c), this verb is irrealis and has volative or directive sense (cf. WO §31.5).

חֶסֶד וּמִשְׁפָּט שְׁמֹר. *Line b*. Independent clause.

חֶסֶד וּמִשְׁפָּט. Acc compls of שְׁמֹר. These words occur together in 2:21 and in 6:4-6. They are fundamental attributes of a life lived in covenant with YHWH.

שְׁמֹר. Qal impv ms √שמר.

וְקַוֵּה אֶל־אֱלֹהֶיךָ תָּמִיד. *Line c*. Independent clause.

וְקַוֵּה. Piel impv ms √קוה.

אֶל־אֱלֹהֶיךָ. The verb √קוה usually takes accusative complements (e.g., Job 7:2) and frequently oblique complements with לְ (e.g., Gen 49:10). אֶל is not common in this role, but it does occur in Pss 27:14 and 37:24. It is difficult to perceive a difference in meaning.

תָּמִיד. A scaler adverb which modifies קַוֵּה, indicating that the action is to be uninterrupted (WO §39.3.1i).

12:8 a כְּנַעַן בְּיָדוֹ מֹאזְנֵי מִרְמָה
b לַעֲשֹׁק אָהֵב:

Lines a-b are a bicolon, distinguished from 12:7 by the indicative verb and from 12:9 by the change to the subject "Ephraim" there. In this verse כְּנַעַן is the antecedent of the 3ms pronoun (בְּיָדוֹ) in line a as well as the subject of the verb אָהֵב in line b. The lines are marked by *Tipḥa* and *Silluq*.

כְּנַעַן בְּיָדוֹ מֹאזְנֵי מִרְמָה. *Line a.* Independent verbless clause.

כְּנַעַן. A *casus pendens*, which is placed at the head of the clause so that it stands aloof from the rest of the syntax but is then resumed by a retrospective pronoun (JM §156a). As a focus strategy, it draws attention to the aspect of Ephraim's character that is now critiqued by Hosea. כְּנַעַן refers to the original inhabitants of the promised land (often in the construction אֶרֶץ כְּנַעַן or מֶלֶךְ כְּנַעַן) as well as a "merchant" or "trader" in mostly later texts (cf. Ezek 16:29; 17:4; Zeph 1:11; 2:5). The gentilic כְּנַעֲנִי can also refer to merchants (cf. Job 40:30; Prov 31:24). The use of the word here may be a double entendre (Stuart 1987:187). Ephraim is being called both a "Canaanite" and a greedy merchant.

בְּיָדוֹ. This PP with a 3ms poss suffix is the subject of the verbless clause (cf. JM §154b). The antecedent of the suffix is כְּנַעַן, which in turn refers to Ephraim (cf. 12:9a).

מֹאזְנֵי מִרְמָה. This construct phrase is the predicate of the verbless clause. It is an adjectival genitive, in which מִרְמָה modifies מֹאזְנַיִם. The combination of these two words occurs three other times (Prov 11:1; 20:23; Amos 8:5) in the context of deceptive business dealings. The "treacherous scale," like the "treacherous weight" (Mic 6:11) is a tool of deception. Hosea used the word מִרְמָה to describe Ephraim/Israel in 12:1.

לַעֲשֹׁק. *Line b.* This Qal inf constr √עשׁק is the complement of the following אָהֵב. The verb √עשׁק almost always takes an accusative complement (37/38). Here the complement is implied (cf. Job 10:3). The verb refers to mistreating or taking advantage of those who are weaker, such as foreigners, orphans, widows, and the poor (e.g., Jer 7:6; Ezek 22:29; Amos 4:1; Zech 7:10).

אָהֵב. *Line b.* Independent clause. The verb is a Qal *qatal* 3ms √אהב.

12:9 a וַיֹּ֙אמֶר֙ אֶפְרַ֔יִם
b אַ֣ךְ עָשַׁ֔רְתִּי
c מָצָ֥אתִי א֖וֹן לִ֑י
d כָּל־יְגִיעַ֕י לֹ֥א יִמְצְאוּ־לִ֖י
e עָוֺ֥ן אֲשֶׁר־חֵֽטְא׃

In this verse Hosea represents Ephraim's perspective as quoted speech. Ephraim confirms his own guilt by announcing that his injustice and fraud have indeed led to wealth. Although he protests that it is not iniquity, the defense is obviously hollow. The quotation consists of two bicola introduced by an introductory line (a) that stands outside of the poetic structure. The first bicolon includes lines b and c. The lines share 1cs verbs as well as the theme of wealth in the terms עָשַׁרְתִּי and אוֹן. The lines are marked by *Zaqep parvum* and *'Atnaḥ*. The second bicolon, lines d and e, comprise one sentence. The lines are marked by *Ṭipḥa* and *Silluq*. It is tempting to place עָוֺן at the end of line d since it is the accusative complement of יִמְצְאוּ. The present layout follows the disjunctive Masoretic accents.

וַיֹּאמֶר אֶפְרַיִם. *Line a*. Independent clause. This clause introduces the (purported) direct speech in lines b-e. The verb is a Qal *wayyiqtol* 3ms √אמר, and אֶפְרַיִם is its subject. This line completes the deliberate link between "Canaan" (12:8) and "Ephraim."

אַךְ עָשַׁרְתִּי. *Line b*. Independent clause.

אַךְ. An adverb which is either asseverative ("surely!") or antithetic ("but") (HALOT 45). The former makes better sense here. Hosea is implying that they are gaining wealth (albeit illegitimately) in 12:8. Thus it makes no sense for Ephraim to protest by saying, "But I have become rich!" Rather, the contrast is between 12:9b-c and 12:9d-e in which he says, "I am rich ... but it is not illegitimate!"

עָשַׁרְתִּי. Qal *qatal* 1cs √עשר. This *qatal*, and מָצָאתִי in the next line, are perfective and refer to a situation that began in the past and persists in the present (WO §30.5.1c).

מָצָאתִי אוֹן לִי. *Line c*. Independent clause.

מָצָאתִי. Qal *qatal* 1cs √מצא.

אוֹן. Acc compl of מְצָאתִי. This word was used in 12:4 of "strength" or "power" to refer to Jacob's adulthood. In this context it means "wealth."

לִי. PP with לְ of interest or advantage. The antecedent of the 1cs suffix is Ephraim, the speaker (line a).

כָּל־יְגִיעַי לֹא יִמְצְאוּ־לִי. *Line d*. Independent clause that concludes in line e.

כָּל־יְגִיעַי. Constr phrase, כֹּל is the subject of יִמְצְאוּ. The word יְגִיעַ refers both to toil and labor as well the profits produced by that labor (cf. Deut 28:33; Isa 45:14).

יִמְצְאוּ. Qal *yiqtol* 3mp √מצא. Note the wordplay between this bicolon (lines d-e) and the previous one (lines b-c). There is the repetition of √מצא (line c—I have *found* wealth//line d—my wealth does not *find* guilt) as well as a similarity between אוֹן ("wealth"; line c) and עָוֹן ("iniquity," line e). Ephraim denies that his wealth comes from injustice and deception.

לִי. PP with לְ of interest (see line c).

עָוֹן אֲשֶׁר־חֵטְא. *Line e*. This is the conclusion of the clause begun in line d.

עָוֹן. Acc compl of יִמְצְאוּ in the previous line. The noun עָוֹן refers to religious and ethical violations as well as the guilt that they incur.

אֲשֶׁר־חֵטְא. Relative clause headed by and defining the preceding substantive (עָוֹן). This is a verbless clause without an overt subject. Holmstedt (2016:175–76) calls it a "one-part relative clause" because its only overt constituent is the complement.

חֵטְא. This noun ("sin," "offense") is derived from the verb חָטָא ("to sin") (cf. HALOT 306).

12:10 a וְאָנֹכִי יְהוָה אֱלֹהֶיךָ מֵאֶרֶץ מִצְרָיִם
b עֹד אוֹשִׁיבְךָ בָאֳהָלִים כִּימֵי מוֹעֵד׃

Lines a-b are a bicolon. The lines are related topically by reference to the exodus from Egypt and subsequent wilderness period. In addition, the speaker is YHWH in contrast to Ephraim (12:9). The lines are marked by *'Atnaḥ* and *Silluq*.

וְאָנֹכִי יְהוָה אֱלֹהֶיךָ מֵאֶרֶץ מִצְרָיִם. *Line a*. Independent verbless clause. The וְ expresses a consequence of the previous clause. YHWH is responding to Ephraim's self-justification (12:9) and announcing that he will bring retribution. This line has wording identical to the first line of Hos 13:4. אָנֹכִי is the subject and יְהוָה is the predicate of the verbless clause.

אֱלֹהֶיךָ. This noun, with a 2ms poss suffix referring to Ephraim (12:9), is in apposition to יְהוָה.

מֵאֶרֶץ מִצְרָיִם. Adjunct PP with מִן prep, which should be understood either as temporal ("from the time of the land of Egypt") or as geographical, if this is a condensed form of a fuller formula: אָנֹכִי יְהוָה אֱלֹהֶיךָ אֲשֶׁר הוֹצֵאתִיךָ מֵאֶרֶץ מִצְרָיִם ("who brought you up from the land of Egypt"; cf. Exod 20:2). The former is more likely since line b mentions כִּימֵי מוֹעֵד ("like the days of the assembly"). The reference is to the past and a return to their status at that time.

עֹד אוֹשִׁיבְךָ בָאֳהָלִים כִּימֵי מוֹעֵד. *Line b.* Independent clause.

עֹד. Constituent adverb modifying the predicate אוֹשִׁיבְךָ (WO §39.3.1d).

אוֹשִׁיבְךָ. Hiph *yiqtol* 1cs √ישב with a 2ms acc suffix referring to Ephraim. In the Hiphil √ישב is transitive and takes two complements: the first is the accusative indicating whom is placed (here the 2ms suffix), the second complement is a PP (usually with בְּ) indicating where they are being placed.

בָאֳהָלִים. Compl PP with בְּ indicating where YHWH is going to settle Ephraim. They gained their great wealth from deception and oppression (12:8-9), now YHWH will remove their wealth and make them live in tents once more, as they did in the wilderness period.

כִּימֵי מוֹעֵד. Adjunct PP with כְּ indicating agreement in kind (cf. 2:5; 2:17; 9:9). The noun מוֹעֵד refers to a "meeting" or "appointed time." AF (618) suggest that this may be a condensed form of the expression אֹהֶל מוֹעֵד ("tabernacle"). In either case, this is a reference to the beginnings of YHWH's dealings with Israel in the wilderness. He is undoing their accumulated prosperity and taking them "back to square one."

12:11 a וְדִבַּרְתִּי עַל־הַנְּבִיאִים
b וְאָנֹכִי חָזוֹן הִרְבֵּיתִי
c וּבְיַד הַנְּבִיאִים אֲדַמֶּה:

Lines a-c are a tricolon. The first-person speech continues from 12:10, and each line contains a verb referencing revelation to the prophets (דמה√//חָזוֹן ;רבה√//דבר√). The word הַנְּבִיאִים occurs in lines a and c as an inclusio around the verse. The lines are marked by *Zaqep parvum*, *'Atnaḥ*, and *Silluq*.

וְדִבַּרְתִּי עַל־הַנְּבִיאִים. *Line a*. Independent clause.

וְדִבַּרְתִּי. Piel *qatal* (irrealis) 1cs √דבר. This irrealis *qatal* (indicated by the prefixed וְ) refers to frequentative action in the past (cf. GKC §112dd; Cook 2012:250, 255). The time/tense is determined by the context. In 12:10 YHWH is speaking about Israel's beginnings in the wilderness, and the verb in the following line (b) is a *qatal*. Here YHWH states that he continually and habitually revealed his word to the prophets to no avail.

עַל־הַנְּבִיאִים. Adjunct PP indicating the recipient of the speech. The usual preposition in this role with דבר√ is לְ. The use of עַל in this verse emphasizes the authority of the speaker (cf. the specific collocation in 2:16; Wolff 1974:207; Macintosh 2014:502).

וְאָנֹכִי חָזוֹן הִרְבֵּיתִי. *Line b*. Independent clause.

וְאָנֹכִי. This pleonastic 1cs independent pronoun, which anticipates the 1cs verb הִרְבֵּיתִי, highlights YHWH as the subject (cf. 12:7). It is *he* who multipled visions.

חָזוֹן. Acc compl of הִרְבֵּיתִי ("I multiplied"). The noun should be understood as collective.

הִרְבֵּיתִי. Hiph *qatal* 1cs √רבה. In each of the four previous occurrences of this verb in Hosea, it is used of the people of Israel multiplying various aspects of rebellion and disloyalty (8:11—illicit altars; 8:14—fortified cities; 10:1—altars; 12:2—lies and destruction). Now YHWH states that during this same time, he has been multiplying prophetic visions and revealing his will, which they have ignored.

וּבְיַד הַנְּבִיאִים אֲדַמֶּה. *Line c*. Independent clause.

וּבְיַד הַנְּבִיאִים. Adjunct PP with instrumental בְּ. The expression בְּיַד indicates agency. YHWH speaks parables (אֲדַמֶּה) by means of the prophets; they speak on his behalf.

אֲדַמֶּה. Piel *yiqtol* 1cs √דמה. The *yiqtol* indicates frequentative action in the past (cf. the context in 12:10 and the *qatal* verb in line b). This verb elsewhere in Hosea means "to destroy" (Qal; 4:5) or "be destroyed" (Niphal; 4:6; 10:7, 15). However, the Piel occurs only in √דמה (I) meaning "to be like," or "to resemble." Given the context of speech and revelation in lines a and b, the sense here probably refers to speaking in parables or using analogies (Macintosh 2014:502).

12:12 a אִם־גִּלְעָד אָ֫וֶן
b אַךְ־שָׁ֫וְא הָי֫וּ
c בַּגִּלְגָּל שְׁוָרִ֫ים זִבֵּ֫חוּ
d גַּם מִזְבְּחוֹתָם֫ כְּגַלִּ֫ים
e עַל תַּלְמֵ֫י שָׂדָֽי׃

The return to third-person verbs distinguishes this verse from 12:11. Lines a-b are a bicolon referring to גִּלְעָד. Each line contains three words and the lines are marked by *Pašṭa* and *Zaqep parvum*. Lines c-e are a tricolon referring to גִּלְגָּל. Each line contains three words and are marked by *'Atnaḥ, Zaqep parvum*, and *Silluq*.

אִם־גִּלְעָד אָ֫וֶן. *Line a*. Subordinate conditional clause. The conjunction אִם introduces the protasis of a real conditional clause (cf. WO §38.2d). The degree of contingency is determined by the context and can range from possible (e.g., Judg 4:8) to realized fully (e.g., 2 Kgs 1:10) (McComiskey 2009:209). Here, the context and other statements in the book (cf. 6:8) indicate that the protasis is fully realized: Gilead *is* wicked. The translation "since" conveys this nuance (2009:209). This conditional clause is a verbless clause (cf. GKC §159v).

גִּלְעָד. Subject of the verbless clause.

אָ֫וֶן. Predicate of the verbless clause. The word אָ֫וֶן is a noun, not an adjective, making the construction seem ungrammatical in English (i.e., "Gilead is wickedness"). However, it is possible in Hebrew (see 5:2, אֲנִי מוּסָר, "I am discipline") (McComiskey 2009:209). Here it is translated as an adjective for sense in English. גִּלְעָד ("Gilead") is mentioned elsewhere in Hosea only in 6:8, where it is described by the construct chain קִרְיַת פֹּעֲלֵי אָ֫וֶן ("a city of doers of evil").

אַךְ־שָׁ֫וְא הָי֫וּ. *Line b*. Independent clause.

אַךְ. Asseverative particle (see 12:9b).

שָׁוְא. Compl of the copular verb הָיוּ. The word שָׁוְא ("worthlessness," "deceitfulness") is used elsewhere only in 10:4, which also contains the construct phrase תַּלְמֵי שָׂדָי in line e below. Because there is apparently an intentional intertextual link between the passages, and because שָׁוְא refers to deceitful or empty words in 10:4, the sense of שָׁוְא in this verse probably refers to Gilead as deceitful (i.e., scheming) rather than worthless (i.e., of no value). This sense also fits the analogy to Jacob, which Hosea will pick up again in the next verse.

הָיוּ. Qal *qatal* 3cp √היה.

בַּגִּלְגָּל שְׁוָרִים זִבֵּחוּ. *Line c*. Independent clause.

בַּגִּלְגָּל. Adjunct PP with locative בְּ indicating the location of the sacrificing. Gilgal was a key religious location in the north (see 9:15).

שְׁוָרִים. Acc compl of זִבֵּחוּ. This form is a *hapax* and the only occurrence of the plural of שׁוֹר ("bull").

זִבֵּחוּ. Piel *qatal* 3cp √זבח.

גַּם מִזְבְּחוֹתָם כְּגַלִּים. *Line d*. Independent verbless clause. The conjunction גַּם associates this clause with the previous one and emphasizes an additional element.

מִזְבְּחוֹתָם. Subject of the verbless clause. The antecedent of the 3mp poss pronoun is the people of Gilgal (line c).

כְּגַלִּים. This PP with כְּ (indicating agreement in kind) is the predicate of the verbless clause. This noun is derived from the verb √גלל ("to roll") and refers to a heap of stones (e.g., Gen 31:46; Jos 7:26) or waves in the sea (Ps 42:8; Isa 48:18). The former is meant here in connection with the field (שָׂדָי).

עַל תַּלְמֵי שָׂדָי. *Line e*. See 10:4e. The image describes the abundance of the altars that Gilgal has multiplied. They are scattered everywhere, just like "heaps of stones along the edges of the fields."

12:13 a וַיִּבְרַח יַעֲקֹב שְׂדֵה אֲרָם
b וַיַּעֲבֹד יִשְׂרָאֵל בְּאִשָּׁה
c וּבְאִשָּׁה שָׁמָר׃

This tricolon (lines a-c) is set apart from the previous verse by the *wayyiqtol* (past narrative) verbs in lines a-b, which signal a return to the historical allusion to Jacob (cf. 12:4-6). There is semantic development from the patriarch's original name יַעֲקֹב in line a to his new name יִשְׂרָאֵל in line b. Lines b-c are arranged chiastically (verb + בְּאִשָּׁה//בְּאִשָּׁה + verb). The lines are marked by *'Atnaḥ*, *Zaqep parvum*, and *Silluq*.

וַיִּבְרַח יַעֲקֹב שְׂדֵה אֲרָם. *Line a*. Independent clause.

וַיִּבְרַח. Qal *wayyiqtol* 3ms √ברח. The *wayyiqtol* refers to simple past-tense action. Hosea uses three *wayyiqtol* verbs in 12:5 in the allusion to Jacob. In 12:9 he uses one for the historical retrospective of Ephraim's guilt. Now, in 12:3 two *wayyiqtol* verbs are again used as Hosea revisits the historical allusion to Jacob.

יַעֲקֹב. Subject of וַיִּבְרַח.

שְׂדֵה אֲרָם. Adjunct PP, with an implied preposition, indicating where Jacob fled. The verb √ברח more often takes PPs with מִפְּנֵי or מִן specifying from where someone is fleeing. When the PP indicates the goal of one's flight, the preposition is אֶל (e.g., Gen 27:43), or it is left implicit (e.g., 1 Sam 27:4; 2 Sam 4:3; Jon 1:3; 4:2).

וַיַּעֲבֹד יִשְׂרָאֵל בְּאִשָּׁה. *Line b*. Independent clause.

וַיַּעֲבֹד. Qal *wayyiqtol* 3ms √עבד.

יִשְׂרָאֵל. Subject of וַיַּעֲבֹד.

בְּאִשָּׁה. Adjunct PP. The collocation √עבד + בְּ refers to the agreed-upon wages for work (see Gen 29:18, 20, 25; 31:41 which refer to Jacob working to get his wives). This is called a בְּ *pretii* (GKC §119p; JM §133c).

וּבְאִשָּׁה שָׁמָר. *Line c*. Independent clause.

וּבְאִשָּׁה. Adjunct PP with a בְּ *pretii* (see line b), indicating the purpose for which Jacob worked.

שָׁמָר. Qal *qatal* 3ms √שמר. This verb normally requires an accusative complement, which is implied here, and should be understood as "sheep" given the historical allusion (cf. Gen 30:31). Perhaps Hosea omitted the complement in order to heighten the wordplay with נִשְׁמָר in 12:14b. There is intensification in the parallelism from the general √עבד ("work") in line b to the more specific √שמר ("keeping sheep") in line c.

12:14 a וּבְנָבִיא הֶעֱלָה יְהוָה אֶת־יִשְׂרָאֵל מִמִּצְרָיִם
b וּבְנָבִיא נִשְׁמָר׃

Lines a-b are a bicolon. Each line is introduced with the PP בִּנְבִיא. The parallel lines contain active (הֶעֱלָה)//passive (נִשְׁמָר) grammatical parallelism. They are of unequal length, yet even though line b is short, it recollects and connects to 12:13c (שָׁמָר). The lines are marked with *'Atnaḥ* and *Silluq*.

וּבְנָבִיא הֶעֱלָה יְהוָה אֶת־יִשְׂרָאֵל מִמִּצְרָיִם. *Line a*. Independent clause.

וּבְנָבִיא. Adjunct PP with instrumental בְּ indicating the agent of the verb. The PP וּבְנָבִיא at the beginning of lines a and b in this verse are intended to recall בְּאִשָּׁה in 12:13b-c (though there the בְּ has a slightly different sense). The "prophet" must refer to Moses in this context of YHWH bringing Israel out of Egypt.

הֶעֱלָה. Hiph *qatal* 3ms √עלה. The Hiphil of √עלה is transitive and takes two complements: an accusative specifying who is brought up and a PP specifying the goal (e.g., Exod 8:3 with עַל) or the original location (e.g., Gen 37:28 with מִן).

יְהוָה. Subject of הֶעֱלָה.

אֶת־יִשְׂרָאֵל. Acc compl of הֶעֱלָה. The name יִשְׂרָאֵל refers to Jacob in 12:13. Now the historical allusion has advanced chronologically and the name refers to the nation that came from that patriarch. As in 12:4-6, Hosea is applying the experiences of Jacob to his own contemporaries in the northern kingdom. Jacob's deception did not result in lasting success; he (and his descendants) only flourished when he submitted to YHWH in the covenant.

מִמִּצְרָיִם. Compl PP indicating from where YHWH brought up יִשְׂרָאֵל.

וּבְנָבִיא נִשְׁמָר. *Line b*. Independent clause.

וּבְנָבִיא. Adjunct PP with instrumental בְּ indicating the agent of the verb (see line a).

נִשְׁמָר. Niph *qatal* 3ms √שמר. The ָ (*qamets*) theme vowel here is due to pause from the *Silluq* accent. The subject of this verb is יִשְׂרָאֵל (see line a). This verb recalls שָׁמָר at the end of 12:13. What Jacob (Israel) did for sheep, YHWH did for Israel. Jacob "guarded and cared for" for his own benefit, but he (i.e., his ancestors) flourished because he was "guarded and cared for" by YHWH.

a 12:15 הִכְעִיס אֶפְרַיִם תַּמְרוּרִים
b וְדָמָיו עָלָיו יִטּוֹשׁ
c וְחֶרְפָּתוֹ יָשִׁיב לוֹ אֲדֹנָיו:

Lines a-c are a tricolon which features an introductory line followed by two lines in parallel. There is semantic correspondence in lines b and c between three pairs of words: חֶרְפָּתוֹ//דָמָיו, ל//עַל, and √נטש//√שׁוב. There is grammatical parallelism between אֶפְרַיִם in line a and the 3ms suffixes in lines b and c. The lines are marked by *'Atnaḥ, Zaqep parvum*, and *Silluq*.

הִכְעִיס אֶפְרַיִם תַּמְרוּרִים. *Line a*. Independent clause.

הִכְעִיס. Hiph *qatal* 3ms √כעס. In the Qal this verb is intransitive and means "to be angry." In the Hiphil it is transitive and means "to provoke (someone) to anger." It is almost always used of provoking YHWH to anger by worshiping false gods, but Deut 32:21 and 1 Sam 1:7 are exceptions. The expected accusative complement יְהוָה or suffix -וֹ is implied (see 1 Kgs 21:22; 2 Kgs 21:6; Neh 3:37; Ps 106:29).

אֶפְרַיִם. Subject of הִכְעִיס.

תַּמְרוּרִים. This noun, meaning "bitterness," is from the verb √מרר. Here, it functions as an adverbial accusative which modifies the preceding verb, הִכְעִיס (see GKC §118q; WO §10.2.2c). It is likely an abstract plural (Macintosh 2014:514).

וְדָמָיו עָלָיו יִטּוֹשׁ. *Line b*. Independent clause.

וְדָמָיו. Acc compl of יִטּוֹשׁ. The word דָּם refers elsewhere in Hosea to the crime of "bloodshed" (cf. 1:4; 4:2; 6:8). Here, however, the context indicates that it refers rather to guilt (i.e., "bloodguilt") that will not be absolved. דָּם is used in the OT for crimes that require the death penalty because they are so serious (e.g., incest, Lev 20:12; necromancy, Lev 20:27; accidental manslaughter, Deut 22:8; cf. also Exod 22:1). The antecedent of the 3ms poss suffix is Ephraim (line a).

עָלָיו. Adjunct PP with עַל indicating where YHWH will leave the bloodguilt (וְדָמָיו) (cf. 1 Sam 17:20, 22 with עַל and 17:28 with בְ). The antecedent of the 3ms suffix is Ephraim (line a). In other words, rather than pardoning or forgiving Ephraim's guilt, YHWH will leave it on him where it will incur certain punishment.

יִטּוֹשׁ. Qal *yiqtol* 3ms √נטשׁ. The subject of the verb is אֲדֹנָיו ("his Lord") in line c. YHWH is frequently the subject of this verb (cf. 1 Sam 12:22; Ps 27:9).

וְחֶרְפָּתוֹ יָשִׁיב לוֹ אֲדֹנָיו. *Line c.* Independent clause.

וְחֶרְפָּתוֹ. Acc compl of יָשִׁיב. The antecedent of the 3ms suffix is Ephraim (line a).

יָשִׁיב. Hiph *yiqtol* 3ms √שׁוב.

לוֹ. This PP is a second complement of אָשִׁיב with לְ indicating the person to whom the deeds are returned. The antecedent of the suffix is Ephraim.

אֲדֹנָיו. Subject of יָשִׁיב. This is the only time that Hosea refers to YHWH as אָדוֹן. The intent may be to emphasize YHWH's superiority and lordship in the covenant which is being broken (Stuart 1987:196; McComiskey 2009:211). The antecedent of the 3ms suffix is, again, Ephraim.

YHWH Has Become Israel's Enemy (13:1–14:1)

In the previous unit, Israel was characterized not just by sin, but by deception. The unit ended with a statement that YHWH would leave them in their guilt and repay them for their deeds (12:15). In the present unit (13:1–14:1), Hosea expands upon the certainty of their judgment. The description of divine destruction reaches its climax at this point in the book. Hosea 13:1–14:1 is a discrete unit constituting a short introduction by the prophet (13:1-3) and then a speech by YHWH (13:4–14:1). The verb √אשׁם ("to be guilty") opens (13:1) and closes the unit (14:1) in an inclusio. The next unit begins in 14:2 with a hopeful word and a call to repentance.

In 13:1-3 the prophet begins by reviewing the guilt of Ephraim in the past, present, and future (Mays 1969:171–73). Verse 1 refers to Ephraim's guilt in the past (two *wayyiqtol* verbs), v. 2 to their guilt in the present (cf. וְעַתָּה; progressive participle), and v. 3 to their ruin in the future (cf. לָכֵן + *yiqtol*). They will be like mist, dew, chaff, and smoke: all of which disappear quickly.

YHWH begins speaking in 13:4-8 (note the first person forms throughout). He gives a historical retrospective, reminding Israel that there has never been a deliverer apart from him (13:4) and reviewing their rebellion in the wilderness period (13:5) and in the land (13:6). In

13:7-8 he compares himself to wild animals (lion, leopard, bear) which will brutally devour them as a result of their rebellion.

In 13:9-11 YHWH speaks to Israel directly with 2ms forms, reminding them again that he *should* be their helper, but they have turned him into their enemy. He sarcastically asks the whereabouts of their human king in which they trusted and states that he will give them a king: the king of Assyria!

In the final section (13:12–14:1), YHWH uses various images to describe judgment: Ephraim's sin is stored up like a written record (13:12), and Ephraim is like an unborn baby that refuses to emerge and end the turmoil of labor (13:13). This lack of wisdom will end in death. In a frightening conclusion, YHWH deliberates whether he will save Israel from the coming destruction and exile (13:14). The answer is no: he will destroy their land and goods (13:15), and the people will be grotesquely killed in the atrocities of war (14:1).

Thus there are two themes that run through the unit. First, YHWH will not be their helper (13:4, 9, 14). Second, YHWH will be their destroyer (13:3, 7-9, 15; 14:1).

¹When Ephraim spoke there was trembling.
He was exalted in Israel,
but he became guilty through Ba'al and died.

²And now they continue to sin;
they made for themselves cast images,
from their silver, according to their skill—idols,
All of it is the work of craftsmen.

They speak to them;
those who sacrifice people kiss calves.

³Therefore they will be like a morning cloud,
and like dew which disappears early,
like chaff that is blown from a threshing floor
and like smoke from a window.

⁴But I am YHWH, your God from the land of Egypt,
and you did not know a god besides me,
and there is no deliverer except me.

*⁵I have known you in the wilderness—
in the land of drought.*

*⁶According to their pasturage, they were satisfied.
They became satisfied and their heart was haughty,
therefore they have forgotten me.*

*⁷And I was like a lion to them;
I will lurk like a panther on the road.*

*⁸I will meet them like a bereaved bear,
and I will tear open the covering of their heart.*

*And I will devour them there like a lion—
a wild animal of the field, which will rip them to shreds.*

*⁹I will have destroyed you, Israel,
for [you rebelled] against me—against your helper.*

*¹⁰Where is your king then,
that he may save you in all your cities—*

*And your judges of which you said,
"Give me a king and princes"?*

*¹¹I will give you a king in my anger,
and take (him) in my wrath.*

*¹²The iniquity of Ephraim is bound up;
his sin is stored up.*

*¹³The pangs of one giving birth will come with respect to him.
He is an unwise son,
because, at the right time, he does not present himself
at the opening of children.*

*¹⁴Will I ransom them from the power of Sheol?
Will I redeem them from death?*

*Where are your plagues, O death?
Where is your sting, O Sheol?
Compassion is hidden from my eyes.*

*¹⁵Indeed he behaves wildly among brothers;
an east wind will come, a wind from YHWH*

going up from the desert.

And his spring will be dry,
and his fountain will be parched.

He will plunder the treasury—
every desirable vessel.

¹⁴:¹ *Samaria is guilty,*
for she rebelled against her God.

They will fall by the sword,
their infants will be smashed,
and their pregnant women will be ripped open.

13:1 a כְּדַבֵּר אֶפְרַיִם רְתֵת
b נָשָׂא הוּא בְּיִשְׂרָאֵל
c וַיֶּאְשַׁם בַּבַּעַל וַיָּמֹת:

Lines a-c are a tricolon that opens the unit and corresponds to a tricolon in 14:1 that closes the unit. There is noun//pronoun grammatical parallelism between lines a (אֶפְרַיִם) and b (הוּא). אֶפְרַיִם is the subject of the verbs in line c, which forms the conclusion to the verse. The lines are marked by *Zaqep parvum*, *'Atnaḥ*, and *Silluq*. This verse is very difficult and the following analysis is tentative.

כְּדַבֵּר אֶפְרַיִם. *Line a.* Temporal clause introduced by a Piel inf constr √דבר with a כְּ prep subordinate to the truncated verbless clause at the end of the line ("[there was] trembling"). This means that Ephraim's speech was accompanied by and produced trembling in those who heard. It (along with line b) is a statement of Ephraim's preeminence, power, and influence, which were lost when he became guilty with Ba'al worship (line c).

רְתֵת. *Line a.* Independent verbless clause. The subject of the verbless clause is implied. The predicate רְתֵת is a *hapax* in the OT but is known in the Qumran scrolls (1QH 4.33) with the meaning "trembling" (HALOT 1301).

נָשָׂא הוּא בְּיִשְׂרָאֵל. *Line b.* Independent verbless clause.

נָשָׂא. In the MT this verb is vocalized as a Qal *qatal* 3ms √נשׂא. Because it is usually transitive, some have suggested that an accusative such as "voice" (AF 629–30) is elided. Alternatively, there are a few verses in the OT in which it appears that the Qal of √נשׂא is intransitive (Nah 1:5; Hab 1:3; Ps 89:10; cf. GKC §117v-w), although the evidence is not certain (see HALOT 726). The difficulty with these explanations is that the independent pronoun הוּא must be the subject, but its location following the verb would suggest that this is a verbless clause with a noun or participle as predicate (WO §37.6a). Accordingly, I tentatively revocalize it as נִשָּׂא, a Niph ptc ms √נשׂא ("he was exalted"). This may be the understanding of S and T (see BHS note [b]). The participle/predicate is fronted for focus: his temporary exaltation is contrasted with his guilt and death (line c). Both verbless clauses in this verse (lines a and b) are translated in the past tense due to the *wayyiqtol* verbs in line c. This verse refers to the past, 13:2 to the present, and 13:3 to the future (see the discussion in 13:2a below).

הוּא. Subject of the verbless clause. Its antecedent is אֶפְרַיִם (line a).

בְּיִשְׂרָאֵל. PP with locative בְּ having the sense "in" or "among." Ephraim was preeminent in the northern kingdom.

וַיֶּאְשַׁם בַּבַּעַל. *Line c.* Independent clause.

וַיֶּאְשַׁם. Qal *wayyiqtol* 3ms √אשׁם. This verb refers to the guilt or punishment that a person must bear for wrongdoing (cf. 4:15; 5:15; 10:2). It is repeated again in 14:1 at the close of the unit. In the context of the preceding clause, the sense is that Ephraim *was* exalted, but that status was ended when he engaged in the worship of Baʿal.

בַּבַּעַל. Adjunct PP with instrumental בְּ indicating the means by which Ephraim became guilty. While it is not common for a PP with בְּ to express agency with √אשׁם, there is another example in Ezek 22:4. In addition, Hosea condemns the addition of בַּעַל to cult practices elsewhere and blames it for Israel's guilt and consequences (e.g., 2:10, 15; 11:2).

וַיָּמֹת. *Line c.* Independent clause. The verb is a Qal *wayyiqtol* 3ms √מות. Ephraim now has a "death sentence" of irrevocable consequences to be described in the following verses.

Hosea 13:2

13:2 a וְעַתָּ֣ה ׀ יוֹסִ֣פוּ לַחֲטֹ֗א
b וַיַּעֲשׂ֨וּ לָהֶ֤ם מַסֵּכָה֙
c מִכַּסְפָּ֣ם כִּתְבוּנָ֔ם עֲצַבִּ֕ים
d מַעֲשֵׂ֥ה חָרָשִׁ֖ים כֻּלֹּ֑ה
e לָהֶם֙ הֵ֣ם אֹמְרִ֔ים
f זֹבְחֵ֣י אָדָ֔ם עֲגָלִ֖ים יִשָּׁקֽוּן׃

Lines a-d are a quatrain, identified by the ellipsis of the verb וַיַּעֲשׂוּ (line b) in line c. Line d is a verbless clause which summarizes the preceding lines. All four lines are related topically, describing the construction of idols. In this alignment, each line has three words/stresses. The lines are marked by *R*ᵉ*bîaʿ*, *Pašṭa*, *Zaqep parvum*, and *ʾAtnaḥ*. Lines e-f are a bicolon. The pronoun הֵם in line e has the same referent as the substantival participle זֹבְחֵי in line f. Both lines describe the worship of the idols. The lines are marked by *Zaqep parvum* and *Silluq*.

וְעַתָּה יוֹסִפוּ לַחֲטֹא. *Line a*. Independent clause.

וְעַתָּה. An adverb of time which signals that the following statements apply to Hosea's contemporaries.

יוֹסִפוּ. Hiph *yiqtol* 3mp √יסף. Following the adverb עַתָּה, the *yiqtol* signals frequentative action in the present. The verb √יסף functions as an auxiliary describing continuation or escalation with the following infinitive לַחֲטֹא as its complement (cf. 1:6; 9:15; JM §177b).

לַחֲטֹא. Qal inf constr √חטא. Compl of יוֹסִפוּ.

וַיַּעֲשׂוּ לָהֶם מַסֵּכָה. *Line b*. Independent clause.

וַיַּעֲשׂוּ. Qal *wayyiqtol* 3mp √עשה. The *wayyiqtol* conjugation indicates simple past action. Hosea's contemporaries are continuing to sin now (line a) with idols that they made previously (lines b-d). There is continuity between their past and present behavior.

לָהֶם. PP with לְ of interest. The 3mp suffix refers to Ephraim (cf. 13:1) and has a reflexive sense (WO §16.4g). Note the PPs with reflexive pronouns in pentateuchal passages prohibiting the construction of idols (Exod 20:4, 23; Deut 4:16).

מַסֵּכָה. Acc compl of וַיַּעֲשׂוּ. This word refers to the idolatrous golden calf in Exod 32:4, 8 (cf. Ps 106:19). Elsewhere it is said to be made from silver (cf. Judg 17:3-4 and line c below) or silver and gold (Isa

30:22). This is likely a collective singular that refers to various cast idols (cf. 2 Kgs 17:16).

מִכַּסְפָּם כִּתְבוּנָם עֲצַבִּים. *Line c.* Independent clause with the verb וַיַּעֲשׂוּ elided (see line b).

מִכַּסְפָּם. PP with מִן indicating the material from which the עֲצַבִּים (idols) were made (cf. WO §11.2.11d). The antecedent of the 3mp poss pronoun is Ephraim (13:1).

כִּתְבוּנָם. PP with כְּ of norm indicating the manner in which they made עֲצַבִּים (cf. WHS §259). Elsewhere this word is feminine (תְּבוּנָה), so here we would expect כִּתְבוּנָתָם. This is either a unique masculine form or, more likely, an abbreviated form before the 3mp suffix (GKC §91e).

עֲצַבִּים. Acc compl of וַיַּעֲשׂוּ, elided here and assumed from line b. This constituent is held to the end of the line in order to create suspense and to give it a place of prominence, emphasizing Ephraim's guilt.

מַעֲשֵׂה חָרָשִׁים כֻּלֹּה. *Line d.* Independent verbless clause.

מַעֲשֵׂה חָרָשִׁים. This construct phrase is the predicate of the verbless clause. חָרָשִׁים is a genitive of agency, expressing the originator of the מַעֲשֶׂה (cf. WO §9.5.1b).

כֻּלֹּה. Subject of the verbless clause. The 3ms pronominal suffix refers to מַעֲשֶׂה, which in turn refers to the whole project of idol construction. On the form of the 3ms suffix with ה, see JM §94h.

לָהֶם הֵם אֹמְרִים. *Line e.* Independent clause.

לָהֶם. PP with לְ indicating the addressee of the verb of speaking (אֹמְרִים). The antecedent of the 3mp suffix is the idols (עֲצַבִּים; line d). The PP is fronted in the clause for focus. The people of Ephraim are speaking to *idols* (not YHWH).

הֵם. This independent 3mp pronoun is the subject of the predicate participle אֹמְרִים. Its antecedent is again the people of Ephraim (13:1).

אֹמְרִים. Qal ptc mp √אמר. This participle is the verbal predicate of the clause and indicates progressive action.

זֹבְחֵי אָדָם עֲגָלִים יִשָּׁקוּן. *Line f.* Independent clause.

זֹבְחֵי אָדָם. Constr phrase. זֹבְחֵי is a Qal ptc mp √זבח. The question here is how one should understand the construct relationship and, therefore, which of the two words is the subject of יִשָּׁקוּן. GKC understands the genitive אָדָם as indicating the genus and providing a definition (§128l). Therefore, the translation would be "sacrificing people" or "people who sacrifice," and אָדָם would be the subject. An alternative analysis sees the genitive אָדָם as the complement of the participle זֹבְחֵי (Wolff 1974:219; AF 632; cf. WO §37.3c). In this case, the translation would be "those who sacrifice people," and the substantival participle would be the subject of יִשָּׁקוּן. If this latter view is correct, Hosea is referring to human sacrifice which would certainly be an intensification of the sin described in line a of this verse. AF notes the irony, "The sacrifice of 'calves' to Yahweh was part of Israel's religion. Here the calves receive religious homage, and human sacrifice is offered to a casting in the shape of a calf!" (632).

עֲגָלִים. Acc compl of יִשָּׁקוּן. The word עֵגֶל refers to idolatrous calves in Hos 8:5-6 as well.

יִשָּׁקוּן. Qal *yiqtol* 3mp √נשק with a paragogic ן (see WO §31.7.1a-b; JM §44e). The initial I-נ assimilates in the closed syllable, causing gemination of the שׁ.

13:3 a לָכֵן יִהְיוּ כַּעֲנַן־בֹּקֶר
b וְכַטַּל מַשְׁכִּים הֹלֵךְ
c כְּמֹץ יְסֹעֵר מִגֹּרֶן
d וּכְעָשָׁן מֵאֲרֻבָּה׃

Lines a-d are a quatrain. The verb יִהְיוּ in line a is elided in each of the following lines (b-d), linking all of them together. In addition, the four lines are related through similar and corresponding metaphors (cloud, dew, chaff, smoke)—all ephemeral substances found in nature. The lines are marked by *Zaqep parvum*, *'Atnaḥ*, *Zaqep parvum*, and *Silluq*.

לָכֵן יִהְיוּ כַּעֲנַן־בֹּקֶר. *Line a*. Independent clause.

לָכֵן. Adverb introducing the logical consequence of what precedes. The prophet has described Ephraim's past and present guilt in 13:1-2; now he describes the consequences.

יִהְיוּ. Qal *yiqtol* 3mp √היה. In the context the *yiqtol* expresses a future prediction.

כַּעֲנַן־בֹּקֶר. This PP with כְּ indicating agreement in kind is a complement of the copular verb יִהְיוּ. This phrase and the three words in line b are identical to those in 6:4 (see below). On the construct phrase, see 6:4c.

וְכַטַּל מַשְׁכִּים הֹלֵךְ. *Line b.* Each of the next three lines in the quatrain begin with a PP with בְּ, indicating that they are additional complements of the verb יִהְיוּ, which is elided. The participle מַשְׁכִּים functions adverbially and modifies the following participle הֹלֵךְ (cf. GKC §120g; JM §177g). הֹלֵךְ forms a relative clause, headed by and modifying כַטַּל, even though it does not have an article (see WO §19.7b). The wording in this line is identical to that in 6:4d, creating an intertextual link. In that verse Israel's covenant love (חֶסֶד) is described as ephemeral and quickly vanishing. They were swift to turn from YHWH. In this verse it is the *people* who will vanish because of their idolatry.

כְּמֹץ. *Line c.* Compl of the verb יִהְיוּ, which is elided. This is a PP with כְּ indicating agreement in kind. מֹץ refers to "chaff," which is known for being helplessly driven away by the wind (e.g., Job 21:18; Ps 1:4; 35:5; Isa 17:13).

יְסֹעֵר מִגֹּרֶן. *Line c.* Asyndetic relative clause headed by מֹץ.

יְסֹעֵר. In the MT this is vocalized as a Poel *yiqtol* 3ms √סער. In the Qal this verb means "to be turbulent" (e.g., the raging sea in Jonah 1:11, 13). It occurs in the Piel one time with the transitive sense "to blow away" (Zech 7:14). In this relative clause, it is difficult to make sense of a transitive Poel since מֹץ is the subject rather than the complement. While AF (633) argue that the Poel *is* passive, that would be unusual (cf. the passive Poal), and there are no other examples to serve as a point of reference. The vocalization is likely an error, and the verb should be vocalized as a passive Pual, which is a difference of one vowel (יְסֹעַר) (see HALOT 762). This analysis is supported by G's passive ἀποφυσώμενος ("blown away").

מִגֹּרֶן. PP with abl מִן.

וּכְעָשָׁן מֵאֲרֻבָּה. *Line d.* Two verbs from the preceding lines (√היה—line a; √סער—line c) are elided in this one.

כְעָשָׁן. PP with כְּ indicating agreement in kind. It functions as a complement of the verb יִהְיוּ, which is elided (see line a).

מֵאֲרֻבָּה. PP with abl מִן. This forms an asyndetic relative clause (headed by עָשָׁן), which assumes the verb יְסֹעֵר (or יְסֹעַר) elided (see line c). The full sense of the line is, "and [they will be] like smoke [which is blown] from a window."

13:4 a וְאָנֹכִי יְהוָה אֱלֹהֶיךָ מֵאֶרֶץ מִצְרָיִם
b וֵאלֹהִים זוּלָתִי לֹא תֵדָע
c וּמוֹשִׁיעַ אַיִן בִּלְתִּי:

Lines a-c are a tricolon. The first line, a repetition of 12:10a, introduces lines b and c which speak to YHWH's exclusive status as Israel's God. Lines b and c are parallel, sharing the corresponding terms אֱלֹהִים//מוֹשִׁיעַ, זוּלָתִי//בִּלְתִּי, and לֹא//אַיִן. The lines are marked by *'Atnaḥ*, *Zaqep parvum*, and *Silluq*.

וְאָנֹכִי יְהוָה אֱלֹהֶיךָ מֵאֶרֶץ מִצְרָיִם. *Line a.* Independent clause. This line is identical to 12:10a (see the discussion there).

וֵאלֹהִים זוּלָתִי לֹא תֵדָע. *Line b.* Independent clause. Just as line a is a restatement of Exod 20:2/Deut 5:6, this line (b) is a restatement of the first stipulation of the Sinai Covenant found in Exod 20:3/Deut 5:7, which reads לֹא יִהְיֶה־לְךָ אֱלֹהִים אֲחֵרִים עַל־פָּנָי.

אלֹהִים. Acc compl of תֵדָע. It is fronted in the word order for focus. It was not *other gods* that they knew but YHWH.

זוּלָתִי. PP with זוּלָה indicating an exception. The antecedent of the 1cs suffix is YHWH, the speaker (cf. 13:4a).

לֹא תֵדָע. Qal *yiqtol* 2ms √ידע. Because line b is a restatement of Exod 20:3/Deut 5:7, one might be tempted to understand this verb as a prohibition (לֹא + *yiqtol*; cf. Exod 20:3). However, the statement here in Hosea is retrospective. YHWH is reminding Israel of the original call to exclusive worship, which has been vindicated: although they have worshiped other deities, those gods were false, and they never did really know a god apart from him. In this context the *yiqtol* תֵדָע should be understood as a past imperfective ("you did not know"). In the preceding verses (2-3), YHWH's people have been referred to in 3mp. For the subject of this singular verb, we may have to go back to "Ephraim" in v. 1.

וּמוֹשִׁיעַ אַיִן בִּלְתִּי. *Line c.* Independent verbless clause.

וּמוֹשִׁיעַ. Hiph ptc ms √ישע. This substantival participle is the predicate of the verbless clause.

אַיִן. Negative copula (cf. JM §154k).

בִּלְתִּי. Adjunct PP. בִּלְתִּי is usually a negative particle but sometimes has the force of a preposition meaning "except" (cf. Exod 22:19; Num 32:12; Jos 11:19; Brockelmann 1956:§118).

13:5

13:5 a אֲנִ֧י יְדַעְתִּ֛יךָ בַּמִּדְבָּ֖ר
b בְּאֶ֥רֶץ תַּלְאֻבֽוֹת׃

Lines a-b are a bicolon, with ellipsis of the verb יְדַעְתִּ֛יךָ in line b. The lines are marked by *'Atnaḥ* and *Silluq*.

אֲנִ֧י יְדַעְתִּ֛יךָ בַּמִּדְבָּ֖ר. *Line a*. Independent clause.

אֲנִ֧י. This pleonastic independent 1cs pronoun underscores that it was YHWH (not Ba'al) who knew and cared for his people in the wilderness period.

יְדַעְתִּ֛יךָ. Qal *qatal* 1cs √ידע with a 2ms acc suffix. The 2ms suffix refers to Ephraim (cf. 13:1) or Israel (cf. 13:9). In the third person, mp forms are used (cf. vv. 2-3, 6-8).

בַּמִּדְבָּ֖ר. Adjunct PP with locative בְּ.

בְּאֶ֥רֶץ תַּלְאֻבֽוֹת. *Line b*. Independent clause in which the verb יְדַעְתִּ֛יךָ (line a) is elided. This is an adjunct PP with locative בְּ. תַּלְאֻבֽוֹת is a *hapax*. HALOT relates it to cognates in Akkadian or Arabic which have the sense "exhausted" or "hot and dry" (1737).

13:6

13:6 a כְּמַרְעִיתָם֙ וַיִּשְׂבָּ֔עוּ
b שָׂבְע֖וּ וַיָּ֣רָם לִבָּ֑ם
c עַל־כֵּ֖ן שְׁכֵחֽוּנִי׃

Lines a-c are a tricolon. The lines are related by their content: a step-by-step sequence describing Israel's apostasy. In line a, their pasturage led to satisfaction (*wayyiqtol*); in line b their satisfaction led to pride (*wayyiqtol*); in line c that pride led to forgetting YHWH. In contrast to vv. 5-6, all the verbs are third person plural. The lines are marked by *Zaqep parvum*, *'Atnaḥ*, and *Silluq*.

כְּמַרְעִיתָם֙ וַיִּשְׂבָּ֔עוּ. *Line a*. Independent clause.

כְּמַרְעִיתָם֙. PP with כְּ of the norm (WHS §259). Their satisfaction (√שׂבע) was proportionate to their "pasturage," which was bountiful. The antecedent of the 3mp poss suffix is the people of YHWH.

וַיִּשְׂבָּ֔עוּ. Qal *wayyiqtol* 3mp √שׂבע. The verb √שׂבע can take an accusative complement (e.g., Exod 16:12; Eccl 5:9) or an absolute sense of being "satisfied."

שָׂבְעוּ. *Line b*. Independent clause. This is a Qal *qatal* 3cp √שׂבע. While the *wayyiqtol* וַיִּשְׂבְּעוּ in line a is a simple past, this *qatal* refers to an action viewed as completed (perfective aspect). In other words, once they became satisfied it led to pride, the next action in the sequence.

וַיָּרָם לִבָּם. *Line b*. Independent clause.

וַיָּרָם. Qal *wayyiqtol* 3ms √רום.

לִבָּם. Subject of וַיָּרָם. The antecedent of the 3mp poss suffix is the people of YHWH.

עַל־כֵּן שְׁכֵחוּנִי. *Line c*. Independent clause.

עַל־כֵּן. The prep עַל ("upon") combined with the adverb כֵּן ("thus") is idiomatic for "for this reason" or "therefore." It expresses the logical consequence of the preceding line.

שְׁכֵחוּנִי. Qal *qatal* 3cp √שׁכח with a 1cs acc suffix referring to YHWH. Israel was warned that riches in the promised land (Deut 8:13) could lead them astray from YHWH when their heart (לֵבָב) is haughty (√רום) and they forget (√שׁכח) him (Deut 8:14). The repeated language in lines b-c of this verse make the claim that this is exactly what happened. They have strayed from YHWH because they were wealthy, and they have gone to Canaanite religion in order to attempt to gain more wealth (cf. 2:15; 8:14). They are unfaithful no matter their circumstances, and now punishment awaits.

13:7 a וָאֱהִי לָהֶם כְּמוֹ־שָׁחַל
b כְּנָמֵר עַל־דֶּרֶךְ אָשׁוּר׃

Lines a-b are a bicolon with a chiastic structure (verb + PP + PP with כְּ//PP with כְּ + PP + verb). The word pair נָמֵר//שַׁחַל is another correspondence between the parallel lines, which are marked by *'Atnaḥ* and *Silluq*.

וָאֱהִי לָהֶם כְּמוֹ־שָׁחַל. *Line a*. Independent clause.

וָאֱהִי. Qal *wayyiqtol* 1cs √היה. This *wayyiqtol* needs some explanation since the other verbs in the subunit comprising vv. 7-8 are all *yiqtols* apparently referring to future violence. This verb takes its place in a temporal progression from the exodus out of Egypt (13:4) to the wilderness period (13:5) to life in the land (13:6) to recent history (this verb; 13:7a) to the present and immanent future (13:7b-8). YHWH has *already* shown himself to be like a lion (this verb); now he will be like a panther, bear, and wild animal of the field toward them as well (13:7b-8). There is a transition from past to present/future between the parallel lines.

לָהֶם. PP with לְ of interest. The antecedent of the 3mp suffix is the people of YHWH.

כְּמוֹ־שַׁחַל. PP with כְּמוֹ, a longer form of כְּ used in poetry (JM §103g), indicating agreement in kind. YHWH compared himself to a violent שַׁחַל ("lion") in 5:14 (see the discussion there).

כְּנָמֵר עַל־דֶּרֶךְ אָשׁוּר. *Line b*. Independent clause.

כְּנָמֵר. PP with כְּ indicating agreement in kind. The word נָמֵר is used six times in the OT. It refers to a wild animal known to be dangerous (e.g., Isa 11:6; Jer 5:6) and swift (e.g., Hab 1:8).

עַל־דֶּרֶךְ. PP with locative עַל expressing either the sense "on" or "beside" (cf. WO §11.2.13b).

אָשׁוּר. Qal *yiqtol* 1cs √שׁוּר. HALOT glosses √שׁוּר (I) as "to look at from a bent position" (1450). The sense seems to be one of lurking or lying in wait for prey that passes by on the road.

13:8 a אֶפְגְּשֵׁם כְּדֹב שַׁכּוּל
b וְאֶקְרַע סְגוֹר לִבָּם
c וְאֹכְלֵם שָׁם כְּלָבִיא
d חַיַּת הַשָּׂדֶה תְּבַקְּעֵם׃

Lines a-b are a bicolon, indicated by the semantic correspondence and intensification of קרע√//פגש√. The image of a violent bear governs both lines, each of which contains a 3mp acc suffix. The lines are marked by *Zaqep parvum* and *'Atnaḥ*. Lines c-d are also a bicolon with 3mp acc suffixes. Line d (חַיַּת הַשָּׂדֶה) is in apposition to לָבִיא in line c. The lines are marked by *Zaqep parvum* and *Silluq*.

אֶפְגְּשֵׁם כְּדֹב שַׁכּוּל. *Line a*. Independent clause.

אֶפְגְּשֵׁם. Qal *yiqtol* 1cs √פגש with a 3mp acc suffix. This verb refers to meeting or encountering someone. In this context it signifies a confrontation that results in an attack (cf. Exod 4:24).

כְּדֹב. PP with כְּ indicating agreement in kind. The image is one of a female bear who has lost her cubs (שַׁכּוּל) and is, therefore, ferocious.

Other passages also use the image of a bereaved bear to illustrate blind or unpredictable rage (e.g., 2 Sam 17:8; Prov 17:12). The noun דֹּב is grammatically masculine, but refers to either male or female bears (cf. WO §6.5.2a).

שַׁכּוּל. A masculine adjective modifying דֹּב.

וְאֶקְרַע סְגוֹר לִבָּם. *Line b*. Independent clause.

וְאֶקְרַע. Qal *yiqtol* 1cs √קרע.

סְגוֹר לִבָּם. Constr phrase. סְגוֹר is the acc compl of אֶקְרַע. This noun is a *hapax*, apparently derived from √סגר ("to shut") and, thus, refers to the covering that encloses the heart cavity. לִבָּם is a possessive genitive. The antecedent of the 3mp poss suffix is the people of YHWH.

וְאֹכְלֵם שָׁם כְּלָבִיא. *Line c*. Independent clause.

וְאֹכְלֵם. Qal *yiqtol* 1cs √אכל with a 3mp acc suffix. The antecedent of the suffix, like the others in this verse, is the people of YHWH.

שָׁם. Locative adverb expressing the location of the verbal action. The referent might be the דֶּרֶךְ ("road") in the metaphor (13:7b), or it could have no stated referent and be intentionally vague (McComiskey 2009:217).

כְּלָבִיא. PP with כְּ indicating agreement in kind.

חַיַּת הַשָּׂדֶה תְּבַקְּעֵם. *Line d*. The noun חַיָּה is in apposition to לָבִיא in line c and is thus situated within that PP. An appositive has the same referent as the lead noun and provides more information about it (GKC §131; WO §12.3). חַיָּה is in construct to הַשָּׂדֶה, an adjectival genitive.

תְּבַקְּעֵם. Piel *yiqtol* 3fs √בקע with a 3mp acc suffix. This verb forms an asyndetic relative clause headed by חַיָּה (cf. WO §19.6). The verb √בקע refers to dividing, cleaving, or ripping something. There is semantic overlap between the Qal and the Piel. Both refer to splitting wood (e.g., Eccl 10:9; Gen 22:3) or the barbaric practice of ripping open pregnant women (Amos 1:3; 2 Kgs 8:12). In some occurrences it seems that the Qal refers to a simple division into two parts (e.g., the sea, Exod 14:16), whereas the Piel refers to multiple breaks and fractures (e.g., Job 28;10; Ps 78:15; Hab 3:9). If so, the use of the Piel here describes an animal ripping the victims to shreds.

13:9 a שִׁחֶתְךָ יִשְׂרָאֵל
b כִּי־בִי בְעֶזְרֶךָ׃

Lines a-b are a bicolon. While there are no obvious correspondences or links between the lines, 13:8c-d and 13:10a-b are cohesive verses, and, therefore, this bicolon is identified by the process of elimination. The lines are marked by *Ṭipḥa* and *Silluq*.

שִׁחֶתְךָ יִשְׂרָאֵל. *Line a*. Independent clause. This verse is very difficult, and the solution to each difficulty impacts how we understand the rest. Therefore, the analysis below must be tentative.

שִׁחֶתְךָ. Interpreters have understood this word in many different ways, but there are three common approaches among modern commentators. First, in the MT it is vocalized as a Piel *qatal* 3ms √שחת with a 2ms acc suffix. The problem with this reading is that the subject is not readily apparent. The noun חַיָּה in 13:8d is feminine. McComiskey suggests that the subject is indefinite: "it has destroyed you, that you are against me" (2009:219; cf. GKC §144b). The difficulty with this is that it does not make adequate sense of the 1cs pronoun in line b. A second solution is to understand שִׁחֶתְךָ as a noun, on analogy with שֶׁלֶם or דֶּבֶר (cf. HALOT 212). Macintosh, for example, translates, "Your destruction, Israel" (2014:535). This solution may find support with G, which has a noun (τῇ διαφθορᾷ σου). However, the noun is unattested elsewhere in the OT. Finally, a third solution is to vocalize the verb as שִׁחַתִּךָ, a Piel *qatal* 1cs √שחת with a defective spelling. This is supported by S, which has a first-person verb. It also makes sense within the context: YHWH is the first-person speaker in 13:4-8 and again in v. 11. In addition, this makes sense of the 1cs suffix in line b (בִי). Even if we maintain the 3ms vocalization in MT, YHWH is the subject. In the context of *yiqtol* verbs (13:7-8), the *qatal* conjugation refers to completed action in the future (future perfect).

יִשְׂרָאֵל. Vocative explicating the 2ms suffix on שִׁחֶתְךָ.

כִּי־בִי בְעֶזְרֶךָ. *Line b*. There are several possible solutions to this difficult line. As indicated by BHS note b-b, G and S translate בִי as מִי ("who") and do not represent the כִּי. As always, it is difficult to know if this represents a Hebrew source text different from MT, or if the versions are making the best sense that they can. Stuart follows this approach in light of the questions that follow in 13:10 (1987:200). Macintosh understands שִׁחֶתְךָ in line a as a noun, so in this line he understands כִּי as asseverative and בִי as instrumental, "by me." In other words, "your destruction" (line a) is "my doing" (2014:535–36). The best solution might be that of AF, who see line b as elliptical and translate, "you rebelled against me" (636). This assumes that בִּי is the oblique complement of an elided verb such as √מרד ("to rebel") (e.g., Num 14:9; Jos 22:29). This, combined with reading שִׁחֶתְךָ in line a as a 1cs verb, would maintain YHWH's first-person speech in the context. Elliptical constructions are also characteristic of Hosea. On this reading, the כִּי introduces a subordinate causal clause, which gives the reason that YHWH destroyed them (line a).

בְעֶזְרֶךָ. This noun is in apposition to the preceding oblique complement בִּי. It further specifies the identity of the 1cs suffix referring to YHWH. It is ironic that YHWH, their helper, is destroying them, but that message has been consistent throughout the book. YHWH has offered himself as their helper (and functioned in that role in history), but if they do not accept his help and run instead to idols, other nations, and any other possible resource, then he will turn on them.

13:10 a אֱהִי מַלְכְּךָ אֵפוֹא
b וְיוֹשִׁיעֲךָ בְּכָל־עָרֶיךָ
c וְשֹׁפְטֶיךָ אֲשֶׁר אָמַרְתָּ
d תְּנָה־לִּי מֶלֶךְ וְשָׂרִים׃

This verse consists of two related bicola. Lines a-b consist of a verbless clause (line a) and an unmarked subordinate clause (line b). The noun מֶלֶךְ in line a is the subject of the verb יוֹשִׁיעֲךָ in line b. The lines are marked by *Zaqep parvum* and *'Atnaḥ*. Lines c-d form a second bicolon in which line d is direct speech introduced by line c (אָמַרְתָּ). The lines are marked by *Zaqep parvum* and *Silluq*. There is also parallelism between the two bicola. The first lines (a and c) of the bicola are linked via the word pair שֹׁפֵט//מֶלֶךְ as well as ellipsis of the interr אֱהִי and the noncopula (line a) in line c.

אֱהִי מַלְכְּךָ אֵפוֹא. *Line a.* Independent verbless clause.

אֱהִי. Interr particle ("where"). This form occurs only three times in the OT, all in Hosea (cf. two more occurrences in 13:14). The similar word אַיֵּה occurs forty-five times outside of Hosea but never in Hosea. Therefore, אֱהִי may be a dialectical (Stuart 1987:200) or alternate form (McComiskey 2009:220). It is the subject of the verbless clause.

מַלְכְּךָ. Predicate of the verbless clause. The antecedent of the 2ms poss suffix is Israel (13:9a).

אֵפוֹא. Enclitic particle which frequently follows interrogatives (e.g., Gen 27:33; Judg 9:38; Isa 22:1) (Brockelmann 1956:§55b).

וְיוֹשִׁיעֲךָ בְּכָל־עָרֶיךָ. *Line b.* Subordinate final clause that expresses the potential actions of the מֶלֶךְ in line a. Final clauses may be joined to the main clause by a simple וְ with an indicative *yiqtol* or jussive verb (cf. GKC §107q, §165a; JM §168b). It is more usual for the verb in the final clause to be a jussive.

יוֹשִׁיעֲךָ. Hiph *yiqtol* 3ms √ישׁע with a 2ms acc suffix. In the Hiphil the indicative and jussive moods are distinguished morphologically. The jussive would be יוֹשַׁעֲךָ (cf. Isa 35:4).

בְּכָל־עָרֶיךָ. PP with locative בְּ. In a time of invasion, the countryside would be difficult to defend so the king would make his stand in the cities.

וְשֹׁפְטֶיךָ. *Line c.* This is the predicate of a verbless clause; the subject אַיֵּה is elided (see line a). שֹׁפְטֶיךָ is a substantival Qal ptc mp √שׁפט with a 2ms poss suffix referring to Israel.

אֲשֶׁר אָמַרְתָּ. *Line c.* Relative clause headed by שֹׁפְטֶיךָ. The verb אָמַרְתָּ is a Qal *qatal* 2ms √אמר.

תְּנָה־לִּי מֶלֶךְ וְשָׂרִים. *Line d.* Direct speech introduced by the verb אָמַרְתָּ in line c.

תְּנָה. Qal impv ms √נתן. This is a long form of the imperative with paragogic ־ָה that occurs in the ms (the short form is תֵּן). It does not appear to add any particular nuance (JM §48d; WO §34.2.2a).

לִּי. This PP with לְ is the first complement of תְּנָה expressing the recipient. The antecedent of the 1cs suffix is Israel, represented in the first person within the direct speech.

מֶלֶךְ וְשָׂרִים. Acc compl of תְּנָה. This verse alludes to Israel's original request for a king and shares language with 1 Sam 8:6 (תְּנָה־לָּנוּ מֶלֶךְ לְשָׁפְטֵנוּ; cf. also 1 Sam 12:13). That request was seen as an act of rebellion and independence since Israel trusted in their potential king for military deliverance rather than YHWH. The allusion is therefore sarcastic: where is that king now that they need him?

a 13:11 אֶתֶּן־לְךָ֤ מֶ֙לֶךְ֙ בְּאַפִּ֔י
b וְאֶקַּ֖ח בְּעֶבְרָתִֽי׃ ס

Lines a-b are a bicolon featuring corresponding word pairs (לקח√/נתן√; עֶבְרָה//אַף) and PPs with בְּ. In addition, the accusative complement of נתן√ in line a (מֶלֶךְ) is implied as the complement of לקח√ in the second line as well. The lines are marked by *Zaqep parvum* and *Silluq*.

אֶתֶּן־לְךָ מֶלֶךְ בְּאַפִּי. *Line a.* Independent clause.

אֶתֶּן. Qal *yiqtol* 1cs נתן√. There is some uncertainty about whether this *yiqtol* (and אֶקַּח in line b) refers to the past, present, or future. A past interpretation is supported by G and S which translate "I gave you a king...." This would make sense following the apparent allusion to Israel's first request for a king in the previous verse (3:10). The imperfective/frequentative aspect of the *yiqtol* would then refer to the succession of kings that YHWH gave the northern kingdom, ending with Hoshea. McComiskey (2009:221) interprets the verb as present tense, arguing that YHWH is referring to the general failure of the monarchy. Garrett (1997:261) makes the intriguing suggestion that the verb is oriented toward the future. It is an ironic statement in which YHWH says something like, "I will give you a king! But it will not be the one you expect—it will be the king of Assyria!" In that case, line b would refer to the future removal of King Hoshea from the Israelite monarchy. In this reading YHWH is connecting Israel's rebellious wish for a human king in the past to their present rebellious desire for deliverance without his help. The punishment is poetic justice for that same sin.

לְךָ. This PP with לְ is the first complement of נתן√ and specifies the recipient.

מֶלֶךְ. Acc compl of אֶתֶּן.

בְּאַפִּי. Adjunct PP with בְּ indicating the mental circumstances of the action (cf. WO §11.2.5d). The antecedent of the 1cs suffix is YHWH, the speaker.

וְאֶקַּח בְּעֶבְרָתִי. *Line b.* Independent clause.

וְאֶקַּח. Qal *yiqtol* 1cs לקח√. The verb לקח√ requires an accusative complement which is missing in this clause. It is understood as the noun מֶלֶךְ from line a.

בְּעֶבְרָתִי. Adjunct PP with בְּ indicating the mental circumstances of the action (see line a).

a 13:12 צָרוּר֙ עֲוֺ֣ן אֶפְרָ֔יִם
b צְפוּנָ֖ה חַטָּאתֽוֹ׃

Lines a-b are a bicolon. Each line has a verbless clause of which the predicate is a Qal passive participle. Two word pairs link the lines semantically (עָוֺן//חַטָּאת; √צרר//√צפן). In addition, there is noun/pronoun grammatical parallelism between the lines (אֶפְרַיִם//וֹ). The lines are marked by *Zaqep parvum* and *Silluq*.

צָרוּר עֲוֺן אֶפְרָיִם. *Line a*. Independent verbless clause.

צָרוּר. Qal pass ptc ms √צרר. This participle is a predicate adjective (cf. WO §37.4c) modifying עָוֺן. The verb √צרר refers to binding or wrapping something. Hosea uses it in 4:19 in reference to the spirit wrapping Ephraim in its wings.

עֲוֺן אֶפְרָיִם. Constr phrase. The genitive אֶפְרָיִם indicates possession.

צְפוּנָה חַטָּאתוֹ. *Line b*. Independent verbless clause.

צְפוּנָה. Qal pass ptc fs √צפן. This is a predicate adjective modifying חַטָּאתוֹ (see line a). The verb √צפן refers to hiding or storing something. Thus there is semantic amplification between the lines. In line a the sin is metaphorically wrapped (√צרר), but for what purpose? In line b the answer is given: it is being placed in storage (√צפן). It is likely that Ephraim's sins are pictured as scrolls being tied up and preserved (Vuillenmier-Bessard 1958:218–12). W. G. E. Watson (1984) has argued that the metaphor indicates that their sins are unabsolved. More recently, Holtz (2012) points to legal practices in neo-Babylonian trial records and suggests that the sins are being preserved until the subsequent trial. YHWH will use them as evidence at the time of reckoning.

חַטָּאתוֹ. Hosea uses עָוֺן and חַטָּאת in parallel in 4:8 and 8:13/9:9. The antecedent of the 3ms suffix is Ephraim (line a).

Hosea 13:13

13:13 a חֶבְלֵי יוֹלֵדָה יָבֹאוּ לוֹ
b הוּא־בֵן לֹא חָכָם
c כִּי־עֵת לֹא־יַעֲמֹד
d בְּמִשְׁבַּר בָּנִים:

This whole verse is governed by the metaphor of childbirth, but it is difficult to identify subgroups of lines. The independent pronoun הוּא in line b corresponds to the 3ms suffix at the end of line a. Line c is syntactically subordinate to line b (a causal clause). Line d is an adjunct PP which further describes the circumstances of the verb יַעֲמֹד in line c. The lines are marked by *'Atnaḥ*, *Zaqep parvum*, *Ṭipḥa*, and *Silluq*.

חֶבְלֵי יוֹלֵדָה יָבֹאוּ לוֹ. *Line a.* Independent clause.

חֶבְלֵי. Subject of יָבֹאוּ. This noun, in construct with יוֹלֵדָה, always occurs in the plural (except Isa 66:7) and refers to labor pains (e.g., Isa 13:8; Jer 13:21). In the present verse, these labor pains are a synechdoche for the time of childbirth. In other words, the verse refers to the proper time (עֵת—line c) that the baby should be born, not the pain of the birth process.

יוֹלֵדָה. Qal ptc (substantival) fs √ילד.

יָבֹאוּ. Qal *yiqtol* 3mp √בוא.

לוֹ. PP with לְ. The antecedent of the 3ms suffix is Ephraim (cf. 13:12). The meaning of the לְ prep in this clause is dependent upon how one understands the verse as a whole. There are essentially three views. First, for some scholars, Ephraim is being compared to a woman in labor (cf. Isa 37:3; Jer 30:6), and *not* to an unborn child (cf. Garrett 1997:261–64; Macintosh 2014:543–44). A second view is that Ephraim is first compared to a mother in labor in line a, but then in a twist the metaphor changes and Ephraim is compared to an unborn child in lines b-d (cf. McComiskey 2009:223). In these two views, the לְ specifies the spatial termination of the action (WHS §266a) ("the labor pains have come *to* him," i.e., he has gone into labor). However, the overall sense of the verse refers not to the process of labor but to *timing* (line c). Furthermore, while line a states that there are labor pains, line b immediately imagines Ephraim as the unborn child. McKenzie (1955:296) writes that it is unlikely the verse refers to both the mother and the child in a single line, while "Israel is certainly likened to the child," and "the mother is mentioned to complete the metaphor." A third view is best: that Ephraim is compared to an unborn child but not to a mother in labor (cf. Wolff 1974:228; Stuart 1987:206–7). Line a is the setting of the metaphor: the labor pains indicate that it is time for delivery and, thus, time for the child to emerge. In this view the לְ indicates specification (i.e., "with respect to") (WHS §273a; cf. Rudolph 1966:239).

הוּא־בֵן לֹא חָכָם. *Line b*. Independent verbless clause.

הוּא. Subject of the verbless clause. The antecedent of this 3ms independent pronoun is Ephraim (cf. 13:12).

בֵן. Predicate of the verbless clause.

לֹא חָכָם. The attributive adjective חָכָם modifies בֵן. (On the negation of the adjective, see GKC §152a, n. 1). Hosea negates substantives in 1:9 (לֹא עַמִּי), 2:1 (לֹא עַמִּי), and 7:16 (לֹא עָל).

כִּי־עֵת לֹא־יַעֲמֹד. *Line c*. Causal clause (with כִּי) subordinate to the verbless clause in line b. This clause gives the reason that Ephraim is "not wise."

עֵת. Adverbial acc ("at the right time") modifying יַעֲמֹד and specifying the time (cf. GKC §118q; JM §126i; WO §10.2.2c).

יַעֲמֹד. Qal *yiqtol* 3ms √עמד. If one takes the view that this verb refers to a mother in labor (see above), then √עמד here means "to endure" or "to survive," perhaps indicating that Ephraim will die in childbirth (cf. Macintosh 2014:544). More likely, it refers to the unborn child positioning himself at the cervical opening in readiness to emerge. Negated by לֹא, the imagery is that of an unborn baby refusing to be born. This results in continued turmoil and eventual death. In the same way, Ephraim, and the nation of Israel more broadly, is in the turmoil of its last days. Yet, it refuses to return to YHWH in repentance and to do what is necessary to resolve the situation properly. The "labor" cannot continue indefinitely, and since Ephraim will not emerge from it, he will die.

בְּמִשְׁבַּר בָּנִים. *Line d*. Adjunct PP with locative בְּ indicating the place where the metaphorical child (should) be positioned (יַעֲמֹד). In the construct phrase מִשְׁבַּר בָּנִים, the genitive בָּנִים is adjectival, specifying the kind of מִשְׁבַּר in view. The word מִשְׁבַּר often refers to waves of water (e.g., 2 Sam 22:5), but in a few instances, to the cervical opening (HALOT 642). A similar expression in 2 Kgs 19:3/Isa 37:3 provides additional support for the view that it is the child who is in view here, not the mother.

13:14 a מִיַּד שְׁאוֹל אֶפְדֵּם
b מִמָּוֶת אֶגְאָלֵם
c אֱהִי דְבָרֶיךָ מָוֶת
d אֱהִי קָטָבְךָ שְׁאוֹל
e נֹחַם יִסָּתֵר מֵעֵינָי׃

Lines a-b are a bicolon with lines sharing four corresponding elements: PP with מִן, the word pair מָוֶת//שְׁאוֹל, the word pair גאל//√פדה, and the 3mp acc suffix. The lines are marked by *Zaqep parvum* and *'Atnaḥ*. Lines c-e are a tricolon. The first two lines (c-d) are parallel questions with the interrogative particle אֱהִי and word pairs קֶטֶב//דֶּבֶר and שְׁאוֹל//מָוֶת. Line e is the conclusion to the tricolon. The lines are marked by *R^ebi^a‘*, *Zaqep parvum*, and *Silluq*.

מִיַּד שְׁאוֹל אֶפְדֵּם. *Line a*. Independent clause. It is possible to understand this verse in two opposite ways. AF (639–40) and McComiskey (2009:222–24) interpret this clause and the parallel clause in line b as statements indicating that YHWH will ultimately deliver Israel. This is in sharp contrast to the surrounding context (e.g., 13:12-13, 15), which describes the inevitability of Israel's destruction. McComiskey (2009:223) admits that the transition is abrupt, but points to the analogy of the sudden shift in 11:7-9. An opposing view interprets the verse in continuity with the context. Chapter 13 not only describes Israel's certain judgment, but it is the climax of YHWH's destructive intentions, culminating in 14:1. Therefore, it makes better sense to regard the clauses in lines a and b as rhetorical questions which expect a negative answer. "Shall I redeem them from the power of Sheol?" No! Questions need not be indicated by explicit interrogative particles (cf. JM §161a). This reading also understands נֹחַם in line e in a more natural way (see line e below).

מִיַּד שְׁאוֹל. PP with abl מִן. The noun יָד ("hand") is used here as a metonymy for "power." The genitive שְׁאוֹל indicates possession.

אֶפְדֵּם. Qal *yiqtol* 1cs √פדה with a 3mp acc suffix. The antecedent of the 3mp suffix must be Israel/Ephraim in the context. The third person singular is used in 13:12-13 and 13:15. YHWH is the speaker and the subject of this first-person verb.

מִמָּוֶת אֶגְאָלֵם. *Line b*. Independent clause.

מִמָּוֶת. PP with abl מִן.

אֶגְאָלֵם. Qal *yiqtol* 1cs √גאל with a 3mp acc suffix.

אֱהִי דְבָרֶיךָ מָוֶת. *Line c*. Independent verbless clause.

אֱהִי. Interr particle. This is apparently a dialectical or alternate form of אַיֵּה (see the discussion in 13:10a).

דְבָרֶיךָ. The predicate of the verbless clause. The word דֶּבֶר ("plague") also occurs in parallel with קֶטֶב (line d) in Ps 91:6. The antecedent of the 2ms poss suffix is the following vocative מָוֶת.

מָוֶת. Vocative. On the lack of an article, see GKC §126e.

אֱהִי קָטָבְךָ שְׁאוֹל. *Line d*. Independent verbless clause.

אֱהִי. Interr particle (see line c; 13:10a).

קָטָבְךָ. Predicate of the verbless clause. The noun קֶטֶב is often translated "sting," but its occurrences point to something more destructive (e.g., Deut 32:24; Ps 91:6). Blau (1957:98) argues that it refers to a "pox"; a disease of death parallel to the plague (דֶּבֶר). On the vocalization, see GKC §93q.

שְׁאוֹל. Vocative.

נֹחַם יִסָּתֵר מֵעֵינָי. *Line e*. Independent clause.

נֹחַם. This noun—the subject of יִסָּתֵר—is a *hapax*. The Jewish medieval exegete Rashi argued that it is derived from √נחם (similar to the noun נֹעַם < √נעם) (Englander 1942:473). The verb √נחם occurs in the Niphal ("to regret," "to change one's mind"), the Piel ("to comfort"), and in the Hithpael ("to plot revenge," "to allow oneself to be comforted") (see HALOT 688–89). McComiskey (2009:222) argues, in connection with his view that the verse is a statement of YHWH's determination to deliver, that the noun here should be translated "relenting." In other words, the possibility of changing YHWH's mind is hidden from his eyes. This seems to stretch the semantic connotations of the verb and to read it unnaturally. The vast majority of occurrences of the Niphal of √נחם, even those that refer to changing one's mind, have the sense of acting in mercy. As mentioned above, the Piel means "to comfort." Overall, the verb has a consistent positive sense and should be translated "compassion" or "pity." If this compassion is "hidden" (יִסָּתֵר), that provides support for reading the entire verse as a continuation of YHWH's statement that judgment is inevitable.

יִסָּתֵר. Niph *yiqtol* 3ms √סתר.

מֵעֵינָי. Oblique compl of יִסָּתֵר with מִן indicating from what compassion is hidden. The antecedent of the 1cs poss suffix is YHWH, the speaker.

13:15 a כִּי הוּא בֵּן אַחִים יַפְרִיא
b יָבוֹא קָדִים רוּחַ יְהוָה
c מִמִּדְבָּר עֹלֶה
d וְיֵבוֹשׁ מְקוֹרוֹ
e וְיֶחֱרַב מַעְיָנוֹ
f הוּא יִשְׁסֶה אוֹצַר
g כָּל־כְּלִי חֶמְדָּה׃

Lines a-c are a tricolon. There are no grammatical or semantic correspondences between the lines, but the preceding lines (13:14c-e) are a tricolon and lines d-e in this verse are clearly a bicolon, so we are left with a unit of three lines in a-c. Overall, the lineation is not certain and the lines do not necessarily correspond to disjunctive Masoretic accents. The lines are marked by *'Atnaḥ*, *Gereš*, and *Rᵉbîaʿ*. As already mentioned, lines d-e are a bicolon, indicated by the word pairs √יבש (see below)//√חרב and מַעְיָן/מָקוֹר as well as 3ms poss suffixes. The lines are marked by *Pašṭa* and *Zaqep parvum*. Lines f and g are a bicolon; line g is in apposition to אוֹצַר in line f. The lines are marked by *Ṭipḥa* and *Silluq*.

כִּי הוּא בֵּן אַחִים יַפְרִיא. *Line a*. Independent clause. The כִּי is asseverative (cf. JM §164b).

הוּא. This 3ms pleonastic pronoun resumes the subject "Ephraim" from 13:13 (interrupted by 13:14) and anticipates the 3ms verb יַפְרִיא.

בֵּן אַחִים. PP with locative בֵּין ("among") written defectively (the י *mater* is present in the Aleppo Codex and Cairo Codex).

יַפְרִיא. Hiph *yiqtol* 3ms √פרא. This verb is a *hapax*. The versions (G, S, V) have "separate," which may represent יַפְרִיד (see BHS note ᵃ) or it may be a guess. Perhaps the simplest explanation is that it is related to the noun פֶּרֶא ("wild donkey"; cf. Hos 8:9) and refers to wild behavior.

יָבוֹא קָדִים רוּחַ יְהוָה. *Line b.* Independent clause.

יָבוֹא. Qal *yiqtol* 3ms √בוא.

קָדִים. Subject of יָבוֹא. The word קָדִים refers to an "east wind," which is scorching and destructive (cf. 12:2). It is often mentioned in the OT as a means of judgment (Ps 78:26; Ezek 17:10; Jonah 4:8).

רוּחַ יְהוָה. This construct phrase is in apposition to קָדִים, emphasizing that it is under YHWH's control.

מִמִּדְבָּר עֹלֶה. *Line c.* This line is also in apposition to קָדִים in line b. It consists of a PP with abl מִן and a Qal ptc ms √עלה.

וְיֵבוֹשׁ מְקוֹרוֹ. *Line d.* Independent clause.

וְיֵבוֹשׁ. In the MT, this verb is a Qal *yiqtol* 3ms √בושׁ ("to be ashamed"). However, fragment 4QXII^c in the Qumran scrolls has ויבש from √יבשׁ ("to be dry") (see Testuz 1955:37; Ulrich 2013:597). It is unlikely that this reading is actually a defective form of ויבוש (which would agree with MT) since the fragment demonstrates a full orthography elsewhere (cf. Gelston 2010:72*). √יבשׁ is also supported by the major versions (G, V, S, T) and the parallel with √חרב in the following line. Therefore, we should read this verb either as וְיָבֵשׁ, a Qal (irrealis) *qatal* 3ms √יבשׁ, or more likely וְיִ(י)בַשׁ, a Qal *yiqtol* 3ms √יבשׁ.

מְקוֹרוֹ. Subject of וְיִ(י)בַשׁ. The antecedent of the 3ms poss suffix is Ephraim (13:12).

וְיֶחֱרַב מַעְיָנוֹ. *Line e.* Independent clause.

וְיֶחֱרַב. Qal *yiqtol* 3ms √חרב. The verbs √יבשׁ and √חרב occur as a word pair in six other passages (Job 14:11; Isa 19:5; 42:15; 44:27; Jer 51:36; Nah 1:4). Interestingly, in each of those cases, √חרב precedes √יבשׁ in sequence or in the parallelism. Here, the terms are reversed.

מַעְיָנוֹ. Subject of וְיֶחֱרַב. The antecedent of the 3ms poss suffix is Ephraim.

הוּא יִשְׁסֶה אוֹצַר. *Line f.* Independent clause.

הוּא. A pleonastic 3ms pronoun which anticipates the subject of יִשְׁסֶה. Its referent may be YHWH or perhaps the king of Assyria, but in any case it is the agent of judgment. This forms a contrast with the pleonastic pronoun הוּא in line a, which refers to Ephraim. *He* (Ephraim) behaves wildly (line a) so *he* (the judge) will plunder Ephraim's treasury (line f).

יִשְׁסֶה. Qal *yiqtol* 3ms √שסה.

אוֹצָר. Acc compl of יִשְׁסֶה.

כָּל־כְּלִי חֶמְדָּה. *Line g*. This construct chain is in apposition to אוֹצָר in line f and further describes it. The phrase כְּלִי חֶמְדָּה occurs in 2 Chr 32:27; Jer 25:34; and Nah 2:10 to describe riches that will be plundered by an enemy conquest.

14:1 a תֶּאְשַׁם שֹׁמְרוֹן
b כִּי מָרְתָה בֵּאלֹהֶיהָ
c בַּחֶרֶב יִפֹּלוּ
d עֹלְלֵיהֶם יְרֻטָּשׁוּ
e וְהָרִיּוֹתָיו יְבֻקָּעוּ׃ פ

Lines a-b are a bicolon with noun (שֹׁמְרוֹן)//pronoun (הָ) parallelism. Line b is a causal clause subordinate to the main clause in line a. The lines are marked by *Zaqep parvum* and *'Atnaḥ*. Lines c-e are a tricolon; each line intensifies the description of horrible acts in the conquest of Samaria (√נפל > √רטש > √בקע). The lines are marked by *Zaqep parvum*, *Zaqep parvum*, and *Silluq*.

תֶּאְשַׁם שֹׁמְרוֹן. *Line a*. Independent clause.

תֶּאְשַׁם. Qal *yiqtol* 3fs √אשם. This is an indicative *yiqtol*, so we would expect SV word order in the clause. The VS word order here has fronted the verb √אשם ("guily") for topicalization. On the semantics of √אשם, see 4:15. Hosea also uses this verb in 5:15; 10:2, and 13:1.

שֹׁמְרוֹן. Subject of תֶּאְשַׁם. Samaria is mentioned elsewhere in Hosea in 7:1; 8:5, 6; and 10:5, 7. Here it is used as a synechdoche for the defeat of the northern kingdom of Israel as a whole.

כִּי מָרְתָה בֵּאלֹהֶיהָ. *Line b*. Subordinate causal clause with כִּי giving the reason that Samaria is guilty (line a).

מָרְתָה. Qal *qatal* 3fs √מרה.

בֵּאלֹהֶיהָ. Oblique compl of מָרְתָה. The verb √מרה also takes accusative complements and oblique complements with עִם. The antecedent of the 3fs suffix is שֹׁמְרוֹן.

בַּחֶרֶב יִפֹּלוּ. *Line c.* Independent clause.

בַּחֶרֶב. PP with instrumental בְּ.

יִפֹּלוּ. Qal *yiqtol* 3ms √נפל. The subject of this verb (and the referent of the 3mp suffix in the following line) is either the people of Samaria (line a) or more broadly the people of the northern kingdom.

עֹלְלֵיהֶם יְרֻטָּשׁוּ. *Line d.* Independent clause.

עֹלְלֵיהֶם. Subject of יְרֻטָּשׁוּ. The SV word order is expected with an indicative *yiqtol* verb.

יְרֻטָּשׁוּ. Pual *yiqtol* 3mp √רטשׁ. In the OT this verb is always used of the slaughter of people in war. It is is used in parallel with ripping open pregnant women (2 Kgs 8:12) and rape (Isa 13:16), so it may have the nuance of an atrocity. In Isa 13:18 young men are √רטשׁ with bows. In Hos 10:14, mothers and children are "dashed" together.

וְהָרִיּוֹתָיו יְבֻקָּעוּ. *Line e.* Independent clause.

וְהָרִיּוֹתָיו. Subject of יְבֻקָּעוּ. This form of the adjective (הָרִיָּה) is a *hapax* (see GKC §84ᵃg). The usual form is הָרָה (see 2 Kgs 8:12; Amos 1:13, which also refer to pregnant women being ripped open). The antecedent of the 3ms poss suffix may be Ephraim (cf. 13:12). Hosea thus moves from references to Samaria with 3ms forms (lines a-b) to the people with 3mp forms (lines c-d) to Ephraim with a 3ms suffix (line e).

יְבֻקָּעוּ. Pual *yiqtol* 3mp √בקע (cf. WO §25.3b). The lack of agreement between this masculine verb and the plural subject is probably due to general aversion to 3fp verbs in Hebrew (see GKC §145u). Hosea used this verb in 13:8 (the covering of the heart).

Relationship Will Be Restored through Repentance (14:2-9)

In this last unit of the book, the prophet looks past the certain judgment to come (13:1–14:1) and gives a final word of hope to the people of YHWH. It is too late to ward off destruction now, but in the eschatological future they can look forward to a restored relationship with YHWH and complete renewal of their land ... if they repent and put their trust in him.

Hosea begins the unit in v. 2 by calling Israel (2ms) to return to YHWH. In vv. 3-4 he provides them (now addressed with 2mp) with the words of a prayer of repentance that they can take to YHWH. The prayer consists of three positive statements of repentance in v. 3 as well as three negative statements in which they disavow those things which drew them away from YHWH: political alliances, military power, and false gods (v. 4). Israel must adopt this repentant perspective and make it their own.

In vv. 5-8 first-person forms indicate that now YHWH responds to the prophet and states that he will accept this prayer. He will love Israel freely and will heal them of their apostasy (v. 5). A string of similes (dew, flowers, trees of Lebanon, olive trees, fragrance, grain, vines, wine) all portray a delightful, fertile land and restoration of the people. These verses contain a number of intertextual connections with language in the Song of Songs (cf. Wolff 1974:234; Pope 1977:304, 372, 621). YHWH alternates between references to the people of Israel and the nation as a whole (14:5a-b = 3mp; 14:5c-7 = 3ms; 14:8a-c = 3mp; 14:8d = 3ms).

The book of Hosea begins with the breaking of an intimate relationship, portrayed as a painful, unfaithful marriage (chs. 1–3). In the final verse, 14:9, Hosea portrays the climax of restoration with a quiet, tender dialogue between YHWH and his people. They declare that they are finished with idols once and for all. YHWH responds that he will care for them. They observe their new status as a mighty, healthy tree. YHWH says that their fruit comes from him. In this short conversation, we are reminded that YHWH was the source of what they wanted all along (2:8). When his people come to that realization and turn to him, he will eagerly love and restore them. That is what *he* wanted all along.

²*Return, Israel, to YHWH your God,*
for you have stumbled in your iniquity.

³*Take with you words,*
and return to YHWH.
Say to him,

"You will forgive all iniquity
and take what is good,
and we will render the fruit of our lips.

⁴*Assyria cannot save us.*
We will not ride on horses.
And we will no longer say, 'our gods!' to the work of our hands.
—for by you the orphan is pitied."

⁵*I will heal their apostasy.*
I will freely love them,
for my anger has turned from him.

⁶*I will be like the dew to Israel;*
he will blossom like the flower,
and strike his roots like the (tree of) Lebanon.

⁷*His shoots will go out;*
his splendor will be like the olive tree
and his fragrance like the (tree of) Lebanon.

⁸*The inhabitants in his shadow will return;*
they will produce grain.

They will blossom like the vine;
his fame (will be) like the wine of Lebanon.

⁹*Ephraim: "What are idols to me anyore?"*
(YHWH:) "I will have answered and I will watch over him."
(Ephraim:) "I am like a luxuriant Cypress."
(YHWH:) "Your fruit is found from me."

14:2 a שׁוּבָה יִשְׂרָאֵל עַד יְהוָה אֱלֹהֶיךָ
b כִּי כָשַׁלְתָּ בַּעֲוֹנֶךָ׃

Lines a-b are a bicolon. The two lines feature 2ms forms in contrast to 14:3 below, and line b is a causal clause subordinate to the main clause in line a. The lines are marked by *'Atnaḥ* and *Silluq*.

שׁוּבָה יִשְׂרָאֵל עַד יְהוָה אֱלֹהֶיךָ. *Line a.* Independent clause.

שׁוּבָה. Qal impv ms √שׁוב. This is a long form of the imperative with paragogic ־ָה (the short form is שׁוּב). The paragogic ending does not appear to add any particular nuance (JM §48d; WO §34.2.2a). √שׁוב is a favorite word of Hosea, frequently used to refer to repentance (e.g., 2:9; 3:5; 5:4; 6:1; 7:10; 12:7).

יִשְׂרָאֵל. Vocative and addressee of the ms impv שׁוּבָה.

עַד יְהוָה אֱלֹהֶיךָ. This PP is the oblique compl of שׁוּבָה. The more typical preposition with √שׁוב is אֶל (cf. 2:9; 5:4, 15; 7:10; 14:3). √שׁוב + עַד occurs thirteen times in the OT (e.g., Deut 4:30; Joel 2:12; Amos 4:6-11). It is difficult to determine the precise nuance vis-à-vis אֶל, but it apparently marks some semantic difference. It may suggest "slowly but surely," a sense of deliberation and seriousness (Macintosh 2014:560) or the emphasis on the action rather than the direction of √שוב (McComiskey 2009:229).

כִּי כָשַׁלְתָּ בַּעֲוֹנֶךָ. *Line b.* Subordinate causal clause with כִּי, giving the reason that Israel should repent. AF (642) understand this as a concessive clause ("although"; cf. JM §171a). However, repentance is not called for *in spite of* rebellion, but in *response to* rebellion. Israel has stumbled and that is the reason they should now turn to YHWH.

כָשַׁלְתָּ. Qal *qatal* 2ms √כשל. This verb refers to tripping or stumbling, often as a result of sin (cf. 4:5; 5:5). The *qatal* conjugation represents the action as completed. They are not being invited to repent in order to avoid destruction, it is too late for that. The doom of chapter 13 has already taken place (or is envisioned as having already taken place), and now they have the opportunity to become the people of YHWH once more.

בַּעֲוֹנֶךָ. Adjunct PP with a בְּ of specification qualifying the realm of the verbal action (cf. WO §11.2.5e). The sense is that it will be their "iniquity" that trips them up and causes them to stumble (cf. 5:5).

14:3 a קְחוּ עִמָּכֶם דְּבָרִים
b וְשׁוּבוּ אֶל־יְהוָה
c אִמְרוּ אֵלָיו
d כָּל־תִּשָּׂא עָוֹן
e וְקַח־טוֹב
f וּנְשַׁלְּמָה פָרִים שְׂפָתֵינוּ׃

Lines a-c are a tricolon, with a plural imperative beginning each line. The lines present a set of progressive instructions: the people should take words (line a), return to YHWH (line b), and speak to him (line c). The lines are marked by *Zaqep parvum*, *'Atnaḥ*, and *Rᵉbiaʿ*. The verb √אמר in line c introduces direct speech in 14:3d-f and 14:4a-d, in which the prophet provides the people with words of confession. AF (645) note that the supplied prayer consists of seven lines: three positive (14:3d-f), three negative (14:4a-c), and a conclusion (14:4d). In this verse lines d-f are a tricolon. Lines d-e consists of instructions/requests with a *yiqtol* (תִּשָּׂא)

and imperative (קַח). Line f is the conclusion. The lines are marked by *Pašṭa*, *Zaqep parvum*, and *Silluq*.

קְחוּ עִמָּכֶם דְּבָרִים. *Line a.* Independent clause.

קְחוּ. Qal impv mp √לקח. After beginning the unit with a a singular imperative addressing the nation Israel in 14:2, the prophet changes to plural imperatives in this verse as he addresses the people.

עִמָּכֶם. PP with עִם indicating accompaniment. The antecedent of the 2mp suffix is the people of Israel, addressed by the imperative verbs.

דְּבָרִים. Acc compl of קְחוּ. The content of the "words" that they are to take to YHWH are given in lines d and following.

וְשׁוּבוּ אֶל־יְהוָה. *Line b.* Independent clause.

וְשׁוּבוּ. Qal impv mp √שׁוב. This is a common word in Hosea, used to refer to repentance (see 14:2a).

אֶל־יְהוָה. Oblique compl of שׁוּבוּ. See 14:2a.

אִמְרוּ אֵלָיו. *Line c.* Independent clause.

אִמְרוּ. Qal impv mp √אמר.

אֵלָיו. Adjunct PP with אֶל indicating the addressee of the speech. The antecedent of the 3ms suffix is יְהוָה (line b).

כָּל־תִּשָּׂא עָוֹן. *Line d.* Independent clause.

כָּל ... עָוֹן. This is a broken construct phrase which is interrupted by the verb תִּשָּׂא. Typically, no element except for an article can occur between the bound form and the genitive, but there are exceptions (cf. GKC §128e; WO §9.3d; Blommerde 1974). Hosea also uses a broken construct phrase in 6:9, (possibly in 8:2), and 14:8. Freedman (1972:536) argues that the unusual wording draws particular attention to כָּל: the expectation is that *all* iniquity will be forgiven. כָּל is the accusative complement of תִּשָּׂא.

תִּשָּׂא. Qal *yiqtol* (irrealis) 2ms √נשא. The irrealis *yiqtol* is identified by the parallel with the imperative קַח in line e. It is used as a volative, expressing a request or even a command: this is what the speaker wants YHWH to do. √נשא is used in a number of passages in the OT to denote forgiveness and the removal of guilt (e.g., Lev 10:18; Isa 2:9).

וְקַח־טוֹב. *Line e.* Independent clause.

וְקַח. Qal impv ms √לקח. On the morphology of this verb, see line a. The ms form is addressed to YHWH. √לקח here has the sense of "accept" or "receive."

טוֹב. Acc compl of קַח. This substantival adjective meaning "what is good" refers to that which is pleasing to YHWH. In the context of שְׂפָתֵינוּ ("our lips") in line c, which is a metonymy for speech, the טוֹב is their humility, contrition, and words of repentance.

וּנְשַׁלְּמָה פָרִים שְׂפָתֵינוּ. *Line f.* Independent clause.

וּנְשַׁלְּמָה. Piel juss (cohortative) 1cp √שלם. The cohortative connected by a וְ copulative to the preceding imperative קַח expresses intention or logical consequence (GKC §108d). Here the people (as projected by Hosea) have decided to render what is due. The verb √שלם refers to paying or repaying what is owed.

פָרִים שְׂפָתֵינוּ. The noun פָּרִים is the acc compl of נְשַׁלְּמָה. It is usually understood in one of two ways. First, we could understand it as from the word פַּר ("bull"). O'Callaghan (1954:170) argues that it is a mp construct form (cf. Jer 50:27) with an enclitic מ. The enclitic מ is well known in Ugaritic literature and sometimes occurs in the midst of a construct phrase. The translation would be "we will render the bulls of our lips." McComiskey (2009:230) understands the plural absolute form פָּרִים as an adverbial accusative ("we will render, as bulls, our lips"). It may also be that שְׂפָתֵינוּ is in apposition to פָּרִים, giving the translation, "we will render bulls, that is, our lips" (cf. Ehrlich and Orlinsky 1969:393). Identifying פָּרִים as "bull" or "bulls" would mean that people are giving YHWH their prayer of confession and true repentance rather than traditional animal sacrifices. This would reflect statements such as those in 1 Sam 15:22; Ps 51:19; or Mic 6:6-8—that faith and fidelity is superior to ritual obligation. The people would be saying to YHWH, "Our penitential prayers are the 'bulls' that you really want." A second option is to understand פָּרִים as the noun פְּרִי ("fruit") with an enclitic מ and translate, "we will render the fruit of our lips" (cf. Gordis 1955:89). This "fruit" would be symbolic of their vows and words of confession, which are delightful to YHWH. Although this would require a revocalization of the MT (to פִּרִים), there are three points in favor of this interpretation. First, there are a number of passages in the OT in which "fruit" is used in a similar way to denote words (e.g., Isa 57:19; Prov 12:14; 18:20). Second, this is the way that G (καρπὸν χειλέων ἡμῶν, "the fruit of our lips") and S understand the clause. Third, the book has described the people's drive to gain fertility, agriculture, and wealth without submitting to YHWH. In a play on words, this reversal involves giving their "fruit" to YHWH in the form of the humble words he wants to hear.

14:4 a אַשּׁוּר | לֹא יוֹשִׁיעֵנוּ
b עַל־סוּס לֹא נִרְכָּב
c וְלֹא־נֹאמַר עוֹד אֱלֹהֵינוּ לְמַעֲשֵׂה יָדֵינוּ
d אֲשֶׁר־בְּךָ יְרֻחַם יָתוֹם:

The four lines in this verse conclude the prayer of confession that Hosea urges the people to take to YHWH (see 14:3). Lines a-c are a tricolon, indicated by the corresponding negated verbs. Each lines suggest possible means of deliverance that the people should reject due to their renewed trust in YHWH: Assyria (political alliances), horses (military power), and the work of their hands (false gods). The lines are marked by *R^ebi^{a‘}*, *Zaqep parvum*, and *’Atnaḥ*. Line d stands apart and concludes the verse with a *Silluq*. This is admittedly odd. Stuart (1987:210) does not even regard 14:2-4 as poetry. However, it does seem that the verse divides into lines, even though line d remains isolated. As mentioned above in 14:3, the entire prayer suggested by Hosea consists of seven lines: three positive (14:3d-f), three negative (14:4a-c), and 14:4d, which serves as a conclusion (AF 645).

אַשּׁוּר לֹא יוֹשִׁיעֵנוּ. *Line a*. Independent clause.

אַשּׁוּר. Subject of יוֹשִׁיעֵנוּ. Elsewhere in the book, Hosea mentions Assyria as not only a threat but as in competition with YHWH for Israel's trust (5:13; 7:11; 8:9; 12:2). Here, the people of Israel should tell YHWH that they recognize Assyria's inability to save them.

יוֹשִׁיעֵנוּ. Hiph *yiqtol* 3ms √ישע with a 1cp acc suffix. In the context of this (proposed) prayer of confession, the negated *yiqtol* probably has the sense of "cannot save us" (cf. GKC §107w).

עַל־סוּס לֹא נִרְכָּב. *Line b*. Independent clause.

עַל־סוּס. This PP with locative עַל is the oblique complement of נִרְכָּב. The noun סוּס is a collective singular. The "horse" is a metonymy for all of Israel's potential weapons and fortifications in which they have trusted (cf. 8:14; 10:13).

נִרְכָּב. Qal *yiqtol* 1cp √רכב.

וְלֹא־נֹאמַר עוֹד אֱלֹהֵינוּ לְמַעֲשֵׂה יָדֵינוּ. *Line c.* Independent clause.

נֹאמַר. Qal *yiqtol* 1cp √אמר.

עוֹד. Temporal adverb ("still," "again" or negated: "any longer") modifying נֹאמַר.

אֱלֹהֵינוּ. Vocative with a 1cp poss suffix. Hosea 14:3c-4 is direct speech suggested by Hosea, and this statement is direct speech embedded within that. The noun is plural, presumably because it refers to the various images made by Israel to represent Ba'al and possibly other deities (cf. 8:6; 13:2).

לְמַעֲשֵׂה יָדֵינוּ. Adjunct PP with לְ expressing the addressee of the speech. מַעֲשֵׂה is a bound form in construct with יָדֵינוּ. The antecedents of the 1cp poss suffix are the implied speakers among Hosea's audience.

אֲשֶׁר־בְּךָ יְרֻחַם יָתוֹם. *Line d.* This is a particularly difficult clause to make sense of in the discourse. GKC (§158b) suggests that אֲשֶׁר is a shortened form of the causal conjunction יַעַן אֲשֶׁר (e.g., Gen 30:18; 34:13; 1 Kgs 3:19; Zech 1:15; see Holmstedt 2016:376–77). If so, this is a causal clause subordinate to the coordinated independent clauses in lines a-c. The reason that they will forsake all other potential sources of salvation (lines a-c) is that it is YHWH who saves the helpless.

בְּךָ. This PP with בְּ indicates the agent of the passive verb יְרֻחַם. BH usually marks the agent of the passive verb with the prep לְ, but בְּ is sometimes used for personal agents (GKC §121f). JM (§132e) regards the present example as text-critically doubtful but gives no explanation.

יְרֻחַם. Pual *yiqtol* 3ms √רחם. The *yiqtol* is present progressive. YHWH's compassion is ongoing and ever available.

יָתוֹם. Subject of the passive verb יְרֻחַם. The line provides a counterpoint to lines a-c. The rejection of political alliances, military might, and cultic images implies that it is YHWH who *can* save. This clause makes that explicit: the person who is humble and without any self-sufficiency (like an orphan) will find his or her hope in YHWH.

14:5 a אֶרְפָּא מְשׁוּבָתָם
b אֹהֲבֵם נְדָבָה
c כִּי שָׁב אַפִּי מִמֶּנּוּ׃

Hosea 14:5

Lines a-c are a tricolon. The first two lines are parallel with two 1cs verbs (אֹהֲבֵם//אֶרְפָּא) and 3mp suffixes. The third line, a causal clause, is subordinate to lines a and b and serves as the conclusion. The lines are marked by *Zaqep parvum*, *'Atnaḥ*, and *Silluq*.

אֶרְפָּא מְשׁוּבָתָם. *Line a*. Independent clause.

אֶרְפָּא. Qal *yiqtol* 1cs √רפא. The switch to first-person singular verbs in this verse signals that YHWH is now the speaker as presented by the prophet. This is his response to the penitential prayer suggested for Israel in vv. 3-4. The use of this verb ("to heal") implies that Israel's problem (מְשׁוּבָה—apostasy) is a sickness that needs to be cured. In 5:13 Ephraim sees his sickness (חֳלִי) but goes to Assyria in an attempt to be healed (√רפא). But only YHWH can cure him (cf. also 6:1; 7:1; 11:3).

מְשׁוּבָתָם. Acc compl of אֶרְפָּא. The 3mp poss suffix refers to the people of Israel. YHWH's words are presented as a response to the prophet, referring to the people in the third person. In this way Hosea's audience gets an "inside look" at YHWH's deliberations and his decision to respond to their prayer with favor and restoration. The word מְשׁוּבָה ("apostasy") occurs elsewhere in this book in 11:7, where YHWH states that his people are "fixed on apostasy." To this point, the people have been characterized as *incapable* of responding in any other way (cf. 5:4; 7:2; 11:5). Now, YHWH will heal them.

אֹהֲבֵם נְדָבָה. *Line b*. Independent clause.

אֹהֲבֵם. Qal *yiqtol* 1cs √אהב with a 3mp acc suffix. YHWH "loved" (√אהב) Israel when he brought them out of Egypt and founded the nation (11:1). In the future Israel's repentance will result in a restoration of this relationship.

נְדָבָה. Noun ("freewill offering" or "voluntariness") functioning as an adverbial accusative modifying the verb אֹהֲבֵם (cf. GKC §118q; WO §10.2.2c). The sense is that YHWH's love is not contingent upon Israel's actions or effort. Because it is voluntary, it is assured.

כִּי שָׁב אַפִּי מִמֶּנּוּ. *Line c*. Causal clause with כִּי subordinate to the clauses in lines a and b and giving the reason that YHWH will heal and love them. His anger is no longer a barrier.

שָׁב. Qal *qatal* 3ms √שוב. Morphologically, this verb could be a Qal ptc ms, but the context suggests a *qatal*. Although the time of this hypothetical speech is in the future, this line occurs chronologically between Israel's repentance (vv. 3-4) and restoration (v. 5a-b).

אַפִּי. Subject of שָׁב. The antecedent of the 1cs poss suffix is YHWH, the speaker. YHWH has spoken in previous verses about his אַף ("anger") (cf. 8:5; 11:9; 13:11).

מִמֶּנּוּ. Compl PP with abl מִן.

14:6 a אֶהְיֶה כַטַּל לְיִשְׂרָאֵל
     b יִפְרַח כַּשּׁוֹשַׁנָּה
     c וְיַךְ שָׁרָשָׁיו כַּלְּבָנוֹן:

Lines a-c are a tricolon containing three similes introduced by comparative PPs with כְּ. The word יִשְׂרָאֵל, in line a, is the subject of the 3ms *yiqtol* verbs in lines b and c. In line a YHWH is compared to dew. In lines b-c Israel is the object of comparison, with plant imagery ("flourish"//"strike roots"). The lines are marked by *Zaqep parvum*, *'Atnaḥ*, and *Silluq*. This verse explains what is meant by √רפא ("heal") in 14:5a: YHWH will reactivate the fertility and flourishing of the land (cf. 2:18-23).

אֶהְיֶה כַטַּל לְיִשְׂרָאֵל. *Line a*. Independent clause.

אֶהְיֶה. Qal *yiqtol* 1cs √היה. The subject is YHWH, the speaker in vv. 5-8.

כַטַּל. This PP with כְּ indicating agreement in kind is the complement of אֶהְיֶה. In two previous occurrences in the book (6:4; 13:3), טַל ("dew") is an image for that which is ephemeral and temporary. Here, however, it is an image of conditions favorable to agricultural.

לְיִשְׂרָאֵל. Adjunct PP with לְ of interest (WO §11.2.10d).

יִפְרַח כַּשּׁוֹשַׁנָּה. *Line b*. Independent clause.

יִפְרַח. Qal *yiqtol* 3ms √פרח. This verb refers to the sprouting, budding, or flowering of a plant (cf. 10:4; 14:8). In 10:4 it was Israel's corruption and (in)justice that sprouted; now they will flower like a beautiful plant. The 3ms subject is יִשְׂרָאֵל, found at the end of the previous line.

כַּשּׁוֹשַׁנָּה. Adjunct PP with כְּ indicating agreement in kind. The noun שׁוֹשַׁנָּה occurs seventeen times in the OT, with the greatest concentration in Song of Songs (8×) where it is used as an image of luxuriant plants in a lush garden. It probably refers to a flower with large blossoms such as the iris or the tulip (see Dalman 1928:357–66).

וְיַךְ שָׁרָשָׁיו כַּלְּבָנוֹן. *Line c*. Independent clause.

וְיַךְ. Hiph (apocopated) *yiqtol* 3ms √נכה. The usual indicative *yiqtol* form of √נכה is יַכֶּה. This apocopated form is normally that of the jussive, which we would translate "let him strike," or a past tense *wayyiqtol*. However, the context dictates that this must be an indicative verb in the future (see also וִיהִי in 14:7). √נכה is used elsewhere of thrusting a fork into a pot (1 Sam 2:14) or a spear into a wall (1 Sam 19:10). That is the idea here: Israel will thrust his roots into the ground.

שָׁרָשָׁיו. Acc compl of יַךְ. The antecedent of the 3ms poss suffix is Israel (cf. line a).

כַּלְּבָנוֹן. Adjunct PP with כְּ indicating agreement in kind. לְבָנוֹן refers to the northern neighbor of Israel, "Lebanon," known for its great trees (1 Kgs 5:13-28; Ps 29:5). Here, it is used as metonymy for those trees, and means, "like the tree of Lebanon."

14:7 a יֵלְכוּ֙ יֹנְקוֹתָ֔יו
b וִיהִ֥י כַזַּ֖יִת הוֹד֑וֹ
c וְרֵ֥יחַֽ ל֖וֹ כַּלְּבָנֽוֹן׃

Lines a-c are a tricolon, the third in a sequence in YHWH's speech (vv. 5-8). Line a serves as an introduction, while lines b-c are parallel, as seen in the ellipsis of the verb וִיהִי, which governs both lines. All three lines are tied together via the 3ms poss suffix and the imagery of Israel as a tree, continued from 14:6. Stuart (1987:216) observes that each line in this verse describes a different desirable aspect of the metaphorical tree: in line a the tree is stable (יֹנְקוֹת, "shoots"), in line b it is visually impressive (הוֹד, "splendor"), and in line c the tree is fragrant (רֵיחַ). The lines are marked by *Zaqqep parvum*, *'Atnaḥ*, and *Silluq*.

יֵלְכוּ יֹנְקוֹתָיו. *Line a*. Independent clause.

יֵלְכוּ. Qal *yiqtol* 3mp √הלך. In the context of plant imagery, √הלך means "to spread out" or "to grow." With indicative verbs (see on וִיהִי below), we would expect SV word order, but the verbs in lines a and b are fronted for topicalization. There is a dynamic aspect to the imagery: the metaphorical tree is growing and flourishing.

יֹנְקוֹתָיו. Subject of יֵלְכוּ. The noun is feminine, whereas the verb יֵלְכוּ is masculine. This lack of agreement leads AF (646) to suggest that the subject is actually the masculine שָׁרָשָׁיו from 14:6c. However, it is common for biblical authors to default to a mp verb with a feminine subject, especially when the verb precedes the subject, as it does here (cf. JM §150b). The noun יוֹנֶקֶת refers to shoots or tendrils that spread out (cf. Job 8:16; Ps 80:12). The antecedent of the 3ms poss suffix is Israel (cf. 14:6a).

וִיהִי כַזַּיִת הוֹדוֹ. *Line b.* Independent clause.

וִיהִי. Qal (apocopated) *yiqtol* 3ms √היה. The apocopated form is usually used of the jussive or the *wayyiqtol*. However, the context dictates that this must be an indicative referring to the future. The prophet also uses a short form for an imperfect indicative in 14:6 (וְיַךְ).

כַזַּיִת. This PP with כְּ indicating agreement in kind is the complement of וִיהִי.

הוֹדוֹ. Subject of וִיהִי. The antecedent of the 3ms poss suffix is again "Israel."

וְרֵיחַ לוֹ כַּלְּבָנוֹן. *Line c.* Independent clause. The verb וִיהִי is elided. This line is very similar to the last clause of Song 4:11 which states, וְרֵיחַ שַׂלְמֹתַיִךְ כְּרֵיחַ לְבָנוֹן ("and the fragrance of your garments is like the fragrance of Lebanon").

וְרֵיחַ. Subject of the elided verb וִיהִי.

לוֹ. Adjunct PP with לְ indicating possession. The antecedent of the 3ms suffix is again Israel.

כַּלְּבָנוֹן. This PP with כְּ indicating agreement in kind is the complement of the elided verb וִיהִי (see line b). The word לְבָנוֹן ("Lebanon") is again used as a metonymy for the trees of Lebanon (see 14:6c).

14:8 a יָשֻׁבוּ יֹשְׁבֵי בְצִלּוֹ
b יְחַיּוּ דָגָן
c וְיִפְרְחוּ כַגָּפֶן
d זִכְרוֹ כְּיֵין לְבָנוֹן: ס

Lines a–d are a quatrain. Lines a and d continue 3ms references (בְצִלּוֹ and זִכְרוֹ) to Israel (the tree; cf. vv. 6–7). The rest of the verse (esp. lines b and c) uses 3mp references to describe the people of YHWH who will find shelter and flourish in relationship to Israel because YHWH

Hosea 14:8

will have restored them. The lines are marked by *Zaqep parvum*, *Tipḥa*, *'Atnaḥ*, and *Silluq*.

יֵשְׁבוּ יֹשְׁבֵי בְצִלּוֹ. *Line a*. Independent clause.

יֵשְׁבוּ. Qal *yiqtol* 3mp √שוב.

יֹשְׁבֵי בְצִלּוֹ. The construct form is a Qal ptc mp √ישב. This substantival participle is the subject of יֵשְׁבוּ. It refers to the people of Israel, mentioned by YHWH in 14:5 at the beginning of his speech. בְצִלּוֹ, the genitive, is a PP with locative בְּ. This is another example of a "broken" construct chain. Normally, only the article can intervene between the construct form and the genitive. However, there are exceptions (see the discussion and references at 6:9 and 14:3). A number of scholars and versions (including the NRSV and ESV) emend the 3ms poss suffix on צִלּוֹ to 1cs and read בְצִלִּי ("my shadow"; see BHS note ᵇ). This is motivated by the fact that YHWH is speaking in this section (vv. 5-8), that he compares himself to a tree in the following verse (14:9), and that elsewhere in the OT he is said to give shade (e.g., Ps 91:1). However, there is no textual evidence for this reading; the versions support the MT. Furthermore, Israel is compared to a tree in vv. 6-7, and it makes more sense for the antecedent of the suffix to refer back to that metaphor already in progress than to anticipate the comparison between YHWH and a tree in the following verse. The 3ms and 3mp forms alternate in this unit (see the unit introduction) and 3ms forms create an inclusio around this particular verse.

יְחַיּוּ דָגָן. *Line b*. Independent clause.

יְחַיּוּ. Piel *yiqtol* 3mp √חיה. In the Qal this verb means "to be alive," whereas in the Piel it is factitive and means "to preserve alive" or "to bring to life" (cf. Hos 6:2). This latter sense is used in some passages of producing offspring (e.g., Gen 7:3; 19:34). In the present passage it similarly refers to producing a crop. The subject of this verb are the inhabitants of Israel (see line a).

דָגָן. Acc compl of יְחַיּוּ.

וְיִפְרְחוּ כַגֶּפֶן. *Line c*. Independent clause.

וְיִפְרְחוּ. Qal *yiqtol* 3mp √פרח. See 10:4d; 14:6b.

כַגֶּפֶן. Adjunct PP with כְּ indicating agreement in kind. In 2:14 YHWH says that he will destroy Israel's vines. In 10:1 Israel is compared to a luxuriant vine that uses its strength to apostatize. Now, YHWH will cause his people to flourish like a vine. The vine is a common metaphor in the OT for health, desirability, and productivity.

זִכְרוֹ כְּיֵין לְבָנוֹן. *Line d*. Independent verbless clause. In this line, the metaphors are mixed: Israel the tree (vv. 6-8a) will have fame like the wine of Lebanon.

זִכְרוֹ. Subject of the verbless clause. The noun זֵכֶר refers to what is known or remembered about someone or something. Here it refers to Israel's reputation. The antecedent of the 3ms poss suffix is "Israel" (cf. 14:6a), picked up from line a.

כְּיֵין לְבָנוֹן. This PP with כְּ indicating agreement in kind is the predicate of the verbless clause. יֵין לְבָנוֹן is a construct phrase. This is the third verse in a row that ends in לְבָנוֹן ("Lebanon") (see 14:6c, 7c).

14:9 a אֶפְרַיִם מַה־לִּי עוֹד לָעֲצַבִּים
b אֲנִי עָנִיתִי וַאֲשׁוּרֶנּוּ
c אֲנִי כִּבְרוֹשׁ רַעֲנָן
d מִמֶּנִּי פֶּרְיְךָ נִמְצָא׃

Lines a-d are a quatrain. Each line contains at least one first-person form, distinguishing this verse from the immediate context. The major question in this verse is the identity of the speaker or speakers. Initially, we might assume that YHWH is the speaker in the entire verse (continuing his speech from vv. 6-8) (see Wolff 1974:233; AF 647). However, what would it mean in line a for YHWH to suggest that he no longer had anything to do with idols? Has he *ever* had anything to do with them? It would also be strange for YHWH to be the speaker of line c and to compare himself to a tree. The tree has been a metaphor for Israel in the preceding verses, not YHWH.

Alternatively, we might understand Ephraim as the speaker in the verse. This is the view of S, which represents וְיֹאמַר אֶפְרַיִם ("Ephraim will say") (see BHS note [a]; T also attributes this line to Ephraim). But the problem with this approach is that it makes no sense for Ephraim to speak line d, in which he says, "Your fruit is found from me." That sounds like YHWH's line, since he is the one who grants fertility and agricultural gifts.

אֶפְרַיִם. *Line a.* Macintosh (2014:576–77) argues that the rhetorical question following אֶפְרַיִם has an adjectival force, portraying and describing Ephraim. In this way it is like a *casus pendens*, but it introduces Ephraim's speech and portrays his perspective.

מַה־לִּי עוֹד לָעֲצַבִּים. *Line a.* Independent clause. Direct speech spoken by Ephraim.

לָעֲצַבִּים ... מַה־לִּי. The collocation מָה־לְ ("What is there to …") refers to the effect that a situation or event has on someone. This can be something that is troubling to someone (Gen 21:17), is desired (Josh 15:18), or is a point of conflict (Judg 11:12). It frequently occurs with a second PP with לְ which indicates the potential effect (such as מַה־לִּי וָלָךְ, "What do I have to do with you?" in 1 Kgs 17:18). That is the sense here; the translation is literally "What are idols to me?" Ephraim is stating (via rhetorical question) that he has nothing to do with idols any longer. The word עָצָב ("idol") occurs three times previously in the book (4:17; 8:4; 13:2) to describe the idols that Ephraim makes and serves. Now, he is abandoning them.

עוֹד. Temporal adverb. In Hos 14:4 the prophet suggests words of repentance to the people including the statement: וְלֹא־נֹאמַר עוֹד אֱלֹהֵינוּ לְמַעֲשֵׂה יָדֵינוּ ("We will no *longer* say 'Our gods!' to the work of our hands.") The repetition of עוֹד here signals that the potential has become reality: they will be finished with competing deities.

אֲנִי עָנִיתִי וַאֲשׁוּרֶנּוּ. *Line b.* Direct speech by YHWH. This line consists of two independent clauses.

אֲנִי. 1cs independent pronoun, which frequently signals a change in speaker or topic in discourse (see 4:14c; 6:7a). Its antecedent is YHWH, the speaker.

עָנִיתִי. Qal *qatal* 1cs √ענה. Given that the entire chapter has a future reference, and this verse is a description of eschatological restoration, this *qatal* should be understood as future perfect: "I will have answered (him)." We expect an accusative complement, which is omitted. It is supplied by the suffix on the following verb (see GKC §117f). √ענה (I) means "to answer," but Hosea uses the verb with a special sense here as in 2:23. In that verse YHWH declares that he will √ענה the heavens, which will start a chain-reaction of blessing and restoration of the land. The sense is that of "reactivating" or "rejuvenating" the agricural processes.

Here, it means something similar: YHWH will "respond" to Ephraim by restoring him.

וַאֲשׁוּרֶנּוּ. Qal *yiqtol* 1cs √שׁור with a 3ms (energic) acc suffix. √שׁור means "to behold" or "regard"; here it has the nuance of giving watchful care.

אֲנִי כִּבְרוֹשׁ רַעֲנָן. *Line c*. Independent verbless clause. Direct speech by Ephraim.

אֲנִי. Subject of the verbless clause. In the previous line אֲנִי referred to YHWH; here it refers to Ephraim, a new speaker.

כִּבְרוֹשׁ. This PP with כְּ indicating agreement in kind is the predicate of the verbless clause. A בְּרוֹשׁ is a mighty tree (at least in the area of Palestine). It could be used for building material (e.g., 1 Kgs 6:15; 2 Chr 2:8). Here it represents strength and health.

רַעֲנָן. Attributive adjective modifying בְּרוֹשׁ. The word רַעֲנָן refers to that which is fresh (e.g., Ps 91:11) or luxuriant and thick with leaves (cf. Thomas 1967:395–96).

מִמֶּנִּי פֶּרְיְךָ נִמְצָא. *Line d*. Independent clause. Direct speech by YHWH.

מִמֶּנִּי. Adjunct PP with מִן expressing the source of Ephraim's fruit (פְּרִי) (cf. WO §11.2.11d; WHS §322). The antecedent of the 1cs suffix is YHWH, the speaker in this line.

פֶּרְיְךָ. Subject of the pass verb נִמְצָא. The antecedent of the 2ms suffix is Ephraim, addressed by YHWH. The word פְּרִי (like עָצָב and √ענה) resolves a pattern previously seen in the book. In 9:16 Hosea says that Ephraim will not bear fruit. In 10:1 Ephraim uses its fruit (i.e., wealth) to further its apostasy from YHWH (in an attempt to get even more fruit). Now, in 14:9 YHWH promises that they will get what they desired all along but from the correct source: himself.

נִמְצָא. Niph *qatal* 3ms √מצא.

Epilogue (14:10)

The book concludes with a brief, one-verse epilogue, offering final advice to the reader and urging the careful study of the preceding contents. The five lines consist of terms that are associated with the Israelite wisdom tradition: חָכָם ("wise"), √בין ("to understand"), √ידע ("to know"), יָשָׁר ("upright"), דֶּרֶךְ ("way"), and √כשׁל ("to stumble") as well as the antithesis between the righteous (צַדִּיק) and the transgressor (√פשׁע). These words are common in the prophecies of Hosea, but now they are clustered here in order to make the claim that faithfulness to YHWH and his ways will bring the reader success. This last verse suggests (as does the book as a whole), that the choice is not between success on the one hand and fidelity to YHWH on the other. The choice is between fidelity to YHWH *and* success, or infidelity accompanied by destruction. YHWH does not demand disinterested loyalty. He offers himself as the true way to a life of flourishing.

¹⁰Whoever is wise, let him understand these things;
understanding—let him know them.

For the ways of YHWH are upright
and the righteous walk in them,
but transgressors stumble in them.

14:10 a מִי חָכָם וְיָבֵן אֵלֶּה
b נָבוֹן וְיֵדָעֵם
c כִּי־יְשָׁרִים דַּרְכֵי יְהוָה
d וְצַדִּקִים יֵלְכוּ בָם
e וּפֹשְׁעִים יִכָּשְׁלוּ בָם:

Lines a-b are a bicolon, indicated by ellipsis of the word מִי and the noncopula in line b. There is also semantic correspondence between ידע√//בין√, which are both jussives. The lines are marked by *Zaqep parvum* and *'Atnaḥ*. Lines c-e are a tricolon consisting of an introductory line (c) that is followed by two parallel lines. Lines d and e are linked via two contrasting word pairs (וּפֹשְׁעִים/וְצַדִּקִים and כשל√//הלך√) as well as identical PPs (בָם). The lines are marked by *Rᵉbîᵃʿ*, *Zaqep parvum*, and *Silluq*.

מִי חָכָם. *Line a*. Free-choice relative clause introduced by an מ-relative and translated "whoever is wise—let him understand these things" (Holmstedt 2016:301; cf. WO §18.2e).

וְיָבֵן אֵלֶּה. *Line a*. Independent clause.

וְיָבֵן. Qal juss 3ms בין√. The subject of this verb has the same referent as that of the interrogative pronoun מִי in the previous clause. The jussive expresses volition: the author is urging the wise to grow in even greater understanding.

אֵלֶּה. This plural demonstrative pronoun is the accusative complement of וְיָבֵן. It refers generally to the preceding contents of the book.

נָבוֹן. *Line b*. A relative clause. See the comment on line a above. This Niph ptc ms √בין is used substantively. It is the predicate of the non-copula which is elided in this line (via the parallelism).

וְיֵדָעֵם. *Line b*. Independent clause. The verb is a Qal juss 3ms √ידע with a 3mp acc suffix. The antecedent of the 3mp suffix is אֵלֶּה ("these things") in line a.

כִּי־יְשָׁרִים דַּרְכֵי יְהוָה. *Line c*. Verbless causal clause with כִּי.

יְשָׁרִים. This plural adjective is the predicate of the verbless clause.

דַּרְכֵי יְהוָה. The bound (i.e., constr) form דַּרְכֵי is the subject of the verbless clause. יְהוָה is an adjectival genitive describing the nature and character of the דְּרָכִים ("ways").

וְצַדִּקִים יֵלְכוּ בָם. *Line d*. Independent clause.

וְצַדִּקִים. Substantival adjective and subject of יֵלְכוּ.

יֵלְכוּ. Qal *yiqtol* 3mp √הלך. This indicative *yiqtol* expresses a gnomic present (cf. WO §31.3e). This is a habitual activity with no specific time reference.

בָם. Adjunct PP with locative בְּ. It specifies the domain in which readers will walk (יֵלְכוּ). The antecedent of the 3mp suffix is the דַּרְכֵי יְהוָה ("ways of YHWH") in line c.

וּפֹשְׁעִים יִכָּשְׁלוּ בָם. *Line e*. Independent clause.

פֹּשְׁעִים. Qal ptc mp √פשע used substantivally. It is the subject of יִכָּשְׁלוּ.

יִכָּשְׁלוּ. Niph *yiqtol* 3mp √כשל. The *yiqtol* expresses a present gnomic sense (see line d).

בָם. Adjunct PP with locative בְּ (see line d).

WORKS CITED

Alter, Robert. 2011. *The Art of Biblical Poetry*. 2nd ed. New York: Basic Books.
Andersen, Francis I. 1970. *The Hebrew Verbless Clause in the Pentateuch*. Journal of Biblical Literature Monograph Series. Nashville: Abingdon.
Andersen, Francis I., and David Noel Freedman. 1980. *Hosea*. New York: Doubleday.
Baumgärtel, F. 1961. "Die Formel *'ne'um jahwe.'*" *Zeitscrhift für die alttestamentliche Wissenshaft* 73:277–90.
Berlin, Adele. 1994. *Poetics and Interpretation of Biblical Narrative*. Winona Lake, Ind.: Eisenbrauns.
———. 2008. *The Dynamics of Biblical Parallelism*. Revised and expanded ed. Grand Rapids: Eerdmans.
Blau, Joshua. 1955. "Etymologische Untersuchungen auf Grund des palaestinischen Arabisch." *Vetus Testamentum* 5.4:337–44.
———. 1957. "Über Homonyme und Angeblich Homonyme Wurzeln." *Vetus Testamentum* 7.1:98–102.
Blommerde, A. C. M. 1974. "Broken Construct Chain, Further Examples." *Biblica* 55.4: 549–52.
Brisco, Thomas V. 1998. *Holman Bible Atlas*. Nashville: Broadman & Holman.
Brockelmann, Carl. 1956. *Hebräische Syntax*. Neukirchen: K. Moers.
Brotzman, Ellis R., and Eric J. Tully. 2016. *Old Testament Textual Criticism: A Practical Introduction*. 2nd ed.. Grand Rapids: Baker Academic.
Callaham, Scott N. 2010. *Modality and the Biblical Hebrew Infinitive Absolute*. Wiesbaden: Harrassowitz Verlag.
Cathcart, Kevin J., and Robert P. Gordon. 1989. *The Targum of the Minor Prophets*. Aramaic Bible. Wilmington, Del.: Michael Glazier.

Comrie, Bernard. 1976. *Aspect: An Introduction to the Study of Verbal Aspect and Related Problems*. Cambridge: Cambridge University Press.

Conklin, Blane. 2011. *Oath Formulas in Biblical Hebrew*. Winona Lake, Ind.: Eisenbrauns.

Cook, John A. 2006. "The Finite Verbal Forms in Biblical Hebrew Do Express Aspect." *Journal of the Ancient Near Eastern Society* 30:21–35.

———. 2008. "The Hebrew Participle and Stative Typological Perspective." *Journal of Northwest Semitic Languages* 34.1:1–19.

———. 2012. *Time and the Biblical Hebrew Verb: The Expression of Tense, Aspect, and Modality in Biblical Hebrew*. Linguistic Studies in Ancient West Semitic 7. Winona Lake, Ind.: Eisenbrauns.

———. 2013. "The Verb in Qohelet." Pages 309–42 in *The Words of the Wise Are Like Goads: Engaging Qoheleth in the 21st Century*. Edited by Mark J. Boda, Tremper Longman, and Cristian G. Rata. Winona Lake, Ind.: Eisenbrauns.

———. 2017. Personal email exchange, February 17–24.

Dalman, Gustaf. 1928. *Arbeit Und Sitte in Palastina*. Vol. 1/2. Hildesheim: Georg Olms.

Dearman, J. Andrew. 2010. *The Book of Hosea*. NICOT. Grand Rapids: Eerdmans.

Dewrell, Heath D. 2016. "Yareb, Shalman, and the Date of the Book of Hosea." *Catholic Biblical Quarterly* 78.3:413–29.

Dobbs-Allsopp, F. W. 2015. *On Biblical Poetry*. New York: Oxford University Press.

Driver, G. R. 1950. "Difficult Words in the Hebrew Prophets." Pages 52–72 in *Studies in Old Testament Prophecy*. Edited by H. H. Rowley. Edinburgh: T&T Clark.

Ehrlich, Arnold Bogumil, and Harry M Orlinsky. 1969. *Mikra Ki-Pheshuto: The Bible according to Its Literal Meaning in Three Volumes*. New York: Ktav.

Emmerson, Grace I. 1975. "Structure and Meaning of Hosea 8:1-3." *Vetus Testamentum* 25.4:700–710.

Englander, Henry. 1942. "A Commentary on Rashi's Grammatical Comments." *Hebrew Union College Annual* 17:427–98.

Eslinger, Lyle M. 1980. "Hosea 12:5a and Genesis 32:29: A Study in Inner Biblical Exegesis." *Journal for the Study of the Old Testament* 18:91–99.

Fisher, Eugene J. 1976. "Cultic Prostitution in the Ancient Near East: a Reassessment." *Biblical Theology Bulletin* 6.2:225–36.

Fokkelman, J. P. 2001. *Reading Biblical Poetry: An Introductory Guide*. Translated by Ineke Smit. Louisville, Ky.: Westminster John Knox.

Freedman, David Noel. 1972. "The Broken Construct Chain." *Biblica* 53.4:534–36.

Freedman, David Noel, James A. Sanders, Marilyn J. Lundberg, Astrid B. Beck, and Bruce E. Zuckerman, eds. 1998. *The Leningrad Codex: A Facsimile Edition*. Grand Rapids: Eerdmans.

Garrett, Duane A. 1997. *Hosea, Joel*. The New American Commentary. Nashville: Broadman & Holman.

Gelston, Anthony. 1980. *The Old Testament in Syriac/ Pt. 3, Fasc. 4, Dodekapropheton-Daniel-Bel-Draco*. Leiden: Brill.

———. 2010. *Biblia Hebraica Quinta: The Twelve Minor Prophets*. Stuttgart: Deutsche Bibelgesellschaft.

Gevirtz, Stanley. 1973. *Patterns in the Early Poetry of Israel*. Chicago: University of Chicago.

Glenny, W. Edward. 2013. *Hosea: A Commentary Based on Hosea in Codex Vaticanus*. Boston: Brill.

Gordis, Robert. 1955. "Text and Meaning of Hosea 14:3." *Vetus Testamentum* 5.1:88–90.

———. 1971. "Quotations in Biblical, Oriental, and Rabbinic Literature." Pages 104–59 in *Poets, Prophets, and Sages: Essays in Biblical Interpretation*. Bloomington: Indiana University Press.

Gordon, Cyrus H. 1965. *Ugaritic Textbook*. Rome: Pontifical Biblical Institute.

Gruber, Mayer I. 1986. "Hebrew *qedešah* and Her Canaanite and Akkadian Cognates." *Ugarit-Forschungen* 18:133–48.

Holladay, William L. 1966. "Chiasmus, the Key to Hosea XII 3-6." *Vetus Testamentum* 16:53–64.

Holmstedt, Robert D. 2005. "Word Order in the Book of Proverbs." Pages 135–54 in *Seeking Out the Wisdom of the Ancients: Essays Offered to Honor Michael V. Fox on the Occasion of His Sixty-Fifth Birthday*. Winona Lake, Ind.: Eisenbrauns.

———. 2009. "Word Order and Information Structure in Ruth and Jonah: A Generative Typological Analysis." *Journal of Semitic Studies* 54.1:111–39.

———. 2010. *Ruth: a Handbook on the Hebrew Text*. Waco, Tex.: Baylor University Press.

———. 2011. "The Typological Classification of the Hebrew of Genesis: Subject-Verb or Verb-Subject?" *Journal of the Hebrew Scriptures* 11.14:2–39.

———. 2016. *The Relative Clause in Biblical Hebrew*. Winona Lake, Ind.: Eisenbrauns.

Holmstedt, Robert D., and Andrew R. Jones. 2014. "The Pronoun in Tripartite Verbless Clauses in Biblical Hebrew: Resumption for Left-dislocation or Pronominal Copula?" *Journal of Semitic Studies* 59.1:53–89.

Holtz, Shalom E. 2012. "Why Are the Sins of Ephraim (Hos 13,12) and Job (Job 14,17) Bundled?" *Biblica* 93.1:107–15.

Hutton, Jeremy M., and Safwat Marzouk. 2012. "The Morphology of the tG-Stem in Hebrew and *Tirgaltî* in Hos 11:3." *Journal of Hebrew Scriptures* 12. DOI:10.5508/jhs.2012.v12.a9.

Jenni, Ernst. 1968. *Das hebräische Pi'el: Syntaktisch-semasiologische Untersuchung einer Verbalform im Alten Testament*. Zurich: EVZ.

Kaiser, Walter C. 1985. "Inner Biblical Exegesis as a Model for Bridging the 'Then' and 'Now' Gap: Hos 12:1-6." *Journal of the Evangelical Theological Society* 28.1:33–46.

Keil, C. F., and F. Delitzsch, eds. 1977. *Minor Prophets. Commentary on the Old Testament*. Grand Rapids: Eerdmans.

Kelley, Page H., Daniel S. Mynatt, and Timothy G. Crawford. 1998. *The Masorah of Biblia Hebraica Stuttgartensia: Introduction and Annotated Glossary*. Grand Rapids: Eerdmans.

König, Eduard. 1897. *Historisch-kritisches Lehrgebäude der hebräischen Sprache*. Leipzig: J. C. Hinrichs'sche Buchhandlung.

Kugel, James L. 1980. "The Adverbial Use of KÎ ṬÔB." *Journal of Biblical Literature* 99:433–35.

———. 1981. *The Idea of Biblical Poetry: Parallelism and Its History*. New Haven: Yale University Press.

Kuhnigk, Willibald. 1974. *Nordwestsemitische Studien zum Hoseabuch*. Rome: Pontifical Biblical Institute.

Lemaire, Andre. 2005. "Éssai D'interprétation Historique D'une Nouvelle Inscription Monumentale Moabite." *CRAIBL* 149.1:95–108.

Lipinski, Edward. 2014. "Cult Prostitition in Ancient Israel?" *Biblical Archaeology Review* 40.1:48–56, 70.

MacDonald, John. 1964. "The Particle את in Classical Hebrew: Some New Data on Its Use with the Nominative." *Vetus Testamentum* 14.3:264–75.

Macintosh, A. A. 2014. *A Critical and Exegetical Commentary on Hosea*. Edinburgh: T&T Clark. Originally published 1997.

Mauchline, John. 1956. "Hosea." Pages 553–725 in *The Interpreter's Bible*. Vol. 6. Nashville: Abingdon.

Mays, James Luther. 1969. *Hosea: A Commentary*. Old Testament Library. London: SCM Press.

McComiskey, Thomas Edward. 1993. "Prophetic Irony in Hosea 1.4: A Study of the Collocation pqd 'l and Its Implications for the Fall of Jehu's Dynasty." *Journal for the Study of the Old Testament* 58:93–101.

———. 2009. "Hosea." In *The Minor Prophets: An Exegetical and Expository Commentary*. Edited by Thomas Edward McComiskey. Grand Rapids: Baker. Originally published 1992.

McKenzie, John L. 1955. "Divine Passion in Osee." *Catholic Biblical Quarterly* 17.2:287–99.

McKenzie, Steven L. 1986. "The Jacob Tradition in Hosea XII 4-5." *Vetus Testamentum* 36.3:311–22.

Miller, Cynthia L. 2003. "A Linguistic Approach to Ellipsis in Biblical Poetry (Or, What to Do When Exegesis of What Is There Depends on What Isn't)." *Bulletin for Biblical Research* 13.2:251–70.

———. 2005. "Ellipsis Involving Negation in Biblical Poetry." Pages 37–52 in *Seeking out the Wisdom of the Ancients: Essays Offered to Honor Michael V. Fox on the Occasion of His Sixty-Fifth Birthday*. Winona Lake, Ind: Eisenbrauns.

Morgan, G. Campbell. n.d. *Hosea: The Heart and Holiness of God*. London: Marshall, Morgan & Scott.

Moshavi, Adina. 2010. *Word Order in the Biblical Hebrew Finite Clause*. Winona Lake, Ind: Eisenbrauns.

Muraoka, T. 1999. "The Tripartite Nominal Clause Revisited." Pages 187–214 in *The Verbless Clause in Biblical Hebrew: Linguistic Approaches*. Edited by Cynthia Miller. Winona Lake, Ind.: Eisenbrauns.

Nyberg, Henrik Samuel. 1935. *Studien Zum Hoseabuch*. Uppsala: A.B. Lundequistska Bokhandeln.

O'Callaghan, Roger T. 1954. "Echoes of Canaanite Literature in the Psalms." *Vetus Testamentum* 4.2:164–76.

O'Connor, Michael. 1987. "The Pseudosorites: A Type of Paradox in Hebrew Verse." Pages 161–72 in *Directions in Biblical Hebrew Poetry*. JSOTSup 40. Edited by Elaine R. Follis. Sheffield: Sheffield Academic.

Patterson, Richard D. 2010. "An Overlooked Scriptural Paradox: the Pseudosorites." *Journal of the Evangelical Theological Society* 53.1:19–36.

Pope, Marvin H. 1953. "'Pleonastic *Waw* before Nouns in Ugaritic and Hebrew." *Journal of the American Oriental Society* 73.2:95–98.

———. 1977. *Song of Songs*. Garden City, N.Y.: Doubleday.

Rashi. 1951. מקראות גדולות עם ל«ב פירושים. New York: Pardes.

Ratner, Robert J. 1983. "Gender Problems in Biblical Hebrew." Ph.D. diss., Hebrew Union College-Jewish Institute of Religion.

Robar, Elizabeth. 2015. *The Verb and the Paragraph in Biblical Hebrew: A Cognitive-Linguistic Approach*. Leiden: Brill.

Rudolph, Wilhelm. 1966. *Hosea*. KAT 13/1. Gütershloh: Gerg Mohn.

Saydon, P. P. 1964. "Meanings and Uses of the Particle את." *Vetus Testamentum* 14.2:192–210.

Scott, R. B. Y. 1952. "Meteorological Phenomena and Terminology in the Old Testament." *Zeitschrift für die alttestamentliche Wissenschaft* 64.1:11–25.

Screnock, John, and Robert D. Holmstedt. 2015. *Esther: A Handbook on the Hebrew Text*. Waco, Tex.: Baylor University Press.

Sivan, Daniel, and William M Schniedewind. 1993. "Letting Your 'Yes' Be 'No' in Ancient Israel: A Study of the Asseverative L' and Hal'o." *Journal of Semitic Studies* 38.2:209–26.

Sperber, Alexander, ed. 2004. *The Bible in Aramaic*. Leiden: Brill.

Stuart, Douglas K. 1987. *Hosea-Jonah*. Word Biblical Commentary. Waco, Tex.: Thomas Nelson.

Testuz, M. 1955. "Deux Fragments Inedits Des Manuscripts de La Mer Morte." *Semitica* 5: 37–39.

Thomas, David Winton. 1967. "Some Observations on the Hebrew Word Ra'eanan." Pages 287–97 in *Hebräische Wortforschung; Festschrift Zum 80 Geburtstag von Walter Baumgartner*. Leiden: Brill.

Tully, Eric J. 2015. *The Translation and Translator of the Peshitta of Hosea*. Leiden: Brill.

Ulrich, Eugene C. 2013. *The Biblical Qumran Scrolls: Transcriptions and Textual Variants*. Leiden: Brill.

Vuillenmier-Bessard, R. 1958. "Osée 13:12 et Les Manuscrits." *RevQ* 1:281–82.
Waltke, Bruce, and M. O'Connor. 1990. *An Introduction to Biblical Hebrew Syntax*. Winona Lake, Ind.: Eisenbrauns.
Watson, Wilfred G. E. 1984. "Reflexes of Akkadian Incantations in Hosea." *Vetus Testamentum* 34.2:242–47.
———. 1986. *Classical Hebrew Poetry: A Guide to Its Techniques*. Sheffield: JSOT Press.
Weber, Robert, et al., eds. 2007. *Biblia Sacra: Iuxta Vulgatam Versionem*. Ed. altera emendata. Stuttgart: Deutsche Bibelgesellschaft.
Wernberg-Møller, P. 1959. "Observations on the Hebrew Participle." *Zeitschrift für die alttestamentliche Wissenschaft* 71:54–67.
———. 1988. "The Old Accusative Ending in Biblical Hebrew: Observations on הַמָּוְתָה in Ps. 116:15." *Journal of Semitic Studies* 33:155–64.
Wolff, Hans Walter. 1974. *Hosea: a Commentary on the Book of the Prophet Hosea*. Hermeneia. Philadelphia: Fortress.
Yamauchi, Edwin M. 1973. "Cultic Prostitition: A Case Study in Cultural Diffusion." Pages 213–22 in *Orient and Occident: Essays Presented to Cyrus H; Gordon on the Occasion of his Sixty-Fifth Birthday*. Kevelaer: Verl Butzon & Bercker.
Yeivin, Israel. 1980. *Introduction to the Tiberian Masorah*. Masoretic Studies 5. Missoula, Mont. Scholars.
Ziegler, Joseph, ed. 1984. *Duodecim prophetae*. Septuaginta: Vetus Testamentum Graecum. Göttingen: Vandenhoeck & Ruprecht.

INDEX OF LINGUISTIC ISSUES

accent (masoretic), 12–13, 28–29, 48–49, 56, 70, 85, 88, 91, 93–94, 97, 107, 109, 137, 143, 153, 158, 160, 190, 192, 195, 209, 243, 247, 262, 272, 278, 302, 309, 334
accusative, 6, 24, 39, 43–46, 51–53, 55, 60, 72–75, 79, 87, 90, 93–94, 101, 105, 107–8, 117, 123, 130–31, 133, 135, 144, 153, 161, 171, 184, 187, 193, 200, 203, 224, 229, 238, 247, 255, 258–61, 272–74, 277, 279, 285, 291, 294, 298, 300–301, 304, 309–10, 315, 321, 328, 342, 345, 351, 354, 361
adjective, adjectival, 6, 10, 21, 24, 32–34, 39, 44, 73, 96, 122, 127–28, 143, 148, 159, 162–63, 165, 170, 178, 194, 196, 200, 204, 208, 210, 213, 217–18, 229, 237–38, 256, 263, 273, 282, 290, 301, 306, 324, 329, 331, 337, 342, 351–52, 354
adjunct, 5–6, 11, 16, 21, 23, 33, 46, 55, 61, 63, 70, 75, 81, 91, 109, 117, 120, 122, 139–40, 147, 151, 158–59, 163, 166–67, 170–71, 174–78, 188–89, 211, 213–14, 220, 234, 243–45, 247, 250, 253, 255, 258, 263, 265, 282, 285, 292–93, 304–5, 307–10, 315, 320–21, 328–31, 340–41, 344, 346–49, 352, 354
adverb, adverbial, 6, 24, 26–27, 33, 39, 42, 48–49, 57–61, 63, 70, 73–74, 78–80, 84, 86–87, 98, 106, 117, 123, 137, 143–44, 146–47, 150, 155, 160, 162, 187, 189, 193, 195, 197–98, 202, 219–20, 226, 230, 239–41, 252, 264, 270, 279, 281–82, 290–91, 298, 300, 302, 304, 310, 316, 318–19, 322, 324, 331, 342, 344–45, 351
adversative, 27, 73, 226, 240
agreement, 32, 39, 42, 62, 105, 127, 132–33, 139, 143, 145, 148, 159, 162–63, 170–72, 178, 181, 193, 195, 200, 207, 220, 222, 225, 242–44,

248, 263, 273, 280, 283, 285, 291, 293–94, 304, 307–8, 318–19, 323–24, 335, 337, 346–50, 352
Akkadian, 321
apodosis, 71, 90, 149, 193, 199–200, 226, 254
appositive, apposition, 18, 23, 29, 40–41, 75, 128, 148, 169–70, 183, 218, 246–47, 249, 253, 262, 265, 273, 280, 282, 299, 304, 323–24, 334–36, 342
Arabic, 129, 167, 191, 228, 237, 321
Aramaic, Aramaism, 263, 271
article, 6, 25, 73, 86–88, 103, 114, 124, 143, 147, 149, 154, 159, 163, 217, 225, 241, 271, 319, 333, 341, 349
aspect, aspectual, 8–10, 32, 42, 55, 121, 163, 242, 264, 270, 290, 292, 322, 328
asseverative, 27, 34, 40, 84, 105, 113, 117, 122, 149, 161, 190–92, 212, 226, 230, 240, 244, 253, 275, 284, 302, 306, 325, 334
assimilation, 23, 39, 45, 49, 72, 91, 212, 254, 263, 271, 274, 318
attribution, attributive, 25, 33, 44, 71, 73, 114, 122, 138–39, 143, 159, 165, 170, 178, 196, 204, 212, 218, 229, 237, 256, 331, 352
auxiliary verb, 21, 27, 44, 48, 75, 231, 282, 316

Canaanite, 15
casus pendens, 95, 164, 193, 215, 219, 221, 225, 241
causal, 22, 24, 27, 30, 34, 40–41, 44, 71, 74, 78, 88, 94, 96, 98, 101–3, 105, 113, 117–18, 122, 128, 132, 136–37, 145, 152–53, 173, 181–82, 191, 196, 207, 213–14, 226, 230, 233–34, 240–41, 243, 245, 261, 275–76, 282, 326, 330–31, 336, 339–40, 344–45, 354
chiasm, 12, 105, 182, 289
circumstantial, 74, 295
cognate, 22, 27, 43, 102–3, 129, 131, 167, 259, 265, 321, 357
cohortative, 41, 44, 134, 136, 138–39, 342
comparative, 44, 71, 89–90, 146, 148–49, 212, 269, 346
complement, complementizer, 5–7, 21–22, 24–25, 27, 29, 37, 41, 44–46, 50–54, 58, 60, 79, 87, 92–96, 101, 104–5, 107–8, 112, 117–18, 120–22, 124, 126–28, 130–31, 133–34, 136, 138, 144–45, 153–55, 159, 161, 166–71, 174, 177–78, 182, 187–89, 194, 198–99, 203, 209–10, 213, 216, 220, 222–24, 227–29, 231, 233, 236, 238–39, 244–47, 252, 256, 258–62, 265, 269, 271–73, 275–77, 279, 285, 293–95, 297–304, 308–11, 316, 318–19, 321, 326–28, 336, 341, 343, 351

Index of Linguistic Issues

concessive, 71, 103, 197, 226, 232–33, 278, 340

concord, 52, 96, 106, 158, 189, 237

conditional, 107–8, 193, 197, 199–200, 226, 306

conjugations, 13, 32–33, 88, 120–21, 126, 136, 149, 198, 214, 223, 280, 298, 316, 325, 340

conjunction, 9, 18, 29, 38–39, 65, 73, 86, 89, 120, 151, 166, 182, 187, 190, 220, 246, 259, 344

constituent, constituency, 5, 7–8, 11, 26–27, 75, 84, 147, 195, 272, 276, 303–4, 317

coordination, 18, 22, 28, 32, 37, 39, 41, 43–44, 46, 49, 64, 71, 81, 121, 128, 133–36, 138, 163, 181–82, 259, 282, 344

copula, copular, noncopula, 27, 78, 113–14, 129, 132–34, 142–43, 150, 178, 193, 241, 276, 307, 318, 320, 326, 342, 353–54

definite, nondefinite, 41, 78, 87, 103, 124, 143, 171–72, 217, 293, 325, 331

demonstrative, 6, 25, 168, 179, 354

dialect, 15, 326, 333

disjunct, disjunction, 12, 28–29, 48, 63, 68, 70, 79, 84–85, 89–91, 93, 97, 103, 106–7, 112, 114, 118–20, 122–23, 134, 137, 143, 153, 158, 192, 195, 201, 243, 247–48, 262, 290, 302, 334

dittography, 85, 108, 198, 272

ellipsis, 12, 14, 34, 37, 100, 123, 129, 132, 139, 143, 145, 152, 158, 160, 213, 243, 249, 260, 284, 288, 316, 321, 326, 347, 353

embedded (clause), 17, 32, 45, 51–54, 81, 102, 154, 195

emendation, 67, 85, 94, 114–15, 122, 159, 178, 183, 198, 201, 207, 224, 278, 297, 349

emphasis, 27, 38, 101, 133, 182, 208, 340

enclitic, 85, 327, 342

epexegetical, 218, 231, 256, 282, 299

exceptive, 226

exclamation, 180, 183, 279

factitive, 138, 157, 349

focus (pragmatics), 11–12, 28, 45, 52, 55, 57, 68, 84, 88, 94, 104, 119, 145, 174, 177, 182, 191, 203, 210, 225, 239, 247–48, 276, 289, 291, 301, 315, 317, 320

fronting, 11–12, 28, 52, 55, 62, 68, 84, 88, 94, 96–98, 100, 104, 109, 119, 126, 145, 157, 174, 177, 182, 191, 194, 203, 210, 222, 247–48, 289, 291, 315, 317, 320, 336, 347

gapping (see also ellipsis), 14

gemination, 7, 25, 176, 187, 263, 318
gender, 6, 45, 168, 193,
genitive, 21, 24, 31–32, 39, 41, 42, 49–50, 59, 71 78, 81, 84–85, 95, 107, 125, 128, 143–44, 149, 153, 163, 171, 179, 200, 201, 208, 213, 216–18, 224, 231, 233, 243, 256, 263, 273, 282, 301, 317–18, 324, 329, 331–32, 341, 349, 354
gnomic, 354

hapax legomenon, 15, 38, 42, 50, 52, 115, 201, 229, 247–48, 253, 307, 314, 321, 324, 333–34, 337
haplography, 110, 256
hendiadys, 295

imperative, 14, 18, 21, 24, 34, 37, 70, 73, 104, 112–13, 124, 257–58, 327, 339–42
imperfect, imperfective, 8–10, 32, 60, 201–2, 270, 272–73, 293, 298, 320, 328, 348
impersonal, 50, 84
inclusion, 3, 82, 95–96, 109, 119, 203, 305, 311, 349
indefinite, 124, 325, 331
indicative, 9–10, 60, 126, 154, 167, 231, 239, 300–301, 327, 336–37, 347–48, 354
infinitive, 5, 27, 49, 71, 79, 88–89, 108, 118, 128, 131, 152–53, 159, 189, 198–99, 207, 224, 227–28, 231, 242, 254–55, 259, 271, 282, 293, 297
interjection, 42, 57, 140, 173, 214
interrogative, 7, 106, 229, 279, 327, 332, 353
intransitive, 41, 87–88, 93, 101, 109, 121, 131, 152, 160–61, 163, 166, 226, 238–39, 246, 273, 310, 315
inversion (inverted word order), 7, 9, 11, 126, 154, 184, 194, 239
irrealis, 7, 9–12, 24–25, 28, 31–34, 39, 43–44, 48–51, 53, 57, 59–63, 65, 67–68, 75, 84, 86–87, 91–93, 108, 119–20, 126, 135, 153–54, 163, 167, 174, 183–84, 193–94, 200, 204, 210, 216, 225, 232–33, 239, 243–44, 246, 250, 254, 256–57, 262, 265, 275–77, 280, 284–85, 300, 305, 335, 341

ketiv, 150, 200, 233, 255

locative, 57–59, 79, 81, 147, 150, 210, 215, 219, 222, 228, 230, 234, 246, 248, 250, 253, 256, 272, 277, 282, 285, 292, 294, 298, 307, 315, 321, 323–24, 327, 331, 334, 343, 349, 354

Masoretes, Masoretic, 12–13, 79
metathesis, 131, 172, 178, 253, 261
mood, modality, 7–11, 39, 174, 197, 327

nominalization, nominalizer, 134, 171, 227

parenthesis, 135
participle, participial, 10, 41–42, 52, 57, 70, 81, 104–5, 107–8, 115, 117, 126–27, 133, 143, 151, 158–59, 163, 169–70, 196, 212, 229, 237, 248, 273, 290–92, 311, 315–20, 329, 349
particle, 7, 26, 29–30, 49, 67, 84, 100–101, 133–35, 142, 155, 164, 178, 193, 226, 229, 233, 241, 246, 253, 275, 306, 320, 326–27, 332–33
perfect, perfective, 8–10, 55, 121, 126, 264, 280–81, 302, 322, 325, 351
Peshitta, 16
phonology, 14, 236
postpositive, 108
pragmatics, 11–12
predicate, predication, predicator, 17, 26–27, 30, 32, 34, 39–40, 44, 52, 68, 71, 78, 81, 84–85, 107, 119, 127–29, 132, 139, 147, 151, 158, 162, 173, 190–91, 196, 212, 215, 217–19, 227–28, 230, 232, 241, 248, 255, 268, 276, 282, 293, 299, 301, 304, 306, 314–15, 317, 326, 329, 331, 333, 354
proleptic, 214
protasis, 71, 193, 199, 226, 306

qatal, 9–10, 18, 21, 24–26, 28, 31–35, 39–41, 43–46, 48–53, 55, 57, 59–63, 65, 67–68, 75, 79–81, 86–88, 90–94, 96, 106, 108–9, 113, 115–17, 119–22, 126, 128, 135–36, 144–45, 147, 149–51, 153–55, 160–61, 163–68, 170, 173–78, 182–83, 187–89, 191, 194–96, 199–202, 204, 207–8, 210, 214, 216, 219–20, 222–23, 226–27, 230–34, 238–39, 241–46, 250, 252–54, 256, 260–62, 264–65, 269–72, 276–77, 280–81, 284–85, 289–90, 294–97, 301–2, 305, 307–10, 315, 321–22, 325, 327, 335–36, 340, 245, 351–52
qere, 150, 200, 233, 255

relative clause, 17–18, 21, 31–33, 46, 49, 51–54, 75, 102–3, 114, 134, 140, 143, 170, 195, 245, 256, 263, 290, 303, 319, 324, 327, 353, 354
restrictive, 32, 84, 226
resumptive, 54, 119
revocalization, 87, 108, 114–15, 162, 183, 224, 274, 297, 315, 342

Septuagint, 6, 361
stative, 5, 9, 232–33,
substantival, 41, 59, 71, 133, 147, 194, 200, 210, 234, 238,

273, 282, 318, 320, 327, 330, 342, 354
Syriac, 16, 131

tense, 7–10, 45, 55, 88, 126, 135, 136, 153, 201–2, 205, 233, 239, 242, 245, 264, 270, 298, 305, 308, 315, 328, 347
topic, 11–12, 45, 48, 62, 80, 84, 91, 97, 109, 116, 157, 184–85, 187, 194, 222, 225, 235, 240, 254, 256, 300, 303, 316, 336, 347, 351
transitive, 28, 41, 101, 109, 121, 131, 152, 160–61, 165–66, 177, 198, 220, 226, 238–39, 273–74, 282, 285, 304, 309–10, 315, 319
triggered inversion, 7, 9, 11–12, 84, 174, 217, 231

Ugaritic, 131, 190, 342,
unmarked, 21, 46, 71, 81, 102, 106–8, 140, 155, 195–96, 203, 210, 244, 253, 259, 263, 269, 278, 280, 326

valency, valent, 5–6, 52, 229
verbless clause, 30–31, 34, 37, 40, 52, 68, 71, 74, 78, 84–85, 106–7, 113, 115, 119, 124, 127–29, 132–33, 139, 142–43, 147, 150–51, 158–59, 162, 164, 169, 173, 187, 190–91, 195–96, 212, 215, 217–19, 226–28, 230–32, 236–37, 241, 248, 255, 258–59, 268, 276, 278, 282, 292–93, 299, 301, 303, 306–7, 314–17, 320, 326, 329, 331, 333, 350, 352, 354
vocative, 34–35, 78, 84–85, 104, 112–13, 117, 124–25, 142, 151, 189, 207, 228–29, 252, 265, 280, 289, 323, 333, 344

wayyiqtol, 7–8, 10, 13, 21, 23, 26, 29–31, 54–55, 70, 72–73, 88–89, 96, 130, 137, 169, 198, 201–2, 204, 222–24, 268, 273–74, 296–98, 302, 307–8, 311, 315–16, 321–22, 347–48
weqatal, 7, 9

yiqtol, 9–10, 13, 22, 24, 27–29, 31–33, 37–38, 40, 43–44, 48–50, 54, 60–62, 65–66, 68, 73–75, 80–81, 88–94, 96–104, 106, 109, 118, 120–21, 123, 125, 127, 131, 133–35, 137–40, 142, 145, 149, 154–55, 157–59, 163, 165, 167, 171–72, 174, 188, 189, 191–94, 197, 199, 203, 209–15, 225–26, 229, 231, 233–34, 237, 239–41, 244–47, 248, 253–54, 256–67, 259, 263, 269–70, 272–75, 279–80, 282–85, 292–94, 296, 300, 303–5, 311, 316, 318–29, 322–25, 327–28, 330–37, 340–41, 343–49, 352, 354